DEMOCRATIZATION AND ETHNIC PEACE

Democratization and Ethnic Peace
Patterns of ethnopolitical crisis management in post-Soviet settings

AIRAT R. AKLAEV
Russian Academy of Sciences, Institute of Ethnology

LONDON AND NEW YORK

First published 1999 by Ashgate Publishing

Reissued 2018 by Routledge
2 Park Square, Milton Park, Abingdon, Oxon, OX14 4RN
52 Vanderbilt Avenue, New York, NY 10017

Routledge is an imprint of the Taylor & Francis Group, an informa business

Copyright © Airat R. Aklaev 1999

All rights reserved. No part of this book may be reprinted or reproduced or utilised in any form or by any electronic, mechanical, or other means, now known or hereafter invented, including photocopying and recording, or in any information storage or retrieval system, without permission in writing from the publishers.

Notice:
Product or corporate names may be trademarks or registered trademarks, and are used only for identification and explanation without intent to infringe.

Publisher's Note
The publisher has gone to great lengths to ensure the quality of this reprint but points out that some imperfections in the original copies may be apparent.

Disclaimer
The publisher has made every effort to trace copyright holders and welcomes correspondence from those they have been unable to contact.

A Library of Congress record exists under LC control number: 99072330

ISBN 13: 978-1-138-61245-7 (hbk)
ISBN 13: 978-1-138-61249-5 (pbk)
ISBN 13: 978-0-429-45803-3 (ebk)

Contents

List of Figures and Tables vii
Acknowledgements viii

Introduction and Overview 1

PART I: DEMOCRATIZATION, CRISES, AND ETHNIC PEACE: A CONCEPTUAL FRAMEWORK

1 Democratic Peace: Considering its Ethnic Dimension 9

2 Ethnic Conflict and Crises in Changing Societies 26

3 Democracy and Multiethnicity: Conditions of Democratic Ethnic Peace 50

4 Democratization and Factors of Ethnic Peace 78

PART II: POST-COMMUNIST DEMOCRATIZATION AND ETHNOPOLITICAL CRISES, CHANGE AND CHOICE

5 Post-Communist Democratization and Ethnopolitical Crises 103

6 From Soviet to Post-Soviet Ethnopolitics: Change and Menu of Choice 125

PART III: MANAGING PROBLEM AREAS (CRISES) IN DEMOCRATIZING ETHNOPOLITICS: FOUR POST-SOVIET CASES

7	Estonia	143
8	Lithuania	178
9	Moldova	197
10	Russian Federation	224
	Conclusion	254
	Bibliography	*262*
	Index	*292*

List of Figures and Tables

Figure 1.1	Ethnic peace and type of rule	25
Table 6.1	Ethnicity in post-Soviet successor states	132
Table 7.1	Dynamics of Estonia's Ethnic Composition	144
Table 8.1	Dynamics of Lithuania's Ethnic Composition	179
Table 9.1	Dynamics of Moldova's Ethnic Composition	198
Table 10.1	Constituent units of the RSFSR	226
Table 10.2	Constituent units of the RF	227
Table 10.3	Ethnic composition of republics within the RF	228

Acknowledgements

The author would like to express his most sincere gratitude to the following organizations and individuals who contributed to the study reflected in this publication.

First of all, I am extremely grateful to the U.S. Institute of Peace owing to whose grant support it has become possible to accomplish the research project and to prepare this book. Obviously, the opinions, findings and conclusions or recommendations expressed in this publication are those of the author and do not necessarily reflect the views of the U.S. Institute of Peace. I am also grateful for the support offered for conducting several portions of the research and some of the research-related travel to the Kennan Institute for Advanced Russian Studies of the Woodrow Wilson International Center for Scholars (Washington, DC) for a 6-month regional scholarship, to the Berghof Foundation (Germany) for a 3-months guest scholarship and to the German Academic Exchange Service (DAAD) for a short-term research scholarship.

Special thanks go to those librarians who granted me access to library resources and pointed me in the right direction as I searched for research materials. Too many people fit into this category to mention them all. I thank the staff at the following libraries: The British Library in London; The Library of Congress, the George Washington University Library, the Smithsonian Institution Library in Washington, DC; the State Library of Literature in Foreign Languages (VGBIL) in Moscow; the Freie University Library and the State Library (Staatsbibliothek) in Berlin.

I want to express my many thanks to Dr. Hanna Newcombe, Betty Truman and Linda Carroll from Peace Research Institute-Dundas for their valuable cooperation during the whole work over the research project. My many thanks also go to the various people who found time in their busy schedules to help me during my field work in Estonia and Lithuania, particularly to Aksel and Marika Kirch, Anu Uljas and Anne Kalling in

Tallinn. For contributing to the development of the ideas in this book I am grateful to numerous people who commented on various papers presented at several conferences and seminars. I want to thank particularly Dr. Norbert Ropers and Anja Weiss from the Berghof Research Center for Constructive Conflict Management (Berlin) who read parts of the manuscript and provided their thoughtful and constructive comments and suggestions. My special thanks also to my research assistants Kara Madison, Steve and Kristiina Watts for the time they devoted to help me with library research and data processing.

I am very grateful to all those people for their interest in my work and for contributions they made to improving the quality of my effort. All errors and mistakes contained in these pages are, of course, my own responsibility.

Introduction and Overview

As we move into the 21st century two major variables emerge as particularly important and interrelated areas of concern for students of peace On the one hand, the past two decades have witnessed remarkable progress for democracy and the whole period has been recognized as democratization's third wave (Huntington, 1991). The upsurge of democratic governments, starting in 1974 and continuing through the early 1990s, is indeed '*the* sign of political change in contemporary world' (Munck, 1994, p. 355). On the other hand, comes the salient role of ethnicity as it affects everything from democratic development to the prospects of peace in multipolar and multicivilizational world.

The widespread proliferation of ethnic conflict across the globe has taken many people by surprise and forced them to reassess prevailing assumptions and beliefs about the direction of historical development and the motive forces of social change. Ethnic conflict has become today's most pervasive and dangerous expression of organized strife. Most of the ongoing violence in today's world are internal conflicts and not classical interstate wars. None of the 31 instances of active hostilities around the world in 1994, for example, were 'classical' interstate wars (Baker, 1997, p. 563). The bitter reality of ethnonationalist strife has prompted many to see in it the seeds of what may become one of the most serious threats to humanity in the coming era. This, in turn, has generated apprehensions about the conflict of civilizations as a sobering prospect for the future course of human development (Huntington 1993; idem, 1997) and a search for approaches by which the clash of cultures and identities can be transcended.

Issues of ethnic peace lie at the core of much of the current debate over the future of the democratic project. The emergence of disruptive ethnic conflicts in many new democracies has led to a pervasive fear that primordial ties can eat away at the democratic process and undermine the foundations of a peaceful, progressive future. The critical question is whether and how ethnic conflict situations can be managed to prevent the turn to violence and be subsequently transformed into constructive arrangements based on democratic principles.

Given the difficulties inherent in mitigating ethnic conflict, some of the analysts were tempted to rush into the conclusion that multiethnicity is bound to overwhelm efforts to consolidate democratic systems. Other scholars contend that this relationship is more complex. An important point made in this regard is that democracy needs to be seen not as part of the problem of ethnic conflict, but as the basis for its solution. This argument is grounded in a strong belief that there are no viable alternatives to democracy as a system of just and stable conflict management. If democracy cannot encompass ethnic diversity, what else can?

The very subject of peace studies warrants interdisciplinary perspectives that transcend traditional academic boundaries and provide for the systematic integration of disciplines relevant for peace. Boulding (1978, pp. 131-2) captured the phenomenon by observing that 'peace research is an interdiscipline rather than a discipline'. It has been rightfully argued by many that disciplinary traditions have created major barriers to the development of theory capable of comprehending new realities in world politics. Precisely because of these boundaries, many comparativists continue to limit their search for causal patterns to the level of the nation-state and rarely develop comparisons or generalizations that incorporate international variables. Many international scholars, on the other hand, err in the opposite direction and attempt to generalize about causation without meaningful reference to political life at the national or sub-state level.

This book makes an attempt to consider issues of ethnic peace through cross-perspectives of comparative and international politics. In searching for ways to think about problems of inter*ethnic* peace in the 1990s it may be useful to consult the achievements made by inter*national* relations scholars. The answers to all today's problems are not to be found there, but some of the right questions and insights are. One of such insights regards the relationship between democracy and peace.

Two centuries ago, the German philosopher Immanuel Kant predicted that republican states would enjoy a 'perpetual peace' with other republics. More recently, many observers have noted that democratic countries virtually never go to war with one another. Since the 1980s, this apparent pattern has been regarded as coming 'as close as anything we have to an empirical law in international relations' (Levy, 1988, pp. 661-62). It thus becomes heuristic to consider if insights originated in the *inter*national relations theory can be fruitfully applied to increase the measure of our intelligence and ability to cope with *intra*national ethnic conflict. In simple words, the democratic peace proposition is about the fact that free peoples make good neighbors. If this is true at international level, does this also hold at the sub-national level as well? Does the democratic peace proposition have an ethnic dimension? Does the establishment of a constructive pattern of ethnic conflict management has anything to do with the type of rule?

The experience of this century offers important evidence in this regard. Nationalism and intranational ethnic differences can and often do lead to war and turmoil. Yet, as the development of many today's established democracies has proved, ethnic diversity does not need to be eradicated or forcefully suppressed for interethnic peace and cooperation to prevail. Countries with democratic governance do have ethnic conflict and even occasional incidents of low level racial and ethnic strife, yet, they manifestly display the capacity to manage their ethnic diversity in constructive and predominantly non-violent ways. These countries have also tended to be substantially less likely to face ethnic insurgencies or civil wars between ethnic segments of their citizenry. As put by Saul Newman (1996), ethnic politics in established democracies represents 'mostly ballots, rarely bullets'. The core of the matter is that the form of ethnic conflict in established democracies has been a function of the nature of their democracy rather than of the nature of ethnic conflict.

A better understanding of the relationship between democracy and peace in today's world has acquired a new (and by no means, an exclusively domestic) facet - probing into the relationship between democratization and ethnic peace in new democracies. It is reasonable to suggest that under certain conditions new democracies can develop the skills to manage ethnic pluralism in modes that are compatible with liberal values.

Conceptualizing democracy and ethnicity within the continuum of the peace relationship and exploring patterns of democratizing ethnopolitics can help to specify, first, which conditions provide for a stable, positive and sustainable quality of the relations that prevail between ethnically identified segments of citizenry in the overwhelming majority of established democracies; second, which critical areas require craftful responses for a fledgling ethnically plural democracy to consolidate into a fully-fledged system and, finally, what issues of the agenda warrant a more concerted attention by scholars and practitioners alike.

A whole web of issues loom large in this regard: What menu of choice is available to promote nonviolent conflict management in democratizing multiethnic systems? When are the critical junctures in ethnopolitical interactions most likely to arise and how can they be managed constructively? How is it possible to prevent aroused ethnic tensions from being inflamed at the stage of democratic transition? What tasks and dilemmas must be dealt with at the stage of democratic consolidation to promote a more positive and stable relationship of ethnic peace?

Many agree that it is fruitful to view both democratization and ethnic peace not as givens or results but as evolving processes, involving the task of allaying ethnic tensions salient in the course of building democratic institutions and forging democracy as discourse. This book argues that a heuristic perspective that would focus on the interplay between the dynamics of ethnic conflict as interwoven with the dynamics of the democratization process can be *a crisis and change perspective*. It involves a close attention to two aspects: 1) the nature and configuration of sequences of systemic crises of post-authoritarian development as they impinge upon the dynamics of intergroup conflict in ethnically-riven societies; 2) the policy choices made by different ethnic elites and accepted by their ethnic constituencies during behavioral (or interactional) crises as specific and observable events in evolving political interaction between the state and ethnic groups.

Concerns with ethnopolitical crises as focal points in the unfolding dynamics of democratizing ethnic peace invite a focused comparison of the patterns by which ethnopolitical crises are managed. Not only can this enable us to surmise the relative strengths and weaknesses of various structural, cultural, political and psychological factors and forces arrayed in different regions, but also to infer insights into what the viable patterns of ethnic non-violence can be in the context of democratization.

This monograph is one of the first undertakings to explore the linkages between patterns of crisis management and the ensuing dynamics of ethnic peace. Therefore, at this initial stage of inquiry its goals can only be reasonably modest. A more specific focus is made on instances of post-communist democratization and a sample of relevant case studies has been taken from the post-Soviet setting. Three major objectives have been set forth in this regard: 1) to survey the theoretical approaches in order to construct a cross-perspective conceptual framework that links the ethnic dimension of the democratic peace proposition with issues of ethnopolitical conflict and crisis management under democratization; 2) to consider comparative histories of ethnopolitical conflict management in a sample of four more or less successful cases of post-Soviet democratization, specifically, Estonia, Lithuania, Moldova, and Russian Federation; 3) to conclude on the specific features of the ethnic peace relationship in democratizing systems and prospects of its evolution.

Part I attempts to delineate a conceptual map of issues of democratization, ethnic peace and crisis management by integrating insights from several disciplinary lines of inquiry.

Chapter 1, 'Democratic Peace: Considering Its Ethnic Dimension', stresses the importance of two avenues in the progressively unfolding agenda of democratic peace research: 1) inclusion of the sub-national (sub-state) level of analysis in addition to the national, dyadic and systemic levels; 2) examination of the effects of democratic transitions upon prospects of ethnic peace. In this connection, it discusses the issues of ethnic peace in relation to the type of rule and suggests a conceptual distinction between two pairs of concepts: 'ethnic peace' vs. 'democratic ethnic peace' and 'democratizing ethnic peace' vs. 'democratic ethnic peace'.

Chapter 2, 'Ethnopolitical Conflict and Crises in Changing Societies', argues that any study of ethnopolitical conflict management under democratization is a study of critical challenges made and critical choices (or non-choices) of responses to make in order to preserve and sustain ethnic peace. Therefore, concerns over problems of ethnopolitical crisis prevention and crisis management inevitably move to the fore. After a brief survey of major approaches to sources, patterns of manifestation and dynamics of ethnopolitical conflict, the discussion turns to the peculiarities of ethnic conflict in changing societies and on how, in this respect, the linkage between political change, ethnic crises and peace can be conceived. It is suggested to distinguish between two basic types of ethnopolitical crises in changing societies: crises at the system level (or systemic crises) and crises at the level of strategic interactions (or interactional crises).

Chapter 3, 'Democracy and Multiethnicity: Conditions of Democratic Ethnic Peace', delineates the field of concerns with regard to a complex web of relationships between ethnicity and democracy's specific mode of processing conflicts and major kinds of challenges that ethnic diversity poses to democracy as a form of rule (the symbolic and identity-related nature of ethnic conflict, the structure of cleavages, the structure of civil society, issues of inclusion and exclusion, problems of majoritarian rule in plural societies, issues of ethnic outbidding). Positive and stable ethnic peace, conceived as constructive process of non-violent conflict management, is the response that only mature liberal democracy can give to the challenges of ethnic diversity. It is argued that analysis of the conditions of democratic ethnic peace can proceed along the lines of two explanatory models - cultural (or normative) and structural (or institutional).

Chapter 4, 'Democratization and Factors of Ethnic Peace', overviews major sets of research concerns in contemporary studies of democratization. Ethnicity closely interacts with the politics of democratic transition, consolidation and sustainability. In this regard the chapter considers factors of ethnic peace in democratizing systems by grouping those into four broader sets of identity, institutional, differential power and leadership/constituency factors. It is argued that problems of democratizing ethnic peace are to a large degree coterminous with the choice and application of patterns of ethnopolitical crisis management.

Part II narrows the discussion to the post-communist cluster of the third-wave democracies. *Chapter 5*, 'Post-Communist Democratization and Ethnopolitical Crises', starts with assessing peculiarities of post-communist transitions and the relevant place occupied by ethnic conflict. It suggests identifying three major system-level problem areas (crises) that derive from the interplay between political legitimacy and salient ethnic identities under post-communist transformations: stateness, state effectiveness, and nationhood. *Chapter 6*, 'From Soviet to Post-Soviet Ethnopolitics: Ethnopolitical Change and Menu of Choice', surveys basic changes in patterns of post-Soviet ethnopolitics and suggests several lines of inquiry into the menu of ethnopolitical choice in the realms of institutions and interactions that are to be considered in the subsequent case studies.

Part III presents a comparative survey of the dynamics of ethnopolitical conflict management in four post-Soviet cases - Estonia, Lithuania, Moldova, and Russian Federation (respectively, chapters 7-10). The central concern is with identifying patterns of manifestation and management of ethnopolitical crises at different stages of post-Soviet democratization.

Conclusion discusses the features of democratizing ethnic peace and new departures that the agenda of future research into the relationship between democracy and ethnic peace can take.

PART I:
DEMOCRATIZATION, CRISES, AND ETHNIC PEACE: A CONCEPTUAL FRAMEWORK

1 Democratic Peace: Considering its Ethnic Dimension

This chapter discusses the implications the democratic peace proposition, originally developed for understanding the phenomenon of an almost total absence of wars between dyads of democratic countries in *international* relations, can have for the sphere of *interethnic* relations. For this purpose I intend, first, to overview basic arguments of the democratic peace theory; second, to map the ethnic dimension of the democratic peace research agenda; and third, to discuss the relationship between ethnic peace and the type of rule.

Democratic Peace as a Phenomenon and a Theory

The Phenomenon of Democratic Peace

The rapidly developing body of scholarly work known as the 'democratic peace' literature asserts the relevance of domestic politics to understanding patterns of international interactions. Extensive research on the relationship between democracy and international conflict has revealed two major empirical patterns that, taken together, constitute a most remarkable phenomenon of human interactions in world politics.

On the one hand, the weight of current evidence suggests that democracy per se does not entail any discernible pacifying effect on foreign policy.[1] Democracies are no less war prone and no less likely to become involved in foreign wars, crises, or potentially violent disputes than states organized under alternative arrangements of political rule (Small and Singer, 1976; Weede, 1984 and 1992; Chan, 1984; Domke 1988; Maoz and Abdolali, 1989; Maoz and Russett, 1993; Rousseau, Gelpi, Reiter and Huth, 1996). On the other hand, an equally compelling set of results shows that democratic states rarely if ever, fight wars against one another. Democracies have been recorded extremely seldom even to engage one another with threats of military violence, and when disputes do arise, they hardly even result in military hostilities (Doyle, 1983 and 1986; Levy, 1988; Maoz and Abdolali, 1989; Bremer, 1992 and 1993; Russett, 1990 and 1993; Weede, 1992; Ray, 1993, 1995b, and 1997; Senese 1997). Taken together, these two empirical patterns have come to be known as the 'democratic peace'.

The core of the democratic peace proposition is that the relationship of peace among democracies is importantly a result of some inherent features of democracy, rather than being caused exclusively by economic or geopolitical characteristics correlated with democracy (Maoz and Russett, 1993, pp. 624-38, Russett, 1993, pp. 11-5 ff). On the whole, recognition of the democratic peace result is probably one of the most significant non-trivial products of the scientific study of world politics. In Jack Levy's words (1988, p. 661-2), the democratic peace proposition 'comes as close as anything we have to an empirical law in international relations'.

Intellectual Roots of the Democratic Peace Proposition

The basic idea that autocracy or dictatorship is an important cause of war that can be eliminated by democracy, because democratic states will have peaceful relationships with each other, has philosophical roots that antedate the current debates by almost two centuries. The proposition that conflict and violence can be overcome if the world is organized according to certain principles flourished during the Enlightenment. It was, for instance, a central part of the political debates which surrounded the American and French revolutions. In explaining the phenomenon of democratic peace, the liberal school of thought departs from the political writings of Immanuel Kant, particularly, his *Idea for a Universal History with a Cosmopolitan Intent* (1784) and *On Perpetual Peace* (1795). Another foundation rests on the Hegelian ideas on the inherent potential for the universalization of liberal values and their internationalization (Ray, 1995, p. 4-6).

In his *Perpetual Peace*, Kant ([1795] 1970, p. 113) envisioned the central role for the liberal republics as the foundation for future peace ('pacific union') in the world: '[the] republican constitution... provides for this desirable result - namely, peace'. Kant's notion of a pacific union of democracies rests on three pillars: first, the mere existence of democracies with their culture of peaceful resolution of conflict; second, the common moral bonds which are forged between democracies on this basis; third, the democracies' economic cooperation towards mutual advantage.[2] The Enlightenment thinking about liberal peace was revived in the early 20-th century in the works of Woodrow Wilson who included Kant's principles of cosmopolitan law and pacific union into his Fourteen Points (Knock, 1992, p. 3 ff.). Wilsonian 1917 war message openly asserted that 'a steadfast concert of peace can never be maintained except by a partnership of democratic nations' (quoted in Russett, 1993, p. 5).

Contemporary Studies of Democratic Peace: Emergence of a Theory

Systematic quantitative and qualitative studies of the phenomenon of democratic peace and its theoretical explanation are quite a recent development. Contemporary studies of the relationship between democracy and peace have passed through four major stages.

The *first stage* can be attributed to the mid-1960s - early 1970s. For the first time the contemporary observation that democracies do not fight each other was made almost three decades ago by Dean Babst (1964, 1972).[3] Babst (1972, p. 10) had examined data on 116 major wars from 1789 to 1941 from Quincey Wright (1965) and found that 'no wars have been fought between independent nations with elective governments'. Applying a probabilistic argument to the two world wars of this century, he concluded that it was extremely unlikely that all the elective governments (10 out of the 33 independent nations participating in World War I; 14 out of 52 in World War II) should be on the same side purely by chance. Small and Singer (1976) attempted to discredit Babst's conclusion. They reported that between 1816 and 1965, international wars involving democracies lasted about as long and involved about as many battle deaths as wars that involved only undemocratic states. They acknowledged, however, that, with a couple of debatable exceptions, there have been no wars between democratic states. They also observed that this was probably due to the fact that 'war is most likely between neighbors' and that 'bourgeois democracies do not border upon one another very frequently' (1976, p. 64). To Gleditsch (1992, p.370), it was the first of many attempts to explain away democratic peace with reference to third variables.

The *second stage* of research on democratic peace refers to the late 1970s-mid 1980s. It was initiated by Rummel (1979 and 1983) who argued that 'libertarian' states were more peaceful and never fought each other.

This argument quickly led to rejoinders by Chan (1984), Weede (1984), and others. During the same period, Doyle (1983, 1986) developed an argument on the foundations of the liberal peace, based on the Kantian views.

The *third* round of debate in the democratic peace studies evolved in the late 1980s-early 90s and proceeded along two major lines. One line involved mostly testing the empirical regularities between regime-type and war involvement. Overall, the findings had given evidence that liberal polities correlate negatively with amounts of foreign violence at the dyadic level of analysis (Geller, 1985; Starr, 1991 and 1992; Bueno de Mesquita and Lalman, 1992, Maoz and Abdolali, 1989; Maoz and Russett, 1992 and 1993; Morgan and Schwebach, 1992; Bremer, 1992; Owen, 1994; O'Neal, O'Neal, Maoz and Russett, 1996, and Rousseau et al., 1996). This research included testing for third variables, eventual 'statistical artifacts', evaluating the possibility that the correlation between regime type and international conflict on the dyadic level of analysis is brought about by other factors, such as contiguity, wealth, alliance ties, and political stability.

Another line of research pursued during the same period paid attention to diachronic aspects of the democratic peace phenomenon. As a basis for understanding better the sources and nature of peace among modern democracies, Russett and Antholis (1992) investigated the only other well-documented state system with a large number of democratic regimes - the city-state system in Greece during the late fifth century BC The authors systematically compiled information on wars and types of political systems in the world of Ancient Greek city-states and discussed the fragile emergence, during the Peloponnesian War period, of some norms that democracies should not fight each other. Using cross-cultural ethnographic evidence Ember, Ember and Russett (1992) explored a similar phenomenon in non-industrial societies. They found that polities organized according to more participatory ('democratic') principles fight each other less often than do polities organized according to hierarchical principles. Stable participatory institutions seem to promote peaceful relations, especially if people perceive that others also have some control over politics.

The on-going, *fourth* stage of research on democratic peace, started in the early 1990s as a parallel endeavor to empirical testing and case studies, is characterized by increasing attention to the theoretical foundations of the democratic peace proposition. Fairly elaborate theoretical arguments have been fashioned to date that account for the connection of democracies to international conflict.

Theoretical Explanations of Democratic Peace

Two major explanations have been advanced to account for the lack of war between democracies; one based on political culture, the other on political structure. Together they argue that democracy is a set of institutions and norms for peaceful resolution of conflict. Both address the issue of the source of peace and the pattern of interaction. Although there is some overlap between these two focuses, each stresses a different causal mechanism in accounting for the peaceful proclivities of democratic states.

Cultural explanations, or the normative model This model defines democracy in terms of political culture and contends that the shared norms fostered by a democratic culture promote non-violent conflict resolution and predispose democracies toward peaceful relations with each other.

A political culture grounded in norms of tolerance and compromise has often been cited as a necessary condition for democracy (e.g., Verba 1965; Almond and Verba, 1963 and 1980; Hofstede 1989; Poortinga and Hendriks, 1989). Democratic regimes are based on political norms that emphasize regulated political competition through peaceful means. Dixon (1994, p. 15) proposed the term 'bounded competition', in this regard. Winning does not require elimination of the opponent, and losing does not prohibit from trying again. Political conflicts in democracies are resolved through compromise rather than through elimination of opponents. This norm allows for an atmosphere of 'live and let live' that results in a fundamental sense of stability at the personal, communal, and national level. The democratic citizenry is informed by powerful norms which discourage the use of lethal force, prioritize peaceful means of conflict resolution and shy away from brute force.

The procedural norms that govern conflict resolution in daily life are externalized. What functions at home is assumed to be viable abroad. Democracies, writes Joffe (1990, p. 125), are prone 'to view the world as an extension of their domestic polities'. Dependence on democratic norms tips rational cost-benefit calculations toward further support of these norms. Empirically, disputes between democracies are more likely to be settled by a third-party mediation, by agreement or stalemate (rather than an imposed solution), and by strategies of reciprocation (Dixon, 1993; Leng, 1993).

A related argument of the normative explanation puts the stress on socialization of political leaders within their domestic political environment. The model argues that decision-makers in democracies follow norms of peaceful conflict resolution that reflect domestic experiences and values (Dixon 1993 and 1994; Raymond, 1994). Experiments in social psychology studying persistent behavior have shown that people tend to cling to their beliefs, so that we repeat accustomed practices in new situations, unless emphatic experience convinces us that we must change (e.g. Bandara, 1986; Levine and Campbell, 1972; Jöhnsson, 1990; Bendor et al., 1991. To Weart (1994, p. 300), these facts suggest that leaders tend to act toward their foreign counterparts in the same way they act towards their rival domestic political leaders. Since democratic leaders are socialized into accepting norms of peaceful political competition, the policies toward foreign democracies, as a result, are likely to be non-violent and to reflect the spirit of compromise. No such expectation exists with regard to nondemocracies where political competition is likely to be more zero-sum in terms of the contention of the parties and its consequences. The winner may take all, denying the loser the power or opportunity to rise again. Such mode of conflict conduct generates an atmosphere of mistrust and fear within and outside the government. Nondemocratic political leaders are socialized in an environment in which coercion and violence are more widely accepted as legitimate means for resolving political disputes. In this way, the norm of peaceful conflict resolution creates a separate peace among democracies, but does not prevent democracies from fighting nondemocracies.

Structural explanations, or the institutional model Structural explanations define 'democracy' in terms of political institutions and focus on the relationship between political structures and the domestic political costs of using force. They draw on decision-making theories to argue that democratic institutions have built-in constraints that limit the ambitions and power of top-level decision-makers (Morgan and Campbell, 1991; Morgan and Schwebach, 1992; Bueno de Mesquita and Lalman 1992; Russett, 1993) In general terms, the institutional model holds that domestic institutional constraints, including checks and balances, separation of powers, and the need for public debate, will slow or constrain decisions to go to war. Leaders in democracies will recognize that other democratic leaders are similarly constrained. As a result, democracies will have more time to resolve disputes peacefully and less fear of surprise attack.

Comparing the two explanatory models, most analysts stress that they are not mutually exclusive but, on the contrary need be viewed as overlapping, complementary and mutually reinforcing. Though Maoz and Russett (1992 and 1993) have found that the data-driven support for the normative model is more robust and consistent, they correctly observed that it would be a mistake to emphasize too strongly the subtlety or persuasiveness of the distinction between [the] cultural-normative and structural-institutional models. Norms, after all, shape institutions and procedures. In addition, both models depend on the presence of reciprocal perceptions, i.e., on whether democracies perceive one another as democracies. The sense of distinguishing between the two explanations as ideal-types is just to highlight two different facets of democratic politics that are presumably responsible for the democratic peace phenomenon.

Recent scholarship has elaborated on a number of more specific causal elements of democratic peace working within one of the two explanatory approaches. Within the normative model, Thomas Risse-Kappen (1995, pp. 502-9) proposed the social-constructivist approach which stresses mutually held perceptions: democracies 'construct' their friends and enemies - 'us' and 'them' - by inferring either defensive or aggressive motives from the domestic structures of their counterparts. They evaluate the external behavior of states as corresponding to their internal treatment of conflict. Nondemocracies are expected to externalize their perceived violent means of conflict resolution and are constructed as potentially dangerous. Other democracies are constructed as friends because they are expected to externalize their peaceful means of conflict resolution. Since these means are perceived to correspond with their own way of dealing with conflicts, democracies form a collective identity, to some extent an in-group, while nondemocracies are constructed as an out-group.

Within the institutional model, refined arguments were built on the organizational and rational choice theories. David Lake (1992) has offered an explanation of what he calls a syndrome of powerful pacifism drawn from the microeconomic theory of the state. Gus diZereuga (1995) who explored organizational dimension of peace between democracies holds that democracies do not fight one another, because they are self-organizing systems and therefore fundamentally distinct from other states. As systems, liberal democracies have more in common with science and the market than they do with undemocratic states. By contrast, undemocratic states are best conceived as instrumental organizations pursuing relatively well-defined goals. Liberal democracies do not normally pursue particular goals, are rarely comprehensible as rational actors, have unusually open boundaries, are self-transforming and are therefore able to handle greater complexity than instrumental organizations. These characteristics provide the foundation for their mutually pacific relationships. Hermann and Kegley (1995) proposed explanations which explicitly incorporate leadership, leaders' perceptions, and their leadership styles.

Karl Deutsch's (1957) model of pluralist security community has been another theory-inspiring concept for democratic peace studies. Building on it, Archer (1996) examines the notion of the 'zone of peace' and then assessed the quality of zones of democratic peace. Kacowicz (1995) has made an attempt to establish a correlation between democracies and territorial demands by posing the hypothesis that well-established democracies do not fight each other since they are conservative powers, usually satisfied with the territorial status quo within and across their borders. Starr (1997) links democratic peace to the Deutschian concept of integration, considering the former as a subset of the processes and results of integration by emphasizing the importance of the mutual perceptions of two democracies, that the other is clearly a democracy.

Democratic Peace and Democratizing Ethnicity

Progressive Research Agenda of Democratic Peace Studies

Based on its progress over the past two decades, the debate over the democratic peace reflects the inherent strength of the liberal argument and its research program. Few other academic debates have generated so much high-quality social science that includes statistical testing. As observed by Doyle (1996), the idea of the democratic peace has produced a progressive research agenda with rich variety of research methods ranging from political theories and historical case-studies to sophisticated large-N statistical testing that includes data on many countries and conflicts over several centuries. Today there even seems to be some degree of cumulation, as studies replicate or challenge the results of the earlier ones. At the same time, the scholarly community is increasingly aware of the fact that many important avenues of research thus far have been underrepresented on the democratic peace agenda (e.g., Chan 1993, Lynn-Jones 1996, p. xxix). I would like to attract attention to two of such underresearched areas.

First, a comprehensive study of the effects of democratization upon prospects of peace. Recent works by Ray (1995a, 1995b) have called attention to the issue of global trends in regime transitions and their bearing on international politics. Many researchers have reached the conclusion that widespread democratization will lead to a more peaceful world. The end of the Cold war made the Kant's ideal of a world of peaceful democracies more attainable than ever before in human history (Russett, 1993, p. 138).

A more peaceful world as a result of the current democratizations - although a theoretical possibility - is by no means assured. In many instances current democratic advancement is taking place in a way that may well jeopardize continued democratic progress. Untamed nationalisms and ethnic conflict represent major challenges in this regard.

Some scholars observe that democracies eventually may become more peaceful but that, in their very early years, they are unusually prone to war involvement. In the historical patterns that emerge from Mansfield and Snyder's (1995 and 1996) research on democratizing states from 1816 to 1992, new democracies with weak institutions result particularly vulnerable to aggressive nationalism pushed by authoritarian elites, and therefore prone to provocative foreign policies and war. Mansfield and Snyder argue that immature democracies are a force for war, not peace. Since new democracies lack the institutional capacity to integrate contending interests and views, the pressures of a cauldron of domestic conditions create incentives to mobilize populations around belligerent nationalist platforms.

Recently, Thompson and Tucker (1997) questioned Mansfield and Snyder's research design and conclusions but agreed that the relationship of regime instability and conflict, as opposed to or in addition to the regime type-conflict relationship, deserves further analysis. Given the number of recent transitions (and reversals), plenty of potential cases provide ample opportunities for researchers. Even if additional research supports the conclusion that democratizing states become more war-prone, such case studies can contribute to an understanding of the democratic peace by helping to specify precisely which conditions need to be present for a stable democracy to become one that avoids wars with other democracies.

Second, a more focused attention is warranted to research into conditions of democratic peace at different levels of analysis. Gleditsch and Hegre (1997) distinguish between three levels of democratic peace analysis: the *national* level ('do democracies more frequently maintain peace overall?'), the *dyadic* level ('do democracies usually maintain peace among each other?'), and the *systemic* level ('is an international system with a high proportion of democratic states a more peaceful system?'). The *subnational level* where the basic question concerns the relevance of democracy for intrastate conflict has received little attention thus far. While some research has been made concerning the impact of the regime-type on the propensity to apply state coercion (e.g., Gurr, 1988) and on the relationship between the degree of democracy and violent domestic conflict (Huntington, 1981; Mueller and Weede, 1990; Ellingsen and Gleditsch, 1997), no systematic study, assessing the democratic peace proposition in relation to the *intrastate* level of ethnic conflict has been undertaken.

At least two reasons warrant a specially adapted application of the democratic peace theory as a source of insights for understanding not only *international* but also *intranational* (ethnic) relations. Both of them stem from the interplay between domestic and international levels of politics. On the one hand, ethnic conflict is a worldwide phenomenon. International relations are far from being immune to the impetus of politicized ethnicity which transcends national boundaries. Boundaries of the nation-state itself are a variable (Lustick, 1993). Recent scholarship has pointed out at the complex nature of a two-fold dynamics of ethnicization of international relations and internationalization of ethnic relations (e.g., Midlarsky, 1992; Schechterman and Slann, 1993; Moynihan, 1993; Ryan, 1995; Esman, 1995). The situation in the former Second world deserves particular attention in this respect. Numerous cases of escalating ethnic strife in post-communist nations have explicitly demonstrated that domestic ethnicity is an important factor of post-Cold War international security.

On the other hand, as correctly observed by Donald Horowitz (1985, p. 30ff), the majority of modern multiethnic countries operate as unranked ethnic systems where parallel ethnic groups coexist, each group internally stratified. Unranked ethnic groups 'act as if they were states in an international environment'. Under conditions of uncertainty generated by rapid socio-political change, particularly during democratization, interethnic relations, engagements and confrontations partake of features that usually characterize international actors. O'Connell (1971, p.334-5) refers to ethnic interaction as 'international relations without safeguards'.

I argue that an important avenue of further research into democratic peace should be the one encompassing the above-discussed two broader concerns, namely, a study of the relationship between democratization and ethnic peace at the subnational level within new democracies.

Ethnic Peace and Type of Rule. Democratic vs. Democratizing Ethnic Peace

The ethnic peace relationship exists within a socio-political structure that qualifies it in various ways. Type of rule is a variable not to be discounted. Differential quality of peace in multiethnic systems can be better understood by considering the properties that the peace relationship assumes in systems with different types of rule.

'Positive' vs. 'negative' peace Varied definitions of peace have given rise to several concepts that highlight important attributes of the relationship. 'Negative peace' is deemed as simply the absence of war or active, organized violence. When Raymond Aron (1966) defined peace as a condition of more or less lasting suspension of violent modes of rivalry between political units, he implied negative peace. His is the most common understanding of 'peace' in the context of international politics which suggests that peace is found whenever war or other direct forms of sustained violence are absent. Such narrow (or passive) conception of peace, however, lacks creative and active instances and though it is obviously relevant in situations of on-going violent strife, its capacity to provide for a broader and longer-term perspective on human interactions is rather limited.

An alternative conception of peace emphasizes the importance of a positive (or active) understanding of the relationship. In scholarly publications the concept of positive peace was pioneered by Johan Galtung (1969, pp.161-191; idem, 1981) with reference to a condition of society where there is neither overt violence nor the more subtle forms of 'structural violence'. In Galtung's somewhat romantic thinking, structural violence stood for almost all imaginable and unimaginable forms of social inequality and injustice taken together. The notion of structural violence has been rightfully criticized for implying too many things at once to be helpful for purposes of analytic precision or rigorous study of identifiable empirical referents and has been left in due disregard. At the same time, the obvious need to address peace in a broader and creative sense does not make 'positive peace' a useless concept, provided it be conceived realistically.

It was Kenneth Boulding (1978, pp.3-5) who proposed a realistically meaningful distinction between the positive and negative aspects of peace:

> On the positive side, peace signifies *a condition of good management, orderly resolution of conflict*, harmony associated with mature relationships... On the negative side, it is conceived as the absence of something - the absence of turmoil, tension, conflict, and war... The positive concept of peace... is seen as a skill in the management of conflict and the development of a larger order than that which involves warring parties... (italics added -A.A.).

The above conceptual distinction has important implications for the perceived tasks of the peace community. Attention on negative peace, or the simple absence of war results in emphasis on peace-*keeping* (the prevention of war) or peace-*restoring* (if war has broken out). By contrast, positive peace focuses on peace-*building*, the establishment of harmonious social structures, and a determination to work toward that goal even when war is not ongoing or imminent. Positive definitions of peace transform conflict resolution into a continuous peace-*making* process to deal with conflict and create the institutions and conditions that guarantee justice.

A realistic positive peace is viewed as *a creative and constructive process of managing and transforming conflict*. The intellectual roots of such conception can be traced back to president John F. Kennedy's vision of peace when he spoke at the American University in 1963. He said: 'I am not referring to the absolute, infinite concept of universal peace and good will. Let us focus instead on a more practical, more attainable peace, based not on a sudden revolution in human nature but on a gradual evolution in human institutions' (quoted in Vance, 1983, p. 20).

Within this understanding of positive peace James H. Laue (1991, p. 301) defines peace not only as a cherished goal sought by all individuals and states, but also as 'a process of continuous and constructive conflict management of differences towards the goal of more mutually satisfying relations, the prevention of escalation of violence, and the achievement of those conditions that exemplify the universal well-being of human beings and their groups from the family to the culture and the state'. In the same vein Rabie (1994, p. 15) holds that realistic positive peace means 'the absence of violence under conditions and relationships that provide for the nonviolent resolution of political conflict, and the freedom to pursue legitimate individual and group goals without threat or coercion'.

The points made by Laue and Rabbie are extremely riveting and revealing. Peace is the result of a conflict management pattern. The distinction between negative peace and positive peace can be conceived as the one based on a choice of conflict management approaches which have come to be known as competitive and cooperative (Deutsch, 1968, 1973 and 1987). Constructive patterns of conflict management are identified with a cooperative social process. Destructive patterns, on the contrary, typically have the social and psychological characteristics of a competitive process (Deutsch, 1994, Rubin, 1994, Boardman and Horowitz, 1994).

To Ropers (1997), the qualification of conflict management as constructive points, first, to the *outcome* of the particular conflictual behavior (Have these been successful in preventing or ending violence, or in attaining other goals considered relevant to peace - e.g., social justice or cross-party loyalties and institutions?). Second, *process-related grounds* are also meaningful:

> If it is assumed that a successful instance of conflict management always entails learning processes that lead to a broadening of perspectives, changing mutual perceptions and to increasing mutual understanding on the part of those involved, then the crucial feature is the presence of indicators of these kinds of constructive-learning processes: agreement on the definition of the conflict, or at least a willingness to 'agree to disagree'; signs that differences in standpoints are recognized as legitimate, a willingness to come to consensually framed rules and procedures for dealing with the conflict (Ropers, 1997, p. 3)

Democracy's developmental strength has been its capacity for constructive and non-violent conflict management. Alone among all forms of government, democracy rests on a minimum of coercion and a maximum of consent in its political culture. There is a near consensus that democracy evolves as contingent outcomes of conflicts and represents a set of institutions and rules for mediating plural and competing interests to provide for peaceful resolution of conflicts -whether these arise from the clash of interests, cultures, or from uncertainty about the future (Rustow 1970, Sartori 1987, Przeworski 1988, Hirshman 1994).

The concept of constructive conflict management illuminates the linkage between democracy and realistic positive peace. While peace is the process and outcome of efficient conflict management, democracy is *a* mode of conflict management. Conceptual distinction between negative and positive aspects of peace can be clarified in this regard.

Negative peace is a product of unsophisticated quality. Its attainment is indiscriminate to the choice of conflict management patterns or their moral outcome. Negative peace is based on a power balance and, thus derives from competitive processes which result in one or another form of forceful imposition. Since destructive conflict management lies at the foundation of negative peace, it precludes the sustainability of the relationship.

Positive peace, on the contrary, is both a higher-quality product and a process. As a process it is grounded in constructive patterns of conflict management identified with a cooperative social process. Positive peace characterizes a state of relationship that is more cooperative than competitive and generally viewed as healthy and mutually beneficial. In this context, conflict becomes a reflection of diversity, not enmity, and conflict-resolution techniques become tools and rules to regulate diversity while preserving unity. Attainment of positive peace represents a superordinate goal of compelling value to all concerned, one that can be achieved only by cooperation. A truly cooperative relationship is only possible between equal individuals and groups of citizenry.

Therefore, positive peace in its mature and sustainable form is necessarily a democratic peace. It is liberal democracy's mode of constructive conflict management which is responsible for the positive quality of peace as its outcome. Democracy is not a means to pursue some other end (in this case - peace), but is itself the reverse side of positive peace. Democracy and positive peace come together and merge as the basic grammar of non-violent conflict management based on the cooperative efforts of free and equal individuals. The progress of human freedom induces the unfolding of positive peace as its necessary concomitant.

An important qualification about the fact of democratic peace is that in modern times democracy has come to mean *liberal* democracy - a political system marked not only by freely and fairly elected government, but also the rule of law, separation of powers, and the protection of basic freedoms and liberties of citizens which make for constitutional liberalism. In no other sphere limited majority rule, institutional safeguards for minority rights and an inclusive discourse of civility are as important as in the ethnic realm. The democratic ethnic peace is actually the liberal ethnic peace.[4]

Positive ethnic peace, conceived as creative and constructive process of non-violent conflict management is the response that only mature liberal democracy can give to the challenges of ethnic diversity. Ethnic peace and democratic ethnic peace relate like the whole and its part. The distinction between these concepts derives from the qualitative dimension of the peace relationship. Negative ethnic peace can be non-democratic or illiberal or both. Positive ethnic peace can only be conceived as both democratic and liberal. In fact, it means more than just the absence of interethnic violence. It is based on cooperative patterns of group interaction, compatible self-images and reciprocal perceptions held by ethnic groups. Under these conditions ethnic groups perceive each other as equal (though culturally defined) segments of citizenry, they share the common civic bond (inclusive of multiple identities of their members) which makes for the the mutual progress of both groups and emergence of interethnic social contract.

'Stable' vs. 'unstable' peace A second basic property of ethnic peace as a function of the type of rule concerns the degree of stability and potential for the endurance of the peace relationship. The distinction between stable and unstable peace highlights its processual dimension as the performance output of conflict management norms and respective and institutions.

Boulding (1978) describes unstable peace as the condition in which peace is regarded as the norm and war is regarded as a breakdown of peace, which will be restored when the war is over. If ethnic groups prepare for or anticipate violent conflict - or if the state controlled by ethnic dominants, eventually forcefully represses ethnic dissent - we have what Boulding terms unstable peace. Unstable peace is almost invariably found in the aftermath of a suppressed violent conflict. It is the relationship enforced by deterrence or fear of violent retribution. Both ethnic dominants and ethnic subordinates continually fear for the continuation of peace under a balance of terror. The same applies to various brands of authoritarian or illiberal regimes which succeed in imposing structured ethnic dominance which is stable only as long as these regimes are in strong phases of their life-cycles. Unstable management of ethnic pluralism in divided societies hinges upon suppressing subordinate ethnic identities and superimposing the hegemony of the dominant group over others. Overwhelmingly, theory and experience show that paths to sustainable ethnic peace are to be sought elsewhere.

Boulding's (1978, p. 17) vision of stable peace between peoples represents a situation in which the probability of war is so small that it does not really enter into the calculations of any of the people involved, bears important insights for the ethnic realm:

> The stable peace relationship is not the same thing as having a common language, a common religion, a common culture, or even common interests... Neither similarities nor differences are any guarantee of peace, though they are not irrelevant and must be seen as part of the larger picture. The only guarantees of peace are compatible self-images...[which] each party in a relationship tends to create... of the other in a very complex, mutual learning process...

The causes of stable ethnic peace are not simply the opposite of the causes of ethnic violence. It is the level of supra-ethnic integration that is relevant. Faith in a secure future and the opportunity for individuals and groups of citizens to choose their own political identities are intimately connected. An ethnically diverse political community with liberal democratic governance can be considered as intranational 'security community', a term introduced by Karl Deutsch (1957, p. 5) to define an area where peace is strongly expected:

> A security community is a group of people which has become 'integrated'. By integration we mean the attainment within a territory, of a 'sense of community' and of institutions and practices strong enough and widespread enough to assure... dependable expectations of 'peaceful change' among its population.

In each of the cases of ethnically plural systems, the issue arises as to whether a political community can be said to exist. The term 'political community' in this context suggests an inclusive code of political understanding, a common political culture, symbols of statehood, and, most critical, a shared view that the outcomes of the political process (most notably, elections) are legitimate. Consolidated democratic systems are the only ones where high level of superethnic integration can be in principle achieved through forging an overarching civic bond.

Both qualitative and processual attributes of ethnic peace with respect to the type of rule are summarized in Figure 1.1.

	Stable	Unstable
Positive	Liberal Democratic Ethnic Peace	Democratizing Ethnic Peace
Negative	Unavailable	• Post-war peace • Ethnic Peace in Autocracies • Illiberal Peace in 'Ethnic' Democracies"

Figure 1.1 Ethnic peace and type of rule

On the side of negative ethnic peace only unstable varieties of the relationship are found. This is the kind of peace that predominates in autocratic and illiberal systems either before or after recurrences of ethnic violence. The positive side of ethnic peace comprises both stable and unstable forms. Stability and sustainability characterize the peace relationship within mature multiethnic democracies. Ethnic peace in democratizing multiethnic systems is a kind of relationship that has already developed some measure of positive quality but at the same time, as regards its potential for endurance, it is an elusive and highly unstable relationship.

Notes

1   Rummel (1979 and 1983) are the most prominent exceptions.
2   For a more detailed exposition of Kant's classical argument the reader is referred to the Kant's (1970) writings as well as to the ever expanding body of present-day debates over Kant's political theory of peace, for instance, Bok (1989, pp. 31-54); Sorensen (1992), Held (1995), Gaubatz (1996), Franke (1995), Huntley (1996).
3   According to Doyle (1986, p. 1166), this empirical observation was first noted by Streit (1938, pp. 88, 90).
4   On the absolute importance of the liberal conception of today's mature democracy see Zakaria (1997). For a review of discussions on non-majoritarian democracy see Ch. 4.

2 Ethnic Conflict and Crises in Changing Societies

Probing into issues of ethnic peace presupposes ethnic conflict analysis as a departure point. This chapter briefly surveys major approaches to sources, patterns of manifestation and dynamics of ethnic conflict in changing societies. It goes on to propose a conceptualization of ethnopolitical crises and makes a distinction between systemic and interactional levels of consideration. It is argued that a focus on modes and patterns of ethnopolitical crisis management has an explanatory potential for better understanding the dynamics of ethnic peace relationship in transitional systems.

Approaches to Ethnicity and Sources of Ethnic Conflict

The term *ethnic conflict* is often used loosely to describe a wide range of intrastate conflicts that are not, in fact, exclusively ethnic in character. As a working definition of an 'ethnic conflict' can be taken the one proposed by Michael Brown (1993, p. 4) where it stands for a dispute about important political, economic, social, cultural, or territorial issues between two or more ethnic communities. This characterization does not imply that it is ethnicity as such which is the conflict issue: ethnicity merely constitutes one special, albeit highly important form of socialization. Only when ethnic memberships are used consciously to distinguish the opposing actors in a conflict situation and become powerful mobilizing symbols then ethnicity becomes a key feature of conflict.

Primordialism and Instrumentalism

In a broader sense, social scientists have taken two major approaches to explain the phenomenon of ethnic conflict which differ by the underlying assumptions about ethnicity - primordialist and instrumentalist.

The *primordialist perspective* explains ethnicity in terms of inherited group behavioral characteristics and puts the stress on primordial attachments that are deemed to stem from the assumed 'givens' - of social existence (mainly immediate contiguity and kin connection) and beyond - the givenness that stems from being born into a particular religious community, speaking a particular language, and following particular social practices. These congruities of blood, speech, custom, and so on, are seen to have an ineffable, and at times overpowering, coerciveness in and of themselves. The emphasis is placed on psychological, spiritual relevance of the ethnic bond which is deemed as one of inherited group behavioral characteristics (Shils, 1957; Geertz, 1963; Van den Berghe, 1981).

Clifford Geertz (1963, pp. 105) notes that one is bound to one's kinsman, one's neighbor, one's fellow believer, ipso facto; as the result not merely of personal affection, practical necessity, common interest, or incurred obligation, but at least in great part by virtue of some unaccountable absolute import attributed to the very tie itself. For virtually every person, in every society, at almost all times, some attachments seem to flow more from a sense of natural affinity than from social interaction. The fundamental human need for identity and self-esteem, arguably, can be met only in collectivities where they connect to others like themselves in the community, and find an identity in something larger than one's own individuality. Primordialists regard ethnicity as a primordial bond between the members of a 'natural' community which precedes modern nation-states and class systems, and transcends them. Ethnic identity is a permanent feature of group life, though at times it may be repressed or exists only latently. The aim and function of ethnic movements is to 'awaken' the ethnic and build up collective awareness about it.

The *instrumentalist perspective* represents a competing approach. It builds on the fact that ethnic group formation is much more than a product of individual need. Ethnic ties are regarded as a social and political resource, a socially constructed repertoire of cultural elements that afford a site for political mobilization, especially where the ties of social class are in decay (Barth, 1969; Glazer and Moynihan; Anderson, 1983; Brass, 1985).[1] The instrumentalists argue that ethnicity is contextual, fluid, and a function of structural conditions in society. This approach derives from Marx Weber's (1968, p. 389) idea that ethnic membership per se does not constitute a group, 'it only facilitates group formation of any kind, particularly in the political sphere'. It is primarily the political community, no matter how artificially organized, that 'inspires belief in common ethnicity'. Instrumentalists have expanded Weber's insight to claim that physical and cultural attributes constitute a resource to organize a collectivity of people in order to advance certain material interests. A group constitutes itself as ethnic because it is politically useful, not because the members feel any psychological bond.

In instrumentalist perspective, ethnicity constitutes a tool to further individual or collective interests and also a potent political leverage and weapon of outbidding elites, to be created, built up, used, manipulated or discarded according to political expediency. Consequentially, ethnic identity is perceived more as a forged or, using Benedict Anderson's (1983) word, 'constructed' product, rather than as a given, i.e., it is a 'question of rational choice' (Banton, 1983; idem, 1995).

Crawford Young (1976, pp. 65, 98) clarified this new understanding of ethnicity as a contextually dependent identity that can be created and re-created anew to suit particular economic and political circumstances:

> Cultural identities are not usefully described as primordial, but are for the most part relatively new, and vastly expanded in scale....[They] focus on certain conditions under which cultural characteristics become politically salient... Identity, at bottom is a subjective self-concept of social role; it is often variable, overlapping and situational.

Paul Brass (1974, 1985) has stressed the role of politicians in mobilizing and maintaining ethnicity. Ethnic groups in the sense of conscious, solidary political entities are no more natural than nations, and are equally artifacts of political processes. Brass argues that elite competition is the basic dynamic which precipitates ethnic conflict under specific conditions. The ability to mobilize large numbers of people around symbols and values with a high emotional potential is a major resource for political parties and ethnic elites.

Comprehensive Theories: Psychology and Politics of Ethnic Conflict

Present-day scholarship of ethnic conflict seems to be in increasing consensus that the primordialist and instrumentalist approaches to ethnic identities and ethnic conflict are not mutually exclusive and can in fact be describing different sides of the same coin: ethnic identity probably has its historical roots in the collective consciousness, but it is also used intentionally by salient elites to mobilize support and stake out at precise area for political action. As observed by Sisk (1996, p. 13), 'at best one should view the two poles of the underlying primordialism - instrumentalism debate about the nature of ethnic conflict in terms of a spectrum'.

Attempts to overcome one-sidedness of either primordialist or instrumentalist approaches to explaining causes of ethnic conflict and to integrate the two approaches into a larger theoretical framework were made in the 1980s - early 1990s.

Rothschild (1981, p. 61) pioneered a conceptual framework of ethnopolitics that introduces ethnic groups and the state as actors with economic and political resources at their disposal. Ethnic assertiveness do not flow automatically out of primordial cultural or naturalistic data and differences but, instead, are the intricate products of politics:

> To stress the emotional potency of the ethnic bond is not to disengage it from hard interest leverage. In fact, the political genius of ethnicity in the contemporary developed world lies in its ability to combine emotional sustenance with calculated strategy.

To Rothschild, it is the intensely felt and deeply rooted personal ethnic identity that functions as a potent political and psychological datum in escalatory processes: 'ethnicity itself constitutes a potent, even if intangible resource for mobilizing and organizing individuals precisely because it combines interest and affective ties'. Ethnic political mobilization occurs when given cultural markers are infused with an intense, differentiating value, and are elevated into an ethnic ideology:

> This ideologization of ethnicity through the sacralization of ethnic markers and the mobilization of the sharers of these markers is the achievement of ethnic leaders and elites. It occurs in times of social strain, competition and confrontation, when the ethnic leaders persuade the bearers and sharers of the ethnic culture-markers to perceive their fate in ethnic, rather than in individual or class terms and convince them that without ethnic communal solidarity their distinctive values, customs, and traits are endangered, their personal life-aspirations are jeopardized, and the very survival of their group is imperiled (Rothschild, 1981, p. 141).

Horowitz (1985) has suggested a psycho-cultural approach to explaining ethnic conflict that stresses the importance of positional group psychology and intergroup comparisons in explaining ethnic mobilization. To Horowitz, 'relative group worth' and 'relative group legitimacy' provide alternative ways of measuring worth and constitute the major cause of interethnic tensions and strife. His argument (1985, p. 228) asserts that differences in perceptions of status are important in understanding the presence or absence of tensions between groups, especially when a given group's status is rapidly rising or falling. These two sets of causal dynamics, arguably, can explain both elite and mass behavior in ethnopolitical conflict:

> There are therefore two imperatives in ethnic conflict: the spontaneous and sentiment-driven versus the institutionally constrained. The more spontaneous the conflict behavior, the more pertinent will be the elements of group entitlement; the more tied into institutional constraints, the more we shall have to probe institutional arrangements. The tension between these two imperatives can result in the violent overthrow of the institutional system when it fails utterly to reflect ethnic sentiment.

In this way, Horowitz emphasizes a psychological dynamic that underlies the relationship between the causes of conflict, the development of an ethnic agenda, and the consequent permutations that these conflicts undergo. This has been an attempt to shift the focus of analysis from the structural conditions underlying ethnic conflict to a Weberian emphasis on *verstehen*: social, economic, and political changes result in ethnic conflict only as they are filtered through the mind of the political animal.

In a number of his works, Milton Esman (1977, 1990, 1994) devotes much effort to analyzing the complex web of interrelationships between psychological and political factors in ethnic conflict, with particular focus on issues of ethnic solidarity, ethnic mobilization and political opportunity. Regime-type is viewed as a dimension of ethnopolitical environment that shapes the course and modes of ethnic political mobilization by offering some opportunities and imposing some limitations for promoting claims on behalf of a mobilized ethnic community.

Most recent theory of ethnopolitical conflict was proposed by Gurr (1993) whose basic assumption is that ethnopolitical activism is motivated by peoples' deep-seated grievances about their collective status in combination with the situationally determined pursuit of political interests, as articulated by group leaders and political entrepreneurs. To Gurr (1993, p. 124), 'ethnopolitical mobilization and strategies in pursuit of collective goals are based on interaction of both kinds of factors'. Gurr's theory thus craftfully synthesizes both primordialist and instrumentalist assumptions. In conflict analysis the competing theoretical perspectives are relative deprivation (that contends that peoples' discontent about unjust deprivation is the primary motivation for political action) and group mobilization (that emphasizes leaders' calculated mobilization of group resources in response to changing political opportunities).²

Recently Newman (1991, p. 452 ff.; 1996) attracted attention to an important fact that students of ethnic politics have so far failed to exploit the theoretical implications of the modernization process to its fullest and badly need to develop a new ethnic modernization theory that highlights the relationship between modernization and the institutionalization, composition, and ideologies of ethnic political movements.

> In the course of modernization ethnic political identities and institutions are repeatedly created and re-created anew, a process that constantly destroys the old ethnic loyalties while creating new ethnic ideologies, institutions, and constituencies. The process of modernization explains not only the origins of ethnic conflict but also the form of that conflict, and the success or failure of specific ethnic political movements.

Structure and Manifestations of Ethnopolitical Conflict

To R. Dahrendorf (1959), the prelude to any social conflict lies in structural situations in which conflict is potential. Ethnic conflict, in fact, takes place within a socio-political structure that qualifies it in various ways. In the realm of ethnic conflict analysis scholarly attention in the realm of ethnic conflict analysis has been attracted to three issues: 1) the configurations between ethnicity and society (particularly, the structure of ethnic stratification and social cleavages), 2) the relationship between ethnic groups and the state, and 3) dynamics of ethnic conflict.

Ethnicity and Society

Several attempts have been made to delineate patterns of ethnic stratification. Two of those models have particular relevance for conflict management – the ones by Rothschild and Horowitz, respectively.

Rothschild (1981, pp. 80-2) suggests that societies may stratify their ethnic groups according to models of vertical hierarchy, of parallel segmentation, or of cross-patterned reticulation. In the vertical hierarchical model, 'there is a correspondence among all dimensions, political, social, economic and cultural - of ethnic superordination and subordination' as it was in South Africa's classical apartheid system. In models of parallel ethnic segmentation, 'each ethnic community is internally stratified by socio-economic criteria and each has a political elite to represent its interest vis-à-vis the corresponding elites of the other ethnic segments'. In the reticulate model, 'ethnic groups and social classes cross populate each other - but the system is not random or symmetrical or egalitarian. Each ethnic group pursues a wide range of economic functions and occupations, and each economic class or sector organically incorporates members of several ethnic categories'. To Rothschild, the reticulate model provides the best conditions for the gradual and peaceful resolution of ethnic conflicts.

Following Max Weber who used 'caste structure' to refer to hierarchically ordered groups and 'ethnic coexistence' to denote parallel groups Horowitz (1985, pp. 21-4) distinguishes between ranked and unranked ethnic groups as resting upon the coincidence of social class with ethnic groups. When the two coincide, it is possible to speak of ranked ethnic groups. Where groups are cross class, Horowitz suggests speaking of unranked ethnic groups.

Effects of ethnic cleavages on prospects for peace and multiethnic democracy vary with the pattern of cleavage and the way they articulate with political structures. In the case of ranked ethnic groups, when social cleavages are reinforcing rather than overlapping, the potential for conflict is more acute. In unranked systems, on the contrary, parallel ethnic groups co-exist, each group internally stratified. Consequentially, when ethnic groups are cross class and/or cross-confessional, ethnic identities result crosscutting and thus are less likely to threaten political stability.

A related factor of ethnopolitical stability is the degree of political institutionalization and the way it affects ethnosocial differentiation. Horowitz (1985, p. 19) observes that in advanced post-modern democracies where political institutions are highly developed 'ethnicity... typically does not displace all other forms of group difference'. Conversely, reinforcing cleavages constitute the hallmark of a deeply divided society. Such kind of societies are likely to experience significant and violent conflict because of the presence of separate organizations that 'permeate and divide every aspect of social fabric on the basis of identity'. Thus, although people in developing countries may maintain the same scale of social roles as people who live in more economically modernized societies, as Huntington (1968) noted, their political institutions are less developed and articulated. As a result, one social identity can more easily be transformed into a dominant political identity and determinant of political debate and behavior. Martin Heisler (1990, p. 26-7) makes a similar observation:

> In the modern West neither individual identity nor the structure of the collectivity is likely to be based in its essence on ethnicity... [rather] the ethnic dimensions of individual and group life [are] fragmented and intermittent.

This is the case because the state, the definer of political relations in the West, relates to its citizens through its conception of individual rights rather than group rights. In this regard, it has been noted that all societies promote the existence of numerous social roles for individuals. But states tend to divide social roles from political roles. 'In societies with stronger and more developed pluralist political institutions political roles are almost as fluid as social roles and thus, it is nearly impossible for one social role to dominate the political agenda' (Newman, 1996, p. 5)[3].

Ethnicity, Political Power, and the State

Ethnically relevant power differences and attempts at redistribution of power arrangements are among the major causes of ethnopolitical conflict. In Horowitz's words (1985, p. 187), power is both an instrument to secure other, tangible goods and benefits and also the benefit itself.

> Power is the main goal at both ends of the spectrum. At one end, power is sought purely for its value in confirming a claimed status. To attain the status, power need hardly be exercised; the main thing is to gain it. At the other end, power is sought as a means to goals so diffuse, so remote, so difficult to specify, that attainment of power becomes, again, an end in itself. Power is sought to prevent the emergence of dire but distant and dimly perceived consequences. So critical and dangerous are those feared consequences that it is deemed vital to take steps to avert them far in advance of their likely occurrence. In short, power may be desired not for the lesser things it can gain, but for the greater things it reflects and prevents.

Power is often sought for the confirmation of ethnic status such as citizenship, electoral systems, designation of official languages and religions, the rights of groups to a 'special position' in the polity. Strategic choices made by ethnic contenders derive not only from their perceived interest but also, and quite often too, from perceived conflict of values and symbols.

It has been observed by many that ethnic groups have the propensity to derive 'prestige and self-respect' from the harmony between their norms and those which achieve dominance in the society. When status uncertainties exist, efforts are made to obtain authoritative allocations of prestige. 'Mass restiveness occurs when the state is not symbolically aligned with those who feel threatened' (Edelman, 1964, p. 167). Ethnopolitics is indeed a blend of both interest politics and symbolic politics. Symbolic politics induces the value dimension to the conflict. One of the reasons why conflicts over symbols and principles are difficult to settle is that the outcome of the dispute cannot be divided in a way that will partially satisfy both parties (Coser, 1956, pp. 118; Obershall, 1973, pp. 49-50). To this kind often belong ethnopolitical conflicts. Azar (1990a and 1990b) has coined the term 'protracted social conflict' to refer to deep-seated cleavages between racial, religious, or ethnic groups, characterized by continuing hostility with sporadic outbreaks of violence, and caused by the frustration of basic human needs for security, recognition, and distributive justice.

For these reasons, ethnic group grievances are commonly targeted at the state, while ethnic conflict is often a competition among groups for ownership of the state. The modern state establishes and enforces the formal rules and the informal practices that determine who gets what-the relative power and status of ethnic communities and, thus, the opportunities and life chances of their individual constituents. Esman (1990, pp. 58-9) points out at three groups of values that are allocated by the modern state (political participation, cultural status, and economic opportunities) that tend to be particularly consequential in the realm of ethnic politics.

Similarly, scholarly research suggests that state responses to ethnic grievances are crucial in shaping the course and the outcomes of conflicts (Rothschild 1981; Brass, 1991; Horowitz, 1985; Esman, 1994; Gurr, 1993).

Dynamics of Ethnic Conflict and Conflict Stages

Ethnic conflict dynamics includes changes in intensity and/or magnitude of conflict feelings and behaviors. To discern specific critical junctions (crises) in conflict dynamics is of prime importance for conflict management, for they represent those turning points that ultimately determine the prospects of ethnic peace. Conceptualization of ethnopolitical crises is warranted with relation to two basic contexts of their manifestation. On the one hand, crises can be viewed as products of group interaction at a particular stage of any conflict case dynamics. On the other hand, there is also the obvious need to conceive of crises in a cross-case context over time when ethnopolitical dynamics is itself a reflection of dynamics of the larger political change.

It has been stressed by many that conflict theory-building would be significantly improved by analyzing conflict in terms of life cycle, or a stage process (Scherer et al., 1975; Eberwein, 1981; Luterbacher, 1984, p. 185; Vasquez, 1993, ch. 5; Hammastrom, 1995, p. 235). The life cycle of the conflict is centered on turning points in its escalation/deescalation. This is relevant for conflict management endeavors and determining the chances of settlement since the factors behind the initiation of a conflict may not be the same as those which account for its escalation or outcome. Zartman (1991, p. 16) holds that the course of the conflict itself can be an effective influence on its management, and an evaluation of when and how to use carrots and sticks is important to assessing possibilities for resolution.

Being an exchange of negative outputs between elements in a competitive relationship, conflict passes through a number of identifiable stages in its development. At the 'precompetition stage' the parties have a cooperative relationship or are relatively independent. The relationship is either positive or no interaction occurs at all. At the 'competition stage', the system changes (due to internal dynamics or to events in its environment) so that the parties enter into a competitive relationship. During the 'conflict proper stage' the parties attack each other. When the magnitude of conflicting interaction intensifies, an escalation is produced. Louis Kriesberg (1982, p. 167) argues that 'escalation occurs as people in a struggle believe that the gains if they triumph and the losses if they are defeated are greater than the costs of raising the magnitude of their own conflict behavior and absorbing the increased burdens that the adversary places upon them'.

Escalation is a 'positive feedback' process in which each event intensifies its own precursors. An action by one party stimulates a reaction by the other party, which is in turn reciprocated, and so on, in a spiral.[4] Cooperative relationships between the parties are destroyed, the damage of battle becomes grounds for further battle, the conflict-oriented constituencies become dominant in each party while other elements tend to align on one side or the other, forming blocs which induce conflict polarization. De-escalation, conversely, refers to a reduction in one or more dimensions of the conflict behavior between adversaries. In addition it also signifies efforts to move towards a settlement of the dispute, at best, negotiations about an agreement that resolves a particular dispute (Kriesberg, 1991).

Interactional crises are intimately related to these two basic processes of conflict dynamics and can be of two sub-types - crises of escalation and crises of de-escalation. Each of the types signifies a turning point reached in the course of conflict. Protracted conflicts are characterized by recurrence of crises when attempts to achieve a desired turn of events in the course of a conflict fail. The stage of crisis can be deemed as the peak of every spiral of escalation or de-escalation. It marks a critical junction when a turn is reached. It is distinguished by a new and different level of interaction, and often a change in patterns of strategic interaction occurs. It is at this point in the escalatory processes that violence is most likely to erupt. The ensuing point of the deescalatory crisis means either resolution or settlement.

On the whole, crises can be viewed as those moments which can help to start conflict transformation (Rupersinghe, 1995, p. viii). Deescalations tend to ensue from the crisis stage when the conflict gets stalemated at a high, mutually hurting level of antagonism. The resulting deadlock keeps both parties from achieving their goals. In this regard, recent scholarship discusses the notion of *conflict ripeness* as a metaphorical way to refer to the right time to undertake an effort to make a desired change, most usually to transform the conflict. Ripeness refers to circumstances when the conflict is ready for an effort to bring about a particular change (Modelski, 1964; Zartman, 1985; Touval and Zartman, 1985; Zartman, 1991).

Socio-Political Change and Ethnopolitical Crises

Comparative cross-case studies suggest that under rapid and profound transformations in society's political system or regime the occurrence of ethnopolitical crises as part of conflict dynamics tends to reflect the larger dynamics of socio-political change. A broader conceptualization of crises at both the system level and the level of strategic group interaction is warranted in this regard. This section intends, first, to overview major sets of factors which affect ethnopolitical dynamics in times of political transitions; second, to propose a broader conceptualization of ethnopolitical crises and their typology; and finally, to conclude on the linkage between crisis management and dynamics of ethnic peace in changing societies.

Socio-Political Change and Ethnic Conflict Dynamics

Socio-political change is an important variable influencing the conflict-peace continuum of ethnicity. 'Times of transition are often times of tension'(Shibutani and Kwan, 1965, ch. 14). The experience of the recent decade clearly shows that in times of transition ethnic relations can escalate to disruptive strife at an extremely precipitous rate. At the same time, as suggested by the developments in Spain and South Africa, the long-standing ethnic conflicts in democratizing systems can de-escalate and relations among ethnic groups can become more accommodative.

More generally, intensified ethnopolitical dynamics in transitional periods is accounted by cumulation of three sets of factors: perceptional, institutional, and security-strategic.

Perceptional factors Transitions generate diffuse uncertainty among all groups in society. Collectively shared perceptions matter most among the causes of conflict-proneness under this uncertainty. Many scholars starting with Horowitz (1985) point at the tremendous conflict potential of anxiety-laden ethnic perceptions and problems of credible commitment that spiral in the conditions of rapid political change. Lake and Rothschild (1996, p. 41), among others, observe that collective ethnic fears of the future contain within them the potential for outbursts of violence.

> Ethnic activists and political entrepreneurs, operating within groups build upon these fears of insecurity and polarize society. Political memories and emotions also magnify these anxieties, driving groups further apart. Together, these between-group and within-group strategic interactions produce a toxic brew of distrust and suspicion that can explode into murderous violence.

Vesna Pešic (1994), an academic and a peace activist in the former Yugoslavia captured this almost aphoristically: ethnic conflict is caused by the 'fear of the future, lived through the past'.[5] In such conditions, the tasks of preserving ethnic peace merge with the endeavors of negotiating the ethnic future. Collective fears of the future receive a redoubled impetus when states lose their ability to arbitrate between groups or provide credible guarantees of protection for groups.

Institutional factors Lake and Rothschild (1996, p. 43) argue that state weakness, whether it arises incrementally out of competition between groups or from extremists actively seeking to destroy peace, is a necessary precondition for violent ethnic conflict to erupt.

Under rapidly evolving change old assumptions become increasingly irrelevant, and established procedures and rules increasingly lose their validity and credibility. As a result of breakdown of general and/or specialized political institutions of the old regime comes the breakdown of its conflict management structures.

When known rules of conflict resolution within a society become outdated or fail to settle conflict peacefully, most disputes tend to escalate into individual, group, and class hostility, leading to confrontation and disruptive strife. The failure of governments to accommodate rising political demands within an institutional context often culminates in political violence. Such dangers are especially acute in multiethnic societies when politicized and discontented ethnic minorities encounter few institutional channels for expressing political dissent. State weakness ('softness' of the state) explains many instances in the context of ethnic violence that broke out in some successor states after the collapse of communist regimes in Eastern Europe and ex-USSR (Snyder 1993).

It has been noted that aggressive nationalism often emerges from breakdowns in state structure and capacity. When states lose their ability to sustain performance legitimacy and to deliver public goods and services, political chaos usually ensues. These periods of transition can trigger the ratcheting up of nationalism through several pathways. Governing elites - or their opponents - may turn to nationalistic appeals to rally popular support and divert attention from domestic woes. The military, seeking to take advantage of the political vacuum to better its own fortunes, may generate nationalistic myths and inflate external threats. The public, in the absence of functioning political institutions capable of channeling mass activism and popular disaffection, may rally around strong and virulent currents of nationalism (Breiully, 1982, ch. 15; Mansfield and Snyder, 1995 and 1996).

Security-strategic factors In multiethnic societies, the crisis of state institutions, which necessarily accompanies any serious political transition, induces a particular kind of security dilemmas. Barry Posen (1993) has considered the motives why ethnic groups would turn to violence to counter real or perceived threats that become salient in the conditions when national, regional, and international authorities become too weak to ensure the security of individual groups. As Posen explains, in systems where there is no sovereign - i.e., where anarchy prevails - individual groups have to provide for their own defense. They have to worry about whether neighboring groups pose security threats and whether threats will grow or diminish over time. Under this condition, which Posen (1993, p. 105) refers to as 'emerging anarchy', security becomes of paramount concern for ethnic groups. In taking steps to defend themselves - mobilizing armies and deploying military forces - they often threaten the security of others. This, in turn, can lead neighboring groups to take actions that will diminish the security of the first group. Thus, the security dilemma is produced.

In this respect, Posen (1993) has pointed out at the collapse of a meaningful security structure in Eastern Europe, the disrepair of national military establishments, and the operation of the security dilemma as the key causes of intensifying ethnonationalist conflicts in the former communist countries in the early 1990s. Threat perceptions were by no means uniform across the region, but uncertainty and insecurity were and, to a considerable extent, remain pervasive. For instance, in East Central Europe, it is the perceived existence of a security vacuum between east and west that heightens a sense of vulnerability. In some post-Soviet successor states (notably, in the Baltics and Moldova) the prospects of a resurgence of Russian imperialism fuel feelings of insecurity. In the immediate aftermath of the Soviet collapse in Russia itself, perceptions of vulnerability were heightened by the loss of empire, concern about the security and welfare of Russians outside the homeland, and the prospect of the fragmentation of the Russian Federation itself. In all of these cases, according to Posen's line of argument, insecurity and the prospective steps needed to redress it serve to increase ethnopolitical tensions both domestically and regionally.

Given the often cumulative action of the above factors, any study of ethnopolitical conflict management in changing systems becomes a study of critical challenges made and critical choice of responses to make in order to preserve and sustain extremely fragile ethnic peace. Concerns with ethnopolitical crisis prevention and management loom large in this regard.

Conceptual Map of the 'Crisis' Concept

The word 'crisis' is frequently used in everyday language. It derives from the Greek '*κρινω*' ('to decide') and in its non-technical usage, originally means the timing when a decision is bound to be taken. Political crises are crises with relevance to the functioning of the political system and, thus, are understood in a wider sense than merely governmental crises; they call for and possibly lead to substantial changes in policies or the political order, not merely a replacement of personnel (Zimmerman, 1983, p. 189).

The problem of providing a satisfactory definition of *crisis* is particularly acute when viewed against the general tendency to use this word indiscriminately and without explaining its precise meaning. Therefore, for the purpose of a more organized reflection on this class of conflict phenomena, it may be helpful to sort out among the flood of outpouring definitions. In contemporary literature one can find three main sub-fields where attempts to elaborate conceptualizations of crises have been made: history research, political development theory, and international studies.

One of the approaches originated in studies of history. The historian's tendency is to start with events as a kind of social sample to be analyzed. The definition of a crisis as any serious threat to the functioning of a political regime is traditionally included in the historical literature (Holsti, 1980). It also allows stress on the element of conflict that is usually part of such crises, while inviting one to see events through the eyes of historical actors. A related conception of a 'crisis' refers it to an important change in the way politics works, to new institutions or changes in the political process. It does not matter whether these changes are 'defensive' or 'innovative', but they must now appear to become irreversible.

A second approach to crises emerged in the field of structural-functionalist theories of modernization and political development. It considers crises as a typology of the problems that governments face. This understanding was advanced by a team of political scientists, invited by the Social Science Research Council, and who over more than a decade were engaged in a collegial search for the understanding of the process of political development. Their conception centered on a 'development syndrome' or the three dimensions of a political system: differentiation ('the process of progressive separation and specialization of roles, institutional spheres, and associations in societies undergoing modernization'), equality ('national citizenship, a universalistic legal order, and achievement norms') and capacity ('how the polity manages tensions and stimulates new change'). In the concluding volume of a series of their studies, political development is seen as the successive resolution of a number of crises that are faced by modernizing political systems in the attempts to develop equality, capacity and differentiation (Binder et al., 1971). Grew (1978) has made a fruitful attempt to apply this perspective to the realm of history studies.

The five crises (or problem areas) are thought as having a close relationship to the process by which the government makes and enforces decisions. The successful or, on the contrary, failed resolution of each of the crises marks cardinal stages in a polity's developmental process and, therefore, in certain respects, parallels stages of psycho-social development of personality, as discussed by Erik Erikson (1958, 1963, and 1968). More specifically, five crises constitute the sequence of political development:

> *Identity* An identity crisis relates to mass and elite culture in terms of nationalistic feelings about territory, cleavages that undermine national unity, and conflict between ethnic loyalty and national commitments. Its resolution implies the extension of an active sense of membership in the national community to the entire population; in essence, this is the issue of making state equivalent to nation.
> *Legitimacy* A legitimacy crisis arises because of differences over authority. Its resolution has to provide for a change from the transcendental to immanent sources of authority, for securing a generalized acceptance of the rightness of the exercise and structure of authority by the state, so that its routine regulations and acts obtain voluntary and willing compliance;
> *Participation* A crisis of participation occurs when 'the governing elite views the demands or behavior of individuals and groups seeking to participate in the political system as illegitimate'. Resolving this crisis means the enlargement of the numbers of persons actively involved in the political arena, from elite to mass and from family to group through such devices as voting and other;
> *Distribution* has to meet the challenge of ensuring that the valued resources in society, such as material well-being and status, are available on equal terms to all persons. Its resolution involves changes in distribution from status and privilege to ability, achievement.
> *Penetration* implies extending the effective operation of the state to the farthest periphery of the system.[6]

To Sydney Verba (1971, pp. 300-1), crises represent situations in which the society moves in a new direction. They are the 'major decisional points at which the society is redefined', they signify 'a change that requires some governmental innovation and institutionalization if elites are not seriously to risk a loss of their position or if the society is to survive'. This definition represents an attempt to distinguish between ordinary governmental performance and responsiveness and particularly crucial periods of governmental innovation. To Verba, crises arise when there is an increase in pressure for change (that is, members of the polity are discontented with one of the five aspects of the decisional process), and some new institutionalized means of handling problems of this sort is required to satisfy the discontent. Identity, legitimacy, participation, penetration, and distribution are thought of as aspects of governmental decision-making that can turn into problems or even lead to crises when they become arenas of overt conflict.

A third cluster of approaches to conceptualizing crises has been developed in the field of international studies. For a long time, international crisis analysis had contained an impressive record of descriptive studies but no general theories.[7] In recent times, the discussion of international crises reflects already a bewildering kaleidoscope of theories. Three different ways have been taken by scholars of international politics to define the concept: systemic, process-related, and decision-making.

A systemic definition sees a crisis as a brief phase in which the breakdown or transformation of a system (a pattern of relationships) is threatened. Researchers who employ the systemic approach are united in viewing crisis as a situation which involves change in the normal interaction patterns between states or in the international system as a whole. Cora Bell (1971), for example, drawing on the original Greek meaning of the term, defines international crises as 'the turning points or decision points in relations between states', when 'conflicts rise to a level which threatens to transform the nature of the relationship'.

The process definitions view international crisis as such turning point at which an unusually intense period of conflictive interactions occurs. According to McClelland (1968, pp. 160-1; 1972, pp. 6-7), a crisis is, in some way, a 'change of state' in the flow of international political actions. Acute international crises are 'short bursts' affairs and 'are marked by an unusual volume and intensity of events.' Similarly, Azar (1972, p. 184) defined an international crisis in terms of interaction above the threshold of a 'normal relations range': 'Interaction above the present upper critical threshold ... for more than a very short time implies that a crisis situation has set in'. Combined structural-process definitions go further, by identifying an international crisis as a situation characterized by basic change in processes that might affect structural variables of a system. Young (1968, p. 15) stated this view clearly: 'A crisis in international politics is a process of interaction occurring at higher levels of perceived intensity than the ordinary flow of events and characterized by significant implications for the stability of some system or subsystem'.

The decision-making definitions, as the name suggests, focus on the process by which decisions are made during a crisis. Crises are conceived essentially in terms of the perception of the decision-makers of a single state. The most representative and most widely quoted definition in this regard used to be the one developed by Charles Hermann (1969, p.29): 'Crisis is a situation that (1) threatens the high-priority goals of the decision-making unit; (2) restricts the amount of time available for response before the situation is transformed; and (3) surprise the members of the decision-making unit when it occurs'. More recently, Brecher (1977), Brecher and James (1988), and Brecher and Wilkenfeld (1989)'s analyses of the findings from the International Crisis Behavior (ICB) project became the most well-known attempt so far to integrate the multitude of approaches in all the subfields of the international crisis research. A crisis is viewed as a situational change in the external or internal environment that creates in the minds of the incumbent decision-makers of an international actor a perceived threat from the external environment to basic values to which a responsive decision is deemed necessary.[8]

In my view, the developmental perspective on the one hand, and insights from process approaches to crises, on the other, help conceptualize two different kinds of crises in ethnopolitics of changing societies.

Typology of Ethnopolitical Crises in Changing Societies

Ethnopolitical crises represent the necessary concomitants of socio-political transformations in multiethnic systems. Depending upon the level of analysis, two basic types of ethnopolitical crises need be distinguished: crises at the system level (or systemic ethnopolitical crises) and crises at the level of strategic interactions (or interactional ethnopolitical crises).

Systemic Ethnopolitical Crises Many agree that the decline in interest in structural-functionalism as a theoretical force in comparative politics may have been premature and that the modernization theory has stood the test of time quite well.[9] Revisiting theories of modernization and political development makes it possible to infer important insights for understanding the linkage between ethnopolitical crises, change and choice.

Processes in multiethnic polities induce the necessity to resolve systemic ethnopolitical crises which can be conceived as ethnically-relevant dimensions of the five crises of the modernization syndrome. Such resolution calls for adequate innovations with the aim to institutionalize a new balance between ethnopolitical identities and legitimacy.

Profound socio-economic and political transformations rarely leave relationships between dominant and subordinate groups undisturbed, and a fundamental change tends to take place in the context of the modern state based on the notion of equality of citizenship. Recent scholarship argues that, over a long time-span, the transition to modern statehood is marked by two phases through which subordinate ethnic groups potentially pass. The first phase, as identified by Coackley (1993, p.4-5), is characterized by a demand for equality of all citizens and for individual rights, resting on an assumption of a basic legal identity of all humans. This phase often begins in a period in which the subordinate group's identity is other-defined (that is, it is the dominant group which is most anxious to highlight and maintain the ethnic boundary) and in which the subordinate group is discriminated against. In the second phase the subordinate group's demand is for recognition of its separateness. While its members may be satisfied with the attainment of at least formal equality, ethnic self-consciousness may, depending on the concrete circumstances, propel subordinate groups to make an additional set of demands that come to base on a new premise which is the claim that members of the ethnic minority are *different*, and that this difference should receive institutional recognition. The demand for individual rights is thus followed by a demand for ethnic group rights (Coackley, 1993, pp. 4-6; Allardt, 1979, pp. 27-30, 43-7).

Participation is another crisis area of modernizing ethnopolitics that warrants institutional innovation. As economic modernization proceeds, growing levels of literacy, higher education, and media exposure contribute to increased social mobilization (Deutsch, 1953). This heightened political awareness inevitably contribute to greater political demands. As Huntington (1968) cogently argued, the processes of economic modernization generate increasing demands for political participation by opening up new opportunities for physical, social, and economic mobility. At the same time, the lack of adequate institutional channels provides for increased political instability of modernizing societies. Research by Myron Weiner (1978), for example, suggests that accelerating mobility in the context of scarce resources in a polyethnic society can lead to mobilization along ethnic lines and result in interethnic tensions. Faced with such increased demands and other ethnic tensions, states can resort to coercive strategies, which are, inevitably, short-term palliatives. Therefore, over the longer haul, states, especially multiethnic, have little choice but to develop institutional capacities for accommodating rising demands for political participation.

In case of profound political change associated with democratization, system-level ethnopolitical crises can be conceived of as a sequence of institutional problems that governments of multiethnic systems face in their attempts to develop systemic pre-requisites for a valid multiethnic democracy. In this understanding, an ethnopolitical crisis relates to an important change in the way ethnic politics work, to new institutions and redistribution of ethnopolitical arrangements.

Identity, legitimacy and participation problem areas (crises) are, obviously, the most important ones in this regard. Transitions unfold from a crisis of legitimacy that the old regime cannot resolve or reabsorb by whatever available and acceptable means. In multiethnic polities, the legitimacy crisis is tightly intertwined with identity crisis differentially experienced by groups of ethnic dominants and ethnic subordinates. Ultimately, completing a democratic transition must produce legitimation of the post-authoritarian regime by both ethnic dominants and ethnic subordinates, that is to say, with ethnopolitical legitimation. This, in turn, hinges upon establishing a certain balance between ethnic and political (civic) identities of nationhood as a necessary precondition for expanding democratic political participation without jeopardizing the system's stability. Consequentially, this can lay the ground for the development of democratic legitimacy and forging interethnic social contract.

Interactional ethnopolitical crises   An interactional crisis refers to an important change in strategic interactions between political ethnic actors - a set of moves and countermoves between the state, ethnic dominants and ethnic subordinates which is aimed at ethnically-relevant proaction, inaction or reaction as regards the direction of evolving political change.

Occurrence of such critical junctions in transitional ethnopolitics can be identified by the simultaneous presence of several immediate constituents:

1) A communally perceived threat coming from environment to basic values of an ethnic group, usually in the form of a stark anticipation of an abrupt change in a group's status within the political system. The anticipated change of status has to do with issues of inclusion or exclusion that become salient during transitional period. Interactions become centerd on elaboration and/or acceptance of new rules of the ethnopolitical game.

2) A sharp increase of anxiety-laden ethnic apprehensions that come to be focused on one single issue. Ethnopolitical interactional crises need be distinguished from general background tension, not because of their short duration (actually, crises can be quite protracted), but because the conflict interaction becomes focused on a particular issue which requires crucial decisions. Such ethnically-relevant focus of crisis can be a border dispute, economic or fiscal boycott against or by an ethnoterritorially defined subnational unit, alleged mistreatment of an ethnically subordinate group, discriminatory legislation, threat to territorial integrity of a state or to the regime of established ethnic dominance and so on. Indeed crises are often named after the principal issue at stake.
3) Under these critical conditions ethnic interaction escalates above the threshold of a normal relations' range and the probability of violence is unusually heightened. Triggering events can easily touch off the transition from non-violent to violent political ethnic action.

In rapidly changing systems, the issues that underlie strategic interactions between ethnic groups, actually, correspond to one of the problem areas (crises) at the system level. Therefore, if system-level problems (crises) are ignored, left unattended or coercively settled, they are more than likely to reemerge as interactional crises with every new shift of interethnic power balance at every new phase of rapidly evolving sociopolitical change.

Ethnopolitical interactional crises partake of process and decision-making instances. On the one hand, they represent turning points in ethnic conflict dynamics when intense conflict interaction results in unusually high volume and intensity of political events. On the other hand, like their counterparts at the system level, interactional crises represent problems that governments face and are decision-making crises. They imperatively demand critical choices in the pursued policies.

Overall, an ethnopolitical crisis (be it systemic or interactional) is, actually, concentrated ethnic politics in microcosm. Such elements as power configurations, interests, values, risks, perceptions, degrees of resolve, bargaining, and decision making lie at the core of ethnic politics. In a crisis they tend to leap out at the observer and to be sharply focused on a single well-defined issue. Concerns about ethnic peace thus, merge with the tasks of ethnopolitical crisis management.

Ethnopolitical Crisis Management and Dynamics of Ethnic Peace

The term 'crisis management' has been appropriated by students of conflict from the field of international politics.[10] The purpose of crisis management is to resolve a dangerous confrontation without fighting, but with vital interests preserved. Under crisis, the tension exists between two objectives - protection of one's interests and avoidance of measures that could trigger undesired escalation. This tension creates the policy dilemma of crisis management (George, 1991, pp. 9-11, 22-4, 377-95).

In ethnopolitical interactions crisis management means dealing with turning points through crafting policies that ethnic leadership must adopt in the conditions of unusually heightened tensions among and within their ethnic constituencies. The context is provided by the salient dynamics of conflict that can easily go beyond the threshold of nonviolent confrontation (in case of escalation) or when possibilities to transform or reduce conflict arise out of mutually hurting stalemate (in case of crises of de-escalation). Crisis management can be metaphorically conceived of as the emergency room in conflict management hospital. Dealing with a crisis in interactions means dealing with a serious conflict that has reached a breakdown point. The first steps to be taken in a crisis situation are measures to arrest escalation with a view to stabilize the conflict at the pre-crisis level.

Agenda-setting is particularly relevant in crisis management. Crisis agenda-setting is the process of raising issues in the process of policy coordination between two or more actors to salience among the relevant community of actors (Winn 1996, pp. 19-23). It thus becomes a primary tool for securing and extending power by the state, and ethnic groups.

Recent scholarship stresses the feasibility of using constructive conflict management to deal with conflicts arising as a consequence of interpersonal or intergroup diversity (e.g., Boardman and Horowitz, 1994; Deutsch, 1987 and 1994; Rubin 1994). In this respect, the variety of crisis management techniques or strategies used to cope with crises can also be considered within these two broad categories.

Destructive patterns involve inaction, deception, and various forms of domination ranging from coercive bargaining to non-violent intimidation and finally, direct violence. Coercive bargaining is the principal form of interaction in crises. It is to be kept present that, competitive processes, however, can produce no real solutions. At best, they can result in settlements that coercion and power-based negotiations impose.

Constructive patterns of crisis management rest on such techniques as negotiations, third-party mediation, arbitration and adjudication. Basically, constructive management of crises requires integrative bargaining, or problem-solving negotiations which are considered as fundamentally different from bargaining as such (Pruitt and Rubin, 1986; Groom, 1990, 1991; Rubin, Pruitt and Kim, 1994). The pursuit of the problem-solving strategy strongly reduces the likelihood of runaway escalation under crisis. On the one hand, it does not pose a threat to Other and is psychologically incompatible with the use of heavy contentious tactics. On the other hand, problem solving encourages the discovery of compromises and integrative options that serve both parties' interests. It goes without saying that under heavy time pressures, which invariably accompany crisis situations, creative and innovative approaches in order to start a problem-solving process are warranted if peace is to be preserved.

Peace as a process and a result of social interactions and its quality strongly depend on the choices made by political actors from the menu of crisis management strategies. Ethnopolitical crisis is closely related to conflict and violence, two other concepts that are essential to understanding politics. The occurrence of violence, at any point in the evolution of a crisis, intensifies disruptive interaction and perceived harm and stress. And these have important consequences for decision-making. Violence, in this perspective, is *one of several crisis management techniques*: verbal, political, economic, non-violent military, and violent; that is, to paraphrase Clausewitz's classic dictum, *violence is a continuation of crisis by other means.* Violence (either state or insurgent) does not eliminate or replace crisis. Rather, crisis is accentuated and aggravated by violence. Crises have - or will be - resolved only if both parties choose to resolve them rather than fight.

It takes one to make a war, but it takes two to avoid it. In this respect, the linkage between democracy and the quality of ethnic peace becomes clear. If both conflicting ethnic parties espouse norms of non-violent conflict management and repose legitimacy in the institutions that function on the basis of these norms, the chances to reach a peaceful outcome of a crisis interaction are greatly enhanced. In the subsequent chapters I am going to consider issues of ethnic peace and ethnopolitical crisis management in their relation to democratization in more detail.

Notes

1. On some of the latest polemics of the two approaches see Grosby (1994). Conversi (1995) proposes a three-fold distinction among contemporary perspectives on ethnicity: ethno-symbolic, homeostatic and transactional approaches.
2. The relative deprivation perspective is developed most fully in Gurr (1970). It is similar to 'emergent human needs' theory used by Azar and Burton (1986). A comprehensive statement of the mobilization perspective is Tilly, Tilly, and Tilly (1975) and Tilly (1978). The approaches are compared in Rule (1988, chs. 6-7).
3. In a series of West European case studies Newman (1996) examines the sustained effort that institutions, both organizations and patterns of behavior, undertake to control and curtail the effect of ethnic perceptions on the political debate.
4. This sort of phenomenon has been called 'a Richardson process' after the scientist who demonstrated that relatively simple mathematical formulas for these reactions could describe the arms race that led to World War I, see Richardson (1960).
5. Vesna Pešic, Remarks to the Institute on Global Conflict and Cooperation (IGCC). Working Group on the International Spread and Management of Ethnic Conflict, October 1, 1994, quoted in Lake and Rothschild (1996, p. 43).
6. Quotes in Binder et al. (1971, pp. 53, 77-8, 187, 205-206).
7. This paucity of broad-range theories applied to all four of the main subfields: (1) origins of crises, (2) behavior during crises, (3) crisis management, and (4) impact of crises on actors and the international system (Hopple and Rossa, 1981, pp. 65-98). For reviews of the state of the art in international crisis studies see Haas (1986), Holsti (1972, 1989), Brecher (1993, ch. 1), Richardson (1994, chs 1-3).
8. In operational terms, Brecher identifies four necessary and sufficient conditions of a crisis situation, as these are perceived by the highest-level decision-makers of the actor concerned: '1) A change in its external or internal environment which generates 2) a threat to basic values, with a simultaneous or subsequent 3) high probability of involvement in military hostilities, and the awareness of 4. a finite time for response to the external value threat' (Brecher 1978, pp. 5-21, Brecher 1993, pp. 6-12).
9. As stressed by Ruth Lane (1994, p. 462), if reformulated in more precise terms, the structural-functional model may also provide a guide in formalizing its successors and, seen in this new terms, represents a theory of state-society relations, as well as potentially a theory of state. Lane proposes to 'invert' structural-functionalism through rational choice theory. On the continued relevance of structural-functionalist perspective of analysis and new institutionalism see also Pye (1990), Fukuyama (1995, pp. 21-4), Sartori (1995, p.105), Remmer (1997).
10. Originally, the term 'crisis management' came into general usage after the Cuban missile crisis in 1962. The term was popularized by Robert McNamara's comment on the Cuban experience: 'There is no longer such thing as strategy, only crisis management', see more in Clutterbuck (1993).

3 Democracy and Multiethnicity: Conditions of Democratic Ethnic Peace

Understanding conditions of democratic ethnic peace requires probing into the relationship between ethnicity and democratic rule. This chapter delineates the field of related theoretical concepts and concerns. Two basic issues are particularly relevant in this regard: first, the manifold linkage between democracy, nation-state and nationhood; and second, peculiarities of the mode by which democratic systems process ethnopolitical conflict. Basing on normative and structural explanatory models of the democratic peace proposition it is proposed to distinguish between cultural and institutional sets of conditions that account for the peaceful pattern of ethnic relations that prevails in consolidated democracies.

Democracy, Nation-State and Nationalism

Modern Democracy

In the burgeoning literature on democracy one can easily observe a pronounced definitional confusion. Enough is to mention that Collier and Levitsky (1997) have identified more than 550 'subtypes' of democracy. Democracy is 'the word that resonates in people's minds and springs from their lips as they struggle for freedom and a better way of life; it is the word whose meaning we must discern if it is to be of any use in guiding political analysis' (Schmitter and Karl, 1991, p. 73). Here the discussion is limited to political democracy, i.e., as a political system, separate and apart from the economic and social systems to which it is joined.

The concept of democracy as a form of government goes back to the Ancient Greek philosophers. Literally translated from Greek it means 'rule by the people'. It is sometimes said that democratic government originated in the city-states of ancient Greece and that democratic ideals have been handed down to us from that time. In truth, however, a distinction between the democracy of the classical world and the modern one is to be stressed. The assumptions of the Greeks, for instance, had almost no notion of the rights and freedoms of the individual, an idea that is tied up with the modern concept of democracy. In its today's sense, the term 'democracy' came into use during the course of the 19-th century to describe a system of representative government in which the representatives are chosen by free competitive elections and most male citizens are entitled to vote.[1]

Contemporary scholarly discourse in mainstream political science has come to favor the narrow, or minimalist, concept of political democracy which focuses on the procedures of democratic rule and civic (political and law-related) equality of citizens, instead of maximalist conceptions of democracy that include such overcharged, romantic and extrapolitical matters as economic equality and social justice. Its most important formulation has been proposed by Joseph Schumpeter (1947, p. 269) who advanced what he labeled 'another theory of democracy'. The 'democratic method', he said, 'is that institutional arrangement for arriving at political decisions in which individuals acquire the power to decide by means of a competitive struggle for the people's vote'.

This procedural approach has by now become widely diffused and is shared by most contemporary scholars of the subject. Seymour Martin Lipset (1959, p. 27) defines democracy as 'a political system which supplies regular constitutional opportunities for changing the government officials, and a social mechanism which permits the largest possible part of the population to influence major decisions by choosing among contenders for political office'. Lipset focuses on contestation, or competition, for office as a key feature of democratic politics. As he put it, elections express the 'democratic class struggle'. Most other modern conceptualizations of political democracy follow the lines of the Schumpeterian tradition, for it provides the analytical precision and empirical referents that make the concept a useful one for a rigorous research.[2]

An important contribution in conceptualizing democracy as a political system was made by Robert Dahl. Dahl (1971) emphasized two dimensions - contestation and participation as crucial to his realistic democracy, or polyarchy, based on the responsiveness of the government to the preferences of its citizens, considered as political equals. Governmental responsiveness requires that citizens must have opportunities to (1) formulate their preferences, (2) signify their preferences to their fellow citizens and the government by individual and collective action, and (3) have their preferences weighed equally in the conduct of the government. Dahl noted that there is no country in which these conditions are perfectly satisfied; he therefore prefers the term *polyarchy* for concrete systems, while reserving the term 'democracy' for the nonexistent, ideal type. Dahl's (1971, p. 3) concept of 'polyarchy' requires not only extensive participation but also substantial levels of civil freedom that enable people to form and express their political preferences in a meaningful way.

Against this background, Diamond, Linz and Lipset (1995, p. 6-7) view political democracy as a system of government that possesses three essential dimensions, summarized as follows:

- Meaningful and extensive competition among individuals and organizations, groups (especially political parties) for all effective positions of government power through regular, free, and fair elections that exclude the use of force;
- A highly inclusive level of political participation in the selection of leaders and policies, such that no major (adult) social group is prevented from exercising the rights of citizenship;
- A level of civil and political liberties-freedom of thought and expression, freedom of the press, freedom of assembly and demonstration, freedom to form and join organizations, freedom from terror and unjustified imprisonment-secured through political equality under a rule of law, sufficient to ensure that citizens (acting individually and through various associations) can develop and advocate their views and interests and contest policies and offices vigorously and autonomously.

The concept of modern democracy is intimately linked with liberalism and the related notion of civil society. The tradition that became liberal democracy was liberal first (aimed at restricting state power over civil society) and democratic later (aimed at creating structures that would secure a popular mandate for holders of state power).

First contributions in the liberal tradition had their primary concern with the restriction of political authority over citizens. The classic function of civil society in political theory, dating back in different respects to such 18th- 19th century thinkers as Ferguson, Hegel, and de Tocqueville, was to limit state power and to oppose and resist the tyrannical abuse of state power.[3] Gradually, liberalism became associated with the doctrine that individuals should be free to pursue their own preferences in religious, economic and political affairs - in fact, in everything that affected daily life. The liberal tradition fought for a rollback of state power and the creation of a sphere of civil society where social relations, including private business, non-state institutions, family, and personal life, could evolve without state interference. An important element in this regard was the support of a market economy based on the respect for private property. Liberty has come to be viewed as individual freedom in the realm of civil society.

Contemporary scholarship conceives of civil society as the realm of organized social life that is voluntary, self-generating (largely) self-supporting, autonomous from the state, and bound by a legal order or set of shared rules (Diamond 1994, p. 52). It is distinct from 'society' in general in that it involves citizens acting collectively in a public sphere to express their interests, passions, and ideas, exchange information, achieve mutual goals, make demands on the state, and hold state officials accountable.[4]

The second foundation of classical liberalism was the claim that state power be based not on natural or supernatural rights but on the will of the sovereign people. Ultimately, this was the claim for democracy and democratically derived legitimacy, that is, for the creation of mechanisms of representation that assured that those who held state power enjoyed popular support. Herefrom, both logically and historically, has arisen a complex web of interrelationship between democracy, nationalism, and nationhood, for the nature of community had become something qualitatively different.

Many theorists view the rise of nationhood as the primary agent of legitimation that was central to the concept of popular sovereignty, a newly reformulated relationship between the rulers and the ruled, giving both the rights and duties toward each other. As put by Schöpflin (1995a, p. 39):

> Nationhood became the tissue that was to connect the entire population of the state with its political institutions and claim to exercise power or control over it in the name of popular sovereignty. This process is the civic core of nationhood, its channel into politics.

In this respect, the linkage between the birth of both modern democracy and nationalism becomes clearer.

Modern Democracy and Nation-State

The emergence of democracy has always occurred in distinct communities; there is no record anywhere of free, unconnected, and calculating individuals coming together spontaneously to form a democratic social contract *ex nihilo*.[5] Ancient Greek democracy was tied almost exclusively to the *polis*, the classical city-state. This democracy was essentially commensurate with human personality: the site of the democratic enterprise was small, and citizens dealt with one another face-to-face.

The origins of both modern democracy and nationalism date back to the period after French revolution and they are linked almost genetically. Prior to this, various ethnic phenomena with political consequences did, in fact, exist and influence political actors, but they were secondary to religion or dynasticism or late feudal bonds of loyalty (Armstrong, 1982; Smith, 1986). Modern democracy extends far beyond the intimate boundaries of traditional communities, and so requires citizens to develop a new sense of community that is based less on their unaided senses and more on the human mind or imagination, in sum, on constructed and imagined identities.[6] In other words, when we speak about modern democracy, it is important to bear in mind that it is not simply democracy of the village, the tribe, or the city-state. It is democracy of the nation-state and its very emergence is associated with the development of the nation-state.

Margaret Canovan (1996, p. 112) stresses some dilemmas posed for contemporary political theory and practice of established democracies by its reliance on nationhood. A most important link between nationalism and democracy lies in the fact that the demands of democracy-building provide incentives for molding nations out of preexistent ethnic material. Many scholars hold that nationalism actually acted as the historical force that has provided the political units for democratic government. On its own, democracy is not capable of sustaining the vision of past and future that holds communities together politically, because it does little or nothing to generate the affective, symbolic, and ritually reaffirmed ties upon which community rests (Keens-Soper, 1989, pp. 698-703). The saliency of nations can be located at the moment when loyalty to the nation became the primary cohesive force in the relationship between rulers and ruled. In this respect, democracy rests on the strongly cohesive identities provided by nationhood. As put by Nodia (1992, p. 4), 'Nation' is another name for 'We the People'.

Recent scholarship has come to view the essence of nationalism in a belief about the social basis of political authority. The modernization thesis, as developed by Ernest Gellner (1983), asserts that nationalism need be viewed as a theory of political legitimacy which holds that the political and the national unit should be congruent. To Gellner, nationalism has its roots not in human nature but in the pervasive social order of industrial societies and commitment to the spirit of rationality. This, in turn gives rise to the need for mass education and training of a generic type. The functional prerequisites of the latter include universal literacy, numeracy and technical sophistication in an age of universal high culture. In Gellner's view (1983, p. 94), 'ethnicity enters the political sphere as 'nationalism' at times when cultural homogeneity or continuity (not classlessness) is required by the economic base of social life'. It is 'nationalism which engenders nations, and not the other way round'.

Unlike Gellner, another thoughtful student of nationalism and modernization, Liah Greenfeld (1993, p. 18) argues that nationhood produced most of the features that we know as modernity: 'Rather than define nationalism by its modernity I see modernity as defined by nationalism'. To Greenfeld, it did so by generating a society in which the traditional barriers between nobles and commoners were transcended in common membership of a people, and that 'people' acquired enough solidarity to replace a king as the bearer of sovereignty. As a consequence, observes Greenfeld (1993, p. 10),

> Democracy was born with the sense of nationality. The two are inherently linked and neither can be fully understood apart from this connection. Nationalism was the form in which democracy appeared in the world, contained in the idea of the nation as a butterfly in a cocon.

Analyzing the intimate connection between modern liberal democracy and nationalism, most scholars admit extremely complex nature of this symbiosis. Besides genetic linkage between the nationalism and democracy, there is also the doctrinal tension between liberalism and nationalism. Nationalism gives preference to collective claims based on ethnicity, culture, or some other communal identity. Liberalism, on the contrary, holds individual human liberty as the foremost political value. At the same time many scholars reject the commonplace view that nationalism is simply an enemy of democracy. The reasons become evident in discussions of the interplay between the ethnic and the civic dimensions of nationalism.

Ethnic and Civic Conceptions of Nationhood and Nationalism

All forms of nationalism contain imagery that gives definition to a unique and distinctive national grouping. These symbols may be either ethnic or civic in character. The idea dates back to Friedrich Meinecke who in 1908 distinguished the *Kulturnation* (cultural nation) from the *Staatsnation* (political nation). Recent scholarship has elaborated on the two principal senses of nation in modern times that have come to known as a relation of citizenship, in which the nation consists of collective sovereignty based in common political participation, and a relation of ethnicity, in which the nation comprises all those of supposedly common language, history, or broader cultural identity (e.g. Hobsbawn, 1982; Smith, 1986 and 1991; Ra'anan, 1990; Verdery, 1993; Kupchan, 1995).

Civic nationalism defines a nation in terms of territory, citizenship rights with a supporting framework of laws, as well as effective institutions. Civic definition of nationhood in terms of citizenship and political participation can exist only within the context of a territorial state. To Smith (1991, pp. 12-4), historic territory, legal-political community, legal-political equality of members, and common civic culture and ideology; make the components of the standard, civic (or Western) model of the nation. Historically, in the West (that is, roughly, Europe west of the Rhine and the Western Hemisphere), a new kind of polity - the rational state, and a new kind of community - the territorial nation developed during the modern era in close conjunction with each other and both having much in common with the legal concept of *jus soli*. A citizen is a national, regardless of ethnicity and lineage. It is the bonds forged through the enterprise of statehood and its territory that serve as the basis for the formation of a national grouping (Ra'anan 1990). Civic nationalism is a rather rare form of nationalism and one that is difficult to nurture; it depends on well-developed political and legal institutions to regulate relations and distribute political power across ethnic as well as other social boundaries. Accordingly, civic nationalism prospers only in relatively sophisticated political communities which have achieved a certain degree of civic consolidation.

Ethnic nationalism, in contrast, depends not on institutions, but on culture. Ethnic nationalism defines nationhood in terms of lineage, culture, religion and language. Ethnic groups do not need states in order to become nations. In a majority of pre-modern communities, as in most contemporary non-Western societies, the criteria that determine a person's nationality were derived not from *jus soli* but rather from *jus sanguinis*. Individuals of a different ethnicity, even if they reside in and are citizens of the nation-state in question, do not necessarily become part of the national grouping.

Obviously, these two kinds of nationalism are only ideal types. In reality, nationalism is always both political and communal. Every nationalism contains civic and ethnic elements in varying degrees and different forms which reflects the profound dualism of the phenomenon that is simultaneously functioning in two dimensions - cultural (ethnic) and political (civic). While the civic aspect of nationhood can generally be regarded as appealing to material interests in political and economic life, ethnicity resonates in the cultural and affective spheres. Political stability in a state depends on a balance between the two (Kertzer 1988, Smith 1991). For the last two centuries in the West and in the East alike, polities have subsided on a mixture of civic and ethnic elements, sometimes in competition, sometimes overlapping, as a continuous process, with the relationship between the two being constantly defined and redefined.[7] The main issue is the quality of the resulting balance between the two constituent sides and which of the two predominates at one period of time or another.

The problems that ethnicity causes for democratic systems can be understood against the theory that underpins the modern state. Since virtually every state in the globe includes citizens of more than one nationality, democracy necessarily means granting some degree of political power to those who are ethnically different. In ethnically plural, or divided societies where ethnic nationalism predominates in the public discourse and state policies, a logical issue arises: Is liberal democracy at all feasible in such societies? This is the matter of the next section.

Democracy and Ethnopolitical Conflict Management

Many scholars have expressed profound skepticism about the possibility of stable democracy in ethnically diverse political setting. Yet many others argue that for managing multiethnicity authoritarian methods are at best only a short-term solution. Democracy, therefore, needs to be seen not as part of the problem of ethnic conflict, but as the basis for its solution.

Ethnic Challenges to Democracy in Plural Societies

Classical statements in the debate go back to the 1860s, when two eminent British philosophers debated the nature of the nation-state. In his essay *Considerations on Representative Government*, John Stuart Mill (1958, p. 230) reached the pessimistic conclusion:

> It is in general a necessary condition of free institutions that the boundaries of governments should coincide in the main with nationalities... Free institutions are next to impossible in a country made up of different nationalities. Among a people without fellow-feeling, especially if they read and speak different languages, the united public opinion, necessary to the working of representative government, cannot exist.

In a response, the historian Lord Acton (1956, p. 169) rejected Mill's views and affirmed his faith in the multinational liberal state, declaring that the congruence of political and national boundaries was a recipe for stagnation, whereas the presence of different nations under the same sovereignty' raised 'inferior' races and revitalized 'exhausted and decaying nations', while simultaneously establishing barriers to tyranny.

> [The multinational state] provides against the servility which flourishes under the shadow of a single authority, by balancing interests, multiplying associations'... [in short] diversity preserves liberty.

More than a century after theses observations were made, one might be tempted to conclude that the evidence supports Mill's views more than Acton's. In fact, democratic government has been exceedingly difficult to sustain in ethnically divided societies. Dahl (1971, p. 110) reasoned that nationality differences within states restricted participation for some citizens, thereby limiting the possibility for a successful polyarchy. His empirical data gave support to his reasoning: among 114 polities, 58 % with a low degree of subcultural pluralism, 36 % with moderate pluralism, and only 15 % with marked pluralism were polyarchies, or nearly so Bingham Powell's (1982, p. 159-61) study of contemporary democracies has shown that countries with extreme ethnic complexity experience high levels of deadly political violence, which severely strains the fabric of their democratic orders.

Ethnicity is indeed the most difficult type of cleavage for a democracy to manage. Overall, the arguments against viability of liberal democracy in multiethnic setting center around six main clusters of concern: the nature of ethnic conflict, the structure of social cleavages, impaired civility and fractures in civil society, issues of inclusion and exclusion in the political community, problems of majoritarian democracy, and ethnic outbidding.

The nature of ethnic conflict Ethnicity taps cultural and symbolic issues - basic notions of identity and the self, of individual and group worth and entitlement. This symbolic charge of ethnicity is one of the reasons why ethnic conflicts it generates are intrinsically less amenable to compromise than those revolving around material issues. Ethnopolitical disputes yield competing demands that tend to be indivisible and therefore are viewed as zero-sum contests. Some ethnic conflicts which center on material issues may be resolved through conventional kinds of bargaining. Yet, because at bottom they revolve around exclusive symbols and conceptions of identity and legitimacy, even in these cases they are characterized by competing demands that cannot easily be broken down into bargainable increments.

The structure of cleavages There is broad scholarly consensus that when social cleavages are reinforcing rather than overlapping, the potential for conflict is more acute. The divide in social fabric of ethnically-riven societies is pervasive and tends to be focused on only one line of identity cleavage, concerning ethnic belonging. In contrast to other political cleavages, such as those of class or functional interest, ethnicity appears permanent and all encompassing, predetermining who will be included and excluded from power and resources (Horowitz, 1985).

Impaired civility and fractures in civil society A vital component of a successful democracy is said to be a healthy civil society. Edward Shils (1991, p. 13) found the essence of civility to be vested in the mutual recognition of the moral dignity of opponents in public life: '[Civility] means regarding other persons, including one's adversaries, as members of the same collectivity, i.e. as members of the same society, even though they belong to different parties or to different religious communities or to different ethnic groups'. In the presence of separate organizations that permeate and divide every aspect of society on the basis of identity, transcending civic formations are unlikely to emerge.

Cultural pluralism perspective (e.g., Furnivall, 1947; idem, 1986; M. Smith 1965, 1969, and 1986) emphasizes how divergent ethnic identities reinforce the fracturing of populations into discrete social compartments, each with distinct institutions of marriage, family, religion, property and /or language. Horowitz (1985, pp. 22-36) observes that such organizational encapsulation finds its optimal expression when different groups in a multiethnic state confront one another in an unranked system of stratification where no group is unequivocally either superordinate or subordinate. In such a competitive relationship each group approximates an 'incipient whole society' and with few, if any, jointly held norms, customs, and traditions to restrain them, civility in the conduct of intergroup relations is bound to be rare. Societal autonomy is liable to emerge in the form of unilateral declarations of rival 'civil' space by ethnic parties and the formation of a contending 'civil' society. For instance, multiple labor unionism youth organizations, and rate payers' associations, though bound to exist, are likely to be grouped into rival formations, each serving a discrete community and hostile to their functional equivalents. Under ethnic conflict, according to Horowitz, civility becomes a yardstick reserved for in-group conduct, while the pursuit of collective esteem for one's own group generates incivility toward ethnic outsiders. Ethnic conflict, consequentially, invariably, threatens to dismantle civil society or to prevent its emergence.

Issues of inclusion and exclusion In each of the cases of ethnically divided states, the issue arises as to whether a political community can be said to exist. The term 'political community' in this context suggests an inclusive code of political understanding, a shared political culture, commonly respected symbols of statehood, and, most critical, a shared view that the outcomes of the political process (most notably, elections) are legitimate. An intimately related issue is whether, in spite of ethnic divisions, there exists a transcending bond of national unity. Few multiethnic states have been political communities in this sense. Divided societies represent a particularly serious threat to democratic polities (Horowitz, 1993, p. 2):

> Democracy is about inclusion and exclusion, about access to power, about the privileges that go with inclusion and the penalties that accompany exclusion. In severely divided societies, ethnic identity provides clear lines to determine who will be included and who will be excluded. Since the lines appear unalterable, being in and being out may quickly come to look permanent... Again and again in divided societies, there is a tendency to conflate inclusion in the government with inclusion in the community and exclusion from government with exclusion from the community.

An identity group that is not listened to is actually excluded from the community, but by the same token it is no longer bound by the will of that community.

Problems of majoritarian democracy under ethnic plurality In view of the above, majority rule is not a solution in culturally and ethnically plural societies, but is itself a serious problem. An oft-noted phenomenon in ethnically divided societies is that parties are often structured and votes are cast along ethnic lines. That is why ethnic contests for state power, though eminently 'thinkable' and 'workable' within majoritarian democratic institutions, tend to 'produce suspicion rather than trust, acrimony rather than civility, polarization rather than accommodation, and victimization rather than toleration' (Horowitz, 1985, p. 86).

If democracy is to survive even in ethnically homogeneous setting, the majority rule principle must be restrained by the wide recognition of minority rights. Sartori (1987, p. 32-3) summarizes it most cogently:

> The people [demos]... cannot literally consist of everybody; but they cannot be reduced to a greater part of the citizenry either... The people are divided into a majority and a minority by the decision-making process and in order to have decisions made... Here, then, the argument is that when democracy is assimilated to pure and simple majority rule, by this assimilation a portion of the demos is eo ipso converted into a non-demos. Conversely, democracy, conceived as a majority rule limited by minority rights corresponds to the people in full, that is, to the sum of majority plus minority. It is precisely because the rule of the majority is restrained that all the people (all those who are entitled to vote) are always included into the demos (italics in the original).

Unlimited majority rule as instrument of hegemonic control in formally democratic states effectively, transforms them into illiberal systems even in ethnically homogeneous context (Sartori, 1987, p. 24).

> If we have a majority that cannot be turned into a minority, then we are no longer dealing with a democratic majority - that is, with a system whose rule of game is the majority principle. For a majority principle requires changeable majorities, with the various parts of the body politic being able to alternate in wielding power... Clearly, if minorities are not protected, the possibility of finding a majority in favor of the new opinion is unlikely, since he whose opinion changes from that of the majority to that of the minority immediately falls into the ranks of those who have no right to make their opinion heard. Therefore, unless the liberty of minorities is respected, not only would the first electoral test determine, once and for all, those who are free and those who are not; but also the liberty of those who voted for the majority on that occasion would be lost because, in practice, they would not be permitted to change their opinion. Thus the first election would be, in effect, the only true election. And this amounts to saying that such a democracy dies at the moment of its inception.

The implications of the above statement for the ethnic realm can be grasped if one assumes that a majority is entitled by its very principles to exercise its power without restraints. Inevitably, and almost by definition, if such a majority is ethnically defined, it can and easily will maintain itself as a permanent majority whose unrestricted rule will equal structured ethnic dominance.

> Where political 'majorities' constantly fluctuate, as people change their minds on the key policy or political issues of the day, then majority rule is a sensible decision rule, infinitely preferable to the kind of minority rule practiced by emperors, military dictators or one-party regimes. However, as it has been correctly observed, where there are two or more deeply established ethnic communities, and where the members of these communities do not agree on the basic institutions and on the policies the regime should pursue, or where the relevant ethnic communities are not internally fragmented on key policy preferences in ways which cross-cut each other, then 'majority rule' can become an instrument of hegemonic control (McGarry and O'Leary, 1993, p. 23-24).

Ethnic outbidding A related ethnic challenge to democracy is the tendency for opportunistic politicians to appeal to communal, ethnic and nationalistic impulses and pervasiveness of radical 'outbidding' or 'flanking' on divisive ethnic issues in intragroup competition. In many multiethnic societies, especially those coming out from under years or decades of authoritarian rule, political accommodation and compromise are truly alien principles. Many radical ethnic parties have an almost naturally emerging incentive to mobilize ethnicity for their own immediate political advantage by exploiting the efforts by more moderate parties in the same ethnic group to seek an accommodation with parties from rival ethnic groups. Ethnic outbidders, sensing political profit, are bound to engage in making divisive ethnic issues salient and to nullify the moderating effects of cross-cutting cleavages.

Alvin Rabushka and Kenneth Shepsle (1972) pioneered an exploration of microfoundations for these dynamic. Examining the wave of African and Asian democratic implosions during the 1950s-60s, they argued that in plural societies political entrepreneurs can win votes among all ethnic groups through the use of ambiguity. Politicians who give ambiguous messages are in essence offering the voters a lottery. And, even if the voters have preferences in favor of their own group's interests, they would prefer a lottery in which their first preference has a small possibility to a sure promise of a moderate policy in favor of their own group. Therefore, politicians can construct broad-based multiethnic coalitions. But the lottery situation is not stable, especially in the case of post-colonial democracies where multiethnic coalitions were based on broad anticolonial platforms.

Once independence is achieved, political entrepreneurs from each community recognize that the multiethnic coalitions were oversized and surmise that they can defeat the coalition within their own community by advocating extreme positions. Where they prevail, a perceptual consensus is established that politics involves a zero-sum contest about indivisible goods, thus precluding strategies of logrolling and negotiation. Multiethnic coalitions inevitably break down in these conditions, brokerage institutions disappear, all distributive issues come to be reflected through the ethnic lenses. This 'outbidding' polarizes the polity and ethnic moderation becomes untenable. In turn, the winner of an election in which each cultural group is promised political dominance is likely to so oppress the losers as to induce violence, civil war, and a breakdown of democracy. Rabushka and Shepsle (1972, p. 217) concluded by arguing for an imminent breakdown in multinational democratic systems: 'Is the resolution of intense but conflicting preferences in the [deeply divided] society manageable in a democratic framework? We think not'.

The Issue of Feasibility of Democracy in Plural Setting

The Rabushka and Shepsle argument, perhaps most explicitly expresses the theoretical stances of those who are deeply pessimistic about the feasibility of democracy in ethnically plural societies. Ethnic divide does cast strong challenges to the democratic rule. At the same time, it must be conceded that the actual relationship between democracy and multiethnicity is much more complex and defies simplicity of one-sided characterizations.

In scholarly debates the critique of the pessimist approach has been based on several grounds. From the normative viewpoint, the pessimist argument is ethnocentric and value-charged. It takes sides with those who are strongly biased against the idea that 'all men are created equal'. It seems to imply that 'plural societies' the world over are condemned to an undemocratic future simply because of their plural composition. If this is correct, it would appear that democratic aspirations are a futile fantasy for the vast majority of humankind which does not seem as too much corresponding to the reality, particularly if we consider the global trend towards democratization and its already third wave unfolding up to date.

From the analytical viewpoint, the pessimist assertion rests on the much contested ground of the essentially static, 'primordially' given and intractable nature of ethnic identifications that are presumed to determine people's deepest commitments and most strongly held values. Contrary to this, much recent scholarship of ethnicity has demonstrated that common cultural roots are neither a necessary not a sufficient condition for ethnic or national membership. Historically, numerous identities have been available to serve as bases for political mobilization. Bates (1983) argues that, since ethnic identity is manipulable and changing, the constructions of similarity and difference must be explained as an outcome, not taken as a given. The true challenge then is to explain why one particular identity (such as, say, Moldovan or Croat or Abkhazian, or Basque) is chosen in preference to several possible alternatives at a certain temporal moment.

It has been observed that to understand why and how ethnic loyalties become salient and exclusive at a certain conjuncture, it is necessary to focus on the role of the modern state in such societies and, in particular, to analyze the policies and actions of strategic elites who control the state apparatuses. Cultural differences can either be magnified and reified as part of a political process, or, conversely, mitigated and depoliticized in relevance. 'Nationhood, the consciousness of a collective identity, is a social and political construct, and the choice of identity is best understood in terms of a societal response to the exercise of power by strategic elites at the helm of the modern state' (Bose, 1995, p. 91).

No analyst argues that politics in deeply divided societies facilitates democracy or that conditions for it were or are favorable in the vast majority of today's multiethnic societies. The ever widening consensus to consider democratic practices in situations of deep ethnic conflict is grounded in the firm belief that there are no viable alternatives to democracy as a system of just and stable conflict management. As observed by Lijphart (1977, p. 277) 'not only have non-democratic regimes failed to be good nation-builders; they have not even established good records of maintaining order and peace in plural societies'.

Lijphart argues that the ethnically plural societies can be altered to sustain democracy, specifically, the adoption of consociational constitutional rules may serve so effectively as a mechanism for conflict resolution that in the long term some of the basic divisive structural features of society can be changed. Horowitz (1985, p. 684) concurs by observing: 'there is no case to be made for the futility of democracy or the inevitability of uncontrolled conflict. Even in the most severely divided society, ties of blood do not lead ineluctably to rivers of blood'.

Human experience has known numerous cases of viable and successful non-majoritarian democratic response to the challenges of the ethnic divide. Scholarly research suggests that at some point many democracies seem to acquire the antidote to ward off the debilitating impact of ethnic conflict. In some cases the emergence of ethnic conflict has even expanded democratic opportunities by leading to a restructuring of government to allow for the decentralization of avenues for political participation (Newman, 1996, p.1). In fact, it has been noted that ethnic pluralism and institutional pluralism may be mutually reinforcing. Safran (1991 and 1995) observes that ethnic-group representation provides a useful complement to the other (for example, socio-economic and ideological) kinds of group representation, if the latter are strongly developed and part of the democratic tradition.

Reflections over democracy's responses to challenges of multiethnicity has produced important insights into what kinds of conditions have tended to provide for the sustainability of the peace relationship that prevails in mature multiethnic democracies. In this respect a consideration of democracy as ethnopolitical conflict management is in order.

Democracy as Conflict Management. Challenges of Multiethnicity

An important dimension of any regime performance is its management of conflict. In fact, one irreducible rule of the political game that precedes all others is the rule that establishes how conflicts are to be resolved. If political actors do not share a conflict-solving rule, they are bound to conflict over each conflict and this is the inescapable way to unending political violence. Disruptive strife ends precisely when the winner establishes which rule will peacefully solve conflicts.[8]

Diamond (1990 and 1993b) identifies the tension between conflict and consensus as the first among democracy's paradoxes. By its very nature, democracy is a system of institutionalized competition for power. Without competition and conflict, there is no democracy. But any society that sanctions political conflict runs the risk of its becoming too intense, producing a society so conflict-ridden that civil peace and political stability are jeopardized. If political freedom and competition are not to descend into extremism, polarization, and violence, mechanisms are needed to contain conflict within certain behavioral boundaries. Democracy, according to Lipset (1981, p. 437), 'requires institutions which support conflict and disagreement as well as those which sustain legitimacy and consensus'.

The focus on democracy as a particular system of conflict management reveals that non-violent mode of conflict management and respective political culture are inherent in the very nature of democratic form of rule. Adam Przeworski (1988; idem, 1991) defines democracy as a particular system processing conflicts, a 'system of ruled open-endedness, or organized uncertainty'. Democratic sustainability is the matter of contingent collective choice or decentralized strategic compliance. To Przeworski (1991, p. 19), 'political forces comply with present defeats because they believe that the institutional framework that organizes democratic competition will permit them to advance their interests in the future'. Democracy thus evolves as 'a contingent outcome of conflicts'. Alfred Hirschmann (1994) concurs by arguing that conflicts and ability to manage them constitute pillars of democratic market society, and it is precisely the capacity of democratic systems to peacefully process conflicts that permits conflicts to play a constructive role in social relations.

In Chapter 1 we saw that the core theoretical explanations of the democratic peace phenomenon focus on cultural (or normative) and structural (or institutional) models which point at reasons for democratic pacificness. As it is in the realm of international relations, so it appears to hold true in ethnopolitics: democracy promotes peaceful interactions. The form of ethnic conflict in established democracies has been a function of the nature of their democracy rather than of the nature of ethnic conflict. *Positive and stable ethnic peace, conceived as constructive process of non-violent conflict management, is the response by which mature liberal democracy meets the challenges of ethnic diversity.*

Successful management of ethnic diversity hinges upon creation, promotion and maintenance of two sets of intimately related conditions which nurture peace relationship between identity groups united into a joint partnership of democratic self-governance. One cluster can be termed *cultural (or normative)* conditions. These include identities, norms, perceptions and discourses that permit peaceful management of disputes which come to apply across ethnic boundaries. They provide for the formation of a specific political culture of interethnic political moderation that pays. The second cluster of conditions is related to the incentives and constraints produced by the functioning of specially devised democratic institutions for ethnic conflict expression and accommodation. These can be termed *structural (or institutional)* conditions. Together these two clusters account for the peaceful structuring of ethnic politics.

Cultural Conditions of Democratic Ethnic Peace

Cultural conditions of ethnic peace under democratic governance emerge from specific features of democratic political culture that comprise multiplicity of identities, the civic/ethnic value balance (value-orientations towards civic unity in ethnic diversity), shared norms of inclusive pluralism, intergroup tolerance, and reciprocative intergroup perceptions.

Multiple identities It is true that ethnic cleavages do not die and neither can they be extinguished through repression or assimilation. However, they can be managed so that they do not threaten the peace relationship among people of different ethnic groups enabling them to coexist tranquilly while maintaining their distinctive identities. An important means by which democracies manage, soften, complicate, and contain conflict has been through the presence or even the generation of crosscutting and malleable cleavages. Multiple identities lie at the root of this pattern. In countries where multiple identities are nurtured, ethnic elements provide only one of many sources of identity and can find expression through institutional and legal arrangements that do not threaten the viability of multiethnic states.

When people who are divided on one line of cleavage, such as ethnicity or religion, interact and find common ground with one another around a different line of cleavage, such as transethnic socio-economic associations or class, they experience psychological 'cross-pressures' (Lipset, 1981, p. 78) that tend to moderate their political views and induce them generally toward greater tolerance and accommodation. In this way different types of pluralism tend to fortify one another.

Overlapping membership tends to reduce social fragmentation and makes it possible for the state to relate to citizens as individuals rather than as members of ethnic groups (Heisler, 1990). Newman (1996, p. 147-8) found that an important component of ethnoregional conflict in advanced industrial democracies has been the balance of identification of citizens with their ethnoregions and with the larger state when, consequentially, many do not find these overlapping identities mutually exclusive. Multiple identities ameliorate the intensity of ethnic conflict and the willingness of activists to resort to force if there are viable institutional avenues present for expression and accommodation of group claims. The costs of violence to the perpetrators in terms of state responses become significantly higher than the costs of peaceful democratic engagement.

Civic/ethnic value balance (Value orientation toward unity in diversity)
The quality of the balance between civic and ethnic values of nationhood, as these are present in public discourses at any given time, is an important variable affecting the peace relationship in a multiethnic system.

Civic elements can serve as an important source of legitimacy and cohesion in ethnically heterogeneous countries. Liberal democracy is based on a philosophy of inclusion. Civic aspects of nationhood are compatible with liberal democracy because of their prevailing orientation towards unity in diversity. Civic nationalism defines nationhood in terms of citizenship and political values and norms rather than in terms of ethnicity, it is more inclusive than ethnic nationalism. In this way, civic nationalism erases rather than reinforces, the lines of ethnic divide and is therefore more conducive to both interethnic and international stability.

At the same time, an important lesson has been that the policies of civic integration must be well-balanced and avoid imposition. Efforts to encourage minority ethnic groups to assimilate into the dominant culture or to replace ethnic with civic identities can actually cause a backlash with renewed calls for a distancing from the state. 'Invitations to participate in the political mainstream may be interpreted not as inclusive largess, but as a threat to group distinctiveness' (Kupchan, 1995, p.9). The problem is precisely the one of striking an adequate balance between the two dimensions of nationhood to ensure that the resultant vector of value orientations point at a unity in diversity. Members of minority communities are more likely to identify with the political system and internalize its values if the legitimacy of their specific cultural aspirations is acknowledged and that is reflected in public policies and institutions. In most cases the prevalence of civic values of nationhood and the stress on individual rights imply neither suppression of ethnic values nor their ignoring.

In this respect, some advance the proposition that the maintenance of, or return to, ethnic group legitimation implies of necessity the protection of ethnic group rights, a protection that is incompatible with the ideology of individual autonomy and, in the long run, functionally incompatible with individual human rights - both vis-à-vis the state and vis-à-vis the ethnic group itself (Patterson, 1977). As observed by analysts, ethnic group rights tend to go hand-in-hand with individual rights; the absence of one is not necessarily conducive to the presence of the other (Safran, 1995, p.3). In fact, the history of most established democracies shows that the re-legitimation of ethnic claims and the pursuit of public policies reflecting an acceptance of ethnopolitical pluralism have in fact gone hand in hand with the enhancement of individual substantive rights, such as welfare benefits, the suffrage, the right to strike, and freedom of speech and association, and the strengthening of due-process protections, particularly habeas corpus and the right to legal council.

Norms of inclusive pluralism and intergroup tolerance A vigorous civil society is an inalienable component of every mature liberal democratic system. Civil society presupposes the presence of diffused norms of civility that guide the individual and intergroup conduct.

Theorists in the liberal tradition identify several values and beliefs of civility as crucial for stable and effective democracy: belief in the legitimacy of democracy; tolerance for opposing parties, beliefs, and preferences; a willingness to compromise with political opponents and, underlying this, pragmatism and flexibility; trust in the political environment, and cooperation, particularly among political competitors, moderation in political positions and partisan identifications (Almond and Verba, 1963; Verba, 1965; Dahl, 1971, pp. 129-62; Lipset, 1979, part 3; Putnam et al., 1993, Diamond, 1993, pp. 10-15).

Ultimately, pluralism lies at the heart of civility. The principles of civil society - such as the equality of human beings - cannot deny the immense variability of human experience, identities and attributes. Pluralism not only fosters the dynamic interplay of ideas, parties and civic associations on the basis of reasonable clear, agreed-upon rules that reflect the norms of tolerance, mutual respect, but displays and promotes sensitivity to fundamental human and minorities' rights. The norms and practices of inclusive pluralism, thus, moderate attitudes and behavior by inhibiting the formation of what is termed as 'clusters of permanent allies and permanent enemies' (Miller, 1983, p. 736).

Tolerance and pluralism, though different concepts, are in fact, intimately connected:

> Pluralism presupposes toleration, which is to say that an intolerant pluralism is a false pluralism. The difference is this: tolerance respects values, whereas pluralism posits values. For pluralism affirms the belief that

diversity and dissent are values that enrich individuals as well as their polities and societies (Sartori, 1997, p. 58, italics in the original - A.A.)

In liberal systems inclusive pluralism is the norm which essence is to deal with any marking, with any identity in the same manner, i.e. forms the basis of reciprocal acceptance.

Reciprocative intergroup perceptions Intergroup perceptions are crucial in understanding the extent to which relations between groups can be peaceful or violent. Donald Rothchild (1986, pp. 87-93) rightly focuses on ethnic groups' perceptions of one another, identifying three basic types: essentialist perceptions, in which groups perceive physical, cultural, or social threats to their vital interests-thereby making compromise seem a sign of weakness; pragmatic perceptions, in which conflicts of interest remain acute but compromise is possible on the margins; and reciprocative perceptions, in which groups 'seek to transform the structure of relations to achieve mutual interest, primarily through the state as a mediator'. Essentialist perceptions tend to lead to violent intergroup conflict, pragmatic perceptions allow for an occasional truce or cooperation in limited spheres, and reciprocative perceptions lay the foundation for long-term peaceful cooperation among groups. In mature democracies it is reciprocal perceptions that mediate political affiliations, engagements and disputes between ethnic groups, which, effectively, permits constructive management of ethnic diversity through problem-solving endeavors that bring about integrative solutions.

Institutional Conditions of Democratic Ethnic Peace

Institutions are stable, valued, recurring patterns of behavior. A political community is not just any 'coming together', but a regularized, stable, and sustained coming together. Institutional conditions of democratic ethnic peace provide for the presence of routinized patterns of interactions that are structured on the basis of widely accepted and consensually framed rules of the democratic political game. The function of these rules is to realize both strong structural incentives and constraints that promote peaceful ethnopolitics. This, in turn, produces the long-term patterns that induce moderation, accommodation and trust among competing ethnic actors.

Sustained interethnic moderation which underlies ethnic peace relationship tends to follow not only from the frank recognition of plural identities, but also from legal protection for both individuals and identity group rights, devolution of power to subnational units, and political institutions that encourage bargaining and accommodation at the center. As observed by Diamond (1995, p.6-7), 'such institutional provisions and protections are not only significantly more likely under democracy, they are only possible with some considerable degree of democracy'.

Four conditions have been identified as particularly important for structuring peaceful ethnopolitics: the rule of law (*Rechtstaat*), institutionalized power-sharing that effectively guarantees ethnic minority rights, the ethnic vs. non-ethnic components in the party systems, the consequences of structuring electoral systems in multiethnic polities. The latter two sets of institutions have already been discussed at much length elsewhere (e.g., Horowitz, 1990; idem 1991; Sisk 1995b; idem, 1996b; Newman, 1996; Newman and Piroth, 1997), so in the subsequent sections I intend to concentrate on the former two.

Rule of law (Rechtstaat) The modern rule of law (*Rechtstaat*) grounded in constitutionalism is fundamental for the viable functioning of democratic institutions in multiethnic systems.[9] Where the state stands above ethnic conflicts and mediates them, employing agreed-upon institutions and practices, differences among communities can be worked out in parliament rather than on the streets (Sisk, 1996, p. 30). The rule of law also has important consequences for ethnic party politics. In fact, it permits party systems act as pressure valves to control the possibility of violence. If democratic movements are able to incorporate the more radical factions in the democratic process they can provide access to selective incentives and limit the possibility of government repression, thus decreasing the likelihood that radicals will see the necessity for violence (Newman, 1996).

Institutions of power-sharing The role of power-sharing in non-violent management of ethnopolitical conflict can hardly be overestimated. Institutions of power-sharing, broadly conceived, represent patterned interactions and mechanisms that sustain the relationship of ethnic peace in democratic systems. Rejection of majoritarianism does not mean the rejection of democratic practices. Consensus or near consensus (coalescent) decision making is the hallmark of non-majoritarian forms of democracy (Rae, 1969, Lijphart 1977).

Power-sharing institutions implement the principle of limited majority rule and the rule of law in the realm of ethnopolitics. As observed by Mayo (1960, p. 206),

> A democratic system can give no certain guarantee that the cultural minority will be protected against majority pressure and 'integration'. Neither can any other system give any such guarantee beyond the reach of political forces. The only unique chance which a democracy offers is the opportunity for a minority to put its case, to share in policy-making, to bring pressure to bear.

In liberal democracies the usual rights and liberties, supplemented by a combination of some of the specific policies and devices, may 'at least provide the ethnic minority with a sufficient number of pieces with which to play the game' (Mayo, 1960, p. 207). Members of ethnic minority communities may or may not utilize these devices, but the symbolism of their existence offers a minority a stake in the political system.

Students of power-sharing are concerned with identifying the kinds of practices that can create sufficient stimuli for ethnic groups to mediate their differences through the legitimate institutions of the democratic state they share. When groups in conflict commit to a common set of rules and institutions, the structure of those institutions does make a difference in containing conflicts, including those along ethnic lines. Two schools of thought that coalesced in debates over democratic politics in multiethnic states have come to be known as consociational and integrative models.

Consociational model This model is most often associated with Lijphart (1968, 1969, 1977, 1985) who places greater accent on institutionalized assurances for minority protraction and constraints on radicalism and ethnic outbidding. Consociationalists suggest that conflict management is best promoted by accommodation among group leaders representative of their ethnic constituencies through cooperative power-sharing in post-election coalitions and by effective constraints included into negotiated agreements. Originally, the very term power sharing was proposed (Lijphart 1977) as a set of principles that, when carried out through practices and institutions, provide every significant identity group or segment in a society representation and decision-making abilities on common issues and a degree of autonomy over issues of importance to the group.

Above all, consociationalism relies on elite cooperation as the principal characteristic of successful conflict management in deeply divided societies. Elites form grand coalitions or engage in extra-parliamentary negotiations to arrive at compromises that seek to defuse social disagreements and allow for the maintenance of social peace. In this perspective, elites, or conflict group leaders, directly represent various societal segments and act to forge political ties at the center. This is the case in many of the consociational democracies-Belgium, the Netherlands, Switzerland, Malaysia (1955-1969), Lebanon (1943-1975). Lijphart (1977, p. 25 ff) discusses four main characteristics of consociationalism - the grand coalition of political leaders that represent all the significant communities; the existence of a veto power for all communities on legislation that affects their vital interests; a system of proportionality in parliament, the civil service and other government agencies; and a high degree of segmental autonomy so that each community has a considerable degree of freedom to run its own internal affairs.

A similar approach to multi-ethnic states was advanced by Eric Nordlinger (1972) who also rejects the majoritarian model and places the stress on elite cooperation. Nordlinger (1972, p. 87) claims that 'structured elite predominance is a necessary conflict regulating condition'. Nordlinger (1972, p. 20) points out six political practices that, in his view, account for successful conflict regulation in the afore-mentioned six cases:

> 1) a stable coalition between governing parties; 2) the principle of proportionality; 3) acceptance of a mutual veto; 4) purposive depoliticization; 4) mutual adjustment of conflicting values and interests through compromise; and 6) concession by the stronger group.

Integrative Approach This approach is associated with Horowitz (1985, 1990, 1991, 1993) as its major proponent. The stress is put on the role of incentives in encouraging interethnic cooperation and in making moderation pay. Horowitz (1985, 1991) argues that the likelihood of violent conflict is reduced more effectively by institutions and practices that create incentives for the formation of preelection coalitions and that encourage intragroup rather than intergroup competition. Ideally, integrative mechanisms would lead to multiethnic or organizations that transcend narrow communal interests. In this respect Horowitz maintains that while deep-rooted issues must be addressed, some ethnic differences may be inherently unresolvable and therefore, conflict reduction, rather than conflict resolution is a more practicable goal in divided societies.

Instead of consociationalism, Horowitz (1985; idem, 1991) argues for kind of institutional devices which are structured to provide incentives for moderation which should be constituency-based, rather that rely on elites.

To Horowitz, political institutions should encourage or induce integration across ethnic divides and thus, 'to engineer a centripetal spin to the political system' and 'disincentives' for radical outbidding. Institutional success of democratic governance in multiethnic system is argued to depend upon tangible incentives that politicians have to appeal beyond their own communal segments for support. Five basic mechanisms of conflict reduction identified by Horowitz (1985, p. 597) comprise:

> 1) creating proliferating points of power; often territorial, which 'proliferate points of power so as to take the heat off of a single focal point'
> 2) raising the saliency of intraethnic conflict, for example, by creating reserved offices for particular ethnic groups to create intraethnic competition at the local level;
> 3) creating incentives for interethnic cooperation, e.g., by establishing electoral procedures that encourage preelection electoral coalition formation involving more than one ethnic group through vote pooling;
> 4) policies to encourage alternative social alignments, such as social class or territory, by placing political emphasis on crosscut-ring cleavages;
> 5) reducing disparities between groups so that dissatisfaction declines, through managed distribution of resources.

An important contribution to the on-going debate on power-sharing has been made by Sisk (1996, pp. 30-4) who argues that power sharing should be interpreted as encompassing both approaches. What unites the two approaches is the belief in coalescent democracy as an alternative to the adverse effects of majoritarianism and the assumptions that support a rejection of majoritarian practices. The challenge, as rightfully observed by Sisk (1996, p. 47), is not to develop a singular model of conflict-regulating practices, but rather 'a menu of conflict-regulating practices that disputants and mediators can choose from and adapt to the intricacies and challenges of successfully regulating any given ethnic conflict'. Sisk (1996, p. 48) holds that neither consociational, nor integrative models can be said to be the best in all circumstances: 'Rather, the two approaches should be seen in contingent terms and in terms of a spectrum of options from the most consociational to the most integrative'.

In developing his broader typology of conflict-regulating practices Sisk (1996, pp. 47-96) differentiates consociational patterns from integrative, but considers both in terms of three sets of variables, specifically: territorial divisions of power, decision rules, and state-ethnic relations. Combining these three sets of variables with the mode of power-sharing, he discusses ten conflict-regulating practices. Five of them pertain to the consociational mode: 1) granting autonomy and creating confederal arrangements; 2) creating a polycommunal federation; 3) adopting proportional representation and consensus rules in decision-making; 4) adopting a highly proportional electoral system; 5) acknowledging group rights or corporate federalism. The other five refer to the integrative mode: 1) creating a mixed or noncommunal federal structure; 2) establishing a single inclusive unitary state; 3) adopting majoritarian but integrated decision-making; 4) adopting a semimajoritarian or semi-proportional electoral system; 5) adopting ethnicity-blind policies.

One more institutional pattern of managing internal peace in plural societies warrants discussion, namely the hegemonic control, alternatively known as 'ethnic democracy'. It should be set apart from power-sharing in either its consociational or integrative options. While power-sharing is compatible with liberal democracy and can, in principle, result conducive to positive and stable ethnic peace, the control model is an institution of a basically negative and unstable relationship of ethnic peace that is characteristic of authoritarian or illiberal democratic systems.

Hegemonic control, or Ethnic Democracy

The idea of control, or structural dominance, has been developed both by Benvenisti (1984) and by Lustick (1979, 1980, 1993, 1997) in analyses of Israeli society. Benvenisti, for example, has argued that the Jews and Palestinians in Israel and the Occupied Territories are locked into a confrontation that cannot, under the existing circumstances, be solved by occupation, annexation or power sharing. All that is available to the Israeli state is a policy of permanent control. As a result of similar analysis Lustick (1979) has developed a 'control model' to explain political stability in certain 'deeply divided societies' where conditions for consociational politics plainly were not present. In normative terms, this model was regarded as a 'second-best' alternative, not as desirable as consociational democracy but certainly more preferable to the existing realistic alternatives such as civil war, genocide or expulsion (see McRae, 1990, p. 100). O'Leary and McGarry (1993, chs. 3-4) and McGarry and O'Leary (1993, p. 23-5) use the term slightly differently. To them, hegemonic control is a 'coercive and/or co-optive rule which successfully manages to make unworkable an ethnic challenge to the state order on the part of the subordinate communities'. It has been widely practiced by imperial or authoritarian regimes, but it is also feasible in *Herrenvolk* and formally majoritarian democracies.

The concept of 'ethnic democracy' is similar to the concept of hegemonic control. It has been originally discussed by Linz (1975, p. 326-30) who characterized ethnic democracies as polities that are democratic for the dominant group but that exclude, on the basis of ethnicity, other groups from the democratic process. While minorities are kept outside the centers of political power, without the influence and legal means to effect change, the controlling ethnic groups may experience intragroup democracy.

More recently, the concept of 'ethnic democracy' received quite an extended application with regard to ethnic conflict in Israel. An important reason behind Israel's ability to manage ethnic conflicts within the framework of the law, it was argued, is the particular character of its political system. As defined by Smooha (1990, p. 391), ethnic democracy stands for a polity combining 'the extension of political and civil rights to individuals and certain collective rights to minorities with institutionalized dominance over the state by one of the ethnic groups'. Smooha's (1992) analysis of the state of Israel (i.e., excluding the Occupied Territories) is based on extensive attitude surveys and identifies some positive developments in Jewish-Arab relations over time. He believes that Jewish attitudes have moved slightly from control to an emphasis on equality and integration. Peled (1992) has argued that the citizenship status of its Arab citizens is the key to Israel's ability to function as an ethnic democracy. The confluence of republicanism and ethnonationalism with liberalism, as principles of legitimation, has resulted in two types of citizenship: republican for Jews and liberal for Arabs. Thus, Arab citizens enjoy civil and political rights but are barred from attending to the common good. The Arab citizenship status, while much more restricted than the Jewish, has both induced and enabled Arabs to conduct their political struggles within the framework of the law, in sharp contrast to the noncitizen Arabs of the occupied territories. To Peled, it may thus serve as a model for other dominant ethnic groups seeking to maintain both their dominance and a democratic system of government.

In sum, ethnic democracy, or control model, can be considered as a specific kind of structural ethnopolitical dominance which preserves a superior status for a certain part of the population. Actually, it stands feasible for illiberal or partially liberal systems. It is not just a system of government that a majority institutes to control a minority. It is also a model used by many regimes in the Third World and, arguably, in some of the countries of the Second. Ethnic democracy is attractive to dominant groups who strive for political democratization, but are not prepared to offer their ethnic dominance. Smooha and Hanf (1992) consider this 'democracy' as being extremely suit for democratizing East European countries.

On the whole, structural dominance, or control models cannot possibly be regarded as a viable long term solution to conflict in multiethnic systems, at least not the kind of strategy that is inherently compatible with principles of *liberal* democracy. For, as well as moral objections to this approach, it has to be suggested that such policies are likely to reinforce intercommunal antagonisms and to deepen conflict. 'The idea of domination and supremacy excludes the principle of equal rights and as long as this idea survives the majority and minority become polarized' (Deletant, 1992). The result is, in Raymond Aron (1966)'s phrase, a 'peace of empire' not a 'peace of law'. Positive and sustainable ethnic peace becomes a reality under those cultural and institutional conditions that only mature liberal democracy can offer in response to the challenges of ethnic diversity.

Notes

1 In the United States this state of affairs was reached in the 1820s and 1830s, as the franchise was extended state by state. In France, there was a sudden leap to adult male suffrage in 1848, but parliamentary government was not established securely until 1871. In Britain, parliamentary government was secure from 1688 onwards, but the franchise was not extended to the majority of male citizens until 1867, see Birch (1994, p.46).
2 For instance, Huntington (1991, p. 7) defines a 20th century political system as democratic 'to the extent that its most powerful collective decision makers are selected through fair, honest, and periodic elections in which candidates freely compete for votes and in which virtually all the adult population is eligible to vote'.
3 See, e.g. Huntington (1984), Keane (1988), Geremek (1992), Gellner (1994).
4 Diamond (1994, pp. 8-9) identifies ten principal functions by which a vigorous civil society effectively serves liberal democracy.
5 On historical transformations of democracy see in Dahl (1994, pp. 25-7).
6 This point has been made by Nodia (1992, p. 7), 'Modern democratic regimes, no less than modern nations, are artificial constructs... For the most part, modern nations and modern democracies alike are too large to do without this 'imagined' quality.
7 To George Schöpflin (1995a, p. 37-47), it is crucial to understand that BOTH these factors have been present, for there is a strong tendency in Western Europe, where democracies have been established and functioning for a considerable period of time, to ignore, if not to deny the ethnic aspects of nationalism and deny them any function.
8 For a discussion of the argument see Sartori (1987, pp. 90-1).
9 On the relationship between constitutionalism and liberal democracy see Elster and Slagstad (1988, pp. 1-18), Zakharia (1997).

4 Democratization and Factors of Ethnic Peace

Both democracy and peace need be conceived and analyzed in their dynamics, not so much as states of affairs or once and for good achieved results, but primarily as unfolding processes of human search for broader freedom and more harmony in social relations. The open-ended, dynamic feature of the progress along the way is captured in the notion of democratization. Ethnicity closely interplays with the politics of democratic transition, consolidation and sustainability. This chapter is concerned with identifying and assessing sets of factors that exert influence upon the relationship of ethnic peace in democratizing systems.

Democratization as Political Change

Democratization's Third Wave. New Democracies

Democratization is the leading vehicle of contemporary political change. It represents a variety of nested processes whereby many formerly autocratic states in the Second and Third world attempt to establish more participatory and responsive political systems. In fact, more than thirty countries made transitions toward democracy between the mid-1970s and the early 1990s. The result has been a near doubling of the number of democratic regimes. The first cluster of transitions took place in the mid-1970s in Southern Europe (Portugal, Spain, and Greece). The second cluster refers to Latin and Central America during, roughly speaking, the first half of the 1980s (Argentina, Uruguay, Peru, Ecuador, Bolivia, Brazil, Nicaragua, Honduras, Guatemala, Mexico and Paraguay). In the late 1980s the transitions engulfed Eastern Europe (Poland, Czechoslovakia, Hungary, Romania, Bulgaria, and the former German Democratic Republic). The most recent transitions occurred in South Africa and in the former Soviet Union.[1]

With the collapse of European communism, democracy has reached every region of the world for the first time in history and has become 'the only legitimate and viable alternative to an authoritarian regime of any kind' (Weffort, 1993, p. 245).

These changes are impressive and they do indeed give evidence of democratic progress in a large number of countries in a relatively short span of time. Yet, it is important to bear in mind that almost all of the aforementioned countries are still in the early phases of a move toward establishing their democracy and should be correctly assessed as being unconsolidated, fledgling, or new democracies. For, if a country can be labeled democratic as soon as it emerges from authoritarian rule, in as much as its authorities are popularly elected (applying the minimal, or procedural definition of democracy), it still usually lacks the characteristics associated with fully-fledged democracies. Essentially, 'new democracies' are democracies-in-the-making. This distinctiveness of the current transitions which Huntington (1991) refers to collectively as the 'third wave' of democratization, has stimulated much rethinking of democratic theory.[2]

The difficulties that new democracies face include problems inherited from their authoritarian predecessors, as well as others peculiar to the specific routes navigated by their societies in the aftermath of transition. Current cases of democratizations are different from the classic cases of transitions to modern mass democracies in Western Europe in a variety of ways. In the first place, the *ancien regimes* from which transitions have recently departed - bureaucratic authoritarian, state socialist, post-totalitarian, sultanistic - are very different from the oligarchic regimes of the late XIXth and early XXth centuries. The actors and strategies involved are therefore quite different. Furthermore, the practical unfeasibility, in the current context, of gradually extending the right to vote to broader sectors of the population forecloses the path of incremental democratization through elite contestation, known as essential characteristics of the West European transitions. Finally, the democratization process itself can create or exacerbate other problems with which new democracies must then grapple. In this regard, analysts mention the problems of communal conflict, foreign war, and social decay (Huntington, 1996, p. 8-10).

Recent Conceptualizations of Democratization

Recent literature views the relationship between democracy and democratization as both process-oriented and action-oriented. O'Donnell and Schmitter (1986, p. 9-10) analyze it on the basis of processual unfolding of democracy's guiding principle of citizenship.

> Democratization ... refers to the process whereby the rules and the procedures of citizenship are either applied to political institutions previously governed by other principles (e.g., coercive control, social tradition, expert judgment, or administrative practice), or expanded to include persons not previously enjoying such rights and obligations (e.g., nontaxpayers, illiterates, women, youth, ethnic minorities, foreign residents), or extended to cover issues and institutions not previously subject to citizen participation (e.g., state agencies, military establishments, partisan organizations, interest associations, productive enterprises, educational institutions, etc.).

Scholars draw a crucial distinction between liberalization and democratization, the two types of political changes that frequently occurred in the Second and Third Worlds. Whereas the former encompasses the more modest goal of merely loosening restrictions and expanding individual and group rights within an authoritarian regime, the latter goes beyond expanded civil and political rights. As a movement toward establishing a popular political regime, democratization involves holding free elections on a regular basis and determining who governs on the basis of these results. Liberalization, on the contrary, is understood as the partial opening of an authoritarian system short of choosing governmental leaders through freely competitive elections (e.g. O'Donnell and Schmitter, 1986, p. 11; Mainwaring, 1992, p. 245). Though liberalization and democratization are closely related, the two may not occur simultaneously during a transition. Liberalization without alterations in the structure of authority has occasionally been given the euphemistic label of 'tutelary democracy' or 'liberalized authoritarianism' (*dictablanda*). Democratization without liberalization, when contentious issues are kept off the agenda of collective deliberation and/or when there exist restrictions on the freedoms of particular individuals or groups to enjoy full citizenship status, is termed 'limited democracy'(*democradura*) (O'Donnell and Schmitter, 1986, p.12).

A major on-going debate concerns the issue of craft vs. preconditions. Some argue that movement towards democracy depends on the existence within society of particular social, economic, or cultural *preconditions*, although there is much disagreement over what those preconditions are. A different school of thought sees democratization as primarily the product of *craft* by political leaders who have the will and the skill to bring it about.

Recent studies of democratization belong to the latter approach and hold that a democratic regime is installed not by trends but by people. 'Democracies are created not by causes but by causers' (Huntington, 1991, p. 77). Much of recent scholarship is optimistic in holding that democracy can be crafted and promoted in all sorts of places, including those in structurally and culturally unfavorable environment. IN other words, democracy is now treated as a product that can be manufactured wherever there is democratic craftsmanship and the proper *zeitgeist* (O'Donnell and Schmitter, 1986; Di Palma, 1990; Bermeo, 1990; Huntington, 1991; Karl and Schmitter, 1991; idem, 1993).

That is why many scholars have come to emphasize the role of elites and political pacts in transitions to democracy. Overall, in a transition process involving a high degree of uncertainty and indeterminacy, pacts enhance the probability that the process will lead to a viable political democracy. A related issue concerns the distribution of popular support among key sectors of society (Zhang, 1994; Diamond and Linz, 1995).

An underlying assumptions of much of the literature on transitions has been that the mode with which new regimes are created has important implications for the stability of the newly emerging polyarchies. Modes of transition are usually distinguished according to the process through which incumbents are replaced by opposition forces (Huntington, 1991, p. 114 ff). Roughly, one can differentiate between transitions from above (transformation /transaction /reform), transitions from below (replacement /breakdown /rupture), and transitions where regime and opposition play a roughly equal role in a system transformation (transplacement/extrication). Based on cross-national comparisons, recent research seeks to identify and compare distinctive patterns of transition across different countries with the aim to determine the relationships between, on the one hand, strategic interactions and the type of democratic transition and, on the other hand, between the pattern of transition and the type of democratic political system that emerges (Karl, 1990; Karl and Schmitter, 1991 and 1992).

As a result of numerous recent discussions, a broad academic consensus has emerged that both preconditions and crafting have roles to play, and certain preconditions can facilitate or, conversely, obstruct democratic crafting. Actors cannot make any kind of choice in a given situation and therefore, one must look at the interplay between economic, social, cultural, and other preconditions created in earlier periods and the decisions taken by current political actors. 'The preconditions set the stage on which the actors play' (Karl, 1990, passim; Sorensen, 1993, p. 14).

Stages of Democratization

The overall process of democratization before and after the founding election is usually complex and prolonged. Basically, four major stages are distinguished: 1) pre-democratization stage, i.e., decay of the authoritarian rule usually, though not often accompanied by attempts at liberalization, 2) the democratic transition proper which culminates in the inauguration of the new regime with the founding elections; 3) the consolidation of the democratic system; 4) mainataining democratic sustainability and preventing its breakdown.[3] Stages of democratic transition and consolidation have received most attention in the recent research and one can even speak of the rise of the sub-disciplines of 'transitology' and 'consolidology'.

What is usually referred to as the *transition* is the interval between one political regime and another. Transitions are delimited, on the one side, by the launching of the process of dissolution of an authoritarian regime and, on the other, by the installation of some form of democracy, the return to some form of authoritarian rule, or the emergence of a revolutionary alternative. Major characteristic trait of democratic transition is deemed to be great uncertainty of its political dynamics and outcomes, one especially fraught with the risk of reversion (O'Donnell and Schmitter, 1986, p.6):

> It is characteristic of the transition that during it the rules of the political game are not defined. Not only are they in a constant flux, but they are usually arduously contested; actors struggle not just to satisfy their immediate interests and/or the interests of those who they purport to represent, but also to define rules and procedures whose configuration will determine likely winners and losers in the future. Indeed, those emergent rules will largely define which resources can legitimately be expended in the political arena and which actors will be permitted to enter it.

From the viewpoint of conflict management, the transition stage features the drafting of methods or rules for resolving political conflicts peacefully. It is considered to have largely ended when a new democracy has promulgated a new constitution and held free elections with little barrier to mass participation. However, such a successful transition to procedural democracy guarantees neither its stability nor survival. Executive arrogation, coups and other calamities can terminate fledgling democracies. For this reason, the establishment of substantial consensus among elites on the recurrent application of rules of the political game and the worth of democratic institutions lies at the heart of democratic *consolidation*.

When an agreement on democratic rules is successfully reached, the transition is essentially over. Democracy enters a new phase in which 'the behavior of the actors is influenced, to an extent not seen before, by the presence of the new rules' (Di Palma, 1990, p. 109). Lawrence Whitehead (1989, p.79) argues that consolidation involves an increasingly 'principled' rather than 'instrumental' commitment to the democratic rules of the game.

Discussing the landmarks of reaching consolidation, John Higley and Richard Gunther (1992) hold that democracies become consolidated only when elite consensus on procedures is coupled with extensive mass participation in elections and other institutional processes. Diamond's (1993a) findings in his comparative study of political cultures in democratizing countries concur: 'Democracy becomes truly stable only when people come to value it widely not solely for its economic and social performance but intrinsically for its political attributes.'

To Linz and Stepan (1996, p. 6), the democratic legitimation must be more than a commitment to democracy in the abstract; it must also involve a shared normative and behavioral commitment to the specific rules and practices of the country's constitutional system:

> Behaviorally, a democratic regime in a territory is consolidated when no significant national, social, economic, political, or institutional actors spend significant resources attempting to achieve their objectives by creating a nondemocratic regime or by seceding from the state.
>
> Attitudinally, a democratic regime is consolidated when a strong majority of public opinion, even in the midst of major economic problems and deep dissatisfaction with incumbents, holds the belief that democratic procedures and institutions are the most appropriate way to govern collective life, and when support for antisystem alternatives is quite small or more-or-less isolated from prodemocratic forces.
>
> Constitutionally, a democratic regime is consolidated when governmental and nongovernmental forces alike become subject to, and habituated to, the resolution of conflict within the bounds of the specific laws, procedures, and institutions sanctioned by the new democratic forces.

Many authors argue that the evolution of a democratic political culture is a key factor in the consolidation of democracy (Inglehart, 1990; Diamond, 1993a; idem, 1996; Putnam 1993). In fact, consolidation conjures up a two-fold process. One of these is institutionalization, as defined by Huntington (1968, p. 12): 'The process by which organizations and procedures acquire value and stability.' The second involves subsequent long-term socialization, through exposure and practice, to institutions and procedures, and development of the skills and attitudes for dealing with them. Thus construed consolidation is simultaneously formed at two levels - of valid democratic institutions and of a political culture. Therein resides consolidation's automatic connection with the acquisition of legitimacy.

Successful transitions from authoritarian rule do not somehow lead more or less naturally to consolidated democracies. The mere retention of a democratic regime does not necessarily consolidate it. Consolidation and stability are not the same phenomenon, although the latter is an attribute of the former (Higley and Gunther, 1992, p. 7; Valenzuela, 1992). Schmitter (1994, p. 59) observes that there is no simple choice between regression to autocracy and progression to democracy, for 'at least two other alternatives are available: 1) a hybrid regime that combines elements of autocracy and democracy; and 2) persistent but unconsolidated democracy'.

Many observers note that a general tendency seems to exist for third-wave democracies to become something other than fully democratic. In its *Comparative Survey of Freedom* for 1995, for instance, Freedom House (1995, pp. 5-7) identified 114 countries as democracies - more than at any other time in history. Yet it also classified 37 (or one-third) of these democracies as only 'partly free', because of their abridgments of basic political liberties and human rights. Huntington (1996, p. 6) very elegantly puts it: 'On the democratic-nondemocratic continuum, in short, we seem to be moving toward a classic bell-shaped curve, with a growing number of countries somewhere in the middle between Denmark and China.' Diamond (1996, p. 23) concurs: 'the gap between electoral and liberal democracy has become one of the most striking features of the "third wave".'

Now that the 'third wave' dynamic proceeds from a phase of riveting expansion to one of a laborious and seemingly unexciting routine of consolidation, the research agenda logically shifts to a greater concern with the viability and prospects for long-term survival of new democratic regimes, as well as to various aspects of the performance of democratic institutions and the quality of political and social life in post-transitional context (Huntington, 1996; Diamond, 1996). The consolidation of new democracies entails much more than a question of time. What is at stake is the institutionalization of a new set of rules for the political game, i.e., the construction of a new pattern of processing conflicts.

Democratization as Conflict and Crisis Management

Democracy is linked to conflict and represents a particular system to peacefully process conflicts which permits them to play a constructive role in socio-political interactions. A successful democratic transition lays the ground for a transition to new patterns of conflict management. Realizing this fundamental task is the task of democratic consolidations.

Helga Welsh (1994) has suggested considering democratization as a transition in the modes of conflict resolution. She departs from a more general distinction between three major modes of conflict resolution: 1)command and imposition, 2)bargaining and compromise, and 3)competition and cooperation. Although these modes are clearly present in all political systems, their relative significance varies considerably. In authoritarian systems conflict resolution is based largely upon methods of command and imposition that take the form of rule by decree, force, or exclusion and the mutual denial of legitimacy. Alternatively, competition, accompanied by cooperation, lies at the heart of pluralist politics. Democratic transition is characterized by the switch from command and imposition to intense bargaining and compromise. Once the transition enters the stage of consolidation, bargaining and compromise decline in favor of more competitive modes of conflict resolution.

Drawing upon the examples from Central and Eastern Europe Welsh (1994, p.382-7) observes that in countries where elite bargaining and compromise are largely absent or limited in their outreach, the successful completion of the transition may be slowed down or jeopardized. While bargaining and compromise contributed to the peaceful and orderly transfer of power and the institutionalization of pluralist political structures in Eastern Europe, further progress toward the consolidation of these emerging democracies has been hampered by unresolved issues of power distribution and, to some extent, by conflictual elite attitudes. To Welsh, many of the current problems in the region, including governmental instability, ethnic conflicts, political apathy, can be traced, at least partly to the premature eclipse of bargaining and compromise. Further progress toward democratic consolidation, however, is dependent on both competition and cooperation.

Democratization must also be viewed as necessarily the enterprise of crisis management, both in system-level terms (as peaceful management of social transformation by means of introducing institutional innovations) and in interactional terms (as management of crises resulting from strategic interactions of salient groups by means of problem-solving negotiation). Successful crisis management is actually the core of the transition from destructive (associated with the authoritarian rule) to constructive patterns of conflict management which democracy makes possible.

If we view democracy in developmental terms (Sklar, 1987 and 1996; O'Donnell, 1994), as emerging in fragments or parts, by no fixed timetable or sequence, then revisited theories of modernization bear important insights for underscoring the essence of democratization as the process of bringing about the peaceful change by means of constructive management of problem areas (crises) of political development. A pre-transitional situation is characterized by the need to overcome the inefficiency (or sometimes, the outright collapse) of authoritarian institutions and practices of conflict management in situations when continuation of coercion and imposition generates increasing disruption of all spheres of political life and blocks political development. Management of systemic crises calls for introducing adequate institutional innovations, i.e., for reconstituting the basic rules of the political game on a new normative basis.

After long periods during which major political, social, and economic changes have been postponed or blocked, a growing impatience of the population intensifies the apparent need for change (Genov, 1991, p. 336). Institutional arrangements regarding the future distribution of power and the requirements for 'founding elections' command immediate action. Under democratic transitions, proaction for, and effective convocation of the founding election is the major turning point that occurs in the process of 'institutionalizing uncertainty', i.e., of subjecting all interests of political actors to uncertainty of democratic outcomes (Przeworski, 1986, p. 60).

Consolidating democracy means to come out with even more serious novations in basic institutions. These novations resolve developmental crises (problem areas) that compose the modernization syndrome (identity, legitimacy, participation, distribution, penetration). Doing this, leaders of new democracies face critical choices while they must build, reform and, in many cases, dismantle institutions. Democracy thus develops as the in-system responses to the problem areas of political development become institutionalized.[4] The embrace of democratic procedures lies at the core of democratic consolidation. In terms of conflict management it means a reduction in the uncertainty of democratic politics that concerns not so much the outcomes as the rules of political contestation. The mode of conducting political competition becomes peaceful. Consolidated democracy comes to rest on the institutionalized 'bounded uncertainty' and the 'contingent consent' of actors to respect the outcomes it produces (Schmitter and Karl, 1990).

Democratization in Multiethnic Setting: Factors of Ethnic Peace

Multiethnicity adds to the tasks of democratization before, during, and after the transition episode. In fact, it often exacerbates existing ethnic problems and is accompanied by ethnic unrest. At the same time, democratization can actually provide an opportunity for resolving ethnic conflict. De Nevers (1993, p. 61) observes that 'since in the vast majority of cases democratization includes a negotiating phase, there is an inherent opportunity in the process to address issues raised by ethnic tensions, especially when constitution-building is part of the democratization process'. Sisk (1996, p. 80) explains why in the field of ethnopolitics transitional periods, are often moments of hope and peril:

> Transitions offer hope because the opportunity for institutionalizing peace exists; intergroup relations and rules of the political game are in flux, and parties may adopt conflict-regulating practices. But such moments are equally perilous, for as an interregnum begins, incentives for ethnic mobilization and aggression may be stronger than those that lead to moderation. The absence of clearly defined rules of the game means a vacuum exists in which politics is confusing and its outcomes are deeply uncertain.

Preserving ethnic peace under democratization thus, requires a particularly skilled crafting. Two major sets of factors that influence democratizing ethnic peace have been discussed in the recent literature. They can be referred to as contextual and stage-specific.

Contextual Factors

Contextual factors are not directly related to any specific stage of democratization, although their influence on the state and prospects of democratizing ethnic peace is substantial. This group of factors comprise legacies of the past and international environment.

Legacies of the past Legacies refer to the history of interethnic relations, including historical evolution of conflict, related collective memories, ethnically relevant ideologies and policies pursued by the regime or its antedates. Legacies are obviously of great importance. Ethnic groups not only inherit but also reshape collective myths and beliefs. In the process the past is redefined almost to the point where what is believed about history, and what is remembered or forgotten, becomes more influential than what actually happened. At the same time, the larger legacies based on ethnic histories, are not so malleable and one can detect a number of determining elements in the ancestry of most multiethnic states. Authoritarian regimes invariably suppress ethnic histories and, in an effort to create their own political myths, manipulate historical facts to suit their own purposes. Furthermore, authoritarian regimes fail to promote objective historical inquiry or scholarly standards of evidence in political discourse. Therefore, liberalization periods tend to be accompanied by potent upsurge of ethnic self-consciousness and ideologization of ethnicity that derive from communally perceived need to overcome the ethnic injustices of the past.

International environment The wide range of events and influences both globally and in the immediate region seriously affect the domestic context of perceived group security, opportunity for action and formulation of policies under democratization. One obvious influence is the snowballing, or demonstration, effect of both earlier transitions and outcomes of ethnopolitical struggles (particularly, for secession or larger autonomy) elsewhere. Another is the presence of transnational ethnic kin (diasporas or potential irredenta) or non-ethnically-based international political and moral support to disadvantaged ethnic groups. International pressures influence the direction of post-authoritarian transformation: the level and kind of foreign aid and investment, conditioned provision of support for reforms through pressures to introduce internationally recognized standards of minority rights, the role of foreign experts in actually devising new institutions, etc. Many rightfully observe that neighboring countries and the international community more generally have an important role to play in ensuring that minorities are treated fairly and that states which do respect individual and group rights can feel secure within their borders (Diamond and Plattner, 1994, p. xxviii).

Outside powers may be able to encourage moderation by providing economic incentives or political advice. For instance, the survivability of moderates in situations of deep ethnic enmity depends much on the international community's role in buttressing attempts to reach and sustain mutual security pacts and to transform these initial pacts into viable, long-term, democratic conflict-regulating practices, usually embodied in new constitutions. De Nevers (1993, p. 76) observes that to the degree that democratizing states look to older democracies for blueprints of ways to shape their own systems, established democracies have both an opportunity and an obligation to provide useful examples of ways to avoid ethnic conflict. International environment can also constructively act as a third party mediating on-going domestic conflicts.

Stage-Specific Factors

Five major clusters can be distinguished within this group of factors: leadership, motivational factors, power-balance factors, institutional factors, and modalities of the transition.

Leadership Leadership composition (the balance between extremists, radicals, and moderates) is an important factor at any stage of democratization. At the pre-transition stage, the emergence of ethnic leadership determines the degree of ethnic groups' organization and their ability to engage into concerted political action.

Under democratic transition when negotiations over new institutional arrangements take place, their outcomes are often shaped by the presence or absence of interethnic coalitions between moderates from different ethnic groups. Ethnic apprehensions can easily spiral out of control as opportunistic politicians begin to play a game marked by escalating demands, hyperbolic rhetoric (possibly encompassing the breakup of the state). The balance between political competition within an ethnic group and inter-ethnic competition or the level of homogeneity of ethnic communities seriously affect efforts to develop policies of inclusiveness and moderation at the stage of democratic transition and even more so, under democratic consolidation.

Many scholars agree that the dialectic of cooperation and conflict leaves moderate elites exceptionally vulnerable to intragroup politics of outbidding, particularly in multipolar ethnic conflicts, often making them hostages of the attempts by outbidders to derail negotiations. In virtually every conflict, accommodative pursuits are limited by the reality of achieving only limited or sufficient consensus on the new rules of the political game. In his study of the South African transition, Sisk (1995) traces a complex process of convergence and reformulation of preferences by ethnic actors during their move from the ideal to the possible.

At the stage of democratic consolidation leadership composition and its level of craftsmanship are particularly important when new institutionalized rules of political game start to function and need sustaining. The more constraining and unfavorable the structural circumstances, the more skillful, innovative, courageous, and democratically committed political leadership must be for ethnic peace to become stable. Because political identities are not fixed and permanent, the quality of democratic leadership is particularly important in ethnic politics. Political leadership can nurture multiple and complementary political identities as well as polarized and conflictual identities. Even when the burden of past legacies and present challenges are formidable, breakdowns in ethnic relations are not inevitable but are accelerated by poor leadership and bad choices.

If elites from the dominant group approach minorities in a spirit of flexibility, inclusiveness, and tolerance, the odds are that post-transitional ethnic tensions can be defused. Hislope (1998, p. 141) discusses the importance of the 'generosity moment' as a normative construct that demands that elites from the dominant group publicly acknowledge minority concerns, invite minority elites into negotiations and the policy-making process, and display flexibility in addressing minority issues. 'In this sense, generosity is akin to a process of political incorporation, in which minorities are assured of a permanent "voice" in the system'.

Motivational factors These factors relate to politico-psychological variables that affect democratizing ethnopolitics through the dynamics of group solidarity. These are level of perceived ethnic tension, identity factors (their salience, shifts and balance), and intergroup perceptions.

The level of perceived ethnic tension at the pre-democratization stage affects the likelihood of interethnic strife and often highlights issues to avoid or address immediately during the transition. De Nevers (1993, pp. 67-8) holds that high level of ethnic tension at the onset of the democratization process significantly hinders prospects for negotiations over new ethnopolitical arrangements. If the old regime was an extension of a minority ethnic group that suppressed demographically larger groups, the ethnic problems will complicate negotiations over new political arrangements from the very beginning. If the old regime exacerbated ethnic problems by engaging in coerced assimilation, forced relocation, ethnic expulsion, or extermination campaigns, then the democratization process is likely to be both highly problematic and emotionally charged.

At different stages of democratization identity factors influence ethnopolitical choices unevenly. At the stage of authoritarian decay (pre-democratization) the identity salience, strength of ethnic loyalties and extent of group cohesion strongly influence the potential for ethnic mobilization. Existing ethnic ideologies (organized systems of identity-based beliefs) shape the prevailing discourses within ethnic group publics which stress differential assessments of conflict issues and diverge on the avenues of their solution.

The interplay between ethnic and political (national) identities is particularly important. It is not always clear-cut what constitutes a nation before, during, or even after democratic transition. If a political community does not exist, relationships among the major actors are likely to resemble international relationships; this implies that careful and sensitive diplomacy is a primary requirement of political stability and a basic pre-condition for any substantial attempts to promote civic unity.

At the stage of democratic transition groups experience identity shifts which result in either crystallization of separate political identities (in the case of partition) or in approximation of a fragile balance between ethnic and political identities. Either way, this signifies that a first agreement on the legitimacy of a political unit has been reached. Progress in forging an adequate identity balance between ethnic and political (civic) identities directly influences the degree of stability that ethnic peace relationship develops at the stage of democratic consolidation.

Perceptions of the opponent focus on the adversary's intent and constitute an essential aspect of any conflict. Improving the quality of democratizing ethnic peace necessarily requires changing the negative perceptions and creating cooperative attitudes and arrangements to tie people together. This, as Saunders (1992, p. 4) says, must include, 'changing the perceptions of each party of the other's character and intent'. Rothschild's (1986) distinction between categories of intergroup perceptions (essentialist, pragmatic and reciprocative) has already been referred to in Ch. 3. One of the challenges on the agenda of ethnic peace is to transform mutual perceptions from essentialist to pragmatic and reciprocative. To Sisk (1995, p. 28, 78), in a divided society, the transformation from an essentialist perception of foes to pragmatic or reciprocative perceptions is in essence the realization of the mutually beneficial nature of a shared or common destiny, that is an awareness of the basic reality that 'groups will in fact go on living together'. Pragmatic intergroup perceptions are the necessary intermediate condition, for it is the pragmatism that leads to colloborative problem solving through negotiation.

At the pre-democratization stage, perceptions are based on underlying grievances and differential assessments of conflict issues and avenues for solution. Under democratic transition, perceptions get new ground in expectations and collective apprehensions of the uncertainty of the transition's outcomes in ethnic terms. Therefore, such aroused fears and mutual perceptions are particularly subject to manipulations. To Sisk (1995, p. 50), the expectations of political actors over the working properties of alternative rules and how they may fare under such rules are critical:

> The expectation, or perception, of a party's majority or minority status relative to others is an important factor in perceiving one's fate in a polarized, conflict-ridden, divided society. Choosing among alternative political institutions in the midst of a period of political transition, when uncertainty is heightened, will improve a reasoned estimate of the party's size relative to others and the perceived degree of variability in that size. This is especially true with respect to a transition that will culminate in a founding election.

Critical to the change to pragmatic or reciprocative perceptions is the changing cost-benefit calculations of political leaders and their ethnic constituencies. In cases of successful transitions, the opportunity emerges for mutual perceptions to start to be formed on the basis of new interests and mutual stakes in the unity of a polity under democratic governance. As a result, the possibility of lasting ethnic peace can be greatly enhanced at the subsequent stage of democratic consolidation. It can be attempted through the changing of competitive states of mind and envisioning and gradually building integrative relationships that separate interest from values, promote cooperation and thus foster peace.

Power balance factors Differentials of ethnic group power strongly influence the potential for ethnopolitical activism, specifically the level of mobilization that can be reached. At the pre-democratization stage, they represent power estimates based on the relative size of the ethnic groups in a country's population, resources under group control which can become involved into political ethnic action, ethnic composition of the regime and agents of the state, ethnic composition of the military, possibilities for potential interethnic alliances and the issue of the (im)partiality of the state. These factors have been extensively discussed in the current literature (Horowitz, 1991; De Nevers, 1993; Gurr, 1993; Sisk, 1995). Changes in bargaining power balance (based on degree of politicization of identities, availability of resources under group control, level of mobilization, degrees of organization, presence of elite split and potential for tactical alliances between sub-elites across ethnic lines) structure prospects for institutional viability of the fledgling democracy.

Institutional factors The importance of institutions for the stability and sustenance of the peace relationship can hardly be overestimated. Institutional factors explain both how actors make choices within a given set of institutional settings and how institutions are created or evolve. At the pre-democratization stage availability/lack of institutions for expression and accommodation of ethnic tensions accounts for the salience of ethnopolitical conflict. The lack of specialized institutions for handling ethnic disputes, as suggested by Gurr (1993, p. 137), invariably tends to result in a resurgence of communal activism, both protest and rebellion.

Institutionalization of power-sharing arrangements and guarantees for minority rights, logically becomes the central task of democratization in multiethnic systems. Many agree that deliberate constitutional engineering can be a vital tool of ethnic conflict management. At the stage of democratic transition, this task is addressed through institutional choice which is the precondition for constitution-drafting. A most thorough and thoughtful analysis of transitional ethnopolitics in terms of institutional choice has been proposed by Sisk (1995). To Sisk (1995, p. 45), institutional choice is a matter of configuring a set of rules to constitute a regime that structures the strategic behavior and relationships among social actors.

> In the course of negotiated transitions to democracy, political leaders, political parties, and their allied forces in civil society make choices over preferred alternative institutions, or rule structures, for the future polity. These choices are selected from a set of alternative decision rules; that is, choices must be made to decide the rules to determine how subsequent decisions will be taken in the political system.

Sisk rightfully draws attention to the fact that democratic transitions occur in a set of analytically distinct stages, with each stage fundamentally linked to the previous stage and to subsequent stages. Thus the nature of the democracy that emerges at the end of the process has its roots in the process itself. Analyzing the South African case, Sisk (1995) constructs a multi-step model by identifying several discrete steps that characterized the rule-making process of a transition toward democratic rule. Uniting each step of the democratization process is the collapse and redefinition of the rules of the political game. At each step of the way, the politics of institutional choice, of political actors assessing alternative sets of rules and choosing among them has been central to the process of democratic transition.

The transition to a democratically elected government actually is only the first step to the process of democratic consolidation. After a successfully completed democratic transition the character of ethnic peace is strongly influenced by ethnically relevant priorities pursued in the course of institution-building and institutional readjustment. Three spheres are important in this regard: state-, nation- and civility-building.

1. State-building. Sisk (1995, pp. 28-9) points out that once parties to a conflict seek to avoid confrontation by choosing negotiations, the institutional reconfiguration of the state plays a pivotal role in the search for more peaceful politics. If post-transitional state institutions are to be capable of performing conflict management tasks, they must be reorganized, rather than simply reduced. An important lesson for the management of ethnic conflict while creating new state institutions is that no salient group should be prohibited from a share of effective power (Zartman, 1990; Horowitz, 1990a, idem, 1990b). The basis of pacts should be agreement on mutual restraint and the protection of vital interests, exactly the type of concerns that drive the divisive politics of divided societies.

A related task of post-transitional state institutions is to create the conditions for the effective exercise of citizenship for all members of a political community. Democratic policies in the state-building process are, in fact, those that emphasize a broad and inclusive citizenship where all citizens are accorded equal individual rights (Linz and Stepan, 1996, p. 25).

It has been noted more generally that, once universal adult citizenship rights have been secured in a society, democratization is mostly a matter of the more authentic political inclusion of different identity groups and categories, for which formal political equality can hide continued exclusion or oppression (Dryzek, 1996). In fact, free societies require a higher level of commitment and participation than authoritarian ones. In new democracies citizens have to do for themselves what the rulers did for them in the past. This can happen only if these citizens feel a strong bond of identification with their political community, and hence with their fellow citizens. Therefore, issues of nationhood form the second crucial determinant of post-transitional ethnopolitics.

2. Nation-building. Much of scholarly debates concerns the conditions under which the logics of state policies aimed at nation-building become congruent with those aimed at crafting democracy. Linz and Stepan (1996) argue that the greater the extent to which the population of a state is composed of a plurality of national, linguistic, religious, or cultural societies, the more complex politics becomes, since an agreement on the fundamentals of a democracy will be more difficult. While this does not mean that consolidating democracy in multinational or multicultural states is impossible, it does mean that especially careful political crafting of democratic norms, practices, and institutions is required.

In all multiethnic societies the problem of forging an adequate balance between civic and ethnic identities and conceptions of nationhood comes to the fore in nation-building processes. Linz and Stepan (1996, p. 33-4) suggest that in a multiethnic, multicultural setting, the chances of consolidating democracy are increased by state policies that grant inclusive and equal citizenship and give all citizens a common 'roof' of state-mandated and state-enforced individual rights.

For those seeking to establish and maintain democratic institutions in culturally diverse societies, the test of whether a country is really free increasingly depend on the security enjoyed by the minorities within that country. Designing and building meaningful institutions of power-sharing and safeguards for minority rights are indispensable components for articulating a democratic polity that has the capacity to deal with ethnopolitical conflict through peaceful means.

3. Civility-building. The (re)-construction and empowerment of civil society in post-transitional polities, along with the promotion of a supportive civilized discourse is crucial for increasing the stability of democratizing ethnic peace.

Civil society is a crucial arena for the development of important values and norms of multiethnic democracy, such as multicultural pluralism, tolerance, moderation, a willingness to compromise, and a respect for opposing viewpoints. These values and norms become stable only when they emerge *through experience* of democratic consolidation. Political learning is crucial for engrounding ethnic peace and transforming the relationship to its sustainable forms.

The adoption of a civilized discourse signifies that greater confidence exists about the stability and viability of mutual interethnic security. At the same time, the pliability of democratic rules and their somewhat open effects leave room for improvement within mutual security; which in turn provides the feedback way to build confidence in the democratic ethnopolitical game.

Modalities of the transition These factors of democratizing ethnic peace include three variables: timing of identification and addressing ethnic tensions; speed of the transition; and the mode of transition.

Transition periods are times of accelerated change. There is a felt need to address certain crucial issues under rather urgent time constraints.[5] Ethnic issues are only one of many complications likely to be present during democratization. Conceding that the myriad issues involved in a democratic transition may make it harder to focus sufficient attention on ethnic problems in a timely fashion scholars observe that it only underscores 'the urgency of addressing ethnic concerns as early as possible' (De Nevers, 1993, p. 75). The opportunity for institutional reform which is the pre-condition for democratic persistence is not always present. In democratizing plural societies the window of opportunity to generate mutual security pacts and to establish accommodative institutions may be only a brief moment in time that is either seized or lost.

Where political institutions that ensure meaningful power-sharing protect minorities and reward moderation are crafted early enough, attempts to consolidate democracy and ethnic peace can prevail. Conversely, if the opportunity for such ameliorative policies is lost, the range of available space for maneuver will be narrowed, and a dynamic of societal conflict will likely intensify until democratic consolidation becomes increasingly difficult, and even impossible. As phrased by Horowitz (1993, p. 37),

> It would have been highly advantageous to have set democratic, conciliatory institutions firmly on course the first time. The same will generally be true elsewhere. To have failed once makes things more difficult the next time. To have failed twice makes the next time problematic altogether... In planning

for a state that is to be democratic and multiethnic, earlier is assuredly better.

Because of the intense nature of conflict in ethnically divided societies, transitions to democracy are unlikely to occur unless they are negotiated. With regard to three different modes of transition, (i.e., regime replacements, transplacements and transformations, as identified by Huntington, 1991), analysts observe that they produce differential opportunities and threats for the successful management of ethnic conflict. De Nevers (1993, p. 75) has attracted attention to the fact that, because of the importance of negotiating adequate power-sharing arrangements, transformations and transplacements may provide a greater opportunity than regime replacement to address ethnic problems early:

> Both of these processes rely on negotiation in the creation of new political structures, which means that mechanisms for addressing possible ethnic conflicts are in place prior to the collapse of the previous regime.

Gradual transition, accomplished sooner are viewed as the best-suited to reduce the risks of communal disruption and violence. Rapid and dramatic pace of transition usually means that some of the most important supports for democracy, first off, the safeguards for minorities' rights are likely to be, at best, imperfectly developed (Horowitz, 1991, p. 111). Conversely, if the demise of the old regime takes place over a period of months or even years, opposition leaders will have more time to address ethnic problems when they go about devising new political institutions and processes. De Nevers (1993, p. 75) mentions one more aspect of the process: the ethnic leaders 'will also have more of an opportunity to develop a broad based political alliance', and 'will have a stronger cooperative foundation on which to build'.

Democratizing Ethnic Peace As Ethnopolitical Crisis Management

Democratizing plural societies must meet additional challenges to create and institutionalize norms and interactions which can provide for peaceful expression, accommodation and management of ethnic conflict. Gurr (1993, p. 138) observes that though democratizing autocracies present substantial opportunities for mobilization of communal groups, the states usually lack the resources or institutional means to reach the kinds of accommodations that typify the established democracies. This is in line with Huntington's (1968) argument that the typical problem of changing societies is the gap between high levels of political participation and weak integrative institutions to reconcile the multiplicity of contending claims.

In fact, the scope for ethnic politics in democratizing polities is dramatically widened. Previously dominated ethnic groups are likely to resent their domination in a seemingly sudden and irrational manner. Initial creation of democratic institutions may contribute to the explosion of ethnic conflicts, by providing the means of free expression, including expression of communal animosities and feelings of oppression. The risks run high that mismanagement of ethnic disputes or rejection of accommodation by ethnic contenders can lead to the emergence of disruptive strife and undermine the foundations of a peaceful and progressive future in fledgling democracies. Therefore, concerns with the institutionalization occupy the prime place among the tasks of ethnic peace-making.

In chapter 2 it has already been argued that revisited theories of modernization and political development provide important insights for understanding the linkage between crises, change and choice in democratizing ethnopolitics. Crises are situations in which the basic institutional patterns of the political system are challenged and routine response is inadequate. Therefore, institutional innovation is the hallmark of crisis resolution. In multiethnic systems all problem areas (crises) of political development (identity, legitimacy, participation, distribution, penetration) invariably acquire an ethnic sounding. Ethnopolitical crises can thus be considered by analogy with developmental crises as a typology of the problems that governments face in their attempts to develop political structural requisites in the transition to multiethnic democracy.

Institutional focus on issues of democratizing ethnopolitics suggests that promotion of peace is pre-conditioned by successful dealing with the system-level problem areas (crises) through crafting appropriate institutional innovations and nurturing norms and practices of respect for minority rights that can permit unity in diversity to become a reality. An ethnopolitical crisis is dealt with through the institutionalization of a new pattern of interaction among ethnic groups and/ or the state. Institutional choices represent the nodes of the process by which the new patterns are introduced to structure political ethnic interactions. Successful institutional innovation is the pre-condition for the subsequent forging of an elusive interethnic contract through which democratic ethnopolitics can effectively become 'the only game in town'. Democracy thus is reached in stages along with the resolution of ethnopolitical crises and transition to institutionalized management of respective problem areas of ethnopolitical development.

An ethnopolitical crisis under democratization is, in fact, a concentrated distillation of most of the elements which make up the essence of politics in multiethnic system balancing between legacies of the past, present imperatives of the transition and apprehensions of the future. The long-term prospects for a stable and sustainable ethnic peace depend not so much upon past legacies, but are mostly a function of differences in critical choices (or non-choices) made under democratic consolidation. For ethnically diverse societies the trick is to make choices (or, non-choices) between alternative institutional arrangements that are compatible with both existing socioeconomic structures and cultural identities.

As in the case of general crises of political development, not all ethnopolitical crises are solved by innovative decisions. Some may lead to the collapse of other institutions or to a general societal collapse. Crises can come and go. If crises are left unattended or mismanaged, they are bound to persist and become protracted either because a system is forced to undergo constant re-institutionalization over an extended period of time, or because it is incapable of institutionalizing a response to a new pressure and, therefore, remains at the brink of violent disruption or dissolution.

Notes

1   Finally, transitions toward democracy have taken place in Asia over the entire period since the early 1970s. Here we follow Weffort's (1993, pp. 245-6) identification of clusters of transitions, also Sorensen (1993, ch. 2).
2   Among comprehensive reviews of themes and issues salient in present-day academic debates on democratization, see e.g. Munck (1994), Munck (1997), Shin (1994), Remmer (1995).
3   See, e.g., Huntington (1991, pp. 3-14), Sorensen (1993, p. 30), Shin (1994, p. 143). Of course, the demarcation of stages within the transition process is not new and goes back to Rustow's (1970) seminal article. For a review of the semantic universe of post-transitional regimes and conceptual approaches to democratic consolidation see Collier and Levitsky (1997), Schedler (1998).
4   One way in which analysts have tried to introduce greater precision into the discussion of critical choices to be made under democratization was through the notion of dilemmas that represent sets of tasks to address under consolidation. Schmitter (1994, p. 62) distinguishes between intrinsic dilemmas (generic problems that stem from the functioning of any modern democracy) and extrinsic dilemmas

100 *Democratization and Ethnic Peace*

(problems that call into question the compatibility of emerging democratic rules and practices with existing social, cultural, and economic circumstances).

5   Time as 'a tactical resource' is discussed by Di Palma (1990, chs. 2, 4).

PART II:
POST-COMMUNIST DEMOCRATIZATION AND ETHNOPOLITICAL CRISES, CHANGE AND CHOICE

PART II.

5 Post-Communist Democratization and Ethnopolitical Crises

Processes of democratization took specific shape and dynamics in various clusters of the third wave countries. This chapter is going to consider the peculiarities of post-communist democratization and, in this regard, briefly overviews two on-going debates among social scientists. It goes on to discuss the ethnic issues of post-communist democratization by identifying three major ethnopolitical problem areas (crises) that multiethnic systems are faced with: stateness, state effectiveness, and nationhood.

Peculiarities of Post-Communist Democratization and Scholarly Debates

Post-Communist Transitions

Post-Communist transitions and issues of democratic consolidation clearly manifest a number of peculiarities which distinguish this cluster from other third wave cases (in Southern Europe and Latin America). Among these features contemporary scholarship points out at the specific nature of pre-transitional regime with its distinctive legacies, particular complexity of tasks on the post-communist agenda, the role played by nationalism and ethnic conflict and, finally, specific international context.

The nature of the pre-transitional regime Transitions in Eastern Europe and the former USSR were preceded by decades of the post-totalitarianism in the form of the party-state socialism. [1] 'Really existing socialism' was characterized by political monopoly of the communist party, specific social structure and political economy, strong influence of official ideology on political culture, and a certain position in the international geopolitical arrangements. The totalitarian legacy shapes in distinctive ways the possibilities and the agenda of democratic transition and consolidation, the interests and resources of major actors and the volatile balance of forces supporting and opposing democratization and market-oriented reforms.

Distinctive legacies of post-communist systems Several legacies are usually stressed as particularly tough and presenting serious, if not overwhelming, difficulties for the success of democratic consolidation in these countries. Among those are political learning (the absence or weakness of democratic tradition), lack of market economy, the legacy of overpoliticized state, absence or serious underdevelopment of civil society, survival of old institutions under post-communism, and one-sided modernization.

Some scholars place a high emphasis on long duration (five to seven decades) of the totalitarian rule as one of most important differences that distinguish post-communist transitions from their earlier counterparts. It is frequently argued - Russia is a favorite example - that the absence of democratic traditions impedes the consolidation of new democratic institutions and, conversely, that democracy has more chances to be stable in countries (like Chile) that have enjoyed it in the past. Some observers note that the history of Latin America and Southern Europe has been, for the most part, a history of alteration between authoritarian and democratic rule and, therefore, the recent transitions in these areas can be more accurately termed *re*democratization. This democratic residue, arguably, points to a fundamental advantage that countries in West and South enjoyed as they embarked on their most recent transition to democracy 'Without this "feel" for democracy, Eastern Europe has faced an especially formidable challenge'(Bunce, 1995b, p.88).

However, the criticisms of such position rightfully observe that what arguments of this brand miss is that if a country *had* a democratic regime, it is a veteran not only of democracy but also of the successful subversion of democracy. Political learning, in other way, cuts both ways.

> Democrats may find the work of consolidation easier when they can rely on past traditions, but antidemocratic forces also have an experience from which they can draw lessons: people know that overthrowing democracy is possible, and may even know how to do it. If the failed Russian hard-liners' coup of 1991 was more of a *coup de théatre* that *a coup détat*, it was perhaps because the coup plotters simply did not know what they were doing - an ignorance for which they were justly ridiculed by their more-experienced Latin American soul mates (Przeworski et el., 1996, p.40).[2]

Lack of market relations and market economy is among the most evident and important peculiarities of post-communist transitions. There is a wide agreement that the correlation between the market economy and democracy is very high indeed (democracy is hardly possible without a market economy, although the reverse does not hold). The lack of a market economy is thus adding to the tasks of transition. Nodia (1996, p. 17) comments on a deeper linkage between private property and human personality that has often been underestimated:

> The market economy is not simply a vehicle for more efficient resource allocation and higher growth, just as the communist economy was not merely an alternative way to provide for the general welfare. A crucial but underappreciated element here is the institution of private property. Communism was primarily about the abolition of private property. But, as Hegel says, private property is the necessary correlate of human personality: the notion of personality emerged thanks to the institution of private property; where there is no private property, personality is not possible. The communist project was to change human nature, and the abolition of private property was communism's major - and indeed very powerful - means of doing so, that is, of destroying human personality...

Overpoliticized state and diffuse alienation is another cardinal legacy that post-communist systems inherited from the past. Diffuse alienation, originally a reaction to the defects of the state socialist system, later developed into a pattern of behavior that, to many observers, is harder to transform than the political and economic institutions that had created it. In fact, mass alienation has deep structural roots in the particular relationships between state and individuals that had formed in such systems. In this regard, Tong (1995, p. 220), among others, attracts attention to two phenomena. First, state socialism lacked a civil society, which could have provided alternative sources of identity, meaning, and empowerment, as well as an institutional outlet for personal frustration through various social organizations. The tragedy was that state socialist systems permitted no autonomous social organizations between family and nation that could elicit such a sense of identification. In conditions of such extreme weakness (or non-existence) of a civil society, alienation from official structures constituted a larger part of individual life and was therefore more pervasive. Second, the public and private spheres of life in state socialist systems were highly fused, both politically and economically. State socialism meant habitual official intervention into what is normally considered private life.

That increasingly generated feelings of powerlessness, meaninglessness, and disgust with authority. At the same time that the state invaded the private realm, the population tried to 'privatize the public sphere'. The public regarded the state as something that could be 'used and exploited when needed', and the resources used in the informal sector were 'borrowed, stolen, or otherwise appropriated from the state' (Sampson, 1986, p.86).

Novak (1997, p. 13), among others, points at important consequences:

> Accompanying the abandonment of communist doctrines came a cynicism toward any values and principles. Together with a desire for freedom went a sense of irresponsibility. Along with the opposition to the old political system emerged a defiance toward any kind of authority. And alongside the disgust with government developed a profound mistrust of one's fellow citizens. Once communism collapsed, all these contributed to the emergence of an extremely fragile democracy and a weakness of the state.

Absence or underdevelopment of civil society redoubles the difficulties of post-communist transformations. The key to reduce alienation and bring the masses back into economic and political system is rightfully viewed in (re)building civil society which only can provide intermediate linkages between state and society, help integrate private and public interests, and create informed and motivated citizens who will support reforms (Sztompka, 1991; Weigle and Butterfield, 1992; Tong, 1995, p. 230). However, civil society cannot be built or sustained without a civic culture to support it. Building new patterns of civility looms indeed large on the post-communist agenda.[3]

There is a general agreement among analysts that this task is going to be among the most difficult ones with which post-communist systems have to grapple. Though creating governmental and nongovernmental institutions is relatively easy, the actual (re)construction of a civil society as a civic culture of high trust, as a particular set of norms, values and legal as well as moral views, is much more difficult. In this respect, Dahrendorf (1990, p.105) cogently observes: 'to [reconstruct civil society] effectively, certain civic virtues are indispensable, including civility, but also self-reliance. This is the facet of civil society which cannot be built at all; it has to grow'.

It has been observed more generally that weakly institutionalized party systems is one of the most difficult obstacles facing third wave democracies in their efforts at democratic consolidation (Mainwaring, 1998, p. 67). For many post-communist systems continued persistence of old institutions is a serious challenge to cope with. Geddes (1995) shows that although the political hegemony of the communist party and the totalitarian state were abolished, some of the political institutions established under communism still exist and now serve to shape the balance of power between old and new elites. Some authors contend that it is debatable if in East European countries democratization is the central political issue or if such issue is post-communism or even doubt if communist is actually so 'post' (Terry, 1993; Bunce, 1995a, Norbu, 1996).

Most of the above features are a reflection of one-sided modernization that shapes the specific context of the democratic project in post-communist countries. Earlier transitions took place at a lower level of socio-economic and industrial development, at stages when both privatization and a change of developmental strategy are far easier to implement than at more advanced stages. The oft-noted paradox about modernization in Eastern Europe is that the logic of efficient market reforms requires that 'these countries must actually face the prospect of dismantling much of their existing industrial capacity, even as they try to restructure and modernize the rest' (Terry, 1993, pp. 334-5). Besides economic re-modernization, concerns the tasks of political modernization are even more pressing. [4]

Tasks of the transitional agenda Many agree that the agenda of democratic transition and consolidation in post-communist countries is unprecedently complex and manifold. In East European and post-Soviet cases a great deal is on the move - and on the move simultaneously. What is actually on the order of the day involves the building rather than rebuilding democratic institutions, alongside with deep transformations extending to politics, economics, and social life. This has come to be termed as the 'simultaneity problem' or the 'dual track' nature of the post-communist transitions - that is, simultaneous attempt to construct both pluralistic democracy and a market economy, both to be constructed virtually from the scratch (Terry, 1993, p.334; Bunce, 1995a, p.121; Bunce, 1995b, p. 94). Offe (1991, p. 865-92) goes further and speaks of the triple (economic, political, and socio-cultural) transformations that are necessary.

Schmitter and Karl (1994, p.183) attract attention to yet another important aspect of the situation: not only are such major transformations all on the agenda for collective action and choice in Eastern Europe, but very little authoritative capacity exists for asserting priorities among them.

There is a great deal more to do than in the south, and it seems as if it must be done at once. The codewords are simultaneity and asynchrony. Many decisions have to be made in the same time frame and their uncontrolled interactions tend to produce unanticipated (and usually unwanted) effects.

The role of nationalism and ethnic conflict A manifest peculiarity of post-communist democratization concerns the role of nationalism and ethnic politics. State, nation, and identity have been at the very center of these processes of change.

First, it is widely acknowledged that nationalism played a decisive role in undermining the socialist states of Eastern Europe and the former Soviet Union and most scholars agree about the understanding of the end of state socialism as a process of national liberation - whether that was a consequence of the end of the Soviet 'Outer Empire' or the end of communist 'federations' in the Soviet Union, Yugoslavia or Czechoslovakia (Bunce, 1995a, p. 120, Ruthland, 1996, p. 4). What is involved here is not simply a return to the pre-communist past with the resurgence of old cultural, religious and territorial conflicts, but also new dimensions and dynamics of nationalism. Rather than serving as a vehicle for mass mobilization, ethnicity is mostly being used by the newly established governments as an instrument for the consolidation of their power.

Second, in the midst of destabilizing effects of rapid transitions ethnonationalist values have become salient in political discourses not only of minority groups seeking greater self-determination, but also of majorities fearful of losing influence or access to key resources. In some instances the aspirations of different communities have clashed, resulting in serious conflicts that threaten to derail the progress of democratic project. To a considerable degree this has to do with the very low margin of tolerance that exists in post-communist context.

> Post-communist states have become notorious for the difficulty they have in coping with diversity. The proposition that 'otherness' may have positive functions is completely alien to large sections of the elite and society. The reasons for this intolerance can be found in the absolute values propagated by communism, with its emphasis on the negative stereotype of the enemy (i.e., 'class enemy'), together with the way in which the anticommunist elites have had to construct their strategies in accordance with the ground rules established by communism. The post-communist elites were themselves unable to deal with challenges and criticism; they tended to regard the

normal workings of democracy as a hostile conspiracy rather than a fairly routinized process of give-and-take (Schopflin, 1994, p. 136).

This inability to deal with the diversity, prominent even in ethnically homogeneous settings, becomes doubly acute when there are deep-seated ethnic cleavages and aroused tensions.

Third, in some cases, the 'nation' has become not only the vehicle for dismantling communism, but also a refuge for those seeking scapegoats for the pain of economic transformation. Given the intensity of the emotions associated with ethnic loyalties, which are exacerbated by the process of democratization, ethnic rivals make particularly good targets for scapegoating by political elites (De Nevers 1993, Schöpflin 1995a).

Fourth, ethnicity has had a powerful impact on definitions and practices of citizenship. In this way it provides a theme not only for domestic politics of post-communist democracies, but also for their foreign policies and security throughout the region. (Schöpflin, 1994; Brubacker, 1994 and 1996; Sheffer, 1996; Linz and Stepan, 1996).

International context of transition Almost all observers agree that the international context was more significant in Eastern Europe than in most of southern Europe or Latin America. Moreover, its impact was ambivalent, since the Eastern European transitions have taken place in an international system which is itself in transition to a post-Cold War state of affairs.

Debates over Post-Communist Democratization

Post-communist transitions has produced a vigorous controversy within academic circles about the sources of successful democratic consolidation in societies that have broken from authoritarian or totalitarian past. Scholarly discussions about post-communist countries have come to center around several issues: What are the dominant constraints and incentives that shape the direction of change? What is to be the response by the political science community to the challenges of post-communist studies? In this regard, two closely interconnected debates have been on-going.

Comparativists vs. Anticomparativists This debate has to do with the issue of comparability between post-communist transitions and their previous counterparts, '[if] the East can and should be compared with the South'. On one side we find 'anti-comparativists' who are represented by many (though, by no means, most) area scholars, predominantly of elder generation who tended to be successful Sovietologists and Kremlinologists during the Cold War and who seem to be romantically nostalgic of the special position they had enjoyed in not too remote and apparently so dear to their hearts time ago. They contend that postcommunism is unique in almost all important respects and it is its inheritance that will ultimately determine its future.

In their logics, the cross-regional comparisons between East European transitions and other third wave counterparts in Latin America and Southern Europe are unhelpful at best and misleading at worst (Terry, 1993; Bunce, 1995a). Therefore, they preach the importance of solely descriptive accounts of individual cases of post-Communist transition. As espoused in one of the radical manifests of anticomparativism, 'in view of these differences we would be better served in the near term to concentrate on empirical inquiry and not to tie ourselves in conceptual knots with an excess of model-building and theory-adaptation' (Terry, 1993, p. 333). A moderate and more enlightened wing makes an effort to admit the relevance of comparisons, but only intraregional ones (Bunce, 1995a; idem, 1995b), while strongly discouraging cross-regional comparativist deviations.

The philosophy of such approach comes close to sectarian obscurantism. Those who try to sell it have been duly criticized for their self-imposed isolation from any disciplinary tradition, lack of interest in theory, disregard of mainstream scientific methodology, allowing Cold War ideology to dictate their dicsipline's direction, and overzealous absorption into nude empirie without any sustained effort at generalizing or even organized thinking beyond commonalities of an informed journalism.[5]

The other side in the controversy is presented by the comparativists who, evidently, have an open mind towards cross-regional comparisons within the human world. They come from different academic disciplines. Students of democratization, for example, counter anticomparativists by making a point that the uniqueness of postcommunism has been exaggerated, that democratization as a process displays fairly regular contours that allow for comparison across diverse cases, and, indeed, that it is precisely through such *cross*-regional comparisons that we can identify similarities and differences, test hypotheses, and thereby enrich our understanding of the democratization processual unfolding (Schmitter and Karl 1994, Karl and Schmitter 1995). For comparativists, the study of post-Communist transitions is particularly intriguing because it provides fertile ground both to test theories of political change developed in other regions and different time periods and to construct new approaches to political and social transformation. Overall, the comparativists offer a positive research program that emphasizes the immediate contextual circumstances that constrain choice and determine the path of transition. To the extent that those immediate circumstances are similar across regions and underpin institution-building cross-regional comparisons can highlight the cases of different responses to similar influences.

Comaparativists' critique of the obscurants is based on the premise that 'if the peculiarity of one's region cultural, historical or institutional matrix is so essential to understanding the outcome, this should emerge from systematic comparison rather than be used as an excuse for not applying it' (Karl and Schmitter, 1995, p. 971). Indeed, it seems reasonable 'instead of simply ruling out cross-regional or even intraregional comparisons on the assumption that they are not useful because of the unique characteristics of countries with a Leninist legacy, these assumptions can be tested and reflected upon' (Crawford and Lijphart, 1995, p.173). Conceding that those who stress the peculiar characteristics of postcommunism have some grounds for their position, many still ask when peculiarity turns into true uniqueness which precludes all comparisons and seals the cases within the narcissistic sect of the older generation communist area students. How unusual does a country's experience have to be to sever the common thread that links democratic transitions and allows us to consider them as a group? Moving from the conceptual to the practical plane, it may also be asked whether the peculiarities of post-communism pose an insurmountable obstacle to the consolidation of democracy (Shevtsova, 1995, p. 56-57).

The fear of the anticomparativists has been that elements that are deemed 'unique' to the East would be lost if they risk to embrace cross-regional comparisons or patterns of thinking. One of the recent works has manifestly demonstrated that such fears are less than reasonably grounded and misguided. Linz and Stepan (1996)'s grand study of the problems of democratic transition and consolidation has made it clear that it is precisely this sort of cross-regional comparison has great insight. 'It is precisely through such comparisons that the significant variation between the experiences of the East and the South can be conceptualized and that the relatively unique experience of the East (and by extension of the South as well) can be described and explained' (Munck, 1997, p.543).

Comparative focus is particularly important in the field of ethnic politics. Post-communist ethnicity is bound to remain a very enigmatic rat if it is cornered into a descriptivist research program of narrowly-conceived area studies. Although it appears to be an expression of individual identity, it is available to be used and misused by political elites for their own purposes. In different circumstances, it can serve as a basis both for the fission and the fusion of the state power. All these features of salient 'identity politics' and rising tensions between ethnic groups dictate the relevance of broad cross-regional comparisons between ethnically complex countries from Latin America, Southern Europe and the recent wave of post-communist transitions. (Karl and Schmitter, 1995, p. 972). Horowitz (1992, p. 20) also holds that with regard to the former Soviet Union, not only will such comparisons help to explain the likely course of conflict, but they also will make clear that these new democracies possess several different kinds of ethnic conflict and it is a mistake to think that all their ethnic problems involve the same grievances, issues, and remedies: 'There are more and less effective policies to increase or decrease ethnic conflict. Again, comparative inquiry is useful and helpful in this regard.'

Another strong argument which is helpful in evaluating the seemingly strange debate among political scientists as to whether post-communist transitions can be usefully compared with other transitions to democracy was made by Nodia (1996, p. 17):

> The only valid argument against the enterprise of comparison would be not that the differences are too great - after all, comparison implies differences as well as similarities - but that post-communist cases aim at some destination other than democracy and hence do not belong to the category of democratic transitions at all. As indicated above, however, most post-communist transitions are indeed transitions from something that is not democracy to something that is or tries to be or at least pretends to be democracy. It is the universality of the modern democratic project that creates a conceptual space in which it becomes sensible - and indeed necessary - to compare different attempts to implement this project.

It has been correctly pointed out by some of the observers, the discipline of post-communist studies is likely to continue to be divided in future. Old-fashioned area students are bound, of necessity, to continue to be journalists as well as scholars, forced to worry in the first instance about simply 'getting the story right' (King, 1994a, p. 296) until they have gradually acquired a sound theoretical guidance from the mainstream science. One can only add that the emphasis here is very much on 'gradually'. It may take decades.[6]

Legacies of the Past vs. Imperatives of Liberalization

The second but closely related debate focuses on differential assessments of the role played by the past vs. the present in explaining how choices and incentives are structured in the post-communist setting and in predicting the direction of change. In addressing these questions, scholars have explored and employed a range of analytic and theoretical perspectives (Bermeo, 1990; Bova, 1991; Crawford, 1995; Di Palma, 1990 and 1991; Ekiert, 1991; Janos, 1991; Jowitt, 1991 and 1992; Horowitz, 1992; Karl and Schmitter, 1991, 1992 and 1995; Terry, 1993; Schmitter and Karl, 1994, Bunce, 1995a and 1995b; Crawford and Lijphart, 1995; Nodia, 1996; Linz and Stepan, 1996; Comisso, 1995 and 1997). Two competing approaches - *legacies of the past* and *imperatives of the liberalization* have emerged.[7]

The 'legacies of the past' approach explains post-Communist transformation as a function of the social, cultural, and institutional structures created under Leninist regimes and Soviet domination in Eastern Europe that persist to date. In this view, the past casts a long shadow on the present, shapes the environment in which the battle to define and defend new institutions takes place, and may ultimately undermine the liberalization process. The institutions are thus viewed as simply 'arenas' within which actors, driven by more fundamental historical, cultural, or ideological factors, seize power or compete for resources.

An alternative approach emphasizes the 'imperatives of liberalization'. It suggests that new institutions can be crafted and new international pressures can be brought to bear that shut out the negative influences of the past and to claim some space for the development of new forces to structure incentives according to the more or less universal rules of liberal capitalist democracy. In this perspective, a craftful management of socio-political change often can provide a necessary condition for the break with the past in that it makes elites and the population at large available for new identities and creates the space for new institutions to structure choices in the innovative ways. As put by Geddes (1995), if new democratic institutions are constructed, then 'vested interests in those institutions will develop rapidly and will have long-term consequences that overshadow past legacies'. Since institutions affect the distribution of resources, this, in turn, will determine the relative power of both political and economic actors. When new institutions dominate the processes of political and economic change, and when liberal norms shape the identity of those institutions, old political and economic elites will be forced to behave in new ways that can support the liberalization process.[8]

Crawford and Lijphart (1995) surveyed the pool of six key legacies present in post-communist setting: 1) the history of 'backwardness', victimization and intolerance; 2) the power of the old elite and the absence of an established successor elite; 3) weak party systems with shallow roots in society; 4) the interrupted process of nation-building; 5) the continued persistence of institutions established under the old regime; 6) the legacy of the centralized state and command economy) and then assess a set of normative, institutional, and international forces in the current period that have either magnified or minimized these legacies. Their examination suggests that neither the past legacies nor the imperatives of liberalization approach can provide an adequate perspective for the study of post-Communist change if they are separated one from the other.

Many findings demonstrate that the distinction between the two approaches is not as sharp as their proponents would claim and that competing arguments must be synthesized and broadened for more nuanced and complete explanations of the direction of post-communist change. Overall, Crawford and Lijphart (1995, p.196) conclude that what unites the various arguments presented in the debate is the view that the constraints and incentives that shape current choices arise from the immediate context in which the actors find themselves. It is this context that will determine both which past legacies become politically central and whether there will be a successful transition to democracy and markets in Eastern Europe.

Ethnopolitical Crises (Problem Areas) in Post-Communist Setting

In chapters 2 and 4 it was suggested that promotion of ethnic peace in new democracies, effectively, depends upon successful resolution of a series of ethnopolitical crises which represent ethnopolitical dimension of systemic (developmental) crises that are generated by the syndrome of post-authoritarian modernization, particularly salient unresolved problem areas of identity and legitimacy. In the analysis of democratizing ethnopolitics three ethnopolitical problem areas (crises) arise as foci of prime concern: stateness, state effectiveness, and nationhood.

Crisis (Problem Area) of Stateness

At its base the crisis of stateness has to do with the problem of boundaries and identities incorporated within the territorial state. Different theorists of democracy conceived the problem in terms of the national unity as the basic background pre-condition of any democratization process (Rustow, 1970), of the prior existence of a legitimate territorial unit (Dahl, 1989), or of the problem of stateness (Linz and Stepan, 1992; idem, 1996). All of those are viewed as prerequisites for the successful completion of a democratic transition and onset of democratic consolidation.

The term 'stateness' itself was suggested by Linz and Stepan (1992) and elaborated in Linz and Stepan (1996). A 'stateness problem' that underlies the crisis 'may be said to exist when a significant proportion of the population does not accept the boundaries of the territorial state (whether constituted democratically or not) as a legitimate political unit to which they owe obedience' (Linz and Stepan, 1992, p. 124). The hallmark of the crisis of stateness is a situation, when the challenge to the old nondemocratic regime is also intermixed with challenges of competing nationalisms to the existing territorial state itself. Schmitter (1994, p. 65-6) concurs by observing that before actors can expect to settle into a routine of competition and cooperation, they must have some notion of who the other players are and what are expected to be the spatial boundaries of their playing field. In this respect, he conceives of boundaries and identities as one of basic extrinsic dilemmas of democratization.

Initially, most of the literature on democratization focused on transitions in Southern Europe and Latin America, where the challenge of competing nationalisms within one territorial state was on the whole not a salient issue and thus, the problem of stateness had not been given much attention. Even the competing Catalan and Basque nationalisms in Spain barely entered the theoretical literature, possibly because the legitimacy of Spanish stateness was managed with reasonable success.

The collapse of former socialist 'federations' in the USSR, Czechoslovakia, and Yugoslavia, followed by divergence of paths of the successor states have put the problem of stateness into the foreground of concerns in any study of comparative ethnopolitics of democratization. One of the major problems of post-communist transition has been the ethnic territorialization of the political. The legitimation of some sort of formally structured state is a precondition for completing democratic transition. Linz and Stepan (1992) have argued this in the case of Spain, and the former USSR and Yugoslavia confirm it *a contrario*. In each of these cases the importance of electoral sequencing in the transition from dictatorship to democracy resulted crucial.[9] Linz and Stepan (1992, p. 124-5) stress that stateness is fundamental for democracy:

> In fact, agreements about stateness are prior to agreements about democracy... In a nondemocratic system, the fact that central authority is not derived and maintained by free electoral competition means that separatist or irredentist aspirations, if they exist, are not routinely appealed to in the course of normal politics and can be suppressed. In sharp contrast, the very definition of a democracy involves agreement by the citizens of a territory, however specified, on the procedures to generate a government that can make legitimate claims on their obedience. Therefore, if a significant group of people does not accept claims on its obedience as legitimate, because the people do not want to be a part of this political unit, however constituted or reconstituted, this presents a serious problem for democratic transition and even more serious problems for democratic consolidation.

Crisis of stateness is two-fold. For a separatist ethnoterritorial unit it is the *crisis of recognition* of its diversity or even independence. For the larger territorial state it is the *crisis of integrity (unity)*. It goes without saying that these, obviously, are two sides of the same coin. Resolution of the crisis of stateness requires the establishment of a legitimate politico-territorial unit through either partition or inclusive nation-building.

Crisis (Problem Area) of State Effectiveness

The relevance of state effectiveness to ethnopolitics stems from the fact that state responses to communal grievances are crucial in shaping the course and outcomes of ethnopolitical conflicts. 'Strong states have the capacity both to suppress rebellions and to make significant concessions to protesters, weak states may be unable to do either' (Gurr, 1993, p. 91).

While the problem area of stateness concerns the legitimacy of democratizing political community, state effectiveness has to do with ethnopolitical dimension of the performance legitimacy of post-authoritarian regime and the state. The question arises whether democratic reforms can succeed in overcoming the 'softness' of the post-authoritarian state. Even in ethnically homogeneous setting elected governments must have the effective power to govern if democracy is to be sustained.

The crisis of state effectiveness relates to the problem of 'softening' of the state as the institution of effective governance. This phenomenon is a common feature in changing societies. The regime change itself undermines the viability of states as organizations. Most students of the state have emphasized the difference between strong and weak states (Badie and Birnbaum, 1979; Evans, Rueschemeyer, and Skocpol, 1985; Evans, 1992) and significantly different consequences of this variable for the consolidation of democracy (Heper, 1992). Democracy is a system of rights and responsibilities, but the conditions necessary to exercise them are not automatically generated by the mere existence of democratic institutions. A viable and effective state is necessary to make their exercise possible.

The process of elite-mobilization of the masses adds to the ungovernability and political impasse of democratizing states. The democratization process brings new social groups with widely divergent interests into the political process at a time when the state lacks the institutional capacity to integrate conflicting interests and respond to popular demands. This strain upon the system creates enormous socio-political conflict. When democratic transitions evolve in ethnically plural setting, the stresses more often than not have the outlet in the realm of nationalism and ethnic politics.

Post-communist democratization has been coupled with the introduction of market forces into nonmarket economies which naturally leads to popular pressures for state protection against the pain of economic adjustment. In this respect, recent scholarship points at the linkage between nationalism and the crisis of post-communist state effectiveness. Snyder (1993, p. 81) suggests that nationalism reflects a need to establish an effective state to achieve groups' economic and security goals:

> Today, nationalism is flaring up where old states have collapsed and where mobilized populations are consequently demanding the creation of effective new states, while new states fail to carry out those tasks. The underlying problem is that many of these new states lack the institutional capacity to fulfill popular demands, particularly in the disarray produced in their economies by the market reforms. These shortcomings redouble the intensity

of nationalistic sentiments, as ethnic militants demand the creation of effective national states to manage social problems.

To Snyder, managing post-communist nationalism, therefore, hinges on improving the effectiveness of post-authoritarian states.

Another widely observed manifestation of the 'softness' of the post-communist state has been its uneven functioning, both spatially and territorially. As the new economic and political order was established, it became evident that certain regions were doing much better than others, that their adjustment to the market was proving easier, and that their local cultures were, in consequence, gaining saliency to the detriment of the state as a whole. Other regions, however, were obviously less able to cope with the challenge of the new system. The democratic reforms are faced with the challenge to overcome the patterns of fragmentation and feudalization inherited from the past. This regional imbalance is conducive to important political results, especially if an ethnic cleavage is involved. Ethnically defined republics within post-Soviet Russian Federation make for a most vivid examples in this regard.

Cirtautas (1995) observes that already the late Leninist state in Eastern Europe, was not strong and was well on its way to becoming a classic weak state, barely able to resist societal and clientelistic pressures, and increasingly unable to determine the behavior of public and private actors. In most cases the reforms seem to have simply served to exacerbate the weakness of the inherited state structures.[10] Consequently, the post-Leninist state may not have the institutional capacity to restore law and order and to combat political corruption combined with the growing autonomy of the 'subunits'. In this respect, Cirtautas (1995, p. 386) warns about the potential for a permanent fragmentation:

> In this context, the restoration of procedural, as opposed to corrupt, administrative linkages between center and periphery will be crucial. If such linkages are not established or cannot be maintained, the fragmentation of post-Leninist polities is likely to become a permanent rather than a transitional feature of the political landscape.

Resolving the crisis of state effectiveness requires state-building as the first order of concern. Without the political order that can be provided only by effective states, the gains of democratization cannot be sustained. Ayoob (1997) convincingly discussed it in relation to post-colonial democratization.

A related broad range of problems that characterizes post-communist development concerns the relationship between the individual and the state, i.e., issues of citizenship-building. Under economic and institutional conditions that undermine the viability of state institutions post-communist democracies face multiple challenges of providing an effective citizenship. To Przeworski et al. (1995, ch. 2 passim), the result is that newly democratizing states are incapable of uniformly enforcing standardized bundles of rights and obligations that constitute citizenship.

> We thus face democratic political regimes without effective citizenship in large geographic areas or for significant sectors. And without effective citizenship, it is doubtful whether such regimes constitute "democracies" in any meaningful sense of the term.

Crisis (Problem Area) of Nationhood

The crisis of nationhood relates to the issue of the inclusiveness of a democratic political community's identity where the citizenry is composed of different ethnic groups. As a matter of fact, no democratic community can exist without some form of identity. Democratic institutions in multiethnic setting cannot gain full legitimacy in and by themselves isolated from identification with the state or a nation or the national identities, incorporated into the state. In almost all new democracies, the question arises how much pluralism is compatible with some form of integration, of loyalty to the institutions of the state, and a new sense of nationhood.

Dynamics of democratic exclusion and various ways of compensating for it or minimizing it have been analyzed by Taylor (1998, p. 143-4):

> Democracy is inclusive because it is the government of all the people; but paradoxically, this is also the reason that democracy tends toward exclusion. The exclusion is a by-product of the need, in self-governing societies, of a high degree of cohesion. Democratic states need something like a common identity... In practice, a nation can only ensure the stability of its legitimacy if its members are strongly committed to one another by means of a common allegiance to the political community. It is the shared consciousness of this commitment which creates confidence on the part of the various subgroups that they will indeed be heard...

In democratizing systems ethnic groups can trust in peaceful change only provided there is no perceived threat to their vital interests as identity communities. When individuals have a choice about identity and are able to feel secure about the future, democratization proves workable. But when individuals live in an insecure environment which precludes individuation and choice, democratization will likely precipitate ethnic conflict.

There is a near consensus among the observers that as the dynamics of postcommunism become clearer, the roles of nationhood and its value foundation (ethnic vs. civic) are emerging among central concerns to the functioning of the new political systems. This critical area with regard to Eastern Europe has been thourougly analysed by Schöpflin (1994, 1995a) who makes it clear that the weakness of civic politics accounts for the overemphasis on ethnicity that has characterized post-communist political development. The ethnic component of individuals' identities - always prominent in Eastern Europe - has become even more important during the turbulent transition period because it provides a unifying sense of communal security. The consequences of the process made the acceptance of institutions and the institutional mediation of interests - the contest for power - far more difficult to bring into equilibrium, since bargaining and negotiation over identities are virtually impossible.

> Democratic stability, involving the distribution of power and contest over the allocation of resources - normal stuff of everyday politics in liberal democracies - can only come into being in the absence of constant explicit or implicit reference to questions of identity and survival as a community. Civic nationhood has to be so rooted as to permit the institutional framework to operate in an authentic fashion...Where institutions are not available to mediate the relationship between the individual and power, the codes of behavior appropriate to persons - patron-client networks; personal coteries and loyalties; exploiting state resources for personal gain; corruption, nepotism and family networks - will be used to structure power... (Schopflin, 1995a, p. 65).

To Schöpflin, it is precisely because civic institutions are weak, that compensatory mechanisms have begun to emerge and ethnic nationhood is called upon to decide the issues of power. This pattern is likely to make institutions weaker still. [11]

The predominance of ethnonationalist discourse in Eastern Europe is particularly problematic for the future of democracy. Recent scholarship points at the legacy of incomplete or interrupted nation-building in Eastern Europe in the sense that the process of creation of a territorial (political) nation which had began in the interwar period was aborted with the advent of communist regimes (Greenfeld, 1993; Chirot, 1995). To the extent that the issue is not resolved, politicians may be tempted to privilege - the members of one ethnic group over those of any other residents of the state in exchange for votes.

Geddes (1995) observes that ethnic differences have been mobilized into political support in almost every East European country and argues that when ethnic divisions become politicized, they are likely to remain so if they become enshrined in new political institution. 'Logically, this leads new elites to define citizenship in exclusive and collective terms and thus to neglect the individual as the basic subject of constitutional law. Illiberal democracies are the likely result if any elements of polyarchy remain at all'(Crawford and Lijphart, 1995, p. 187).

The focus on national and ethnic questions inhibits the formulation of clear socio-economic programs and identities among political parties. The dividing line between 'civics' and 'ethnics' can cut across the left-right continuum, often confusing the ideological identity of specific parties. In fact, the emergence of a traditional democratic left-to-right political spectrum have been impeded by the entangling embrace of ethnonationalist and regionalist politics.

In the post-communist countries the construction of democracy inevitably means coming to terms with the resurgence of nationalism and, equally, finding the necessary instruments for integrating ethnic elements into new systems, even making special provisions for ethnic minorities.[12] In this respect, coherently promoting civil society rather than ethnic community liberal forces not only can propose a wholly new way of defining 'us' an 'them', but also suggest a different way of looking at both the past and the future.

Resolving the crisis of nationhood imperatively demands coming up with a certain integrative balance between ethnic and political (civic) identities, that is to say, building civility which can accommodate ethnic diversity. Liberal democratic community is the community of inclusive pluralism and multiple identities, it presupposes tolerance and compromise as its *sine qua non*. The adequate balance between civic and ethnic identities must be integrative and aim at the promotion of multiple identities, not at suppressing either of them. Consequentially, what is crucial in this respect is not complete replacement but striking a balance between individual and group rights. A realistic approach to this task cannot possibly ignore and oppose any form of collective right whatsoever. The classical postulate that group-based rights are *prima facie* incompatible with the individual-based tenets of liberal democracy, though true for monoethnic setting, does not hold in multiethnic milieu where the group-versus-individual rights dichotomy is neither an accurate nor a particularly useful distinction. As argued by Linz and Stepan (1996, p. 34), in a multicultural society and the state, combining collective rights for nationalities or minorities with individual rights fully protected by the state is the least-conflictual way of articulating a democratic policy.[13]

Sequences of Ethnopolitical Crises

All the above-reviewed three problem areas of stateness, state effectiveness, and nationhood coexist at any point of time in multiethnic systems that undergo democratization. Yet, it also important to stress that, if managed constructively and innovatively, these problem areas are not necessarily bound to assume critical salience or to cumulate in every single case. At some points problems of stateness, state effectiveness, and nationhood are merely aspects of decisions; at others they become problem areas, at others they turn into crises. At every stage of democratization the central problem of ethnopolitical development can manifest differentially, ranging from 'recognition of diversity' at the stage of authoritarian decay to the problem of 'stateness' under democratic transition, further on to the problem of 'state effectiveness' at the earlier phase of democratic consolidation, and, finally, to the problem of nationhood and finding avenues to ensure civic unity in ethnic diversity at the more mature phase of democratic consolidation. While resolving the crisis (problem area) of stateness is the precondition for successful democratic transition, successful dealing with the crises (problem areas) of state effectiveness and of nationhood is the irreducible requisite of consolidating democracy in multiethnic setting. In this sense one can speak of a sequential relationship between systemic ethnopolitical crises as types of problems on the agenda of different stages of the democratization process. Multiethnic democracy thus need be viewed in developmental terms, as emerging in fragments and parts.

Successful resolution of ethnopolitical crises is the basic task on the agenda of democratic ethnic peace. Efficient crisis management calls for making coherent institutional and strategic choices in ethnopolitics. In every specific case it is particularly important to understand how the menu of ethnopolitical choice is structured by the general context of the on-going change where past legacies interact with imperatives of democratic transformation.

Notes

1. See Linz (1975) for the analysis of regime types and particularly, post-totalitarian regimes. Poland is usually viewed as the only country that had always been closer to an authoritarian than to totalitarian regime. Romania occupied a specific position among post-totalitarian regimes in that it displayed strong sultanistic tendencies in the later years of the Ceausescu rule (Linz and Stepan, 1996, chs. 16, 18).
2. One of Przeworski et al.'s (1996, p.40-1) major findings was that an overthrow of democracy at any time during the past history of a country shortens the life expectancy of any democratic regime in that country. 'To the extent that political learning does occur, then, it seems that the lessons learned by antidemocratic forces from the past subversion of democracy are more effective than the traditions that can be relied on by democrats'.
3. Smolar (1996, p. 25) observes that a civil society whose essence was radical opposition to the communist state could not possibly survive the disappearance of that state.
4. The ambivalent character of post-communist modernity and its linkage to political activism is discussed by Eisenstadt (1992, p. 32-3). Schöpflin (1995a, p. 54-5) discusses the impact of the one-sided modernization in Eastern Europe upon areas directly affecting nationalism in the area.
5. The critique of such stances have found expression and thorough elaboration in Schmitter and Karl (1994), King (1994a) and Karl and Schmitter (1995): 'The field of post-communist studies - and especially its subfield of Sovietology - has long suffered a partially self-imposed isolation from the major social science disciplines. Many Sovietologists and Kremlinologists explicitly argued that communist systems were so distinctive as to preclude comparison... on assumptions about the allegedly unique legacy of 'totalitarianism', 'marxism-leninism-stalinism', 'Soviet political culture', etc... Just because area studies were born in the contested notion that specific geocultural regions were somehow 'unique' does not mean this comfortable assumption should remain forever unexamined...'(Karl and Schmitter, 1995, pp. 966, 968, 971). For the overview of the history of the discipline of Soviet studies on this issue, see e.g. Fleron and Hoffman (1993).
6. King (1994a, p. 297) observes in this regard 'Although the integration of post-Sovietology and the social sciences is to be welcomed, it will thus be a long time before the study of the Soviet successor states, at least from a practical perspective, can be treated as anything even resembling the study of Southern Europe or Latin America.'
7. The labels for the two approaches have been proposed by Ellen Comisso (1995). In surveying this debate I draw on and adapt from Crawford and Lijphart (1995) for whose thoughtful article the reader is referred for more details and insightful understanding.

8   As observed by Crawford and Lijphart (1995, p. 179), 'actually, each perspective emphasizes opposite forces shaping the calculations and choices of the central actors in the post-Communist environment. The legacies approaches emphasize the importance of political culture, social structure and institutions created under communism in those calculations and choices; the liberal imperatives approach emphasizes the dominance of liberal capitalist democracy as the institutional structure that shapes choice.'
9   The first democratic elections in Spain encompassed the entire country, even if this meant that the new constitution would have to include substantial transfers of power to Catalonia and the Basque regions. It has been cogently argued that, likewise, at the beginning of 1990 in Yugoslavia, the inability of Markovic's federal government to hold free elections over the whole of the territory marked the end of the Yugoslav federation. The federal state was delegitimized as soon as the first free elections took place in Slovenia and Croatia. Power and legitimacy shifted from the federation to the republics, which soon opted for independence to complete their own democratic transitions. The end of communism thus became entangled with the end of Yugoslavia. A roughly similar sequence broke up the USSR where nationalism did create pressures which challenged the legitimacy of the Soviet federation, which the Soviet federal state was unable to renew. See Linz and Stepan (1992, pp. 129-139), also Tedin (1994), McDonough, Barnes and López Pina (1994), Emizet and Hesli (1995), Moreno (1995).
10 See Jowitt (1992) for an analysis of post-Leninist fragmentation in its social, political and economic forms and with the evidence that states in Eastern European region are undergoing a potentially more permanent process of fragmentation.
11 In this respect, Schöpflin (1995a, p. 63) points out at two developments that seriously obstruct democracy-building in post-communist countries: 'One regards the increasing tendency of governments to rely on ethnic nationhood as a means of legitimating their power. This signified that although they had achieved power through popular election, the nexus between the rulers and the ruled was regarded as too weak to carry them through the harsh problems of creating markets and facing the criticism that accompanies competitive politics. Unfortunately, making governments ethnic tended to make the states ethnic, which promoted collectivist, anti-individualist values; it made it that much more difficult to establish genuinely legitimate institutions. The second is the threat of neo-ideologization when the rules that are supposedly derived form the civic dimension being actually based on ethnic criteria. Consequentially, the offices of state will largely be filled on grounds of ethnic loyalty, presumed or real, rather than competence, while members of minorities will find themselves suspect.'
12 Braumoeller (1997, p. 375) observes in this regard that the claim that liberalism is associated with non-violent means of conflict resolution, in particular, is questionable in the case of most newly independent states of Eastern Europe, in which liberalism bears a closer resemblance to 19th-century European liberal nationalism than it does to the universalist (civic) liberalism envisioned by theories of the democratic peace. As long as this nonuniversalist form of liberalism is in fact widespread in multiethnic post-communist states, liberalism's implications for peace may not be strongly benign.
13 For interesting arguments that some notion of group rights is, in fact, necessary to the very definition of some types of individual rights and necessary to the advancement of universal norms in rights, see Raz (1986, pp. 165-217), Kymlicka (1995, pp. 107-30).

6 From Soviet to Post-Soviet Ethnopolitics: Change and Menu of Choice

The demise of the Soviet Union in 1991 was a hallmark of profound change. At the global level this change marked not only the fall of the world communism and end to bipolarity but also by the creation of a multiplicity of new states. At the regional level of post-Soviet Eurasia one of most important facets of this change concerns the growing importance of the politics of identity that followed the disintegration of the last modern empire. This chapter intends to survey major changes in issues and patterns of ethnopolitical conflict which took place in post-Soviet successor states and to assess larger contextual factors that influence ethnic peace in the area. It concludes by discussing the menu of ethnopolitical choice that democratizing countries are faced with in the realms of institutions and interactions.

Ethnopolitical Change of Scene in Post-Soviet Setting

Post-Soviet ethnopolitics displays both structural continuity and new patterns that have become manifest after the Soviet collapse.

The continuity follows from tough legacies. While precise estimates vary, there were more than a hundred nations in the Soviet Union, most of which laid claim to Soviet territory as their homeland. All of these nations were incorporated into a single state, creating what was - considering the geographic, cultural, economic, and religious implications - a state of virtually unprecedented diversity. The former Soviet Union was a severely divided multiethnic state with a highly articulated system of ethnopolitical stratification. Unlike most other states, it was consciously created in order to accommodate the political aspirations of a large number of constituent nationalities by means of institutionalizing ethnoterritorial divisions.

It is crucial to bear in mind the critical role of the articulated ethnohierarchical structure of the USSR 'federation', the 'matrioshka' - type federalism as the structural setting of ethnopolitical conflict. Many of these conflicts came from the peculiar existence of nations within nations. Victor Zaslavsky (1992, p.99) calls it institutionalization of ethnicity.

> One of fundamental innovations of federal state formation under Soviet rule was the Stalinist linkage of ethnicity, territory, and political administration. Ethnicity was institutionalized on the group level by the creation of a federation of ethnoterritorial units, governed by indigenous political elites and organized into an elaborate administrative hierarchy. Ethnicity was also institutionalized on the individual level through the introduction of a comprehensive passport system which immutably fixed the ethnic affiliation of every Soviet citizen.

The specific institutions of the Soviet Union 'federation' created incentives and resource mobilization for the politicization of ethnicity with the onset of the *perestroika* liberalization under Gorbachev. The Soviet ethnopolitics for decades had been structured by the federalism of nominally autonomous ethnic homelands. The degree of economic, cultural, political and other rights as well as the opportunities to satisfy the interests of many peoples depended on the status that was ascribed to an ethnicity within the rigid structures of the USSR federation.

Only fifty-three of the over one hundred Soviet nationalities were officially identified with a particular territory and so afforded rights by virtue of their ethno-territorial status. They were the so-called *'titular'* nationalities. The *titular nationality* status implies a nation which, for any number of economic, demographic, cultural, or political reasons, was vested with administrative power in a given region. In Russian SFSR it was the Russians, in Moldovan SSR the Moldovans, in Abkhazian ASSR within Georgia Abkhazians, like in Tuvinian ASSR within RSFSR the Tuvinians, and so on. The titular nationality had a special relationship with the state, being in a position of privilege *vis-á-vis* those nations not so empowered - the *non-titular nationalities*. Some 60 million people (20 percent of the total population) in the former Soviet Union lived outside of their home ethnoterritorial units or were members of groups without such home units.

Moreover, the status of even the titular nationalities varied widely. Fifteen nations were designated the highest status of Soviet Socialist Republics (SSRs) or 'Union republics', which together encompassed the USSR. Directly accountable to and within the territories of the Union republics, in order of descending status, were 20 Autonomous Soviet Socialist Republics (ASSRs), 8 Autonomous regions (*oblasti*), and 10 Autonomous districts (*okruga*). The rights of these sub-units included areas of dependence, guaranteed institutions and spheres of autonomy. 'Significantly, obligations of obedience under Soviet rule were the same for all national groups while only the fifteen union republics were given the right to secede' (Bremer and Taras, 1993, p. 5).

Despite great cultural diversity, there was an important structural similarity between all Union republics in regard to their place in ethnopolitical structures of the Soviet federation. Each Union republic (SSR) had its own flag, national legislature (Supreme Soviet) and government. One of the houses in the Union's Supreme Soviet in Moscow, the *Soviet of Nationalities*, was made up of representatives of the republics. Under the constitution, the Union government dominated some fields of policy, notably foreign affairs and defense while certain other competencies were largely reserved to the republics. Although the names, number and boundaries of the republics changed slightly over time, the basic federal constitutional structure survived intact for seven decades.

Like almost any 'Soviet-made' political product, from the very start, much of this 'federalism' was a fraud. The Union was not voluntary and claiming the right of secession until perestroika had been beyond any imagination. The role of the terroristic central state with its powerful coercive apparatus in destroying both real and imaginary ethnic opposition has been well documented (e.g. Medvedev, 1989; Conquest, 1990). The division of rights between the center and the republics was couched in vague legal terms whose meaning was determined by the central authorities. The 'federalist' form actually served as a means of accommodating major nationalities within a unified multiethnic state, with Union republics serving as units of central planning and instruments of personnel and cadre policy. This extreme centralization almost nullified any real federalist contents. In its relations to any Union republic, the Union center represented not only the decision-maker, but also both the producer and the distributor.

Inspired by an ideology which did not make any distinction between state and society or any allowance for the separation of powers, the Soviet regime assumed that all nations would accept the Communist Party of the Soviet Union (CPSU) as the ruling party and that its leadership alone would make political decisions. Throughout the existence of the Soviet Union, the CPSU was the supreme political force. The Soviets, in theory elected by the local population, were in fact rubber-stamp bodies whose members were nominated by the Communist Party officials. Although the state apparatuses were federated, the Communist party was not a federated structure. 'Democratic centralism' meant that all decisions of the CPSU leadership would be binding on lower bodies regardless of their national composition.

The republican communist parties were subordinate to the CPSU Central Committee, while their control over all republican and local institutions signified the undermining of the already curtailed authority of republican governments. Within each Union republic the regime created a cadre of party and state officials drawn from the indigenous ethnic group but dependent on Moscow for its members' positions. As this cadre was assigned a monopoly over the mobilizational resources within the ethnic community, it determined when ethnic group would be mobilized to action. It was a strategy that achieved interethnic peace not so much by removing the root causes of ethnic grievances as by eliminating mobilizational opportunities for independent ethnic protest.

The intermixed policies of both cultural accommodation and cultural destruction by the Soviet leaders created a paradox within the system that prevented the emergence of a new Soviet identity (*Sovetsky Narod*) and led to the perception by citizens that they were coerced into accepting the authority of the communist state. Despite attempts to 'create a genuine legitimacy', the Soviet quasi-empire-state 'never managed to free itself from confusion over identities' (Beissinger, 1995, p. 152).

As a matter of fact, many non-Russians, particularly, those belonging to titular nationalities of allegedly 'equal among equals' and even 'sister' republics perceived the government in Moscow as a stranger, robbing them of their identity. It appears quite reasonable that most ethnic non-Russians were not overwhelmingly happy with the way the words like '*indissoluble* union', '*free* republics', 'rallied *forever*' and '*the Great* Russia' sounded in the anthem of a country, ostensibly representing the 'free Union' of 'the equal among the equal'. Unlike the Byzantine patriarch, Russia was not only wordly, but also more than effectively 'the first among equal' *sister-republics*. Justly or less than always so the non-Russians had many reasons to see Russian interests and identity as being projected onto other ethnic groups with communism serving as an instrument of Russian dominance.[1]

Few of those subsided after the Soviet disintegration. The very structure of the Soviet federal system was conducive to the emergence of tensions at all levels of the ethnopolitical hierarchy. In the last years of the Soviet existence previously suppressed ethnopolitical issues reemerged within almost all Union republics. The disintegration of the USSR into independent republics, though it has removed one level of conflict (between the Union center and Union republics), has not essentially affected other levels of interethnic conflicts.

As a consequence, the hierarchy of conflicts reflecting the hierarchy of ethnoterritorial statuses has largely persisted. Bremmer and Taras (1993) analyzed patterns of ethnic interactions and conflict between the Union Center, first-order titular nationalities, second order titular nationalities, and non-titular nationalities in terms and types of cooperation, integration, assimilation, competition, domination, liberation, and collusion. This general framework, used in describing national relations within a Soviet Union in transition also applies to the Soviet successor states as long as power structures among national groups remain hierarchical.

After the removal of the Soviet political and economic structures, a redistribution of power arrangements within the former Union republics and formation of new political and economic systems (by no means the same in different republics) came to the fore in all successor states. Titular nationalities of ethnoterritorial divisions within newly-born or restored states displayed significant degrees of ethnic separatism. Sensing opportunity after the Soviet collapse, many of them came out with separatist claims, like the Chechens and Tatars in Russia, the Poles in Lithuania, the Abkhazians in Georgia, the Gagauz in Moldova. In republics where open ethnic conflict had already been escalating the post-Soviet tensions intensified even more with the end of Soviet power (South-Ossetia-Georgia, Nagorny Karabakh, Moldova-Transdniestria) escalating to warfare.

A second widely observed feature of post-Soviet ethnopolitics was the evident re-emergence of a dominant center seeking regional hegemony in Central Eurasia. Bremmer (1997, p. 20-1) put is quite succinctly:

> Never having forgotten its imperial roots, the Russian government quickly began to see its own state interests as contiguous with those of the former Soviet landmass. This was evidenced concretely by Russian efforts to coordinate military defense zones throughout the former Soviet Union, control key economic infrastructure (in particular, energy import and export), and push through policies of dual citizenship... Also not to be ignored is the widespread currency among Russian policymakers of the term 'Near Abroad', referring to the non-Russian states of the former Soviet Union. This has shown clearly the extent to which Russia believes that

there remains a special entity which can be accurately conceived through traditional interpretations of international relations.

Contextual Factors of Post-Soviet Ethnic Peace

In the specific milieu of post-Soviet ethnopolitics the relationship of peace is shaped by two sets of immediate contextual factors. On the one hand, post-Soviet ethnopolitics is imbued with *past legacies*. On the other hand, new issues of ethnopolitical contention have arisen under *imperatives of a manifold socio-political transformations* that vary in different successor states who took divergent trajectories in the course of market reforms and processes of state-, nation- and - in some cases - democracy-building.

Past Legacies

Past legacies act as important constraints upon patterns of post-Soviet ethnic conflict management. They include a broadly conceived legacy of the empire, a legacy of metaconflict, and the issue of new Russian diaspora.

Legacy of the empire The Soviet Union was often conceptualized as an empire, and its breakup was sometimes seen as falling into the category of decolonization. [2] In this respect, post-Soviet states share the legacy of empire with their counterparts elsewhere in the world. (Katz, 1993, idem, 1997).

On the one hand, the structural continuity of several features of former Soviet ethnopolitics (particularly, the linkage between ethnicity and territoriality and the division into titular vs. non-titular nationalities) has endured after the Soviet disintegration. In numerical terms the minority problems in some of them are just as big as in the former Soviet Union, or bigger. None of the successor states is anything near empirically homogeneous. In many of the new states rich ethnic diversity has existed for centuries. Some of this diversity is due to the creation of or changes in territorial boundaries during the Soviet years, and especially to labor migrations. The closest approximation to a monoethnic nation-state might is Armenia where 93,3% of the population are ethnic Armenians. Russia, the biggest among the successor states, has 21 ethnically defined sub-units (republics), which is more than the Soviet Union had. There are also ten autonomous districts, some of which are territorially considerably larger than most European states. The same legacy is also found in patterns of mutual perceptions between Russia and non-Russian successor states.

The legacy of metaconflict This is another important constraint in post-Soviet ethnopolitics. The term 'metaconflict' has been originally proposed by Horowitz (1991, p.27) with reference to the presence of two kinds of conflicts in societies with long history of unresolved ethnic tensions: 'There is the conflict itself, and there is also the metaconflict-the conflict over the nature of the conflict. Neither is coterminous with the other; neither can be reduced to the other'. In many divided societies, and former USSR is not exception, there are differences among participants and observers in characterizations of the conflict and even a special language code has been used for speaking about such 'hot topics' as ethnopolitical disputes.

As a matter of fact, many believe that talking about ethnicity creates or reinforces ethnic divisions, even when the talk is directed at how to prevent such divisions from overwhelming a future democratic state. In post-Soviet setting, the struggle over interpretative paradigms is, indeed, part of the wider struggle for differential power and security guarantees between ethnic groups. With regard to the management of system-level ethnopolitical problem-areas or crises, the metaconflict is likely to function as a constraint on imagination and creativity that are vital for designing an efficient institutional innovation. This suggests that managing crises under post-communist democratization, if to be successful, should necessarily include the stage of pre-negotiation (talks about talks) when primarily metaconflict and not conflict itself needs be addressed and resolved, before actually passing to negotiating issues of interethnic contention. Many failures in ethnopolitical conflict management in successor states can be attributed to a premature eclipse of the pre-negotiation stage or actual lack of such.

The issue of Russian diaspora in successor states According to the 1989 census data, 25.3 million ethnic Russians resided in parts of the Soviet Union outside Russia. In almost all of these states, the Russians make up the largest minority group, and in several cases they account for more than 70% of the non-titular population (see Table 6.1).

Much has been written of late (and quite rightly too) about the destabilizing role of Russian minorities within the former USSR successor states in the future (e.g. Jackson, 1994; Klatt, 1994; Porter and Saivetz, 1994; Payin, 1994; Barrington, 1995; Brubaker, 1992 and 1995; Kolstoe,

1993 and 1995; Dmitriev, 1996). Both the scope and urgency of the problem of Russian minorities in the former Union republics are great if one takes into consideration the size of that group, the imperial type of the Soviet state, and its citizens' sense of justice as distorted by decades of totalitarian rule.

Russians occupied a distinct position in the Soviet Union. They formed a majority of the population, and they controlled the central state apparatus in Moscow. To the extent that the Soviet state had an ethnic and cultural identity, it was Russian (Dunlop, 1997). As a result, Russians by and large had began to identify their interests and aspirations not with Russia but with the Soviet Union as a whole.[3]

Table 6.1   Ethnicity in post-Soviet successor states
(in percentage of the total population)

	Titular (majority) Group		*Largest Minority Group*		*Next-Large Minority Group*	
Russia	81.5	Tatars	3.7	Ukrainians	2.9
Estonia	61.5	Russians	30.3	Ukrainians	3.0
Latvia	51.8	Russians	34.0	Belarusians	4.5
Lithuania	79.5	Russians	9.4	Poles	7.0
Belarus	77.8	Russians	13.2	Poles	4.0
Moldova	64.4	Ukrainians	13.8	Russians	13.0
Ukraine	72.7	Russians	22.1	Jews	0.9
Georgia	70.0	Armenians	7.9	Russians	6.3
Armenia	93.3	Azeris	2.5	Kurds	1.7
Azerbaijan	82.6	Russians	5.6	Armenians	5.5
Turkmenistan	71.8	Russians	9.5	Uzbeks	8.8
Tajikistan	62.2	Uzbeks	23.3	Russians	7.6
Uzbekistan	71.2	Russians	8.3	Tajiks	4.6
Kyrgyzstan	52.2	Russians	21.5	Uzbeks	2.9
Kazakhstan	39.6	Russians	37.8	Germans	5.7

Source: 1989 USSR Census Data

Already in 1990-91, the 'Middle Empire' of the 14 union republics around the periphery of the USSR became the conflict zone between resident authority and oppositional nationalism. After the Soviet collapse

Russian minorities had faced a reverse identity crisis which continued to agitate them particularly in regions where they are concentrated on specific territories, such as in northeast Estonia, Crimea within Ukraine, northern Kazakhstan, and Transdniesteria in Moldova. The loss of the empire deprived Russians of the advantages and status affiliated with their role as the leading element. The Russians in many successor states seem to have found the material and psychological forced conversion from dominant local representatives of the central authority, a so-called 'imperial minority' (Payin, 1994) to unwanted, ethnically alien and often presumably disloyal subjects of newly independent, nationally exuberant states extremely difficult to stomach.

The problem of citizenship of ethnic Russians in the 'near abroad' has gained much international attention. While the question has been a central issue in the discussion of the situation in the Baltic States, particularly, Latvia and Estonia, it is also relevant to the other successor states of the USSR.[4] Russians outside Russia are in a doubly complicated position. In forming their national identities, the new states have had to consider the question of who should be considered alien. In the newly independent countries in which they have found themselves, Russians are often seen as the representatives of an imperial system, the effects of which are best erased. In Russia, their fate is both a rousing issue in domestic politics and a useful justification for projecting influence into strategically key areas of the former Soviet Union.[5] In a sense, the Russian diaspora has been taken hostage by the nonexistent Soviet imperial state (Dmitriev, 1996, p. 18-21).

Imperatives of the Transformation Processes

While past legacies act as ethnopolitical constraints, imperatives of democratic transformation act as incentives. These new imperatives have been generated by processes of state-building, nation-building and (in some post-Soviet cases) democracy-building.

State-building Fifteen new states appeared in Central Eurasia with the demise of the USSR. Yet 'states' in the true sense do not spring full-grown from declarations of independence or extensions of international recognitions. A truly sovereign state must guarantee territorial integrity and physical security. It must mobilize public savings, coordinate resource allocation and correct income distribution. An administrative apparatus equal to these tasks is needed, as well as a broad social consensus on the rules and routines to be used. In the process of state-building the policies of constructing bureaucracies and forging new elite cadres (with respective salience of intergroup competition for prestigious positions) have important ethnic consequences, as do the actions to promote newly-defined national interests (such as territorial integrity, social unity, and national security).

Nation-building When political independence had been achieved, the authorities in post-Soviet states embarked on a policy of nation-building - a perfectly common process in all modern states. All the successor states, save Russia proclaimed themselves 'national states' or 'nation-states'. In the current post-Soviet context, the interplay between the ethnic and civic projects of nation-building is extremely complex. In fact, the ethnically conceived nationalism remains central to politics in and among the new nation-states. Far from 'solving' the region's national question, the post-Soviet reconfiguration of Eurasian space has only reframed it, recast it in a new form. Rogers Brubaker (1995; idem, 1996) discussed this new phase and form of the national question, focusing on the triadic relational nexus linking national minorities, nationalizing states, and external national homelands. Though he takes former Yugoslavia as a case in point, this analytical perspective is also valid for considering the post-Soviet Eurasia. Three points warrant mentioning in this respect.

First, like in Eastern Europe, political authority in post-Soviet successor states has been reconfigured along ostensibly national lines. Almost everywhere the titular nationality has placed itself implicitly or explicitly at the center of the nation-building project awarding certain prerogatives to its language as well as some privileges for its culture in state symbols and in state-controlled means of socialization, such as state-run media and school textbooks). In many non-Russian successor states the strivings for maximal correspondence between *ethnos* and polity make the incumbent elites see the existence of national minorities as a problem to be solved or at least marginalized - culturally, politically and demographically. This desire is reinforced by the suspicion that the minorities, especially the Russian diaspora, may be susceptible to revisionist propaganda emanating from certain circles in Moscow, and may thus represent a threat to the very existence of the state.

Second, recent scholarship correctly points out at another important complication facing many post-Soviet states, namely, the unconsolidated condition of the titular nationality itself:

Many of the 'nations' of Central Asia, for instance, are inventions of modern ethnographers or commissars eager to counteract the possible influence of pan-Turkism or the Muslim ummah (community). One's identity as, say a Kazakh or a Kyrgyz may pale beside the intensity of one's ties to a certain tribe, clan, or region. Even in a more 'Western' land like Ukraine, ethnic consolidation is incomplete. There are strong cultural (including religious) differences between Galicia in the west and Donbass in the east, for instance. Ethnic consolidation and political nation-building may thus proceed in tension with each other, a tension that some may be tempted to resolve by collapsing both into a unified venture in ethnic nation-building (Kolstoe, 1996, p.121).

Third, almost all observers agree that it would at the same time be an overstatement to claim that the new states of Eurasia that emerged after the Soviet disintegration are based exclusively upon the ethnic principle. According to their constitutions, at least, most have claimed to represent all the peoples on their territories, not just the titular group. Many of them are in fact oriented towards the Western world in their search for new values, and are anxious to live up to the generally accepted standards set for a democracy and for a law-governed state. Their new state structures display 'civic' as well as 'ethnic' elements. 'In country after country, these rival conceptions of nationhood can be found dwelling in uneasy cohabitation' (Kolstoe, 1996, p.120).

Democracy-building It is not only cultural factors that increasingly come to account for the differences in trajectories taken by different post-Soviet countries. Differential experience with democracy is a variable not to be underestimated. Not all post-Soviet countries have undergone a real democratic transition, even less of them have started to consolidate democracy. For instance, it is difficult to speak in any meaningful sense about *completed* democratic transition with regard to most former union republics in Central Asia or Transcaucasus, with the exception of Kyrgyzstan and Armenia, respectively. Belarusan semi-democracy with the Lukashenka's 'auto-golpe' has already suffered democratic breakdown. Those successor states, who did step on the way of democratic consolidation, have proceeded along it at different pace and with differential and uneven success.

In general, the changes which post-Soviet successor states are undergoing in the wake of communism do not fit neatly into the 'classical' model of democratic transition, but rather are multilayered, complex, and even contradictory. Trends and countertrends jostle, intertwine, and collide as post-Soviet space undergoes a fitful evolution away from the Soviet past.

New international imperatives that influence ethnic conflict include at least three aspects: 1) new role of Russia in post-Soviet space; 2) the change in geopolitical balance after the Soviet collapse and increased potential for both conflict mediation and intervention into domestic ethnic conflict because of solidarity with ethnic or religious kin by the bordering countries besides Russia, e.g. Roumania, Turkey, Iran, etc.; 3) the new role of international organizations in monitoring or mediating ethnic conflict, as manifested for instance, in the activities of CSCE (now OSCE) in the Baltics, Moldova, and Caucasus, UN mandated peace-keeping forces in Tajikistan, etc.

Overall, post-Soviet setting in the early 1990s, along with displaying significant continuity with the issues and patterns from the previous period, has undergone a markedly rapid and profound ethnic and political change. The change is on-going and though becomes slower, it does not stop to be less profound. Recent scholarship has rightfully stressed that besides the importance of legacies, the *choices* made during and shortly after the democratic transition can significantly increase or decrease the possibilities for democratic consolidation (Linz and Stepan 1996, p. 414). In assessing the state and prospects of democratizing ethnic peace, a focus on ethnopolitical menu of choice commands particular attention.

Menu of Ethnopolitical Choice at Critical Junctions: Institutions and Interactions

Two areas of choice emerge as critical in democratizing systems. The first is the instituional field. In the longer-term, institutions matter most. By their very nature, institutions cannot be perfectly neutral: rather, they define available political options, wholly excluding some otherwise-feasible alternatives from the array of choices presented to the public, making others less likely to be chosen, and positively favoring still others.[5] The second is the realm of 'strategic' interactions. Post-transitions are often a time of great uncertainty for all political actors. The various 'strategic' behaviors that they choose in the face of an unknown future bear on conflict dynamics.

Political choice and decision-making lie at the core of crisis management. Basically, managing crises means making choices at critical junctures of unfolding political dynamics. Not for nothing does the word *crisis* derive from the Greek κρινω, meaning 'sorting out, choosing, deciding'. As already discussed in Chapter 2, the two areas of choice in democratizing ethnopolitics relate to the two kinds of ethnopolitical crises - systemic and interactional. Crisis management endeavours are structured into patterns which can be distinguished on the basis of the certain priorities which underlie and order the sequences of choices as well as their outcomes. The chosen pattern of crisis management significantly affects the state and quality of the peace relationship in democratizing systems.

Systemic ethnopolitical crises (stateness, state effectiveness, nationhood) can be conceived of as respective areas where institutional choice is warranted. Crisis management at the system level requires craftful institutional choice with the aim to enhance new, democratic legitimacy. The menu of choice ranges from institutions of hegemonic control to power-sharing arrangements in either consociational or integrative options.

A pattern of crisis management at the system level is formed by sequences of steps leading to the formulation, negotiation, agreement and introduction of the institutional innovation as regards the establishment of a specific type of power-sharing and safeguards of the minority rights.

Constructive management of systemic crises proceeds along the path of integrative bargaining. They rely on negotiations over new institutions and represent sequences of steps leading to the formulation of and agreement on an institutional innovation through adopting one or another form of power-sharing and introducing effective safeguards of minority rights. Negotiated inter-elite agreements on new institutions (pacts) come as the products of such constructive crisis management endeavours.

The central challenge in the institutional field becomes elaboration and/or acceptance of new rules of the ethnopolitical game. The major issue is how new rules of ethnopolitics relate to the rules of democratic political game, to what extent they form complementary and not conflicting logic. This issue can be resolved only through innovative change. If the institutional innovation is appropriate, ethnopolitical crisis results downgraded to the level of a problem area and becomes amenable to management within the newly create or re-adjusted institutional framework. Successful handling of systemic problem areas prevents them from assuming critical salience and, thus, can also be conceived of as system-level crisis prevention.

Conversely, lack of agreements on new institutions is a concomitant of destructive pattern of systemic crisis management. Besides inconclusive negotiations, destructive patterns of systemic crisis management involve inaction (ignoring the problem area until it becomes a crisis and threatens political stability) or deception (imitation of attempts to realize a reform in ethnopolitical arrangements without actually intending to do so). Unresolved or mismanaged problem areas (crises) tend to be reproduced over time. Complications produced by unfavorable legacies of the past and wrong choices at the onset of democratization are likely to result in the simultaneity of crises occurrence and their superimposition. Inefficient or failed crisis management at the system level (i.e., inadequate institutional choice or failure to reach an agreement on the matters of institutional choice) exacerbates ethnic tensions and, effectively, poses a serious threat to the relationship of peace between ethnic groups. When either ethnic dominants or ethnic subordinates do not accept the way things are done in relation to a problematic aspect of decision-making, it becomes an issue or an arena of an intense conflict interaction and thus entails an interactional ethnopolitical crisis. Ultimately, this can lead to either democratic breakdown or persistence of democratic unconsolidation.

Interactional ethnopolitical crises relate to important changes in groups' strategic interactions - a set of strategic moves and countermoves between the state, ethnic dominants and ethnic subordinates which is aimed at ethnically-relevant proaction, inaction or reaction as regards the direction of on-going socio-political change. Crisis management at the interactional level requires policy choices to address the focal issue under interethnic contention.   Different actors become engaged in strategic interaction: agents of the central government, agents of subnational (local) government, political elites of both ethnic dominants and ethnic subordinates (e.g., leaders of organized ethnic movements), ethnic consituencies and third parties. Specific configurations of their strategic interactions form the pattern of crisis behavior. Configurations of political, legislative and ideological choices made by ethnic elites and accepted by their ethnic constituencies form the pattern of interactional crisis management. Acceptance of one or another decision by their ethnic constituencies settles or resolves a crisis.

Constructive management of interactional crises promotes non-violent policy change. In fact, constructive patterns themselves make important precedents of new behaviors coined in accordance with the incipient new rules of ethnopolitical game. Such endeavors include peaceful proaction and third-party activities. Peaceful proaction can result from a government's initiative (reform from above) or come as a product of negotiations at which both the government and ethnic leadership take part. Problem-solving negotiations (conceived as efforts to locate a mutually acceptable solution to the controversy) are likely to be the most effective and viable avenue for crisis management. Problem solving also encourages the discovery of compromises and integrative options that serve both parties and are more likely to create a win-win situation, not all-or-nothing contests. Other important strategies within the constructive pattern of crisis management at the interactional level include instances of arbitration, adjudication and third-party mediation or intervention.

Conversely, destructive patterns of interactional crisis management rely on various forms of coercive reactions, ranging from power-based contentious bargaining and non-violent intimidation to threats of violence and its actual application. Though they can impose a settlement, destructive patterns do not solve the underlying crisis problem which is bound to be reproduced with every next round of ethnopolitical mobilization.

A comparison of patterns of ethnopolitical crisis management and of crisis outcomes in different cases can help get a better understanding of the complexity of tasks and available avenues on the road to consolidating ethnic peace in new democracies. The subsequent part III presents a comparative survey of the dynamics of ethnopolitical conflict and crisis management in a sample of four post-Soviet cases putting the focus of discussion on 1) identifying systemic ethnopolitical problem areas (crises) as well as critical periods in ethnic interaction that manifested at different stages of post-Soviet democratization, and 2) assessing the linkages between patterns of crisis management and the resulting quality and potential for the endurance of ethnic peace in each case.

Notes

1   Schöpflin (1995b, p. 89) observed in this regard: 'Although after Stalin's death, the superior status of the 'Elder Brother' was no longer as explicit as it was before, Khrushchev's project for the long-term merger of all cultures was understood as a form of Russification by non-Russians and probably gave a certain satisfaction to Russians, who felt that at the end of the day the state was theirs, however much they

have resented some or many of the ways in which it impacted on them. In this sense, communism and the Soviet state did help to sustain a Russian identity and conversely the Russian identity helped to underpin the Soviet Union. For the non-Russians, on the other hand, the Soviet State was alien, its power over them was resented and when the communist ideology that sustained it collapsed, they opted out.'

2 On the application of the term *empire* to the former Soviet Union see Emizet and Hesli (1995, p. 494-505), also Beissinger (1995), Suny (1995).

3 Payin (1994, p. 22) reports in this regard: 'A poll conducted in Georgia, Moldova, Uzbekistan, and Estonia by the IAE RAS in the early 1980s shows that, regardless of their place of residence, Russians in most cases (70 % or more) named the Soviet Union as their homeland while most members of the titular nations referred to their republics as their homelands. In December 1990 the All-Russian Center for the Study of Public Opinion carried out a survey in 18 cities of 10 republics and found that, despite the proclaimed sovereignty of many republics, the majority of Russians (70-80 %) continued to consider themselves first and foremost to be citizens of the USSR, which means that they perceived their state (all-Union) consciousness.'

4 In June 1992 the Defense Minister, Pavel Grachev, declared that the army would defend the 'honor and dignity of the Russian population' in any region.(Izvestiya 5 Jun. 1992, p. 1). Two important points were noted here by observers: first, that it is the army which will defend, and second, that it will defend ethnic Russians rather than the citizens of Russia (Müllerson, 1994, p. 113).

5 Regarding the 'return' to institutions in political science, see, e.g. Linz (1990), Colomer (1995) and Remmer (1997).

PART III:
MANAGING PROBLEM AREAS (CRISES) IN DEMOCRATIZING ETHNOPOLITICS: FOUR POST-SOVIET CASES

PART III
MASKING PROBLEM AREAS (CRISIS) IN DEMOCRATIZING ETHNOPOLITICS: FOUR POST-SOVIET CASES

7 Estonia

Historical and Demographic Background

Estonia belongs to the group of Baltic states (together with Latvia and Lithuania) which have always occupied a very specific position among former Soviet Union republics and post-Soviet successor states. On the one hand, in the 1920-30s, the Baltic states were not part of the USSR and, unlike the other Union republics, had a recent history of independent statehood.[1] The collective memory of the interwar republics survived the years of oppression. In this respect, the Baltic republics resembled the Eastern European countries, where the interwar period of national states had remained an important focus of identification for individual dissenters and oppositional movements during the Soviet period (Clemens, 1997; Muiznieks, 1995; Gerner and Hedlund, 1993). On the other hand, the three states had been subjected to political control and repression to the same extent as other Union republics (Norgaard, 1996, pp.12-3).

The entire dynamics of ethnic relations in Estonia was shaped by rapid and dramatic changes in the ethnodemographic patterns. Before the Soviet occupation, according to the census of 1934, Estonians comprised 88%, Russians made 8% and other nationalities accounted for some 4% of the country's population (Vetik, 1993, p. 273). Russians lived mainly in the border regions of Peipsi and Petseri. When in 1945 the Soviet authorities in Moscow changed the border, Estonia lost to Russia regions inhabited by native Russians. This left Estonia a very homogeneous country where Estonian-speakers formed 97.3% of the population (Raun, 1997a, p. 406; Vetik, 1993, p. 273). The 1940s became years of demographic catastrophe for Estonia. The country lost about 20% of its pre-1940 population as a consequence of war, emigration and post-war massive deportations that accompanied sovietization.[2] The industrialization of 1960-70s, planned by Soviet Union authorities in Moscow, attracted influx of Slav migrants. By the end of the 1980s the share of Estonian

Population dropped down to 61.5% with Russians accounting for 30.1%. All these dramatic demographic changes have been due to both migrations and to the differences in fertility. Estonian birth-rates remained lower than non-Estonian rates throughout the Soviet years. Since 1991 the death-rate for Estonians has exceeded the birth-rate.[3]

Table 7.1   Dynamics of Estonia's Ethnic Composition

	1934 1000s	%	1959 1000s	%	1970 1000s	%
Estonians	993.5	88.2	892.6	74.6	925.1	68.2
Russians	92.7	8.2	240.2	20.1	334.6	24.6
Ukrainians	-	-	15.8	1.3	28.1	2.1
Belarusans	-	-	10.9	0.9	18.7	1.4
Finns	1.1	0.1	16.7	1.4	18.5	1.4
Jews	4.4	0.4	5.4	0.4	5.3	0.4
Germans	16.3	1.5	0.7	0.1	7.9	0.6
Latvians	5.4	0.5	2.9	0.2	3.3	0.2
Swedes	7.6	0.6	-	-	-	-
Others	5.4	0.5	11.5	1.0	14.6	1.1
Total	1,126.4	100.0	1,196.8	100.0	1,356.1	100.0

	1979 1000s	%	1989 1000s	%	1997 1000s	%
Estonians	947.8	64.7	963.3	61.5	950.1	65.0
Russians	408.8	27.9	474.8	30.3	412.6	28.2
Ukrainians	36.0	2.5	48.3	3.1	37.3	2.5
Belarusans	23.5	1.6	27.7	1.8	21.9	1.5
Finns	17.6	1.2	16.6	1.1	13.6	0.9
Jews	5.0	0.3	4.6	0.3	2.6	0.2
Germans	3.9	0.3	3.5	0.2	2.7	0.2
Latvians	4.0	0.3	3.1	0.2	2.7	0.2
Swedes	-	-	-	-	-	-
Others	17.9	1.2	23.8	1.5	20.0	1.4
Total	1,126.4	100.0	1,196.8	100.0	1,356.1	100.0

Sources: The USSR 1989 Census, *The Baltic States* (1991), Raun (1997a, p. 405), *Demographic Data Collection of Estonia, Latvia and Lithuania* (1998).

During the Soviet years, the number of non-Estonians increased from 23,000 in 1945 to 602,000 in 1989. Since a majority of the immigrants (mostly ethnic Russians or of other Eastern Slav origin) differed from the indigenous populations in several important respects, the demographic change also led to new political and socio-economic cleavages. The Soviet era immigrants took over all sensitive institutions in the Baltic states: security services, police, communications and managerial positions in enterprises (Norgaard, 1996, p.169). The considerable size of the immigration increased the indigenous Balts' feelings of powerlessness and marginality. Most Estonians had come to view the Russian residents in Estonia as settlers who were moved there by the Soviet state in order to 'solidify the conquest'. Given their low birth-rates and an age structure weighted towards the elderly, Estonians feared becoming a minority in their own country.

The pattern of geographic and economic concentration by ethnic group promoted separate societies in which either Estonians or Russian-speakers dominated. Geographically, the immigrant population tended to concentrate in large cities where there was industrial growth. Even in mixed areas, such as Tallinn, jobs and housing were frequently segregated.[4] Entire areas of Northeast Estonia have become ethnically Russian. As of 1989, in the Northeast cities of Narva and Kohtla-Järve, Russians constituted respectively 85.1% and 60.4% of the population. While the Russians predominated in the cities of North-East Estonia, the countryside remained almost exclusively Estonian. The population of Tallinn, Estonia's capital was almost evenly divided between Estonians and non-Estonians.

One of the hallmark of Estonia's existence in the Soviet years, particularly in the 1980s, was the emergence of an ethnically divided society. During the entire Soviet period, a discourse on how to maintain the border between 'us' and 'them' had taken place, especially among the titular nationality. In many instances Estonians, like other Balts, were drawing on pre-Soviet components of their identities and non-Soviet background influences (Norgaard, 1996, p. 16).[5] It has been rightfully observed by many area students that the resulting plural society was among crucial factors shaping interaction in Estonia between Estonians and non-titular national groups on one hand, and between Estonians and the USSR's center on the other (e.g., Kaplan, 1993, p. 208-10). Groups of Estonians and Russian speakers lived separated lives defined by language, education, jobs, occupational structures, and attitudes. Contact between Estonians and Russians was for the most part been limited to official levels with modest interaction at the personal or social levels (Ott, Kirch and Kirch, 1996, p.24).

The feeling that 'foreigners' were privileged in 'our country' and the cultural and social segregation between the titular nationality and the Russophone minorities have facilitated the persistence of historically conditioned prejudices between the groups. To a considerable extent, ethnic agendas had not coincided in the Soviet past and indeed differed during the triple transition to independence, political democracy and market-based economy on the verge of the 1980s-90s.

Ethnopolitical Problem Areas and Crises under Democratization

Stages of Democratization in Estonia

Overall, the democratization in Estonia falls into three distinct periods: 1) authoritarian decay (roughly 1987 - February 1990) when *perestroika* of the Soviet system took on political dimension; 2) successfully completed democratic transition starting with first free elections within the Soviet institutional framework (March 1990) and ending with the 'founding elections' (September 1992) based on new Estonian constitution; 3) democratic consolidation (since fall 1992-onwards) when the enacted constitution was actually put into practice and democratic rules of political game started to determine modalities and outcomes of political life. At each of these stages, ethnopolitics played an important role.

Political and Ethnic Mobilization under Authoritarian Decay (1987-89)

The liberalization attempted under *glasnost* and *perestroika* encouraged aspirations among Estonians. Emerging political pluralism and popular mobilization in Estonia manifested in the form of environmental protests in Spring 1987, especially by students at Tartu University, against the threat of expanded phosphate mining. On the anniversary of the Molotov-Ribbentrop Pact (23 August 1987), Estonian dissidents organized a major demonstration that publicly questioned the legitimacy of Soviet rule for the first time (Taagepera, 1989, p. 15; Zvidrins, 1994, p. 366; Lieven, 1993). In

September 1987 a group of intellectuals came out with a project for self-management and autonomy in Estonian economy (IME), that is, radical economic reform within the Soviet system. (Miljan, 1989; Raun, 1997b).

In 1988 political organizations outside the Communist Party of Estonia (CPE) itself began to appear. In terms of size and influence, the most important was the Popular Front of Estonia (PFE). PFE became the first organization of its kind with initially rather modest aim of channeling the reawakening civic energies of the population and pushing the leadership of the CPE towards fundamental reform. On April 1-2, 1988, the Joint Plenary Session of creative unions of Estonian intellectuals was held in Tallinn, where opponents of the regime openly decried the evils of administrative command socialism, and the republican authorities' resistance to *perestroika* and *glasnost*. In a letter, addressed to the upcoming XIXth CPSU Conference, the plenum expressed concern about the growing complexity of interethnic relations and urged the elaboration of constitutional guarantees to ensure effective decentralization of the Soviet system. It ended by advancing the initiative to form the mass popular movement and set up its organizing Center, headed by Edgar Savissaar and Marju Lauristin.

Within a matter of weeks, local Popular Front organizations sprang up throughout Estonia. PFE represented the true upsurge of civil society, so typical an element of democratization dynamics. One of its first mass actions was the gathering on 17 June, 1988 of over 150,000 sympathizers on the Camp of Songs in Tallinn to greet the Estonian delegates to the upcoming CPSU Conference in Moscow. Estonians openly reclaimed their ethnic identity by unfolding the blue-black-white tricolor and claiming recognition of Estonian as the republic's state language.

Estonian national movement combined the issues of national liberation with the tasks of advancing political democratization. The PFE Constitutive Congress, held on 1-2 October 1988, adopted the movement's Program and the Chart with the declared aims to promote the *perestroika* and *glasnost*. The PFE's documents openly called for 'dismantling of the state-oriented administrative system', the reformation of the Soviet Union on the principles of confederation and transformation of Soviets into competent decision-making bodies outpowering any CP committees. At the same time, *glasnost* in Estonian context implied first of all restoration of historical truth about the circumstances of Estonia's incorporation into the USSR in 1940.

In the fall of 1988, the popularity of PFE became almost overwhelming as a result of Estonia's coherent non-violent protest action against the draft

USSR Law on the Constitutional Amendments and the draft USSR Election Law, published in late October. These drafts made it explicitly clear that the Union Center was not going to extend liberalization to the sphere of the federation politics. On 29 October, the first meeting of the just formed PFE's Council of Authorized Representatives (leaders of the movement's support groups that operated at the communal level) expressed strong concern that the draft USSR legislation would curtail the already only nominal sovereignty of the Union republics. The meeting called upon Estonia's Supreme Soviet to officially express against the draft Union laws and to take a preventive action at the level of republican parliament which would permit to denounce the new USSR laws which violate Estonia's sovereignty (*Sovetskaya* Estonia, hereafter SE, 1 Nov. 1988). In less than two weeks anti-amendment petition drive gathered over 900,000 signatures (SE, 17 Nov. 1988). Given that total population of Estonia was slightly over 1.5 million, this petition campaign equaled a republican-wide referendum.

This peaceful protest received support from the reformed leadership of CPE, and its new secretary Vaino Väljas. On November 16, 1998, Estonia pioneered an unprecedented action. The VIII th extraordinary session of the Estonian Supreme Soviet voted Declaration on Sovereignty of the Estonian SSR which contained explicitly formulated provisions on the supremacy of republican laws over the USSR laws, the inalienable right of the republic on the resources on its territory and legalized the private property relations in Estonia. Special parliamentary resolutions rejected many of the amendments to the USSR Constitution proposed by the Union Center and called upon the USSR authorities to initiate the conclusion of new Union Treaty among the republics (SE, 17 Nov. 1988).

On November 26 the USSR Supreme Soviet's Presidium denounced the decisions of the Estonian Parliament. Gorbachev vehemently opposed the idea of a new Union Treaty and called for the formula 'Strong Center-Strong Republics'(*Izvestiya*, 28 Nov. 1988). Despite the harsh rebuttal from Moscow, the Estonian parliament, acting on the legal basis of the adopted supremacy of Estonia's legislation over the Union laws, re-confirmed the Declaration on sovereignty (SE, 6 Dec. 1988). On January 18, 1989, the law on state languages made knowledge of Estonian a prerequisite for many jobs and gave a 3-year period for acquisition of the necessary language skills (SE, 22 January 1989).

Many ethnic Russians took these developments with growing apprehensions. The majority of them did not view themselves as trespassers, nor did they find that their status in Estonia was different from the one of ethnic Estonians - all being citizens of the Soviet Union. Not all of the Russian population in Estonia shared ethnic Estonian aspirations for autonomy and self-rule nor did they wish a complete break with the Soviet Union. In this context a part of the Russian speakers became susceptible to the conservative rhethorics of communist hard-liners (Raun, 1995; Ott, Kirch, and Kirch, 1996, p. 24).

While the PFE sought to play a stabilizing and centrist role in the republic's re-emerging political life, two new political forces, also appeared in 1988, took the opposite sides of the spectrum. Led by former dissidents, the Estonian Party of National Independence (ENIP) unequivocally advocated the restoration of Estonian independence on the basis of the legal continuity of the Estonian republic which had existed before 1940. The party's declaration asserted the illegality of Soviet rule in Estonia viewed from the international law and rejected any collaboration with the CPE and official structures of authority (Samorodny, 1989, p.51). In contrast, the United Council of Labor Collectivities (OSTK) and the International Movement of Workers of the ESSR (IM) emerged as radical organizations at the other flank of the political spectrum. They became strongholds of conservative Russian speakers, mostly workers at Union-subordinated industrial enterprises and the Soviet military based in Estonia who declaredly opposed both democratization in the USSR and Estonia's strivings for independence and sat the task 'to wage the struggle for the preservation of the socialism on the Estonian soil'. Subsequently OSTK and IM staged a series of small-numbered but generously-sponsored protest rallies in Tallinn, Kohtla-Järve, and Sillamae against Estonian sovereignty and legislation on languages (SE, 7, 15 March 1989).

In 1989 major ethnic tensions in Estonia aroused as a product of differential perceptions with which ethnic groups took the new republican legislation that started to implement the declared principles of Estonian sovereignty. Particularly sensitive were the legislation on languages, re-introduction of traditional Estonian symbols instead of Soviet-style surrogates, pushing for official re-evaluation of the events in 1940 accompanying Estonia's incorporation into the USSR, demands of larger economic autonomy for the republic, and the new legislation on local elections. Overall, supporters of democracy took the lead. In late March of 1989, the PFE-supported candidates won the balloting during the election of the USSR People's Deputies in overwhelming majority of constituencies in Estonia (SE, 28 Mar. 1989).

An episode related to the re-introduction of national tricolor as Estonia's new official symbol was quite emblematic for the atmosphere of those days. In February 1989 Estonian authorities decreed 24 February as the Independence Day in memory of the day of proclamation of independent Estonian Republic in 1918 and announced the decision to raise the national tricolor on the 'Long Hermann' tower in the center of Tallinn to replace the socialist Estonia's red-banner flag (SE, 18 Feb. 1989). On 24 February tens of thousands of Estonians attended the ceremony of raising Estonian tricolor flag on the Toompea hill in Tallinn and on the Observatory tower in Tartu. The socialist era flags were reverently deposited to the ESSR State Museum by processions headed by city mayors (SE 25 Feb., 1 Mar. 1989). The Russophone conservatives actively protested against Estonia's new symbols, particularly the tricolor, and pledged their 'eternal allegiance' to the communist symbols. In Tallinn red flags were raised on almost all chimneys of the factories with predominantly Russophone workers but, since means of ecological protection at Union-subordinated enterprises were war from minimally good, very soon those red banners turned black because of the dirty gas coming out of the factory chimneys.

The same day was marked by two other important episodes at different margins of Estonia's political spectrum. Protesting against re-introduction of the Estonian tricolor the OSTK leadership declared the formation of the All-Estonia Strike Committee. At the same time, the joint meeting of the radical nationalist Estonian Heritage Society (EHS), the Estonian Christian League (ECL) and ENIP convened in *Estonia* Concert Hall to declare the constitution of Estonia Citizens' Committees (ECC). The ECC leadership also strongly pronounced against adoption of the national tricolor as long as Estonia remained within the USSR and accused the Estonian government of populist speculations with ethnic symbols, allegedly, to divert attention from the struggles for real independence (SE, 1 March 1989).

New round of political confrontation was touched off by the draft local elections legislation which provided for 2 to 5 years term of permanent residence in Estonia as a requirement for legal voter registration. On July 21, 1989, the IM and OSTK declared against the draft law and threatened political strike of Russophone workers unless the Estonian Supreme Soviet excluded the bill from the agenda of its upcoming session (SE, 26 July 1989). On July 24, Russophone workers and dockers went on strike drawing estimated several thousands of people (SE, 11 Aug. 1989). Two days after the strike was suspended after the government started talks with the Russophone leaders. (SE, 28 Jul. 1989).

On 31 July, the ESSR Supreme Soviet's Presidium established a standing commission to hold talks with the Russophone leaders (SE, 3 Aug. 1989). The passage of the draft law on August 8 led to the resuming of the strike. Initially, Estonian authorities issued a decree that declared the strike anticonstitutional and threatened responsibility for the strike organizers, but a week later the decree was repealed and it was promised that the application of the voter registration would be reconsidered (SE, 17 Aug. 1989). After a new round of negotiations, the strike was suspended in Kohtla-Järve and Tallinn (SE, 25 Aug. 1989). The Estonian parliament, though did not amend the law on local elections itself, voted the compromise decision to waive the application of permanent residence restrictions at the upcoming December elections (SE, 6 Oct. 1989).

An event of outstanding importance in political life were massive demonstrations in the whole of the Baltic region on August 23, 1989, the day of the 50th anniversary of the 1939 Molotov-Ribbentrop Pact (MRP). The action *Baltic Way*, organized by Baltic Popular Fronts, mobilized nearly 2 million people, both Balts and Russians, who formed an uninterrupted human chain stretching for over 1000 km from Tallinn through Riga to Vilnius to condemn the Molotov-Ribbentrop Pact and to make clear the intense strivings of the Baltic peoples for freedom and independence from the Soviet empire (SE, 24 Aug. 1989).

An extremely harsh statement by the CPSU Central Committee was quick to follow. It denounced nationalism in the Baltics and called for 'urgent measures' to prevent the threat to the 'vital interests' of the USSR. (*Pravda*, 27 Aug. 1989). The day after local communist party leadership in the Baltic republics met at their emergency sessions and issued statements straddling line between Moscow and the overwhelming majority of the Baltic population (SE, 29 Aug. 1989). These events made unequivocally manifest *urbi et orbi* that popular mobilization in the Baltic republics was proceeding mostly along the non-ethnic political divide between conservatives forces prepared to obey to some degree of liberalization (to the extent sanctioned by Moscow) and forces that were pushing for real democratization.

A new crucial component of political dynamics in Estonia became the increased differentiation within the national movement itself. During 1989, the competition between the PFE and the ECC revealed the basic fault line and outbidding rivalry in Estonian politics between those whom Toivo Raun called the *fundamentalists* and the *pragmatists* (Raun, 1997b, p. 345). The fundamentalists argued on the basis of principle and demanded the strict return to the status quo before Soviet rule, while the pragmatists proceeded from the concrete situation confronting them and were willing to make compromises in a less than ideal world. This fault line started to determine the thrust of political dynamics in renewing Estonia.

The ECC feared that the PFE would make too many concessions to Moscow and the existing authorities. On 7 October 1989, the ECC Conference adopted the Declaration stating the re-establishment of independent Estonia on the principle of legal continuity with the republic of Estonia which existed during 1918-40 as the major goal. The only feasible way to restore the Republic of Estonia, as declared, was by completing the registration of Estonia's citizens (SE, 10 Oct. 1989). The ECC organized a massive voluntary registration campaign of individuals who were citizens of independent Estonia (before 1940) and their descendants. During March-November 1989, ECC had registered 330,000 citizens and applicants for citizenship of the Estonian republic. By February of 1990, this number grew up to over 600,000, or over 70% of the adult Estonian population (SE, 12 Nov. 1989; SE, 7 Feb. 1990).

In fall of 1989, the PFE explicitly endorsed independence, mirroring the shifts in political dynamics. From September 1989 to May 1990, support for independence among Estonians increased from 64% to 96%; among non-Estonians it grew from 9% to 26% (Kivirahk, 1992, p. 24).

Ethnopolitics and Democratic Transition (1990-92)

Towards Restoration of Independence (1990-91) Politics of democratic transition in Estonia to a large extent overlapped with politics of restoring independence and an increased differentiation among political actors as regards the choice of principles on which future Estonia was to be built.

In the early months of 1990 a crucial struggle over who should lead the movement for renewed independence emerged on Estonian agenda. During the week between 24 February and 1 March of 1990, ECC successfully organized elections to the non-Soviet Congress of Estonia (CE). Reportedly, 502,445 registered ER citizens and 26,000 applicants came to the polls. Among the elected 439 deputies to the ECC, 109 were independent candidates, while others were distributed between supporters of the PFE

(107 deputies), ENIP (105 deputies), independent Estonian CP (39 deputies) (SE, 3 March 1990; *Ekspress-Khronika*, 13 March 1990). Conceived as an alternative representative body of authority, CE quickly claimed the moral and legal right to negotiate independence on the principle of legal continuity of the pre-1940 Republic of Estonia. The CE expressed for cooperation with the Estonian Supreme Soviet on issues concerning the formation of lawful bodies of power, provided the representatives of what was called the occupation regime (having in mind the Russophones arrived in the republic after 1940) be excluded from the process.

Official elections into Estonian Supreme Soviet, held on 18 March 1990, also resulted in definite victory of the pro-independence forces. New Estonian parliament voted at 73 to 8 with 29 abstentions the *Declaration on State Status of Estonia* which proclaimed juridical *restitutio ad integrum*. The Soviet power in Estonia was declared illegal from the moment it was established and the start of a transition period to the complete restoration of the country's independence was announced. The transition period was to last 'until the formation of the constitutional organs of state power of the Republic of Estonia'. (SE, 31 March 1990). The PFE, which dominated this new and democratically elected Supreme Council, argued that Moscow would be more willing to negotiate with an existing institution. A resolution was passed on collaboration with the Congress of Estonia in the cause of restoration of Estonia's independence on the principle of legal continuity (Nutt, 1990, p. 42).

Both CE and Estonia's new Supreme Soviet agreed to cooperate and there was substantial overlap in their composition. However, the Supreme Soviet possessed the clear advantage of commanding legislative authority within the existing system, and it dominated the day-to-day political life. On 18 May 1990, Estonian parliament voted the decree *On the Fundamentals of the Provisional Governing Order in Estonia* which declared Estonia's intention to base its relations with the USSR on the 1920 Tartu Treaty which had recognized Estonia's independence (SE, 18 May 1990).

The last year of the Soviet history in Estonia saw increasing political differentiation among the Russian speakers. On the one hand, Estonia's thrust for re-independence triggered increasing counter-action on behalf of conservative forces pro-Union oriented forces. IM and OSTK tried to earn support among communist leadership of local Soviets in North-East and to instigate local-based separatism through appeals to create territorial autonomy in North-East Estonia. On the other hand, reform-oriented groups of Russophones sided with the Estonian national movement.

On 26 May the Congress of 'deputies at all levels of authority' who stood for the preservation of the USSR federation was held in Kohtla-Järve. The organizers managed to gather mainly Russophone deputies sharing the ideas of IM, OSTK and Committee for the Defense of Soviet Power formed by Russian speaking conservative MPs in February (SE, 4 Feb. 1990). Numerically, the Congress deputies 'at all levels' comprised 4 out of 41 Estonia's deputies to the USSR Congress of People's Deputies, 20 out of 105 Estonian MPs, and 144 out of 2000 deputies of local Soviets within Estonia (SE, 26 May, 7 Jun. 1990). The gathering proclaimed itself an alternative representative body expressing 'true interests of all Estonia's citizens' and set up an Interregional Council of Deputies and Laborers (ICDL) and Soviet of National Economy (SNE), designed as alternative provisional government for North-East Estonia with the purpose to promote the application of the USSR laws on the territory of local soviets which would recognize their authority (SE, 29 May 1990).

Pro-Soviet agitators got only limited success. Already on 7 June, the Narva City Soviet passed a resolution denying legitimacy of the Kohtla-Järve congress of deputies at all levels and refusing to recognize the authority of the ICDL and SNE (7 Jun. 1990). The actual split among Russophones on issues of furthering democratization and independence could also be inferred from the results of referenda conducted in spring 1991. On 3 March, 1991, the nation-wide referendum was held in Estonia on the issue of restoring independence. All permanent residents were eligible to participate, the total turnout was at 83% and the result was a 77.8% 'yes' vote, including nearly all ethnic Estonians and, by some estimates, perhaps 25-30% of the non-Estonians.[6] On 17 March 1991, the All-Union referendum on preservation of the USSR, officially boycotted by Estonia, was held clandestinely in some districts of north-east and in constituencies established in Soviet Army units. Only 222,240 voters (approximately 23% of the total number of registered voters in Estonia) participated in the event (*Izvestiya*, 27 Mar. 1991).

On August 20, 1991, during the communist coup in Moscow, Estonian parliament voted Estonia's complete independence from the USSR. Following talks with representatives of the CE, it was agreed that both the Congress and the Supreme Soviet would send representatives to a Constitutional Assembly for the purpose of drafting the Constitution and presenting it to the people for a referendum'. The elections to the new Estonian parliament (*Riigikogu*) were to be held in 1992 (Kiionka, 1992, p.56; Bungs, 1993; Raun, 1994, p. 171; on the history of Estonian Constitutional Assembly see Taagepera 1994).

Estonia at Independence: Ethnopolitical Problem Areas After first free elections were held in March 1990, Estonia was well on its way to completing a transition to democracy and independence decided by elected representatives. The elections had been competitive and fair. After independence, during 1991-92, a second transition was in the making. Political discourse came to be 'not so much a debate about democracy, but about what kind of democracy: an inclusionary liberal democracy based on citizenship for almost all permanent residents or an exclusionary 'ethnic democracy' only for 1940 descendants (Linz and Stepan, 1996, p. 408). At the same time, from mid-1993 ethnopolitical evolution aimed at striking the balance between those two options and taking a centered position.

It is important to take into account that during all post-independent years ethnic relations in Estonia have represented an extremely complex set of unfolding dynamics which requires a careful and nuanced assessment. Ever since the task of restoring independence had been put onto political agenda, national identity and ethnopolitical legitimation became major decisional points in redefining Estonian's society. The three problem areas - stateness, state effectiveness, and nationhood - took specific configuration.

Stateness The problem area of stateness did not acquire critical salience before independence. With some smaller exceptions, there were no concerted separatist attempts or politically significant forces which questioned Estonia's territorial state under democratic transition. Neither at independence nor after, did Russian-speaking minority ever seriously questioned the legitimacy of Estonian state, except for a short period of unrest in mid-1993 resulting after the adoption of the initial version of the *Law on Aliens*. On the contrary, it was the radical political groups and the public opinion among the dominant Estonian ethnicity who questioned the legitimacy of Russian-speaking post-war immigrants as the would-be citizens of the restored Estonian state.

Effectiveness of the state State effectiveness is merely an aspect of decision-making. In comparison with other post-communist countries in Eastern

Europe, transition to market economy in Estonia so far have resulted truly successful and the performance legitimacy of the government, as regards market transition and macroeconomic stabilization, has always been quite high. Estonia's success in economic reforms has been reported by Girnius (1993), Laar (1996), Norgaard (1996, ch.4), Gray (1996), Girnius (1993), Lauristin and Vihalem (1997, p. 99-116), Raun (1997a). Overall, for the time being, it appears highly unlikely that the effectiveness of Estonian state can generate serious ethnopolitical disputes or constitute a serious source of aggressive nationalism in Estonia. The economic prospects generally favor democratization in Estonia, particularly since increasing prosperity improves the prospects for the sort of interest group politics common to Western civic democracies.

Nationhood Nationhood, its definition (ethnic or civic) and principles of the citizenship policies was the only problem area that actually became a crisis in Estonian ethnopolitics. The source of the crisis is to be sought in the peculiar features of the discourse of statehood and sovereignties which determined the policies of state- and nation-building. Unlike most of the other post-Soviet states, the Baltic States regarded themselves officially as 'restored' rather than the 'new' sovereignties. This emphasis on continuity with the interwar republics implied an approach to citizenship that tended to be rather exclusivist, or at least, much narrower than those found elsewhere within the borders of the former USSR.[7] The crisis of nationhood derived from the obvious contradiction between the logic of democratization and the logic of initially adopted approaches to the nation-building project.

In following the legal approach of restoring the previously-existing states, all three Baltic nations linked their citizenship in 1991 to citizenship in 1940. Those who were citizens as of the earlier date retained that citizenship, as did their descendants. Only Lithuania's law admitted post-1940 immigrants automatic citizenship on a par with the main body of citizenry. Many analysts agree that such an approach to determining the initial body of citizens was reasonable: had the independent statehood not been forcibly interrupted by Soviet rule, this group of individuals would have constituted the citizenry of the individual states (Chinn and Truex, 1996, pp.133-7; Weigant, 1995, p. 121). At the same time, the normative aspects of the 'restored-state' approach to nationhood have had obvious ethnic implications and clearly served the political interests of the titular nationality. The problem is highlighted by Chinn and Truex (1995, p. 135):

The difficulty with the 'restored' approach arises from the presence of large numbers of immigrants, mostly Russians who came to the Baltics during the Soviet years. When they or their parents or grandparents moved to the Baltics, they had no notion of going abroad. With Soviet dissolution and Baltic independence, this population suddenly found itself living in other countries. With citizenship going only to those who had been or were descended from citizens of the interwar republics, Soviet-era immigrants became stateless. The ethnic consequences result not from the citizenship laws themselves, because all citizens of the interwar republics - whatever their ethnic group - retain their citizenship and pass it to their descendants, but from the republics' change in demographic composition as a consequence of the Russian and other immigration that took place during the half-century of the Soviet rule.[8]

Theoretically, this pattern may or may not lead to so-called 'ethnic democracy', i.e. polities that are democratic for the dominant group but that exclude, on the basis of ethnicity, other groups from the democratic process. A nuanced assessment of consequences of such an approach depends upon the strategic choices made in addressing the issue of naturalizing non-citizens who were resident at the time of renewed independence. Generally speaking, such strategies can range from complete to partial inclusion/exclusion. Complete exclusion, if based on ethnically-defined nationhood, obviously, paves the way to 'ethnic democracy'. This, definitely, is *not* the case with any of the Baltic states. Complete inclusion, based on a civic definition of nationhood, obviously, is an immediate choice for liberal democracy.

Partial (incomplete) inclusion that can be observed in Estonia stands halfway between ethnic and civic definitions of nationhood and is elusive in the longer-run. It can lead to either ethnic or liberal democracy. In this process, very much depends upon ethnopolitical dynamics and implementation of the chosen policy priorities in dealing with nationhood and citizenship. For the time being, it is indicative of the fact that nationhood remains a system-level crisis, and no immediate choice as regards an appropriate institutional innovation is available. It means that either the balance between civic vs. ethnic definitions of nationhood, which is required for such innovation to become a way out of a crisis, has not yet been formed or that it is impossible to find such a balance within the existing institutional framework. Anyway, in the short-run it means a delayed institutional choice.

On September 9, 1991, the ECC and ENIP leadership strongly declared against the zero-variant draft law on citizenship proposed by the PFE faction of the Estonian parliament. One of their more reasonable argument was that the PFE-backed bill would allow tens of thousands of retired servicemen of the occupationist Soviet Army to receive citizenship of Estonia (Barrington, 1995, p. 735). In view of the delicacy of the issue, the provisionary government that ruled in Estonia until post-independence elections postponed the treatment of the citizenship question for fear of committing itself to a long-term policy.[9]

On 6 November 1991, the Estonian parliament reinstated the citizenship law of 1938, followed up by enabling legislation on 26 February 1992.[10] Together, the two laws limited automatically recognized citizenship to those who were citizens of the interwar republic and their descendants, regardless of ethnicity. It has been estimated that approximately 100,000 Russian speakers came into this category. The legislation also laid down the conditions for naturalization which included two years' residence in Estonia (starting from 30 March 1990) and a one-year waiting period for the official review of their application for citizenship, competence in the Estonian language, and the swearing of an oath of loyalty to the state and the constitution. Some 35,000 or so more permanent residents who had registered for Estonian citizenship with the ECC before 24 February 1990 were granted this right without having to taking a language examination (Sheehy, 1993a, p. 8; Weigant, 1995, p. 121).

The language requirement was that the would-be citizens were to demonstrate conversational ability in Estonian, requiring a knowledge of about 1,500 words. Since the high-school language requirement would also satisfy the citizenship language requirement, most young Russians in Estonia would be able to acquire Estonian citizenship if they so wished. For most Russian adults, however, this provision required an effort that they were unwilling to make, particularly given the fact that during the Soviet period, they had had little opportunity or incentive to do so.

An important caveat, contained in the enacted legislation was the requirement to wait a year before citizenship was granted. The pre-war law had been very liberal and had, besides knowledge of the Estonian language, only required two years of residence. However, par.5 of the Citizenship Resolution of 1992 stipulated that the duration of the permanent residency in Estonia was not to begin before March 30, 1990. Since nearly five sixths of all Russians and other non-Estonians in 1991 were immigrants, the first naturalized citizens among them could appear only in spring 1993 (2+1) years after March 30, 1990), i.e. after the September 1992 'founding' elections in independent Estonia. Moreover, the fact that the initial term of the *Riigikogu*, the Estonian parliament, was restricted to two and a half years, as compared to the regular constitutional four-year period, made some speculate whether the goal of this provision was to exclude the bulk of Russian-speakers, who will have first to learn Estonian before they can apply for citizenship, even from the next elections on March 5, 1995 (Weigant, 1995, p. 120-1; Sheehy, 1993a, p. 9). The *Citizenship Resolution* thus not only effected, in the Russian perspective, a 'disenfranchisement' of most Russian-speakers, it was also the best expression that Estonians wanted to be 'among themselves' in the early phase of their new statehood.

Under the pressure of moderates, in May 1992, Estonian parliament included into the ballot lists for the referendum on Estonian constitution an additional question on whether, as an exclusion, to grant the non-Estonian applicants for citizenship the right to participate at the first elections to the new legislature on a par with citizens. Yet, at referendum in June 1992, 53% of the voters expressed against registration of non-Estonian applicants for citizenship as voters in the upcoming parliamentary elections.(*Estonia*, hereafter, ES, 29 Jun. 1992; Clemens, 1994, p. 367).

In making an assessment, it is important to note that, strictly speaking, the adopted approach to citizenship and the initial definition of nationhood were by no means exclusionary. In fact, they were couched not in ethnic, but in civic terms, in the sense that the nation's core (those citizens of the pre-1940 Estonia and their direct descendants) was defined on the basis of civic criteria and included both ethnic Estonians and non-Estonians. Yet, the consequences of this process, nonetheless, have been only partially inclusive. While this approach was justified by the argument of legal continuity, it effectively excluded the larger part of non-Estonian population from participation in the political process that set the initial course of the state. At the time of the 28 June 1992, referendum on the constitution, there were 600,000 registered voters out of a total population of 1.6 million; only about a sixth of the 600,000 non-Estonians living in the republic were eligible to vote. The first post-Soviet parliament, *Riigikogu*, chosen in September 1992, likewise was elected by the same group of interwar citizens and their descendants. Its 101 seats were filled entirely by ethnic Estonians.[11] Thus, Estonian approach to citizenship has left the larger part of Russian minority population outside the political community.

Overall, Estonia's democratic reforms and resolute movement away from communist past were impressive. In June 1992, with 66.3% of the eligible voters participating, 91.2% approved of the new constitution (*The Baltic Independent*, July 3-9, 1992, p. 1). Estonia was the first among successor states to hold the 'founding' post-Soviet parliamentary elections (September 1992). The new cabinet formed by a 32-year old Mart Laar in October 1992 represented a new political generation which was largely free of previous communist ties (Raun, 1977a, p. 417).[12]

The makers of the new constitution returned to the parliamentary tradition of the 1920s and assigned political supremacy to the *Riigikogu*, a unicameral parliament with 101 members elected for a four-year term while the powers of the president are more ceremonial than real. Nevertheless, the President represents the state in international relations, has first two choices in nominating a prime minister, and can force parliament to reconsider legislation by possessing the authority to promulgate the laws*)*. As shown by developments during the crisis in summer 1993, this authority of the President proved an effective instrument for conflict management.

Democratic Consolidation and Nationhood (1992-96)

Crisis of Nationhood in Estonia (1992-93) At the initial stage of democratic consolidation issues of nationhood and citizenship became the focal point of ethnic apprehensions and strategic interactions in Estonia. Actually, citizenship policies had become trapped into metaconflict of differential perspectives, prevalent among both Estonian and Russian speaking communities at indepemdemce. Estonian perspective was rooted into the concept of a 'restored' statehood and was restrictive on issue of citizenship enlargement. It was widely held that only citizens can and should determine the rules by which others can subsequently become citizens. Indeed, Estonians had every interest and emotional feeling militating to the view, that theirs had been an *end of* occupation rather than a successful case of decolonization. Reminiscences of the interbellic Estonia were strong and people had not forgotten the immoral way in which their state had become victim of Soviet aggression in 1940. Soviet rule was of course experienced as alien and Russian speaking post-war immigrants as its bearers (whether voluntary or involuntary). This feeling could not be lightly dismissed (Driessen, 1994, p. 120).

Recent history of ethnically perceived political tensions between conservative opponents and supporters of Estonian independence, also was an important politico-psychological variable not to be discounted. The unsavory activities of the Intermovement and OSTK during the Estonian struggle for independence had created much animosity between the ethnic groups, at least at the unsophisticated level of mass consciousness. Many Estonians found it hard to accept that people who had tried to deny basic rights to others should become entitled to such rights themselves. Still, on a second and a deeper thought it was understood that, under international law and principles of liberalism, they are so entitled and 'it was both unjust and unsavory indulging into seeking an ethnically-based revenge with the whole of Russian-speaking community' (Kolstoe, 1995, p. 137).

Situational politics and ethnic outflanking had come to the fore of political discourse and action in the first years after restoration of independence, particularly, while ex-Soviet Army troops were still stationed on Estonian soil (until end summer 1994). Advocacy of uncompromising stances and 'principled coherence' in relation to de-colonization and legacies of the Soviet period had become a handy tool in power struggles between outbidding ethnic Estonian elites. Priorities of citizenship policies were an issue of heated debates between Estonian elites. Parties of radical nationalist orientation dominated the coalition government, while moderate Estonian elites, mostly associated with the PFE, had resulted in parliamentary minority. Dynamics of radicalization of Estonian elites on issues of citizenship policies is well-reported (Park, 1993; Clemens, 1994; Kask, 1994; Metcalf, 1996; Steen, 1996 and 1997).

From the Estonian point of view, the resulting citizenship legislation was a hard-won compromise between two seemingly conflicting goals. First, lawmakers had sought to assure the survival of the Estonian nation by limiting citizenship to those who understood the country's language and culture. Second, the Supreme Council intended the laws to integrate those who had settled in Estonia under Soviet rule and thus to ensure a stable and loyal population (Kiionka, 1991 and 1992; Sheehy, 1993a; Klatt, 1994).

The perspective of Russian speakers (who in 1989 accounted for some 39% of the population) was quite different. They felt threatened and discriminated against by this approach and regarded Estonia as an independent state of which they unexpectedly found themselves a second category subjects, deprived of political rights and insecure about their further cultural and political existence and even threatened by allegedly planned deportations. In conjunction with these market-induced anxieties, the Russian population had been put under a double stress developed from increased awareness of their alien status both economically and politically.

Ethnopolitical Crisis Interaction: The Law on Aliens (Summer 1993)
Summer of 1993 saw an extremely sharp escalation of interethnic tensions. By mid-1993 anxieties of Russian speaking non-citizens had reached their peak. Ethnic apprehensions and disputes had become concentrated on one single issue - the status of non-citizens. Nationhood manifested as a crisis not only at the system level, but also at the level of group interaction as a series of events where strategic moves and countermoves had acquired an unusually high probability of escalation to violence.

The triggering role of the initially adopted version of the *Law on Aliens* in the outbreak of interactional crisis need be seen in the context of several pieces of earlier legislation. *The Law on National Elections*, adopted on 6 April 1992, stipulated that only citizens could vote and run for election in national elections. The Estonian Constitution, approved by referendum on 28 June the same year, contains the same stipulation. On 19 May 1993 the Estonian parliament, after much discussion, passed a law on local elections, which allowed resident non-citizens to vote but barred them from running as candidates (ES, 20 May, 21 May 1993). Actually, this provision was severely limiting the choice of candidates in such overwhelmingly Russian cities as Narva and especially Sillamäe. Finally, on 16 June 1993, the parliament voted the law *On Schools and Gymnasia* decreeing the phasing out of education in Russian in grades 10 to 12 of state schools by the year 2000. Anticipating harsh reactions, President Meri sent this law back to the parliament where it stayed for amendments until 1996 (ES, 18 Jun. 1993).

From the moment when the Estonian parliament started discussing the *Law on Aliens* in early June 1993, the law was the subject of fierce condemnation by the Russian speaking community, particularly in North-East Estonia. On June 19, over 10,000 supporters of the radical Russophone 'Russian Obshina' marched along the streets of Narva, protesting against placing the bill onto the agenda of the upcoming parliamentary session. The demonstrators declared they would consider eventual approvation of the *Law on Aliens* as declaration of war against Russian speaking community. The protesters threatened railway blockade and suspension of electricity supplies to Estonia via North East (Sheehy, 1993a; Hanson, 1993).

The initial version of the *Law on Aliens* was passed by *Riigikogu* on June 21, 1993, by a vote of 59 to 3 (ES, 1 Jul. 1993). The purpose of the law was to regularize the position of non-Estonian citizens and to supersede the 1990 law on immigration. All non-citizens residing in Estonia, as of July 1, 1990, were termed *aliens* (foreigners) and deemed illegal immigrants without official authorization for residence. The law required all non-citizens to apply for a temporary residence permit within one year and, if the latter is not granted, they have to emigrate from Estonia. Such residence permits were to be renewed every five years. At the same time, applicants for a temporary residence permit were supposed to decide whether they wish to apply for Estonian citizenship, take out Russian or other non-Estonian citizenship, or apply for an alien's passport. Ex-Soviet Army servicemen were excluded from the number of potential applicants whatsoever. Obviously with the intention to arrive as soon as possible at a situation when the status of all people living in Estonia would be cleared, the law set up certain time limits. Two years were given for obtaining authorization for permanent residence. Accompanying the adopted law was a special decision that all permanent residents, regardless of ethnicity, would be allowed to vote in local elections on 17 October, if registered before 12 August (ES, 20 Jun. 1993).

The initial version of the *Law on Aliens* had evoked an outraged critique from members of the Russian minority and had led to massive protests in the Northeast Estonia. Already incited by the Law on Local elections which had excluded non-citizens from holding offices in the local government, local party and government officials in Narva and Sillamäe led the protest against a law that was denounced as turning non-citizens into illegal immigrants. The chief objections to the *Law on Aliens* as originally passed were to its provisions regarding those who came to Estonia before 1 July 1990. The loss of occupation (lawful income) would entail loss of authorization for residence which obviously could be perceived as creating conditions for legal ousting of non-residents from Estonia under transition to market economy. Since the law gave no guarantee that they would be granted a residence permit, in any case would to be renewed every five years, it was seen by members of the Russian-speaking community as giving the Estonian authorities the opportunity to expel noncitizens who had lived much, if not all, of their lives in Estonia (ES, 30 Jun. 1993).

Harsh critique of the *Law on Aliens* came from Moscow. Deputy Russian Foreign Minister Vitalii Churkin told the press on 22 June that

Moscow was considering economic and political measures in response to Estonia's controversial new law on foreigners. The dispute over the *Law on Aliens* continued on 23 June as Russian Foreign Minister Andrei Kozyrev made the claim that the Council of Europe had given an 'indulgence for the continuation of the practice' of violation of human rights by admitting Estonia as its member. Finally, in his special statement of June 24, Russian President Yeltsin accused Estonia of unfriendly actions and charged that 'there is ethnic cleansing similar to apartheid going on in Estonia'. Stressing that he would not tolerate infringement on the legitimate rights of ethnic Russians in Estonia, Yeltsin said that appropriate measures would be taken 'to protect the honor, dignity, and legitimate rights of our compatriots'(RFE/RL Daily Report, 30 Jun. 1993; ITAR-TASS, 23 Jun. 1993; *Rossijskaya Gazeta*, 25 Jun. 1993, idem, 1 Jul. 1993).

By end June crisis escalation reached its peak. On June 28, the city council of Narva held its extraordinary closed door meeting where it was decided to call for local referendum about 'national-territorial autonomy within Estonia' to be held on July 16 and 17. Few days later the local council of Sillamäe took a similar decision (ES, 30 Jun. 1993; RFE/RL Daily Report, 7 Jul. 1993; *Izvestiya*, 8 Jul. 1993). Both local councils adopted resolutions stating that recent Estonian laws discriminated against many of residents. This pattern of developments indicated that stateness could also become a crisis, a development particularly threatening in view of apparently similar events that had taken place in Moldova-Trans-Dniester conflict in 1991-92 when spiraling confrontation between local and central authorities had led conflict escalation to the level of interethnic warfare.

On 30 June the trip from Tallinn to Narva by CSCE High Commissioner for National Minorities Max van der Stoel was temporarily blocked by about 6,000 demonstrators in the city of Sillamäe. Having submitted their petition, the demonstrators marched to the Sillamäe city council, urging immediate local referendum on the creation of Narva-Sillamäe territorial autonomy of Russian speakers within Estonia. Van der Stoel held meetings with Narva municipal officials who told him that they had decided to use 'the most peaceful means of resolving a conflict', holding a referendum instead of resorting to strikes or blocking roads (RFE/RL Daily Report, 1 Jul. 1993).

The uproar of protests and sharp escalation of interethnic tensions met with immediate and efficient crisis management endeavors, undertaken by both Estonian authorities and third parties. The terms of the *Law on Aliens*, like those of the other legislation to which strong objection has been taken, were the subject of much dispute among the Estonians themselves. On June 30, a group of Estonian intellectuals addressed the Estonian nation with an Open Letter which criticized the policies towards Russian-speaking community and called to prevent further escalation of interethnic tension and to abrogate the *Law on Aliens* (ES, 1 Jul. 1993). Instead of promulgating the law, on June 30, Estonia's President Meri, submitted the text to the CSCE High Commissioner for National Minorities, van der Stoel, and sent it to the experts of European Council pending subsequent re-examination by Estonian MPs (RFE/RL Daily Report, 5 Jul. 1993). Estonian government declared illegal and juridically invalid the local referenda to be held in Narva and Syllamäe, but, at the same time, it was stated that Estonian authorities would not oppose holding referenda by force (RFE/RL Daily Report, 4 Jul. 1994).

The Council of Europe's panel of experts found the provisions of the *Law on Aliens* perfectly acceptable with regard to anyone outside Estonia who might wish to live or work in Estonia in the future. However, since, in their opinion, laws should recognize acquired rights it was wrong to equate the status of those already resident in Estonia with that of noncitizens not currently resident there. The panel also found the wording of the law imprecise and thus open to arbitrary interpretation by the authorities (Sheehy, 1993a, p.9; Chinn and Truex, 1996, p. 138). Upon examination of the *Law on Aliens*, Max van der Stoel and Catherine Lalumiere, Secretary General of the Council of Europe, both declared that most of the provisions of the law were very similar to legislation in other states. Their points of critique were essentially the same, the major issue being the vagueness of some of the language which gave the authorities too much discretion in deciding applications for resident permits.[13]

On July 8, a special session of the Estonian parliament approved, by a vote of 69 to 1, with 2 abstentions, 20 amendments to the *Law on Aliens* as recommended by the CSCE and Council of Europe. One important change provided that registered residents need not repeat the registration process every five years and, therefore, the stipulation that permanent residence permits had to be renewed every five years was dropped. The Estonian parliament also voted to include a new article in the law, retaining for noncitizens who had arrived before July 1, 1990 all the rights and responsibilities laid down in previous laws and guaranteeing them residence and work permits, as long as the alien's status was in accord with all other requirements of the law. The amendments also spelled out what was considered lawful income - and stated that those refused residence or work permits have the right to appeal to the courts. The residence permits were still to be denied to anyone who had served in a career position in the armed forces of a foreign state, which meant that the many thousands of former Soviet Army and KGB officers who had retired in Estonia would face expulsion (RFE/RL Daily Report, 9 Jul. 1993).

CSCE High Commissioner for Minorities van der Stoel commented that Estonia had taken a 'major step' forward by revising the law and noted that a number of old formulations that might have led to arbitrary decisions had been removed. In a similar vein, President Meri said that the revisions brought the law into line with similar legislation in other European countries which made it possible for him to sign the revised version of the law (RFE/RL Daily Report, 12 Jul., 13 Jul. 1993).

Efficient functioning of Estonian democratic institutions and constructive intervention of European organizations and leaders as third parties succeeded in bringing down the passions and in defusing the crisis. The fact that Estonian president consulted the Council of Europe and the CSCE about the *Law on Aliens* and that the Estonian parliament acted on most of their recommendations reduced the level of hostile rhetoric emanating from Russia.

After amendments to the law had been made, third party activities continued to play an important stabilizatory role in addressing the pending local referenda whose results might provoke an upsurge of ethnoterritorial separatism in Northeast Estonia (See on CSCE activities Lange, 1994; Birckenbach, 1997). On 11 July, during his third within the two weeks visit to Estonia, Max van der Stoel was reassured by the Estonian government that it would not use force to halt the referenda in North-East. Visiting Narva, he also held talk with the mayors of Narva and Sillamae, as well as with the leaders of the Representative Assembly, a more liberal oriented organization of Russian speakers. As the result of the talks, the mayors called on the Estonian authorities not to interfere with the referendums, but said that the cities would respect the 'territorial integrity' of Estonia and comply with any decisions of the Estonian Supreme Court on the referenda. (RFE/RL Daily Report, 12 Jul. 1993). On July 15, the city council of Kohtla-Järve voted to reject a proposal to hold a poll on local autonomy, arguing that it would be a violation of the Estonian Constitution and decided not to follow the example of its neighbours, Narva and Sillamäe (RFE/RL Daily Report, 16 Jul. 1993).

On 16 and 17-July over 90% of referendum participants in both Narva and Sillamäe expressed support for declaring their towns autonomous territories within Estonia, but the turnout in Narva in particular was much lower than the organizers had hoped. According to Baltic and Russian media of 18 July, voter participation in the municipally organized referendums was about 54% in Narva and 61% in Sillamäe. The organizers had said the referendums would be binding if more than 50% of electorate voted. Since many irregularities were noted in the voting and ballot-counting processes, the actual turnout figures were likely to be lower and the Estonian government claimed that in fact less than the required 50% of the eligible voters participated (ES, 18 Jul. 1993). Since the chairmen of the Narva and Sillamäe city councils had agreed beforehand that they would abide by the ruling of the Supreme Court, the referendums seemed to have been more an exercise in letting out steam than anything else. On 18 July Premier Mart Laar thanked the predominantly Russian residents of the two towns for maintaining calm and promised that the government would strive to improve the economic situation, particularly since both towns have been heavily hit by unemployment (RFE/RL Daily Report, 19 Jul. 1993).

The reaction of Estonian authorities to deal with the perennial complaint of the Russian-speaking minority that it had not been consulted beforehand about laws affecting its interests was constructive and accommodative. On 6 July the Estonian government officially registered the *Representative Assembly*, the more liberal of the two organizations representing Estonia's Russian speaking community. The government said it planned to involve the assembly in drafting supplementary acts to the *Law on Aliens* and other legislation affecting them (ES, 7 Jul. 1993). At the beginning of July President Meri announced the establishment of a *Roundtable of Noncitizens and Ethnic Minorities* under his auspices, which has already met several times. Reportedly, third parties contributed material resources for administrative costs of holding round-table talks between national minorities and the government.[14]

Managing the Problem Area of Nationhood: The Strategy of Integration.

Efficient and constructive management of the interactional crisis in 1993 contributed to the preservation of ethnic peace in Estonia. However, nationhood remains a system-level crisis that waits for its resolution. Historical and demographic legacies, prevailing political discourses among the titular nationality, and ethnic outbidding initially had precluded the choice in favor of a totally inclusive approach to citizenship. The logic of nation-building, thus, contradicted the logic of consolidating liberal democracy. The initial version of the *Law on Aliens* represented an attempt to resolve the crisis of nationhood through an institutional innovation that proved insufficient. The intent was to institutionalize the divide between citizens and non-citizens, effectively keeping the larger part of Russian speakers beyond the political community, at the same time leaving room for acceptance into the polity on the terms, established by the Estonian majority. The developments of the mid-1993 made it manifestly clear that the initially chosen solution in the realm of nationhood was inconclusive and could even trigger serious ethnic disruption.

Overall, there were at least three negative consequences of the initially adopted partially inclusive approach to nationhood. First, the fact that a large portion of resident population could not possibly participate in the development of political democracy and thereby became merely an object of policy. Second, and directly related to the above was the fact that a large portion of the non-Estonian population (non-citizens) were not participating directly in the building of the post-Soviet state. This was producing the danger for ethnization of the problem area of state effectiveness which thus far had been free of ethnically charged potential. Due to on-going market reforms, the extremes of wealth, redistribution of property, increasing harshness of the employment and the marginalization of certain groups of people all fostered societal stress, dislocation and dissatisfaction.

Third, politico-psychological consequences of the ethnic divide, specifically, accumulation of discontent and ethnically charged grievances, were laying the ground for a serious threat to communal peace and stability in the long-run. Great social upheavals produced a deep identity crisis among non-Estonians. It was above all that of rootlessness, a feeling of not belonging anywhere. This could be defined as a completely 'alien existence', since Estonia, as a country of residence (and the place where more than half of non-Estonians were born), was not legally their own. Russia and other countries of origin were similarly perceived by many as alien. And therefore, there was no place which they could truly call their own and to which they could be recognized as belonging.

In sum, it had become increasingly clear that challenges of managing nationhood at the stage of democratic consolidation strongly required a new trial in finding a more adequate institutional response to overcome the division of the political community into the included and the excluded lots. This challenge seems to have been met by endorsing the strategy of integration of non-Estonians into Estonian society.

The roots of this new strategy go back to 1993 when after his first visits to the Baltic states in 1993, UN High Commissioner Max van der Stoel made a series of recommendations to the Estonian foreign ministry, all aimed at a fair and impartial application of the laws. In his most direct letter to the Estonian foreign minister T. Velliste of April 6, 1993 (see published in Birckenbach, 1997), van der Stoel suggested an alternative policy aiming

> at the integration of the non-Estonian population by a deliberate policy of facilitating the chances of acquiring Estonian citizenship for those who express such a wish, and of assuring them full equality with Estonian citizens. In my view, such a policy would greatly reduce the danger of destabilisation, because it would considerably enhance the chances of the non-Estonian population developing a sense of loyalty towards Estonia.

The core of the suggestions stated that since it was unrealistic to think that most noncitizens wanted to leave Estonia, it would be wise to try to integrate them by making it easier for them to get the country's citizenship. It was similarly acknowledged that it was up to the non-Estonians to adapt to the new realities and learn Estonian and that matters would be helped by the withdrawal of Russian troops from Estonia.

Integration of non-Estonians has come to be conceived as the mutual acceptance and tolerance of ethnolingual groups, where general discourse takes place in Estonian and all residents are loyal to Estonia. The ultimate strategic goal of integration is to ensure lasting stability and peaceful change. The more immediate objective is to improve the manageability of the current transitional period, relying on the legal order and international norms (Käärid and Valter, 1997, p.3). In Estonian discourse, the integration process has been formulated as a set of components, organized into a logical chain of 'information - mindset - language - citizenship - mindset'. Obtaining citizenship on the one hand assumes and on the other - entrenches loyalty (Käärid and Valter, 1997, p.13-25).

Adopting the strategy of civic integration of non-Estonians into Estonian society, together with respective serious corrections in the pursued priorities in citizenship policies, have tended to be successful in the context of effectively functioning democratic institutions of independent Estonia and the mode the enacted legislation was implemented, especially since 1995. Public opinion polls suggest that, while public discussion and subsequent enactment of laws affecting non-citizens caused tensions and anxiety among resident non-Estonians, the successful implementation of these acts by the Estonian Republic has given a clear signal to the population, Estonian and non-Estonian alike, that democratic rules will be followed, rights protected, and responsibilities defined (Ott, Kirch, and Kirch, 1996). Altogether these efforts have downgraded nationhood from the crisis level to the level of a problem area that is amenable to management within the framework of existing institutions. Further success in dealing with nationhood in Estonia, to a large extent, depends on finding an adequate balance between its civic and ethnic conceptions.

Any unbiased analysis cannot but admit that ethnopolitical developments since 1993 have been characterized by unfolding dynamics which has been coherently working towards increasing political participation of Russian speakers and enlargement of their share in the citizenry through naturalization and gradual engrounding of a civilized discourse of tolerance. The milestone contextual event in the process of a constructive redirection of ethnopolitical processes was the final withdrawal of all ex-USSR troops from Estonian territory in August 1994.

Russians and other non-Estonians became more actively involved in politics already with the first post-Soviet local elections in October 1993. Only citizens could be candidates, but all permanent residents 18 years of age and older who had lived in a given locality for five years were eligible to vote. It is noteworthy that non-Estonian voters participated in the election much more actively than Estonian ones. In Tallinn, where one-third of the country's population is located, ethnic Russian candidates won 42% (27 of 64) of the seats in the city council. There, and in other areas where non-Estonians were elected, moderate Russian candidates who supported an independent Estonia, were more successful than opponents (*The Baltic Independent*, 22-28 Oct. 1993, pp. 1,4; Norgaard, 1996, p. 419). An important confidence-building note was given on the eve of the elections. At a meeting of the Russian-Speakers' Representative Assembly in Tallinn delegates from the Narva and Sillamäe declared their city councils would not hold alternative local elections on 17 October and were going to comply with all Estonian regulations (RFE/RL Daily Report, 24 Sept. 1993).

Initially, the majority of non-Estonians took a wait-and-see position on the issue of citizenship and while many requested residence permits, the number of applicants for citizenship was not very high. By December 1994, only about 40,000 persons had become naturalized as citizens of Estonia, while another 50,000 or so opted for Russian citizenship. By 1 February 1995, 61,401 residents of Estonia had obtained Russian citizenship (RFE/RL Daily Report, 7 Feb. 1995). It appears that many non-Estonians, including those for whom the language test presented no obstacle, feared the consequences of making a choice. In terms of integration, the most challenging region were the urban areas of North-East, like Narva where ethnic Estonians comprised only 4.0% of the population. Obviously, such non-choices of Russian speakers in relation to Estonian citizenship increased apprehensions among Estonians.

On January 19, 1995, the *Riigikogu* adopted a new Law on Citizenship that brought all citizenship regulations into one document. The most noteworthy change to the old regulation was that the residence requirement had been tightened. In order to be able to apply for citizenship an applicant was to have lived for 5 years in Estonia on the basis of a permanent residence permit. One more year had to pass from the date of the registration of the application on (Art. 6-2). It was noted though that this provision did not apply to persons who had settled in Estonia prior to July 1, 1990, if they were legal aliens with permanent residence permits (Art. 33). Any person who was to submit an application prior to the entry in force of the law (April 1, 1995) would be treated according to the old naturalization conditions (Weigant, 1995, p. 122). Obviously, this provision was made in order to speed up the application process among non- Estonians. At the same time, on 6 February, Estonian authorities reported that 48,491 mostly Russian speakers had become naturalized Estonian citizens since 1992 (RFE/RL Daily Report, 7 Feb. 1995).

The 1995 elections showed that increased participation of Russophones has become a tendency. The growth in the number of eligible voters was from 661,074 in 1992 to 766,626 in 1995, an increase of 16.0% (Raun, 1997b, p. 355). This change reflected the growing number of non-Estonians who were acquiring citizenship. The ethnic Russian share of eligible voters had risen to slightly over 10% which obviously made possible the electoral success in 1995 of *Our Home is Estonia* (6 seats), a Russian-based alliance.[15] The Russian presence in *Riigikogu* has served as a mitigating factor. Most observers agree that *Our Home is Estonia* has played the role of a constructive opposition and found its niche as an advocate for the interests of the Russophones while being at the same time also loyal to an independent Estonia (Raun, 1997b, p. 361). Another sign of the new times was the passage of radical nationalist parties into parliamentary opposition.

The growth in numbers of applicants for Estonian citizenship reflected the increasing acceptance by non-citizens of the actual change in politics of nationhood. By 12 July 1995, the expiration date for registration of non-citizens, reportedly, some 324,000 non-Estonians had applied for residence and work permits in Estonia. In all, there are around 380,000 non-citizens living in Estonia, so this figure means that 80% of them have applied for legal status to remain (RFE/RL Daily Report, 13 Jul. 1995). Overall, since the second half of 1995, the naturalization has been proceeding steadily. By October 1996, already 83,536 people had applied for and received citizenship. Future citizenship applicants are mostly those who are currently stateless, which is almost 300,000 persons plus a certain number of Russian and other citizens and their children. It is believed that granting and acquisition of citizenship will occur more rapidly in the future, at least for the youth who have acquired the necessary proficiency in Estonian.

At the same time, by January 1, 1997, nearly 120,000 people in Estonia had Russian citizenship (RFE/RL Daily Report, 2 Jan. 1996). Estonian leaders have aired concern that the large number of Russian citizens on its territory poses a potential threat to Estonia's security. Obviously, this was one more perceived reason to go ahead with policies of integration. In view of this, new amendments were passed to the *Law on Aliens*, making easier the procedure of applications for citizenship. Thus, on 1 July 1997, despite opposition of the *Pro Patria* radicalists, Riigikogu passed amendments to the *Law on Aliens* granting the right to apply for permanent residence permits to non-citizens. Under the amended law, aliens who applied for a temporary residence permits before 12 July 1995 will be eligible to request permanent residency. It has been estimated that the amendment will apply to some 200,000 aliens, mostly from Russia and other CIS countries (RFE/RL Daily Report, 2 Jul. 1997).

The general discourse on nationhood has considerably changed among ethnic Estonian majority and integration comes to be perceived as an increasingly more reasonable option. The granting of citizenship was difficult in the case where a state has inherited a large number of immigrants with questionable loyalties, especially when the state itself is not yet built. Seven years have passed for Estonia since the restoration of independence.

The state has stabilized as much as it is possible in seven years. So has the population: a noteworthy portion of the non-Estonians have left, the majority have stayed and do not plan to leave.

Major change has also occurred with respect to the immigrants' view of themselves. Whereas a few years ago the majority of immigrants identified themselves mainly with the Soviet Union or Soviet culture, far more now identify themselves with Russia and Estonia (Kirch and Kirch, 1996, p. 202-4; Norgaard, 1996, p. 207). Furthermore, it is characteristic that many of the immigrants see themselves as a kind of diaspora Russians, not really part of either Russia or Estonia. Recently conducted surveys give grounds for optimism about the possibility of Russophones developing multiple and complementary identities (Vetik, 1994; idem, 1995; Linz and Stepan, 1996, p. 410-24; Kirch, 1994; Kirch and Kirch, 1996; Kirch, 1997).

Patterns of Ethnopolitical Crisis Management and Ethnic Peace: The Case of Estonia

There is a general agreement among scholars and observers alike that the most remarkable theme in Estonia that needs to be stressed throughout the last decade has been its exclusively non-violent nature of the transition from Soviet rule to a developing democratic system despite the existence of considerable ethnic tensions and much economic hardship. Haas (1996) has examined several psychological factors that account for ethnic non-violence in Estonia at three levels: each nationality group's attributes (real or imagined), the process of interaction at the social level, and the wider context of international relations (Haas, 1996, p. 48).

At the level of modalities of democratization processes, Raun (1997b, p. 342-6) has identified a larger number of factors: 1) the role of Estonia's previous historical development and inherited traditions, the fact that the use of violence was never part of modern Estonian political culture; 2) the recent origin of the ethnic tensions in Estonia, the fact that Russians and other non-Estonians are overwhelmingly recent immigrants and there are no deep-seated historical antagonisms to contend with 3) the ever decreasing potential for violence after the Soviet collapse has been on the side of non-violent development; 4) the favorable foreign policy situation in the region which contributed to the peaceful transition: Estonia had no territorial problems or serious disputes of any kind with its Baltic neighbors; it also benefited from the positive attitude of the Scandinavian states and their strong engagement in supporting Baltic integration with the West when the Scandinavian states seemed to begin to view the fate of the Baltic countries as an integral part of their own security; 5) the favorable international context when young Estonian democracy received significant backing from the major European powers, the US, and leading international organizations.

One more important factor needs be stressed. It concerns efficient and constructive pattern of management used in dealing with the interactional crisis in ethnic relations in connection with the *Law on Aliens*. The pattern reflected the viability of political institutions of Estonian democracy, particularly, the functioning of institutionalized checks and balances in relations between the *Riigikogu* and the presidency, constructive third-party mediation offered by European organizations and leaders, as well as restraint displayed by Russia. Overall, the joint action of the above has succeeded in preserving peace in intercommunal relations in Estonia.

An assessment of the quality of ethnic peace in present-day Estonia needs to take into consideration specific configuration and patterns of ethnopolitical crisis management at the system level. Nationhood has emerged as the major ethnopolitical problem area and the one which did indeed become a crisis in the first two years of restored independence. Building a new democratic system in Estonia has proved to be a daunting task. Above all, the most lasting legacy of Soviet rule - the drastically changed ethnic composition of the country - has militated against any rapid solution to the problem area of nationhood and political integration which remain on the agenda of democratic consolidation. Legacies of the past and core issues of identity are likely to continue to affect Estonia and its ethnic communities, as they attempt to shape multiethnic democracy. The key problems have revolved around the still-developing citizenship and language policies of the new governments.

In fact, in 1995 the Estonian political system was still absorbing both exclusionary and inclusionary pressures. Subsequent political developments in 1996-97 have demonstrated continuously unfolding dynamics and the capacity of the Estonian democracy to progress in the liberal direction increasingly involving the sphere of ethnic relations as well. The strategy of integrating non-Estonians, if successfully implemented, provides a reasonable chance to meet the challenges of ethnic divide in building a higher quality democracy. The issue is how quickly the 'titular' nationality will go through this period of soul-searching and crystallization and become ready to re-orient itself to the current multicultural society paradigm.

The most workable solution to the challenge of further democratic consolidation would focus on the process of integration, as opposed to assimilation, that is, encouraging non-Estonians to develop a multiple identity - retaining their ethnic roots, but also learning to participate and function in the Estonian political environment. Efficient and coherent policies of integrating non-Estonians into Estonian society seem to hold the keys for the successful dealing with the problem area of nationhood.

Ethnic peace in Estonia is much more than negative peace. Recent ethnopolitical developments, particularly since 1995, have demonstrated the gained momentum of the movement away from the extremes of ethnically perceived democracy towards an increasingly liberal foundation of the still elusive interethnic contract. The major gain achieved along the way has been that, in the current context, the problem area of nationhood increasingly finds its constructive and efficient management *within* the existing framework of Estonia's democratic institutions which is an evidence of viability and adaptability of the latter. At the same time, the peace relationship between ethnic communities in Estonia still cannot be considered a stable one. Russia is one of important external variables in this regard. Consolidation of democratic practices and institutional patterns within Estonia is another crucial variable. Realization of the existing potential for crafting democratic ethnic peace in Estonia, in the final analysis, hinges upon unfolding policies, discourse and institutional re-arrangements within the newly adopted strategies of integration. Influences incoming from European processes and established democracies are more than likely to result decisive for the final outcome. In this regard, the recommendation of the European Commission that Estonia begin negotiations on accession to the EU, expressed in July 1997 is an emblematic sign of the time.

Overall, the pattern of ethnopolitical dynamics in Estonia, as well as most recent developments in the international environment give reasonable grounds for a cautious optimism in assessing the prospects for the consolidation of both liberal democracy and ethnic peace in Estonia.

Notes

1   On history of Estonia in 1918-80s see, e.g. Raun (1987), Hiden and Salmon (1994), Norgaard (1996, ch.2), Lauristin and Vihalem (1997, ch.5).

2   Kirch and Kirch (1992, p. 94), see also Vetik (1993, p. 273). The deportation in June 1940 led to the loss of 10,157 people; in 1944 about 80,000 emigrated to the West; about 100,000 people were killed in the war, and 20, 702 were removed in another deportation in March 1949 (Misiunas and Taagepera, 1983, pp. 272-3).

3   Katus (1992, p. 2-3).

4   Housing patterns have been a consequence of special provisions provided for migrants. This policy was at least prceived to be at the expense of Estonians who had waited long years in queue (Ott, Kirch and Kirch, 1996, p. 13).

5   Norgaard (1996, p. 16). Raun (1997b, p. 335-8) observe, in this regard, that in view of Estonia's strategic geopolitical location on the southern shore of the Gulf of Finland, its role as a historical crossroads in the Baltic region is not surprising. 'Despite Russian and Soviet hegemony during much of the modern era, the formative influences in historical times in such key areas as education and religion came from the German states and Scandinavia. Thus, Estonia retained a 'pre-Russian' identity in terms of cultural background, and tsarist attempts at integration of the Estonians areas into the Russian cultural and political world came far too late to be successful. During the XXth century, especially in the interwar era and in the decades after 1956, Estonia developed a strong connection to Finland that also served as a counterbalance to great power influences from both east and west.'

6   *Molodezh Estonii*, March 5, 6, 1991. On differences between rural (where the population was mostly ethnically Estonian) and urban (mixed or predominantly Russophones) districts, see in Vetik (1993, p. 271). In areas of the non-titular nationalities, those for complete independence accounted for 65.7% in districts of Tallinn, 25.5% in Narva, in Kohtla-Järve approximately 46% (Saar, 1991, p. 13; Taagepera, 1992, p. 126). A survey carried out right before the referendum revealed that three main factors influenced support for independence among the non-Estonian population: (1) knowledge of the Estonian language; (2) number of years lived in Estonia; and (3) a perception that the standard of living in Estonia is higher than in other regions in the Soviet Union (Saar, 1991, p. 16).

7   With certain exceptions, like Georgia, the other states that gained independence as a result of the Soviet breakup defined themselves as 'new' rather that 'restored' states and, therefore, in 1991 these new states used some variety of the 'zero-option' approach to define citizenship: all legal residents at the time of independence were considered citizens

8   Chinn and Truex (1996, p. 134) rightfully stress that the citizenship laws of the "restored" Baltic democracies must be seen in their larger context, including not only the distinction between the restored state and the new state, but also the distinction between citizenship based on descent and citizenship based on residence; the citizenship laws in other states in the former USSR, and the policies used by several democracies in Western Europe.

9   Estonia's constitution, adopted in the referendum in June of 1992, confirmed the *ius sanguinis* as the basis of the citizenship right (Art. 8-1) and left the concretization of the conditions and procedures for the acquisition, loss, and restoration of citizenship to the simple law (Art. 8-5). See also Kask (1994, p. 381), Norgaard (1996, p. 197).

10 Estonian laws and their compliance with the international human rights standards are examined in Ginsburgs (1993), Drieesen (1994), Kask (1994), Weigant (1995).

11 Later, a non-Estonian was elected to fill a vacancy. In the previous parliament, elected in 1990, there had been more than 20 Russian speakers among the 105 deputies.

12 Among the latest works on post-Soviet Estonian elites see Steeen (1996) and (1997), Metcalf (1996), Liuhto (1996).
13 See collection of relevant documents published in Birckenbach (1997, pp. 117-299).
14 On 26 July a State Department spokesman announced that the US is contributing $15,000, while Swedish Foreign Minister Margaretha af Ugglas announced in Stockholm that Sweden would give 50,000 kronor for the same purpose. See also Sheehy (1993a, p. 10).
15 Raun (1997b, p. 362) observes that, however, not all eligible non-Estonian voters supported *Our Home is Estonia*. Of the major competitors, the Center party proved most successful with non-Estonian voters, presumably because of its advocacy of a strong social safety net and the popularity of its leader, Edgar Savisaar, among non-Estonians.

8 Lithuania

Historical and Demographic Background

Like Latvia and Estonia, during the two decades of 1918-40, Lithuania was an independent nation-state. Lithuania shares with the other two Baltic states the same experience of Soviet annexation and dominance. Unlike Estonia and Latvia, Lithuanian statehood has much deeper historical roots going back to medieval times, as well as a history of nationalist resistance within the XIXth century Russian empire. Another important difference is the fact that Lithuania had not suffered such dramatic demographic changes under the Soviet rule as Estonia and Latvia had. Post-war Lithuania was far less modernized and had a work force surplus, therefore, the immigration rate of non-Lithuanian population there was far lower (Zvidrins, 1994, p. 366).

The limited demographic pressure has been an important factor behind the absence of major ethnic conflict in Lithuania. Since Lithuania's incorporation into the USSR, the Russian share of the population had remained constant at the low level of around 8-10%, which is much the same as in the interwar period (see Table 8.1). At independence, the Russian minority was only 9.4% of the total population of the republic's 3.7 million. Russians in Lithuania seem better integrated than in any other former Soviet republic. The proportion of Russians who speak Lithuanian makes 37% which is much higher than in any other successor state.

There is also an important Polish minority of 7.0%, which presence has roots in the pre-Soviet era and by no means can be related to the Soviet occupation (Senn, 1997, p. 356). In contrast to Russians, the Poles in Lithuania have a territorial basis, being compactly concentrated in and around Vilnius in Eastern Lithuania. Most Lithuanians regard the 'Polish question' as much more acute than the problems in Lithuanian-Russian relations. Particular tensions exist in the Polish-populated Salcininkai rural district which is very isolated and characterized by low education and living standards. Area students point out at Lithuania's bad historical experiences with Poland which apparently overshadow the bad relations with the Soviet Union or Russia. The Polish occupation of the Vilnius area during the interwar years and historical conflicts have resulted in a perception of the Poles as a kind of fifth column aiming to incorporate parts of Lithuania into Poland (Zubek, 1993; Norgaard, 1996, p. 175, 185; Burant, 1996).

Table 8.1   Dynamics of Lithuania's Ethnic Composition

	1970		1979	
Nationality	in 1000s	in %	in 1000s	in %
Lithuanians	2,506.8	80.1	2,712.2	80.0
Russians	268.0	8.6	303.5	8.9
Poles	240.2	7.7	247.0	7.3
Ukrainians	25.1	0.8	32.0	1.0
Belarusans	45.4	1.5	57.6	1.7
Jews	23.6	0.8	14.7	0.4
Other	19.1	0.5	24.5	0.7

	1989		1997	
Nationality	in 1000s	in %	in 1000s	in %
Lithuanians	2,924.3	79.6	3,024.3	81.6
Russians	344.5	9.4	304.8	8.2
Poles	250.0	7.0	256.6	6.9
Ukrainians	44.8	1.2	36.9	1.0
Belarusans	63.2	1.7	54.5	1.5
Jews	12.4	0.3	5.2	0.1
Other	27.6	0.8	24.9	0.7

Source: Demographic Data Collection of Estonia, Latvia and Lithuania (1998).

As a result of the small proportion of non-Lithuanians, less demographic 'anxiety' and the heterogeneity of the minorities, the

Lithuanians never introduced an exclusionary policy on citizenship and thus, present-day Lithuania is viewed as a country that does not really have significant tension between the logic of a nation-state and the logic of a liberal democracy (Linz and Stepan, 1996, p. 405). This does not mean, however, the absence of ethnopolitical problem areas under democratization.

Ethnopolitical Problem Areas and Crises under Democratization

Stages of Democratization in Lithuania

Overall, the dynamics of democratization processes in Lithuania falls into three main periods: 1) decay of authoritarian rule and upsurge of ethnopolitical mobilization (1988 - February 1990); 2) democratic transition, falling between first free elections held to the Lithuanian SSR's Supreme Soviet in February 1990 and the 'founding elections' to the Seimas of independent Republic of Lithuania in October-November 1992 followed by presidential elections in February 1993; 3) the on-going period of democratic consolidation (since 1993 onwards).

Political and Ethnic Mobilization Under Authoritarian Decay (1987-89)

During the last years of Soviet history, the conflict between separatist Lithuania and less than reformed Soviet federation was manifestly the most intense and dramatic. In origin, the confrontation between the Lithuanians and the central authorities in Moscow involved a clash of fundamentally opposed ideas of 'statehood'. Soviet ideologists had claimed that a nationality could best realize its potential as part of a multinational state directed from Moscow, and they denounced the 'bourgeois nationalism' as a false doctrine built on class oppression. Asserting a stronger national consciousness in the late 1980s, Lithuanians insisted that a nationality could best realize its potential when it ruled itself as a sovereign national state. In this respect, Senn and Motulaite (1993, p. 25) have pointed out that the Lithuanian concept of statehood, as perceived by the majority of intellectual and political elites, was intimately linked to the national pride.

> Lithuania, they insisted, had a right and a historical destiny to be an independent state. In contrast to the concepts of sovereignty (*suverenumas* or *severenitetas*) or self-dependency, (*savarankis kumas*), both of which could be just 'partial', *valstybingumas* was generally understood as an absolute

right, an indivisible ideal. The resulting conflict shook the Soviet state to its foundation.

At the onset of the Gorbachev liberalization Lithuanian intelligentsia grew enthusiastic. In June of 1988, an 'Initiative Group' of 36 prominent scholars and intellectuals was formed at Lithuanian Academy of Sciences with the declared aim to organize the Lithuanian Movement in Support of Perestroika (*Lietuvos Persitvarkymo Sajudis*), or, as it became better known, *Sajudis* (Sovetskaya Litva, hereafter SL, 24 Jun. 1988). Initially, *Sajudis* spokespersons, all of whom held responsible positions in Soviet society, eschewed political goals and declared the movement to be a response to calls for *perestroika* and the establishment of a government 'ruled by law'. Therefore, at first, they limited themselves to stressing concerns about the cultural rights and the environmental protection of the Lithuanian nation (On the events of 1987-88 in Lithuania see Senn, 1990 and 1991; Lieven, 1993).

Being perceived as an expression of Lithuanian national feeling, *Sajudis* quickly won broad support and became the focus of a powerful national movement. On 24 June, 1988, in the Cathedral Square of Vilnius, *Sajudis* called an open 'send-off' rally with Lithuanian delegates elected to the XIXth CPSU Conference, attended by estimated 50,000 participants (SL, 25 Jun. 1998). On 23 August, the day of the anniversary of the Molotov-Ribbentrop pact, *Sajudis* rally at the Vignis park in Vilnius gathered already over 250 thousand sympathizers (SL, 25 Aug. 1988).

The Founding Congress of *Sajudis*, held in Vilnius on October 22-23, was televised throughout Lithuania. The new movement, reportedly, united over 1000 local groups of support. The adopted Program defined the specific goals of *Sajudis* as restoration of political, economic and cultural sovereignty of Lithuanian SSR, as well as introducing republican economic self-management, proclaiming the supremacy of republican legislation over the USSR laws on Lithuania's territory and the right of Lithuanian SSR to independent diplomatic relations and participation in international organizations (SL, 23 Oct., 24 Oct. 1988).

After its founding convention, *Sajudis* came into rapid ascendance as a republican-wide organization with ever growing number of supporters and progressively radicalizing its politics. As in Estonia and Latvia, the same divide between moderate pragmatists and radical fundamentalists manifested among Lithuanian elites. One group, mostly intellectuals from Vilnius, tended to advocate reform and favored using the momentum of the late 1980s to adapt Soviet institutions to the new life. Their opponents, more radical activists from Kaunas and other parts of the republic did not consider anything in the Soviet system to be worth saving and demanded that all institutions associated with it should be razed' (Senn, 1994, p. 81).

In October 1988 Algirdas Brazauskas became First Secretary of the Lithuanian Communist Party (CP), not without support of *Sajudis* sympathizers. Like in Estonia, the fall of 1988 in Lithuania saw impressive popular mobilization against the draft constitutional amendments proposed by the USSR's central authorities which aimed at reducing the already curtailed sovereignty of Union republics. During that period, however, Brazauskas urged moderation on his compatriots, fearing that Moscow might establish a tougher direct control over the republic. On 18-19 November, 1988, Lithuanian Supreme Soviet sharply criticized a number of provisions of the USSR draft laws on constitutional amendments and electoral system reform. At the same time, the Lithuanian parliament refused to vote Declaration on Sovereignty like the one adopted in Estonia, but instead, expressed for elaboration of a new draft republican constitution. In order to placate national feelings of Lithuanians, the parliamentary session voted amendments in the acting republican Constitution which legalized the use of Lithuanian national tricolor as Lithuania's new official flag and gave the *National Song* the status of Lithuania's new anthem (SL, 19 Nov., 20 Nov., 1988). After the session, *Sajudis* activists staged piquet of protest decrying 'coward' decisions of the MPs who were afraid to follow Estonia's example in directly challenging the USSR central authorities (SL, 23 Nov. 1988).

The situation changed already in spring of 1989 when *Sajudis* achieved an overwhelming victory in the election of deputies for the USSR Congress of People's deputies to be held Moscow. Sajudis-supported candidates won 36 of the 42 seats contested in Lithuania (SL, 28 Feb. 1989).

By mid-1989 *Sajudis* openly started to speak of the desire to re-establish Lithuania's independence. On 18 May, 1989, the eve of the forthcoming USSR Congress of People's Deputies (CPD), the Lithuanian Supreme Soviet adopted the Declaration on the State Sovereignty of Lithuania proclaiming the supremacy of republican legislation over the USSR laws and voted constitutional amendments granting the republic the rights to veto Soviet laws, to control immigration, and to possess exclusive ownership rights on its land and natural resources (SL, 19 May 1989).

On the eve of the 50th anniversary of Molotov-Ribbentrop pact the Lithuanian Supreme Soviet commission published its report which qualified the 1940 events as occupation and forced annexation of Lithuania by the USSR and suggested the Lithuanian Supreme Soviet should annul its 1940 Declaration on Lithuania's entry into the USSR (SL, 22 Aug. 1989). On the day of the pact's anniversary, massive demonstrations and the human chain 'Baltic way' were held throughout the Baltic region (SL, 24 Aug. 1989).

Further progress of Lithuania's taking distance from the Soviet framework was made in December of 1989 when the Lithuanian parliament voted at 243 to 1 to exclude the provisions on the guiding role of the Communist Party from the LSSR Constitution. Other amendments provided for legalization of the multi-party system (SL, 8 Dec. 1989). On December 20, the Lithuanian Communist Party (LCP) Congress voted a declaration of independence from the Communist Party of the Soviet Union (SL, 21 Dec., 24 Dec. 1989). The minority of the congress delegates, constituted the rump Communist Party of Lithuania on the CPSU Platform (CPL/CPSU).

Countermobilization among pro-Union forces in Lithuania was considerably weaker than in either Latvia or Estonia. In November 1988, local representatives of Union-based industrial enterprises and of some cultural institutions of Vilnius attempted to organize the *Yedinstvo* movement deemed as an alternative to *Sajudis*. The majority of the *Yedinstvo* activists denied the priority of the language of the titular ethnicity in Lithuania and demanded a resolute 'struggle for broad use of Russian in the state-run offices, enterprises and institutions' (SL, 18 May, 1989). *Yedinstvo* failed as a movement. Already its first congress on 13-14 May 1989, saw its fragmentation because of personal ambitions of different leaders of hard-line 'defenders of socialist choice' (SL, 16 May 1989).

Single time actions, sponsored by the communist party officials and management of the Union-subordinated industrial enterprises, apparently, had more success among large masses of workers at those factories, if held during the working hours. On 3 February, some 20 thousand residents of the city of Snieckus, mostly personnel of the Ignalina power station and their relatives, were drawn to the protest rally against the recently adopted decree on languages (SL, 4 Feb. 1989). On 8 February, reportedly, 'tens of thousands' of workers at the Vilnius electro-motive factory took part at a similar rally organized by the management and activists of *Yedinstvo* during the lunch break (SL, 9 Feb. 1989). Overall, political mobilization among Russian speakers had been limited precisely because it evolved not along the ethnic lines, but was, instead, based almost exclusively on the divide between conservatives and supporters of the reforms.

Mobilization among ethnic Poles, though also to a large extent inspired by local communist authorities, was somewhat different. Basically, it manifested in locally-based separatism of Polish-populated areas. On February 8, 1989, the session of local Soviet of Rukainjai *apilinka* (district) where ethnic Poles made up 82% of population declared district autonomy within Lithuania and demanded legalization of three official languages - Lithuanian, Russian and Polish in the area (*Komjaunimo Tiesa*, 10 Feb., 14 Feb. 1989). In April, the Voluntary Association of Polish Culture announced its separation from the Lithuanian Fund of Culture and renamed itself into the League of Poles of Lithuania. Reportedly, the League united about 12 thousand supporters. Its Chart announced the protection of political and civil rights of Poles as its main goal, while the conference's resolution demanded to legalize application of Polish as the official language on the territory of Vilnius region and called to set up Polish territorial autonomy within Lithuania (*Komjaunimo Tiesa*, 19 Apr. 1989).

In September 1989, the session of local Soviets in Vilnius region and in Salcininkai district unilaterally proclaimed the formation of self-governing Polish national-territorial districts within Lithuania. The majority of local deputies pledged allegiance to the 'socialist choice' and 'indissoluble unity of the USSR' and proposed that three languages (Russian, Polish, and Lithuanian) be given the status of official languages on the territory of the would-be autonomy (SL, 8 Sept. 1989). Lithuanian authorities responded by inviting those local Soviets to submit draft amendments to the Law on the Application of Official Language and established the Committee for Nationalities under the aegis of the Lithuania's Council of Ministers. Actually, the Committee for Nationalities was the first organization of its kind in the former Soviet Union which explicit aim was to monitor and address the problems of ethnic minorities (Vaitiekus, 1992, p. 10).

Ethnopolitics and Democratic Transition

Lithuania pioneered proclamation of independence among former Soviet Union republics in 1990 and openly challenged the Soviet rule. The resulting crisis of recognition, in fact, was a manifestation of the crisis of stateness that had plagued the USSR during the last years of its existence. The developments also became an interactional crisis in relations between the Soviet and Lithuania. Attempted crisis management by the Union center was predominantly destructive and included coercive bargaining, economic blockade, threats of violence and actual small-scale violent repression, unilaterally applied by agents of the Soviet central state against non-violent protesters. Third-party activities involved diplomatic pressure of Western and East European countries upon Gorbachev government and large-scale protest campaigns throughout the Soviet Union against application of force in Lithuania. The end result was the ultimate delegitimation of the Soviet rule in Lithuania among both the titular nationality and the larger part of ethnic minorities and, effectively, restoration of Lithuanian independence in the wake of the failed Moscow coup of August 1991.

The same period was marked by new outbreaks of assertive ethnoterritorial separatism of Polish-dominated rural districts which indicates that the problem of stateness was present within Lithuania itself. At the same time, the nature of Polish-Lithuanian disputes, the limited objectives pursued by Polish separatists (not secession, but autonomy), and the constructive position taken by the Lithuanian authorities, succeeded in keeping the problem of stateness short of critical level.

Transition to Independence and Crisis of Recognition (1990-91)

Overall, the Lithuanian crisis of recognition lasted for over a year and had passed several stages. First crisis escalation occurred in winter of 1990. The triggering event which unleashed crisis interaction between Lithuania and the Soviet Union authorities were the first democratic elections to the Lithuanian republican parliament (the LSSR Supreme Soviet) and the atmosphere of anticipated imminence of proclamation of Lithuania's independence.

On February 24, 1990, Lithuania moved up run-off elections for republican Supreme Soviet, a week earlier the initially scheduled date, in show of concern that Gorbachev might have emergency presidential powers by mid-March. *Sajudis*-backed candidates won about 80% of the seats to the new Lithuanian parliament with the reported voter turnover of 71%. Among the newly elected MPs 115 were ethnic Lithuanians, 9 ethnic Poles and 5 ethnic Russians. As regards differences in affiliation, 90 MPs supported the *Sajudis* program, 38 were members of independent Lithuanian CP, 9 - Social Democrats, 4 - members of the rump Lithuanian CP/CPSU, 3 members of the 'Green' party, 2 Christian Democrats and 1 member of the Lithuanian Democratic Party (SL, 6 Mar. 1990, *Letuvos Rytas*, 3 Mar. 1990). *Sajudis* leader Vitautas Landsbergis was elected Chairman of the new Lithuania's parliament while Kasimera Prunskiene, affiliated with the independent Lithuanian CP, was nominated prime-minister (*Soglasiye*, 18 Mar. 1990).

On March 11, Lithuanian parliament voted the *Act on Restoration of Independent Lithuanian State*. All 124 MPs who were present during the voting unanimously approved the act. The Provisional Basic Law of Lithuanian Republic was adopted to replace the acting Constitution of the Lithuanian SSR. The Basic Law included provisions of the 1938 Lithuanian Constitution with amendments made in 1988-1989.

On March 15, the USSR Congress of People's Deputies declared invalid the Act and resolutions adopted by Lithuanian Supreme Soviet (*Izvestiya*, 16 Mar. 1990). Communist conservatives in the former Soviet Union urged increased pressure on the republic. Some of the milder demands were making Lithuania pay $33 billion in hard currency as price of secession and challenging republican boundaries, suggesting Lithuania was to surrender first the port of Klaipeda and Vilnius rural area which were added to Lithuania after its entry into the USSR (*Izvestiya*, 17 March 1990). Simultaneously, instances of pro-Soviet activism were orchestrated. In late March, the USSR loyalists from CPL/CPSU in Vilnius announced the founding conference of the so-called Committee of Soviet Citizens of Lithuania, or CSCL (*Ekho Litvy*, hereafter EL, 28 Mar. 1990). On April 4, the rally of Russophone workers and CSCL activists in Vilnius demanded resignation of Lithuania's government and abrogation of all latest decisions of the Lithuanian Parliament. In case of refusal to satisfy their claims the CSCL declared its plans of a preventive strike at Union-subordinated enterprises, simultaneously appealing to the USSR President requesting the presidential rule (i.e. martial law) in Lithuania (EL, 5 Apr. 1990). On April 7, an estimated 250-300,000 supporters of Lithuanian independence held a counter-rally in support of the proclaimed independence (EL, 8 Apr. 1990).

Trying to regain control over the situation, Gorbachev threatened to impose direct control over Lithuania in case of civil conflict while still calling for political resolution and holding both republican and Union-wide referenda on the future status of Lithuania. In their ultimatum letter to the Lithuanian parliament USSR President Gorbachev and Premier Ryzhkov threatened Lithuania with a ban on crucial supplies if the republic's authorities would not rescind the Act on Independence giving 48 hours to respond. On April 19, the Soviet authorities imposed a blockade on Lithuania, stopping the shipment of oil and gasoline while permitting only about 20% of the normal deliveries of natural gas to the republic (*Izvestiya*, 20 Apr. 1990). Gorbachev leadership also banned the shipment of other goods, such as coffee and sugar, that supposedly could be sold for hard currency. At the same time, reportedly, Gorbachev made sure the Moscow loyalists in the Polish regions received supplies as usual (Senn, 1997, p. 359).

On May 15, 1990, the session of Salcininkai district Soviet voted non-recognition of Lithuanian independence and decreed to continue application of the USSR laws on the territory subject to its authority, calling in the meantime for the USSR-wide referendum on future status of Lithuania (EL, 16 May 1990). With the USSR central authorities advanced the idea of a new Union treaty, some communist nomenklatura leaders among Poles came out with the idea to establish a Polish Soviet Socialist Republic as part of the 'renewing' USSR (Senn, 1997, p. 359).

Although the blockade seriously disrupted the Lithuanian economy, the republic resisted the pressure from Moscow. While Gorbachev found himself increasingly embarrassed by the lingering impasse, Lithuanian leadership was split on the issue as to what to do. Parliamentary debates on the proposed moratorium marked the beginnings of party politics in Lithuania. At the end of June, Lansbergis finally agreed to promise a 'moratorium' on legislation supporting the Act of March 11, and Gorbachev immediately lifted the imposed restrictions on deliveries to Lithuania (EL, 22 Jun. 1990).

Frustrated by the failure of the blockade, the CPL/CPSU leaders in Lithuania set about to imitate mobilization of Russian and Polish workers for an assault on the government, simultaneously launching continuous appeals for Gorbachev to establish 'presidential rule' and to ensure 'true proletarian internationalism' in Lithuania. The culmination of this process came in January 1991 in the shadow of the beginning of the Gulf war in which western powers engaged Iraq. This time, the crisis escalation was even more dramatic (Vebra, 1994, p. 187).

The triggering event was the January 2 declaration by Landsbergis that Lithuania withdraws the moratorium on its Act of Independence (*Letuvos Rytas*, 3 Jan. 1991). On January 8, the CPL-CPSU and activists of CSCL mobilized small-numbered groups of dissatisfied workers of the Union-subordinated enterprises for a protest rally against the sharp rise of prices on food products announced by the Lithuanian government. A group of the rally's participants attempted to attack the parliamentary building by rushing into it. Parliament's guards used cold water and fire-pumps to prevent rioting and disperse the crowd. The rally leaders presented the MPs with a petition threatening general strike if their demands be unmet by January 9. The same day Lithuanian parliament suspended the government's decree on price hikes (EL, 9 Jan. 1991). Prunskiene resigned on January 8 and was replaced by A. Simenas (Krikus, 1993, p. 175).

Reports of Soviet troops' moves to and within Lithuania appeared over the next several days, punctuated by everyday threats from Gorbachev that Lithuanians had to 'stop breaking the law'. Protests of workers, organized at Union-subordinated enterprises, went on escalating. On January 9, Russian speaking workers of Vilnius factories rallied again, this time they numbered several thousand and demanded immediate dissolution of the parliament, restoration of the supremacy of the USSR legislation in Lithuania, dissolution of the Lithuanian parliament and introduction of presidential rule from Moscow. In counteraction, groups of Lithuanians started to arrive *en masse* in front of the parliament and governmental buildings to defend them from eventual attack by the Soviet forces. Police managed to separate the opposing crowds and to prevent clashes. The USSR President addressed the Lithuanian MPs calling to return to the status *ante* March 11, 1990 and to abrogate all previously adopted acts that contradicted the Soviet constitution. Gorbachev kept stressing that representatives of public organizations in Lithuania were urging upon him to introduce presidential rule (EL, 10 Jan. 1991).

On January 11, as the Siemenas government took office, Soviet troops began occupying strategic buildings in Vilnius. USSR paratroopers took the buildings of the House of Press, Department for the Defense of Homeland, international telephone and telegraph offices in Vilnius. The same afternoon, 60,000 Russian-speakers were mobilized in front of the building of the Lithuanian Supreme Soviet, urging dissolution of the parliament and introduction of presidential rule (EL, 12 Jan. 1991).

The political tangle in Lithuania took a new twist on Sunday, January 13, when the *Sajudis* majority in parliament installed a new prime minister, G. Vagnorius. On the following night, Soviet paratroopers and KGB forces attacked the Vilnius TV tower and the nearby Radio center. These assaults seemed to be a part of a series of steps that would precipitate a declaration of presidential rule from Moscow and the eventual replacement of the Lithuanian government with Lithuanian communists who remained loyal to the CPSU and had formed the so-called Committee for the National Salvation (CNS). In clashes with the crowd of unarmed civilians Soviet troops opened fire in which 14 Lithuanians were killed, hundreds wounded and three went missing (EL,13 Jan. 1991; *Izvestiya*, 14 Jan. 1991). CNS declared emergency and imposed curfew in Vilnius and Kaunas.

The potent wave of protest across the Soviet Union and around the world prevented further violence by the Soviet troops. On January 14, the commission of the USSR Supreme Soviet arrived in Vilnius. The day after, the curfew was rescinded in Vilnius and Soviet troops started to leave city. Military patrols remained for indeterminate period. Soviet troops, now clearly playing the role of an occupying army, controlled the streets and supported the rump CPL/CPSU (*Respublika*, 15 Jan. 1991).

The bloodshed in Vilnius, unleashed by Soviet troops with the plan to suffocate emerging Lithuanian democracy and to reinstall the communist-run CNS, de-ethnicized the conflict over Lithuanian independence and, actually, contributed to the mitigation of tensions between Russian speakers and Lithuanians. At the peak of the January crisis, Russians responded positively to Landsbergis calls upon the Russian-speakers for solidarity in the name of democracy and freedom. Many ethnic Russians came to the parliamentary square protesting together with Lithuanians against the USSR military. An influential leader of the Russian community, archbishop Khrysostom joined president Lansbergis in the barricaded parliament building. Attitudes of many ethnic Russians changed after the 'Bloody Sunday'. In mourning over the casualties of the Soviet assault, the Ignalina workers on 14 January called off an economically motivated strike scheduled for the following day (RFE/RL Daily Report, 25 Jan. 1991).

Gratitude and generosity of the Lithuanian majority were quick to follow. On 29 January, the Lithuanian law on ethnic minorities was amended to give the non-Lithuanians many new rights. According to the amendments, a minority language may be used on a par with the state language in areas with 'substantial numbers of a minority with a different language'. The state pledged to provide financial aid for the development of minorities' culture and education (Kolstoe, 1995, p. 141; EL, 30 Jan. 1991).

On February 9, at the plebiscite on independence the Lithuanian legislators received solid support from the non-titular ethnic groups. A turnout of 84% of the voters and 90% 'Yes' votes, meant that a large number of Russians supported Lithuanian independence. At the same time, tensions in Lithuanian-Polish relations were slower to subside. Only 20.8%

of the voters in the Vilnius and Shalchininkai rural districts declared in support of Lithuanian independence (EL, 12 Feb. 1991). Polish-populated areas remained strongholds of conservatives. Their local Soviets held on their territories the USSR referendum on the preservation of the Soviet Union which was officially boycotted by Lithuania. (EL, 24 Mar. 1991).

The last months of Soviet control over Lithuania saw a new wave of separatist demands in Polish-dominated districts. III rd Congress of deputies at all levels of Vilnius and Shalchininkai rural districts, held on May 22, demanded speeding up of the work of the State Commission on the problems of East Lithuania set up with the task to propose a bill on the status of Polish-populated area. 199 out of 201 deputies voted in favor of territorial autonomy for the Vilnius rural area with the capital in Novo-Vilnja where non-Lithuanians make up 72% of the population. The projected autonomous region was thought to be ruled by a representative body - Seim Vilenzchizna, to have 3 official languages and a triple citizenship (Polish, Lithuanian and Soviet) for the region's residents. Subsequently, the Lithuanian parliament declared void these resolutions, while inviting local governments to participate more actively at the State Commission (EL, 24 May, 25 May 1991).

Many observers agree that much of the illiberal energy in Lithuanian nationalism seems to have been spent in the confrontation between the independence movement and the Polish separatists. The conflict reached its climax in August 1991, when local Polish leaders openly supported the conspirators in Moscow and demanded the creation of an autonomous Polish-Lithuanian socialist republic on Lithuanian territory (EL, 24 Aug. 1991; Norgaard, 1996, p. 184). After the failed coup, on September 4, local Soviets in the Polish districts were dissolved on the grounds of their declared support to the Moscow coup leaders. Later the same month, Lithuanian parliament introduced direct rule in Vilnius and Sialcininkai rural districts for the period of six months which was prolonged in 1992. In addition, in 1992, the administrative borders were changed in such a way as to render the Poles a minority in all electoral districts.

Lithuania At Independence: Ethnopolitical Problem Areas

The August coup of 1991 in Moscow finally resolved the impasse in Lithuania. After the successfully completed transition with the parliamentary elections in October 1992 Lithuania went ahead with consolidating its democracy. During the six years since those 'founding elections', democratic institutions in Lithuania have experienced progressive and consistent development. Many observers note that Lithuania has particularly succeeded in establishing a truly democratic political party system. While much remains before democracy is consolidated in Lithuania, the current party system indicates that the republic's political elites and general populace have demonstrate a significant degree of acceptance of democratic rules and procedures (Clark, 1995, pp. 41-62).

Stateness continued to be a problem area in relations with the Polish minority during the first post-independence years. First wave of post-communist Polish leaders were primarily persons with strong affiliations with the Lithuanian Communist Party/CPSU, and only initially it had been easy for them to convince the Poles living in the countryside that an independent Lithuania would not adequately safeguard their interests. The skepticism of the Polish minority did not decrease when in September 1991 the *Sajudis* government dissolved the local community groups who had supported the coup in Moscow and the demand for autonomy. At the same time, the conflict between Lithuanians and Poles was intensified by problems related to privatization and restitution of farm land. In 1994 Lithuania and Poland signed a friendship treaty, which was ratified by a large majority of the Lithuanian parliament. Subsequently, the Polish organizations, i.e., primarily the Union of Poles and the leading Polish media, adopted a conciliatory line towards collaborating with the government. The Union of Poles obtained four seats in parliament, though their poor election results show that very few people vote according to ethnic affiliation. Recent opinion polls suggest that the Poles' satisfaction with the government, the state and the country's status as an independent republic has been steadily in ascendance (Kolstoe, 1995, p. 141-2; Norgaard, 1996, p. 184).

Lithuanian Conservatives returned to power at the national elections in fall of 1996. Though this can somewhat increase the level of Lithuanian-Polish tensions, on the whole, it seems that those can still be managed constructively within the framework of democratic institutions of Lithuanian state, so the likelihood that stateness can emerge as a crisis appears decreasingly low. The other two ethnopolitical problem areas (stateness and nationhood) have been much less salient on the agenda of democratic consolidation in Lithuania and the general tendency has been towards their effective management.

Towards Consolidation of Multiethnic Democracy (1992-onwards)

Most observers agree that ethnopolitics in independent Lithuania has been mostly benign because based on two implemented strategies - civic integration and multiculturalism (Resler, 1997, p.101).

The strategy of civic integration takes ground in liberal citizenship policies. In defining its citizenry Lithuania took the same approach of a 'restored state' like Estonia and Latvia, i.e., the principle of legal continuity. Unlike its two neighbors, Lithuanian approach to naturalizing noncitizens who were resident at the time of independence, was different and it has managed to avoid creating large group of stateless population. The Lithuanian government accepted the 'zero-option' concept of citizenship, making all persons residing and working in Lithuania as of 1989 eligible for citizenship. Lithuanian inclusive and liberal approach to citizenship policies have been based on its *Law on Citizenship*, adopted on 3 November 1989, several years before the real independence. The Lithuanian law contains a provision basing automatic citizenship on the pre-Soviet period.[1] In addition, however, two provisions of the law broadened the base of initial body of citizens. First, all permanent residents born in Lithuania or those who could show one of their parents or grandparents was born there were also granted automatic citizenship, provided they did not have citizenship from any other country. Second, those residing on the territory as of November 1989 when the law was enacted and who did not meet the other criteria could still become automatic citizens by signing, within two years, a loyalty declaration stating that they would support the Lithuanian constitution and laws as well as 'respect its state sovereignty and territorial integrity'(Girnius, 1991, p. 21; Brubaker, 1992b, p. 281).

According to a treaty between Lithuania and Russia in July 1991, the option of automatic citizenship without naturalization was extended to those who entered Lithuania after November 1989 but before the signing of the treaty. For those choosing this option under the 1989 law and 1991 treaty there was no language requirement. Taking Lithuanian citizenship, however, meant renouncing Soviet citizenship. The final solution, however, was a compromise: citizens were to carry USSR passports until 'full state sovereignty' was regained (Barrington, 1995, p. 734).

According to the Lithuanian citizenship law (Art. 15), naturalization was possible by showing a knowledge of the Lithuanian language, maintaining permanent residence for ten years, possessing a permanent source of income, promising to obey and showing a knowledge of the Lithuanian constitution, and signing a loyalty statement similar to that for automatic citizens but also stating a respect for Lithuania's state 'language, culture, customs and traditions'. While the naturalization demands were not easy, the requirements for automatic citizenship were quite inclusive, so that nearly everyone of residents was eligible for citizenship. Out of a population of over 3.5 million, roughly only 350,000 permanent residents did not receive citizenship before the 2-year period expired. Today, 95% of those living in Lithuania are citizens through either their birth or naturalization, and can participate fully in the state's political life (Chinn and Truex, 1996, p. 136).

With the end of the 2-year period and with independence a reality, a new citizenship law was put in place on 5 December 1991. The major difference between the new law and the 1989 law was the elimination of automatic citizenship without naturalization. Naturalization requirements, however, remained mostly similar to the 1989 law.[2] One difference was a line inserted at the end of Article 12 in the 1991 law, which stated: 'Persons meeting the conditions specified in this Article shall be granted citizenship of the Republic of Lithuania *taking into consideration the interests of the Republic of Lithuania*'. This statement seemed to open the door for the refusal of naturalization even for those who met the requirements, though so far, there have been no protests on any implementation of this provision claiming denial of naturalization for qualified applicants.

On the side of the integrationist policies, in addition to supporting the development of national cultures, Lithuania has tried to integrate minorities into the economic, political, and cultural life of the country, enabling their equal participation. Under a policy of integration, the state encourages the national groups to engage in economic activities and compete in political process on an equal footing with the dominant nationality. To this end, the state is trying to decrease the economic and educational disparities between nationalities and to train national specialists (Resler, 1997, p. 103).

Multiculturalism has been another corner stone of ethnopolitics in Lithuania. Actually, almost since its very inception, the intensity of the Lithuanian nationalist movement, did not pose a serious threat to Lithuania's minorities or to interethnic relations, because the republic had already adopted significant guarantees of minority rights. It was also a conscious action taken to prevent minority unrest, particularly among the Poles and the Russians, in the event that Lithuania regained its independence. Political leaders wanted to reassure the countries' minorities that their rights would be safeguarded in an independent Lithuania.[3]

At independence, Lithuania developed a general conception of nationalities policy and began actively promoting a group-oriented policy of multiculturalism. The concomitant guarantees of individual and group rights were deemed as integral parts of the effort to promote the multicultural society (Kobeckaité, 1992, p. 7). Indeed, the republic's constitution, adopted on 25 October 1992, stresses both the guaranteed rights of individuals, regardless of nationality, and the rights of national communities. The framers of Lithuanian constitution conceived of individual-level and group-level rights as complimentary, not contradictory. All citizens have the right to foster their native languages, customs and cultures, and national communities may independently administer their cultural, educational, and charitable associations.

In cooperation with a network of state-supported associations of ethnic minorities, the government has been seeking to actively promote their development first by supporting schools or programs offering some level of instruction in the native languages of minorities. According to Lithuanian Law on National Minorities teaching in the relevant minority language should be offered in areas where the minority in question lives compactly and is in the majority.[4] The Lithuanian government has strictly adhered to its program, e.g., a Belarusan school with only nine pupils has been established (Norgaard, 1996, p. 187). Contrary to Estonia and Latvia, the requirement that employees should master Lithuanian at a certain level applies only to public employees and not to those in the private sector. The government is also trying to ensure that minorities have the opportunity to participate in their own religious observances and is trying to return churches, mosques, and synagogues to respective communities and to assist them in renovating the facilities (Vaitiekus, 1994, p. 33-5).

At the same time, analysts observe that Lithuania's emphasis on multiculturalism and minority rights did not always include as many freedoms and rights for minorities as it now does. The development and implementation of the Law on National Minorities was an evolutionary process involving substantial lobbying by ethnic minorities to change some provisions of Lithuanian law that they found restrictive. Several of the amendments on language and education were proposed by the Council of National Communities, an organization composed of delegates from minority associations and affiliated with the Department of Nationalities.[5] Chief among their concerns was the requirement that all citizens of

Lithuania become proficient in Lithuanian. Minorities succeeded in having the deadline for proficiency extended to 1995 from 1993 and also won the right to use minority languages along with Lithuanian in offices in their areas of compact settlement.

Integrationist priorities seem to have come to the fore in the sphere of language policies after the Lithuanian parliament adopted a new language law on 31 January 1995, according to which Lithuanian is established as the only state language. According to this law, all legislation will be adopted and published only in Lithuanian, and the language used in central, regional and local administrations must be Lithuanian as well.

Patterns of Ethnopolitical Crisis Management and Ethnic Peace: The Case of Lithuania

Lithuanian case is similar to Estonian, as regards the predominantly non-violent nature of the country's democratic transition and consolidation. During the Soviet period, more radical and assertive stances taken by Lithuanian authorities in transition to independence, effectively, provoked more aggressive response on behalf of Soviet Union authorities. The crisis of recognition following Lithuania's proclamation of independent statehood in 1990, actually, was the reverse side of the crisis of stateness of the Soviet Union itself that together with similar developments in other Union republics led to the its disintegration in 1991. The USSR government used mostly destructive patterns of crisis management, like coercive bargaining, economic blockade, and violent repression.

In systemic terms, patterns by which ethnopolitical problem areas were managed in post-Soviet Lithuania are impressively telling of the success of the liberal approach to nationhood, based on inclusive citizenship policies and strategies of civic integration and multiculturalism. Unlike its two other Baltic neighbors, Lithuania has succeeded in dealing with problem areas of stateness, state effectiveness and nationhood *within* the viable framework of its democratic institutions and to keep ethnopolitical issues short of critical level. Relatively harmonious ethnic relations in post-Soviet Lithuania have not experienced interactional crises.

In general, the management of ethnic diversity in democratic Lithuanian state has been successfully institutionalized and does not depend on merely *ad* hoc decisions. Actually, the dialogue between the government-bearing Lithuanians and the minority groups is more formalized than in the other two Baltic countries and includes special provisions for minority parties in the electoral law, and institutional collaboration with minority representatives that takes place in parliament rather than anywhere else. This gives reasonable grounds to believe that in future the minorities will engage themselves more in organizations and parties with a broader point of departure than narrow ethnic interests. Furthermore, Lithuanian parliament collaborates with those regional councils where the minorities are heavily represented. The Department of Regional Problems and National Minorities also serves as a forum for dialogue with organizations of minorities on a number of issues.

There seems to be a general consensus among students of the area that overall, culturally, demographically and institutionally, Lithuania apparently presents the easiest case for consolidation of a liberal multiethnic democracy.[6] The quality of ethnic peace in contemporary Lithuania can be assessed as the closest approximation to the liberal ideal that can be found in any of post-Soviet states. It is an increasingly positive, stable and well in the process of becoming consolidated as democratic ethnic peace.

Notes

1. This passage is adapted from Ginsburgs (1993, pp. 233-66) and Barrington (1995, p.733-35).
2. As outlined in article 12 of the law, naturalization required passing a written and spoken test in Lithuanian, permanent residence in Lithuania for 10 years, employment or a constant legal source of income from within Lithuania, knowledge of the Lithuanian constitution, and renunciation of prior citizenship. New citizens also had to take an oath similar to the one in the 1989 law (Kolstoe, 1995, p. 141).
3. This review of Lithuanian policies of multiculturalism is adapted from Resler (1997, pp. 100-3) and Norgaard (1996, p. 183-8).
4. The majority of Lithuanian schools (88.5%) contain ethnic Lithuanian children. Russian schools make up 4.1% and Polish schools 2.5% of all schools. The remaining 4.9% are ethnically mixed schools where Lithuanians and minority pupils are taught in separate classes. This kind of school can be found especially in the Vilnius area, which is the most ethnically mixed area in Lithuania (Norgaard, 1996, pp. 186-7).
5. In March 1994 Department of Nationalities was merged with State Commission for Regional Problems into a Department of Regional Problems and National Minorities.
6. Linz and Stepan (1996b: 405, 432) argue that though Lithuania has not gone very far in the consociational direction, its inclusionary strategy towards citizenship for almost all permanent residents at the start of independence puts Lithuania in the type of a pluralist nation (recognizing that demos and ethnic nation can be different) with inclusionary state-building strategy.

9 Moldova

Historical And Demographic Background

Two major areas can be distinguished within Moldova: the *Right-Bank Moldova* (Bessarabia proper), extending between the Prut and the Dniester rivers to the west of the Dniester; and the *Left-Bank Moldova* (Transdniestria, or Transnistria, or Dniester area) situated to the east.

The collapse of the Russian empire in 1917 permitted the national liberation of the Moldovan people but after World War I the territory of Moldova was divided once again. The forces who came to power in the Right-Bank Moldova proclaimed independence of the Bessarabian People's Democratic republic. The Bessarabian parliament (*Sfatul Tserij*) appealed to the Western powers for recognition and assistance. In December 1917, Romanian troops marched into the Bessarabian republic. In 1918, the Sfatul Tserij voted for union with Romania. Left-Bank Moldova, however, became a Ukrainian possession eventually becoming in 1924 the Autonomous Soviet Socialist Republic (ASSR) of Moldova with the capital in Tiraspol and administered as part of the Ukrainian SSR.

Along with the Baltic states, Moldova was among those territories whose fates were determined by the Molotov-Ribbentrop Pact. On 28 June 1940, Romania yielded to the Soviet ultimatum and ceded Bessarabia. On 2 August 1940, the Moldovan SSR (MSSR) was formed, a new Union republic within the USSR which included five western districts of the abrogated Moldovan ASSR within the Ukraine and most of the incorporated Bessarabia. The area between the Dniester and the Prut to the south were incorporated into Ukraine, leaving thus Moldova landlocked.

Moldova was unique among the Soviet republics in that it has a counterpart across the border of the same ethnic group and with which the republic had been historically united - Romania. Soviet authorities dogmatically asserted that Moldova's national identity was distinct and separate from that of Romania. In the realm of linguistic policy, the decision was taken in the mid-1920s to employ the Cyrillic script for writing the Moldovan language on the grounds that it could be better expressed graphically in this form (Crowther, 1997, p. 319). Effectively, this generated high animosity because of the artificial nature of Moldova's cultural divide from Romania.

Demographically, Moldova has never been anything like monoethnic. Besides the ethnic Moldovan majority, Moldova is home to five significant ethnic minorities - Russians, Ukrainians, Gagauz, Bulgarians and Jews. Dynamics of Moldova's ethnic composition are presented in table 9.1.

Table 9.1 Dynamics of Moldova's Ethnic Composition

Nationality	1959		1970	
	in 1000s	in %	in 1000s	in %
Moldovans	1,887.5	65.4	2,303.9	64.5
Ukrainians	420.8	14.6	506.5	14.1
Russians	292.9	10.2	414.4	11.6
Gagauz	95.8	3.3	124.9	3.4
Bulgarians	61.6	2.1	73.7	2.0
Jews	95.1	3.3	98.0	2.7
Other	25.5	1.1	47.2	1.7

Nationality	1979		1989	
	in 1000s	in %	in 1000s	in %
Moldovans	2,525.6	63.9	2,790.7	64.4
Russians	505.7	12.8	560.4	12.9
Ukrainians	560.6	14.2	599.7	13.8
Gagauz	138.0	3.4	152.7	3.5
Bulgarians	80.6	2.0	87.7	2.0
Jews	80.1	2.0	65.6	1.5
Other	58.8	1.4	78.1	1.8

Sources: Kozlov (1992, pp. 117-22), *USSR Census Data* (1989).

Torn apart on several fault lines, the main ethnic split has been between ethnic Moldovans and Russians, though additional problems divided each of the ethnic groups from the mainstream. Demographically, Moldovans are the largest ethnic group in both Right- and Left-Bank Moldova. However, while in the Right-Bank the Moldovans predominate both among the urban and the rural population, in the Left-Bank the Moldovans represent only a plurality (39.9%) against 53.3% of the Russophones. The Moldovans predominate in rural areas, while the Russophones form an almost overwhelming numerical majority in the large industrial centers like Tiraspol, Rybnitsy, Bendery, and Dubossary. In Tiraspol, the Russophones comprise 87% of the city population, in Rybnitsy 64%.

Another important minority are the Gagauz, a Christian Turks group which migrated to Bessarabia from Bulgaria in the early XIX century. In 1989, the Gagauz numbered 153,000 in Moldova, (3,5% of the total population) and settled in the south of the country, at a strategic crossroads near the borders of Ukraine, Moldova and Romania. Population density being relatively low in South Moldova, the Gagauz and other small ethnic groups predominate in disproportionately large areas and can thus bid for control of a far larger share of Moldova's territory (12%) than their share of the country's total population would seem to warrant (Socor, 1994b, p. 19).

Many observers have noted that the impact of Soviet development policy acted to intensify hostility toward Russia that had already been engendered by annexation. Industrialization in Moldova transformed the distribution of occupations among ethnic groups. Non-Moldovan presence in the urban economy was reinforced, leaving Moldovans in less skilled and less paid urban occupations, and in the agricultural sector. At the end of the Soviet period, in 1987, non-Moldovans accounted for 52% of positions in industry, 49% in party and state leadership positions, and 63% in scientific work (Patrash, 1990, p. 6). As regards its socio-economic development, Moldova entered into the political transformation of the late 1980s under difficult conditions. In 1987 Moldova was the fourth least urbanized of the Union republics, followed only by Central Asian republics of Uzbekhistan, Kyrgyzstan, and Tajikistan. With respect to its attainments in education, Moldova occupied the last place within the USSR (Bater, 1989, p. 84).

Ethnopolitical Problem Areas And Crises Under Democratization

Stages of Democratization in Moldova

Moldova's evolution away from authoritarian regime started in the late 1980s. Periods of democratization in Moldova can be distinguished on the basis of following landmarks: 1) decay of authoritarianism (the end 1980s-1990); 2) a rather prolonged period of democratic transition falling between first free elections in February of 1990, held within the Soviet system, and first post-Soviet elections in February of 1994; 3) on-going efforts to consolidate democracy.

Ethnopolitical Mobilization Under Authoritarian Decay (1988-89)

Already in 1988, prominent members of the Moldovan cultural elite came out with the idea of organizing the *Moldovan Democratic Movement in Support of Perestroika* to press both for democratization and the end of cultural decay in the republic. In May of 1989 the movement was founded as the *Moldovan Popular Front* (MPF). It comprised a number of independent cultural and political groups, united by their common aspirations for separation from the USSR and eventual reunification with Romania (Sovetskaya Moldova, hereafter as SM, 21 May 1989).

The prospect of the Moldovan nationalist movement gaining political influence led to countermobilization among minority groups. Many Russians gravitated toward *Edinstvo*, a pro-Soviet movement, formed in July 1989, whose strongest base of support was in the Left Bank cities. The Gagauzi Popular Front, *Gagauz Halky* aligned itself with the Russian activists and demanded political autonomy for South Moldova.[1]

The MPF campaign to improve the status of the Moldovan-Romanian language became the main rallying cry in the early period of Moldovan self-assertion. On July 30, tens of thousands participants assisted at the MPF rally in Chisinau urging immediate adoption of the language laws that would proclaim Moldovan as the only official language of the republic and re-introduce the Latin-based script (SM, 1 Aug. 1989). On the eve of the MSSR Supreme Soviet's session, on 27 August 1989, MPF activists organized over 400 rallies in favor of the new bills on languages in the constituencies of the Right-Bank. In downtown Chisinau, the MPF rally gathered almost 100,000 supporters. The rally also claimed official revision of the evaluation of the historical events of 1812, 1918 and

1940 and Moldova's incorporation into the Russian Empire and subsequently, into the Soviet Union (SM, 29 Aug. 1989).

The highly-charged atmosphere surrounding the language debates politicized non-Moldovans and polarized the republic as the language laws promised to affect each community differently. The Gagauz and Transnistrians were initially concerned that the pan-Romanian euphoria would lead to their forced 'romanization' and a quick union with Romania. The new language laws were part of an acute concern. The census of 1989 recorded less than 4% of non-native Moldovan speakers who considered Moldovan their second language, while nearly 60% of Moldova's population considered Russian a native or second language.

In late August-September of 1989, protest strikes were organized in almost all major cities on the Left-Bank. The driving force behind them was the Tiraspol-based United Council of Work Collectivities (OSTK), an organization which united workers and managers of Union-subordinated enterprises. As in the Baltic states, the OSTK in Moldova cooperated closely with the Communist Party and *Yedinstvo* Intermovement, and defended not so much the ethnic rights of the non-titular ethnic groups but mostly the entire political and social system of the Soviet Union itself. On August 19, thousands of participants were drawn by the Yedinstvo Intermovement rally in Chisinau urging to exclude the draft language laws from the agenda of the upcoming parliamentary session. The day after, the Moldovan Supreme Soviet's Presidium held consultations with the representatives of MPF, Intermovement, *Gagauz Halky* as well as of the Left-Bank city councils. The talks resulted in making modifications to several articles of the language bills without excluding the bills from the agenda of the upcoming parliamentary session (SM, 20 Aug. 1989).

Dissatisfied with this decision, the Tiraspol-based OSTK renamed itself into United Strike Committee and called for resuming the protest strike on August 21. Very soon, solidarity strikes spread all over the Left-Bank and South Moldova. On August 29, the opening day of the parliamentary session, 80,000 Russophone workers were reported on strike at 116 factories. Bendery railway node and the Moldovan Airlines joined the strike, while railway workers effectively blocked 98% of incoming trains to the Right-Bank. The day after, over 200 factories were reported on strike which they were ready to stop only upon arrival of a special commission from the USSR Supreme Soviet (SM, 30 Aug., 1 Sept. 1989).

The parliamentary session lasted for 4 days amidst a highly charged atmosphere of strikes, rallies and piquets all over Moldova. On August 31, the language laws were approved. Moldovan was declared the only official language in the republic. Conferring the status of state language on to Moldovan was declared 'one of the basic precondition for the existence of the Moldovan nation in her sovereign national-state formation'. Public recognition was made that Moldovan and Romanian are one and the same language, while the Cyrillic alphabet was abandoned and the Moldovan returned to the Latin script. The new legislation also stated that it would 'provide conditions for a *genuine* national-Russian and Russian-national bilingualism', implying that all state employees were obligated to know both Moldovan and Russian. State enterprises and offices were expected to switch to Moldovan as their working language in 5-years' term where Russian was used in that function. A concession made to Russophones was a formula declaring Russian 'the language of interethnic communication in Moldova'. The law contained a special provision, permitting the use of Gagauz for official purposes in the Gagauz-populated areas.

A spectacular rise of mass political activism began in the context of campaigning for legislative elections, scheduled for February 1990. The activists from both the Moldovan and minority communities depicted their opponents in threatening terms in order to secure electoral support. The MPF aired its pre-election program that combined affirmation of republican sovereignty and Moldovan ethnic revival with appeals to declare official re-evaluation of the 1940 events as Moldova's forced incorporation into the USSR. Reportedly, these rallies numbered tens of thousands participants only in Chisinau (SM, 11 Oct., 12 Nov. 1989).

Already at the stage of authoritarian decay, stateness and ethnopolitical legitimation of the Moldovan territorial state manifested as a serious problem area of ethnopolitics. The language laws, in fact, triggered first serious confrontation between Moldovans and non-titular groups. After the laws were adopted, the strikes in Transdniestrian cities of Tiraspol, Rybnitsy, and Bendery intensified and would continue for over a month. The sessions of city councils in Tiraspol, Rybnitsy and Bendery voted to ignore the newly adopted legislation on languages and called the Russophones for civil disobedience (SM, 3 Sept., 17 Sept. 1989). In the cities of Rybnitsy (on 3 December, 1989) and Tiraspol (on 28 January, 1990), local referenda expressed in favor of granting those cities the status of autonomous self-governing and self-managing territories and for the appropriateness of the formation of the larger Transdniestrian Autonomous Soviet Socialist Republic (ASSR) within Moldova (SM, 30 Jan. 1990). The same pattern was replicated in South Moldova where on December 12,

1989, a mass rally of the *Gagauz Halky* in Comrat proclaimed itself the Congress of representatives of the Gagauz people and claimed the establishment of the Gagauz ASSR within Moldova (SM, 14 Dec. 1989).

Democratic Transition in Moldova and the Crisis of Stateness (1990-91) [2]

First free parliamentary elections in Moldova were held in February of 1990. The elections got a turnout of 83,4% of the listed voters. Among the elected MPs 256 resulted ethnic Moldovans, 57 Russians, 36 Ukrainians, 12 Gagauz and 8 Bulgarians. Approximately one third of those elected were supporters of the MPF (SM, 24 Feb., 3 Mar. 1990). With the additional support of centrist deputies, the MPF was able to command a majority in the new legislature. It was the MPF that backed the appointment of Mircea Snegur as the Supreme Soviet Chairman, despite his prominent position on the Moldovan CP. Ion Hadarca, the MPF Executive Council President, became his deputy while Mircea Druc, the leader of the MPF radical (irredentist) wing, was appointed Prime Minister (SM, 27 Apr. 1990).

The shift in political control to the nationalist opposition was accompanied by increasing ethnic confrontation. Major intensification of minority concerns about their future in a republic controlled by the titular nationality resulted from a series of legislative acts introducing new state symbols. On April 27, Moldovan parliament approved the Romanian tricolor as Moldova's new official flag and announced the competition for the republic's new coat of arms (SM, 1 May, 1990). The Tiraspol City Soviet refused to recognize the tricolor on the territory subject to its authority. Bendery, Rybnitsy and Comrat city soviets followed the suit and continued to fly the communist flags (SM, 4 May, 15 May 1990).

Passions over symbols ran so high that several incidents of after-rally rioting were reported. On May 11, two opposing groups of the Gagauz and the MPF activists demonstrated in Slobodzeja with two different flags. Despite forceful resistance, the Moldovans managed to raise the tricolor over the building of the local authorities (SM, 25 May 1990). On May 20, at a MPF rally in Varnitsy the demonstrators called for raising the tricolor over the official buildings in Russian-speaking city of Bendery. Two buses with the MPF activists attempted to enter Bendery but were stopped by some 2000 Russophone workers from self-defense units. Larger clashes were prevented, yet the fighting resulted in 5 injured (SM, 27 May 1990).

Subsequent developments in Chisinau did not encourage ethnopolitical moderation. On May 22-23, a group of some twenty Russophone MPs, reportedly, were furiously beaten by the crowd of radical nationalists picketing the Moldovan parliament, presumably, because of their anti-Moldovan speeches at the televised parliamentary sessions. Following a series of street confrontations in the capital, 100 Russophone deputies from the opposition bloc 'Soviet Moldova' walked out from the parliament. The initial parliamentary experience of Russophone MPs thus gave them little reason to develop confidence in emerging Moldovan institutions. The conciliatory talks resulted in a special resolution which gave guarantees of the personal immunity for the Russophone deputies and banned the MPF piquets in front of the parliament building (SM, 23 May, 14 Jun. 1990).

New legislative acts voted in June were met by Russophone minority with even more hostility. On June 23, the Moldovan parliament adopted Declaration of Sovereignty and approved the conclusions of its commission on political and legal evaluation of the 1939 Molotov-Ribbentrop pact which stated the illegitimacy of the 1940 incorporation of Bessarabia by the Soviet Union and proposed to consider it 'the Day of national mourning' (SM, 25 Jun., 28 Jun. 1990). While solemn mourning ceremonies were taking place in the churches of the Right-Bank, the Left-Bank kept on celebrating the 'Reunification Day' with military parade (SM, 29 Jun. 1990).

In summer of 1990, separatist forces were consolidating. Local governments in the cities of Tiraspol, Bender and Rybnitsy suspended application of recent Moldova's legislation in their territories. On June 2, the Russophone deputies of legislative bodies of all levels of authority elected in the Left-Bank constituencies convened in Parkany for the so-called I Congress of People's Deputies of Transdniestria. The Congress adopted the resolution that called Russian speakers to hold elections of the Supreme Soviet of Transdniestria which was to proclaim territorial autonomy of the Left-Bank unless it be granted by the central Moldova government (SM, 6 Jun. 1990). Within a month, the respective local referenda were held in favor of the creation of Transdniestrian ASSR (SM 7 Jul. 1990).

In Comrat, the Gagauz center in South Moldova, the II Congress of *Gagauz Halky* movement, held on July 22, once again called the central authorities of Moldova to review the petition of the Ist Congress which had claimed national-territorial autonomy to the Gagauz districts a year before and declared the intention to proclaim such autonomy unilaterally unless it be granted (SM 27 Jul. 1990). The Moldovan parliament annulled the decisions of the Gagauz congresses as exceeding their authority. At the same time, Moldovan MPs eventually took up a discussion on the Gagauz issue, confirming the guarantees of cultural autonomy for the Gagauz community. The language of the parliamentary report termed the Gagauz as 'a not-indigenous ethnicity' which therefore was to be viewed as an 'ethnic group' and not as a 'nation entitled to have their own national territory [autonomy] within Moldova' (SM, 29 Jul., 5 Aug. 1990). Official approval of this report only heated passions in South Moldova.

Crisis escalation in ethnic interaction was triggered on August 21, 1990 when the Gagauz representatives announced the formation of their own ASSR in the five districts populated by ethnic Gagauz (SM, 23 Aug. 1990). Local authorities in the Transdniestrian region followed suit days later. In early September, the IInd Congress of People's Deputies of all levels of authority elected in the Left-Bank constituencies was held in Tiraspol. The Congress proclaimed the formation of the Transdniestrian Moldovan SSR (the PMSSR) as independent from Moldova 'subject of the USSR federation' and a legal successor to the Moldovan ASSR which had existed within the Ukraine before 1940. Only the USSR legislation and the MSSR laws adopted prior to August, 31, 1989 (the date of the adoption of the laws on languages), were declared valid on the territory of PMSSR. The Congress urged the Left-Bank population to go to the polls on 25 November. In its 'Appeal to the South Moldova', the Congress recognized the Gagauz ASSR (SM, 4 Sept. 1990).

Within hours of the PMSSR decisions, the MSSR Supreme Soviet Presidium denounces them as illegal. The day after, the Moldovan parliament institutes the presidency, dissolves all local soviets in the Transdniestrian area and declares presidential rule and curfew in the area. Snegur is designated acting Moldova's President (SM, 5 Sept. 1990).

On 16 September, the II-d Congress of the Gagauz deputies of all levels recognized independence of the PMSSR and, in its turn, declared the Gagauz Soviet Socialist Republic (the GSSR) within the USSR and scheduled the Gagauz elections for 28 October (SM, 22 Sept. 1990). The same day, large-scale rallies with the participation of tens of thousands of demonstrators were held in Chisinau and all major centers of the Right-Bank. Moldovan government was urged to take decisive measures. Attending one of the rallies, President Snegur and Prime-Minister Druc promised not to negotiate with the separatists leaders.

Acute escalation of ethnic tensions occurred after October 23, when Premier Druc issued the decree N 407 legalizing the detachments of Moldovan volunteers to be subordinated to the republican Ministry of Defense. The same evening first groups of armed volunteers mobilized by the MPF marched along the Chisinau streets with cries 'Moldovans - take the arms!' Shortly thereafter formations of volunteers were reported to start arriving *en masse* in the Gagauz districts of South Moldova with the aim to prevent the announced elections, if necessary, by force (SM, 24 Oct. 1990).

The Gagauz local bodies declared countermobilization of the Gagauz volunteers into groups of self-defense. Transdniestrian authorities promised support and, reportedly, dispatched thousands of workers. Tension mounted as the 28 October, the date set for the Gagauz elections approached. In Comrat and other Gagauz cities, people digged trenches and created barriers out of bulldozers and trucks. Groups of Transdniestrian workers blocked the Dubossary bridge connecting the Right-Bank with the Left-Bank (SM, 27 Oct. 1990). On October 27, the concentration of opposing formations of Moldovan, Gagauz and Russophone volunteers in Comrat, Chadyr-Lungi and Vulkanesht districts, reportedly, reached 80,000 people from each side (SM, 29 Oct., 30 Oct. 1990). Moldovan Parliament declared emergency in South Moldova and called upon the USSR central government to send internal troops to help the republican police. Their joint action succeeded in separating the semi-armed crowds (SM, 31 Oct. 1990).

Gagauz elections were held as scheduled. After the elections, the tension seemed to subside and the volunteer formations started to leave the area. At the same time, on November 2, an armed clash between the Moldova police and Russophone civilians near Dubossary bridge resulted in 3 casualties and 9 wounded among the Russophones (SM, 4 Nov. 1990).

The danger that further violence might provoke the USSR central authorities to impose martial law in the republic promoted moderation. Special reconciliatory commission headed by the MCP First Secretary Luchinsky was formed to negotiate with the separatist leaders (SM, 5 Nov. 1990). The Moldovan parliament also set up a special commission including representatives of all ethnic minorities with the task to elaborate draft amendments to the laws on languages.

Both Moldovans and Transdniestrians responded to the mediation talks offered by the USSR President Gorbachev on November 4 in Moscow. (SM, 5 Nov. 1990). On November 14, the Moldovan parliament voted a special resolution drawing a strict boundary between the policies of

Moldova government and the irredentist claims of reunion with Romania of 'some radicals from the MPF' (SM, 15 Nov. 1990). Despite the appeals made by Gorbachev, the elections to the self-styled Supreme Soviet of the PMSSR were held on November 25. The first session of the body recalled all deputies elected in the Left-Bank constituencies from the Moldovan parliament (SM, 26 Nov. 1990). In mid-December, the Russophone deputies returned but walked out for good when Moldovan authorities refused to start the Union Treaty talks (SM, 20 Dec. 1991).

Moldova's official refusal to participate at talks on new Union Treaty was widely supported among the titular nationality. The second Great National Meeting of the Moldovans on December 16, reportedly, had drawn over 800,000 people from all over Moldova. The rally categorically expressed against Moldova's signing new Union treaty and urged the parliament to withhold from even discussing the draft. The MPF leaders called for reunification with Romania and denied that Moldova had any ethnic minorities until it remained within the USSR (SM, 17 Dec. 1990).

On December 22, a Gorbachev's decree attempted to call Moldova to order by threatening presidential rule from Moscow. The decree recognized the illegality of the unilaterally proclaimed Gagauz and Transdniestrian republics, insisting at the same time that Moldova's central government repeal its 'objectionable' laws, including the creation of a separate republican guard, Declaration on Sovereignty, the language law and official evaluation of the events of 1940 (SM, 24 Dec. 1990). Several days later, the Moldovan authorities complied by disbanding the national guard and revising the laws on languages. At the same time, the Moldovan parliament rejected any modifications to the Declaration on Sovereignty and refused to recognize the supremacy of the USSR legislation in Moldova.

In response the Transdniestrian self-styled Supreme Soviet reconfirmed the region's claim to become a new Union republic and be given the right to sign the Union Treaty independently from Moldova. (SM, 27 Jan. 1991). On March 17, the USSR referendum, officially boycotted by Moldova, was held in the Dniester area and in South Moldova. Reportedly, 700,893 voters came to the polls, some 30 % of the listed voters (*Izvestiya*, 27 Mar. 1991).

In late May of 1991, Premier Druc received a no-confidence vote and resigned. Rather than a change of policy priorities, however, that reflected more an interpersonal feud between ex-premier and President Snegur.

Newly appointed Premier Valeriu Muravschi espoused the same radical national viewpoints like his predecessor (SM, 29 May 1991; Socor, 1992).

During the August coup in Moscow Moldova's parliament declared independence of the Republic of Moldova on August 27, 1991. Leaders of the separatist regions, in contrast, pledged their support for the coup. When their hopes were dashed by events in Moscow, they asserted their independence from Moldova and their commitment to uphold the values of the former Soviet Union (*Sfatul Tserij*, hereafter ST, 28 Aug. 1991).

Moldova at Independence: Cumulation of Ethnopolitical Crises

Moldova began its independent existence with its political elite internally divided, its government controlled by nationalist ideologues and the legitimacy of its territorial state critically challenged by ethnically based separatism in Gagauzia and Transdniestrian. At its independence, Moldova has come to face a particularly challenging cumulation of crises feeding one onto another. Stateness, state effectiveness and nationhood all cumulated as crisis area of post-Soviet Moldovan ethnopolitics.

Stateness Stateness became the crisis of prime importance. Underlying the crisis were issues of national identity and ethnopolitical legitimation of independent Moldovan state. Since 1990, the existence of secessionist republics in South Moldova and Transdniestrian had given a special urgency to the problem of national identity over Moldova's future territorial organization. Moldova represents a Romanian irredenta, and vocal groups on both sides of the border demanded immediate unification upon Moldova's independence. If this were to happen, the Russophones in Moldova would end up as citizens of another state which happens to have a bad reputation for the treatment of its national minorities.

The crisis of stateness was redoubled by an intense identity crisis of 'Moldovanness' which pervaded the titular nationality itself and caused disarray and outflanking among ethnic Moldovan elites. For many of Moldova's intellectuals, Moldovan independence represented but the first step toward reunion with the Romanian motherland and 'Moldovan' was to be no more than a regional identity in a reconstituted 'Greater Romania'. Area specialists have suggested the label 'pan-Romanianists' for this group (King, 1994b, p. 345). Their opponents ('Moldovanists') wanted Moldova to remain independent. In their perspective, Moldovans are related to Romanians by a shared language and culture, but history 'had condemned

Moldova to be a state' and its citizens did not have to wait for union like 'manna from heaven'. Therefore, Moldovans would rather reject the ethnonym 'Romanian' altogether and get on with the task of constructing an independent Moldovan state. To 'Moldovanists', any talk of pan-Romanian integration, in either a cultural or political sense, is merely using 'high ideals' to 'cover up personal interest in the territorial break-up of the republic.' (Fane, 1993; Mikhailov, 1995).

Although the construction of new post-Soviet identities has been a common feature of political life in the successor states, in the Moldovan case the salience of identity politics has been particularly profound.

> A significant amount of space in major newspapers is taken up by discussions of linguistics, ethnography, and medieval history; letters from cultural and professional organizations castigating the Moldovan government for betraying the pan-Romanian ideal are frequent; and Moldovan politicians themselves have presented historical or literary arguments to defend their own conceptions of Moldovanness. Pressing the identity question, though, represents more than political rhetoric. Indeed, given the deep divisions within Moldovan society, with the mass of its pan-Romanian intelligentsia denying the legitimacy of the state itself, seemingly esoteric disputes about ethnography or linguistics necessarily have genuine political consequences, particularly in the areas of party politics, ethnoterritorial conflict and relations with Romania... Moldova provides a fascinating case of the gravity of identity politics when the image proffered by politicians diverts sharply from that advocated by intellectuals (King, 1994b, p. 364)

Nationhood The searches for a balance between ethnic and civic bases of Moldova's nationhood related more to the crisis of Moldovan identity than to the fears of ethnic minorities. Actually, nationhood was being managed more efficiently than other crises areas. Since 1991, moderate Moldovan elites with President Snegur have been relatively successful in attempts to alleviate fears caused by the MPF's pan-Romanianism.

Moldova adopted its citizenship law on 5 June 1991, at a time when the future of the Soviet Union was uncertain but when its dissolution was by no means a foregone conclusion. Moldovan law was quite liberal. While it required 10 years of residence for all future applicants for citizenship, this proviso did not apply to people who already lived in the country. The law granted the right of citizenship to everyone who had permanent residence in Moldovan territory at the time when Moldovan sovereignty was proclaimed (23 June 1990), and who had a legal source of income. In addition, if they or one of their parents had been born in the territory of the state, citizenship was granted automatically. The possibility that Moldova would follow the Estonian and Latvian examples and deny post-war Slav immigrants the status of original citizens was therefore excluded (Kolstoe, 1995, p. 151).

Some of the first acts of the Moldovan parliament at independence were to suspend the language examinations mandated by the 1989 language law and to affirm Moldova's membership in the CIS. There is, however, generally admitted uneasy relationship between the civic conception of Moldovanness offered to the separatists and the ethnic image which Snegur stresses in his battles with the pan-Romanists. King (1994b, p. 366) argues that this promoting different images to each audience is illustrative for the government's skill at adapting the political message to fit the political milieu:

> With the ethnic Moldovan/Romanian population, the Snegur government has been able to cast itself as the defender of national sovereignty and an independent Moldovan identity, an image which appeals to the mass of Moldova's peasants. With the Transnistrians and Gaguzi the government has forged a non-ethnic concept of citizenship as a bulwark against the pan-Romanian aspirations of the Moldovan intelligentsia, a tactic which has helped to reduce tensions between the center and the separatist regions.

Effectiveness Effectiveness of the post-Soviet Moldovan state had been a serious problem which increased the assertiveness of Transdniestrian separatism. Transdniestrian represented an advanced industrial region within the former MSSR that accounted for the major part of the industrial capacity of the republic. This region accounted for 33% of all industrial goods and 56% of all consumer goods produced in the republic as a whole (*Nezavisimaya Gazeta*, 19 Sep. 1992). When Moldova began to gain real sovereignty in 1990-91 and the power of the central authorities was seriously shaken, it is not surprising that the Dniestr communist nomenklatura and factory directors became increasingly concerned: their positions depended on retaining links with Moscow (Kolstoe, 1995, p. 157). In the post-Soviet period, Transdniestrian loyalty to the Soviet style made its socio-economic situation even worse and by the mid-1990s its economy had transformed into a true 'black hollow' [3].

Escalation of Crisis Interaction to Ethnic War (September 1991-June 1992)

Since the collapse of the Soviet Union, the Republic of Moldova has been asserting its political identity as an independent sovereign state. On the day of the proclamation of independence, the Parliament passed a decree rescinding all articles in the republic's constitution that related to Moldova's membership in the Soviet Union. Simultaneously, a state delegation was appointed to negotiate with the USSR on issues arising from Moldova's secession (ST, 29 Aug. 1991). A series of other measures included the Moldovan government's September 11 decision to set up checkpoints on the republic's borders. The Republic also set up a Ministry of National security to replace the disbanded KGB (ST, 7 Sept. 1991). On October 30, the decree on nationalization of all Soviet enterprises in Moldova's territory stipulated taking over these enterprises together with their bank accounts without providing any financial compensation. Among the affected enterprises were the heavy-industry combines in Transdniestrian (*Nezavisimaya Moldova* - hereafter, NM, 2 Nov. 1991).

The initial approach towards management of ethnoterritorial separatism by the authorities of independent Moldova was far from constructive and mostly aimed at coercive suppression. This, in turn, only exacerbated ethnic tensions and produced a new crisis escalation in ethnopolitical interactions. In the wake of the failed communist coup in Moscow, on August 23, the Moldovan Parliament set up a special commission to review the action of the Transdniestrian and Gagauzi leaders and authorized the arrests of those who supported the coup (ST, 31 Aug. 1991). Shortly after, the leaders of Gagauzia and Transdniestria national movement including S.Topal, E. Kindegelyan and I. Smirnov, leader of Transdniestria, were put under arrest (ST, 4 Sept. 1991).

On 1 September the Russophone population of the Dniester area started protest strikes and the railway blockade of Moldova claiming the release of the arrested leaders and threatened interruption of electricity and gas supplies to the Right-Bank. On September 21, the Transdniestrian parliament approved the Law on the Creation of the PMSSR Republican Guard. These formations were deemed as regular armed forces. Few days later Transdniestrian guardsmen stationed sentries and checkpoints on all roads on the Left-Bank (ST, 21 Sept. 1991).

Particularly explosive situation created in Dubossary, a district center on the borderline between the two banks of Moldova. The city police and executives were controlled by the Moldovans, while the local representative bodies were under control of the Russophone majority of the city population. The population of the rural areas of the Dubossary district, surrounding the city was almost exclusively ethnic Moldovan. The arrest of five Russian civilians by the Moldovan police was followed by a riot among Russian speakers who attacked the city police office and the building of the Dubossary branch of the Moldovan State Bank. Police action led to three casualties. After the clashes Russophone policemen resigned from the Moldovan police and joined the Russophone militia, an alternative to Moldovan police (ST, 2 Oct. 1991).

In late September, a delegation of Russian Federation's MPs arrived in Moldova to mediate the conflict. By 1 October, their mission had brokered an agreement which envisaged liberation of the arrested separatist leaders, mutual withdrawal of additional Moldovan police forces and of Transdniestrian guards from Dubossary, and suspension of the railway blockade against the Right-Bank. The agreement legalized the creation of Russophone municipal militia in Transdniestrian cities, ostensibly, to be subordinated to both local soviets and Moldovan police. The checkpoints of the Transdniestrians remained intact (ST, 4 Oct. 1991).

In mid-September, the Moldovan parliament fixed December 8 as the day for a nation-wide presidential ballot. The presidential elections campaign further polarized the republic. The Transdniestrian and Gagauz republics declared that they would not participate in 'the elections of a foreign state' and were to hold their own presidential elections a week earlier. Moldovan elites themselves split when the MPF set itself in opposition to the Moldovan elections and the Democratic Youth Party joined the Front in the boycott (NM, 24 Oct. 1991).[4]

This led the MPF into overt conflict with Snegur. Consequently, the Front's large bloc in parliament - comprising about 30% of the seats - switched to the side of the opposition. The MPF tried to shift the election issue to holding a referendum on the question of immediate reunification with Romania, but did not get the approval from the parliament (NM, 8 Nov. 1991). On 1 December the MPF leaders announced the formation of a so-called 'Pan-Romanian Council on the Reunion of the Great Romania' (NM, 2 Dec. 1991).

On December 8, the nationwide presidential elections in Moldova got the turnout of 83,9%. Snegur won the presidency receiving 98% of the votes. Reportedly, only 17% of the registered voters in the Dniester area and 29% in the Gagauz area come to the polls (NM, 13 Dec. 1991).

A series of instigating events dramatically increased tensions in mid-December. Meetings of officers in some regiments of the ex-USSR 14th

Army that is located in Moldova declared ready to interfere into ethnic conflict unless the parties reached a compromise (NM, 7 DE., 17 Dec. 1991). The IIIrd Congress of the MPF in late February 1992, renamed the Front into Christian-Democratic Popular Front (CDPF) thus stressing thus its link to the right-wing Romanian parties. Its new program documents set prospected restoration of the Great Romania as its major goal (NM, 24 Feb. 1992). Meanwhile hundreds of semi-armed Cossacks from the Don region of Russia were reported to arrive to the Left-Bank in response to the appeals by local Cossack groups. Soon afterwards, groups of Romanian volunteers appeared in the Right-Bank (*Izvestiya*, 5 Mar. 1992). During January - March 1992, numerous facts of armed assaults at military depots of the ex-USSR 14th Army were reported in the Left Bank. These developments brought the opposing parties to the brink of ethnic warfare.[5]

Escalation peaked in March 1992 with numerous violent clashes between Moldovan policemen and Transdniestrian militia and guardsmen in Dubossary district. Applying armed carriers, Transdniestrians took by storm the Dubossary policy office. Moldovan policemen transferred from Dubossary to Kochiery, a nearby Moldovan populated village. When Moldovan policemen attempted an assault at an ex-Soviet Army arms' depot Transdniestrians attacked Kochiery. Violent clashes, reportedly, resulted in 17 victims (NM, 4 March 1992).

After the incident, Transdniestrian authorities declared the state of emergency in the Left-Bank and called for armed resistance to the Moldovan police. Hostilities assumed the character of daily fire-exchanges in Dubossary and neighboring villages with ethnically mixed population. On March 15-17, Moldovan policemen and Transdniestrian guardsmen engaged in combat at Kochiery, reportedly, numbered over 600 from each side (NM, 17 Mar. 1992; *Kuranty*, 18 Mar. 1992).

On March 16, the Moldovan government, surrounded by the MPF pickets urging resolute measures, addressed Tiraspol with a 24-hour ultimatum to stop hostilities. Reconciliatory talks between Moldova's premier Sangeli and the Dniester Supreme Soviet Chairman Marakutsa produced an armistice (NM, 17 Mar. 1992). The Moldovan side conceded to grant economic and taxation autonomy to the Left-Bank and to introduce new amendments into the law on languages. A new draft law under discussion suggested the creation of Transdniestrian district centered in Dubossary and giving Tiraspol the status of a free city. Nevertheless, Left-Bank leaders insisted on at least politico-territorial autonomy for the whole of Left-Bank with the capital in Tiraspol and the right to free secession in case of its reunion with Romania (*Izvestiya*, 18 Mar. 1992).

By mid-March, the crisis in Transdniestrian invited first mediation attempts of third-parties. On March 17, the Romanian government urged the Russian Federation to undertake urgent measures to mediate the conflict. Moscow was hesitant and gave ambiguous signals. On the one hand, Russian government had recognized the principle of non-interference into domestic affairs of the CIS countries. On the other hand, protection of rights of Russophone minorities has been declared important priority of Russia's foreign policies. Political opponents of the Yeltsyn government accused it of betraying the ethnic kin. Critically complicating the situation became the declared intention of the 14th Army officers to provide military support to Transdniestrians in case ethnic hostilities were to repeat (*Izvestiya*, 18 Mar., 2 Apr. 1992).

Reacting to the note by Snegur, the Ukrainian President L.Kravchuk decreed the creation of a 50-km special zone on the Moldova-Ukraine border to prevent further influx of the Don Cossacks from Russia through the Ukrainian territory (*Izvestiya*, 18 March 1992). On March, 19, Moldova President Snegur stated not to exclude the possibility of Moldova's turning to Romania for military help, since the Cossacks had already intervened in the conflict on the side of the Russophones and good reasons existed not to trust the promises of Moscow that the 14th army would keep neutrality in internal conflict in Moldova (*Izvestiya*, 19 March 1992). During his emergency visit to Moscow the day after, Romanian foreign minister repeated appeal to initiate four-lateral peace-seeking talks. The Russian parliament addressed Moldovan colleagues urging a peaceful resolution of the crisis, suggesting at the same time that economic autonomy of Transdniestria be supplemented with recognition of a special political status to guarantee the right of the Left-Bank to self-determination in case Moldova should lose her independence (*Izvestiya*, 21 Mar. 1992).

New outburst of violence followed President Snegur's decree that introduced emergency in the whole of Moldova. Moldova's authorities demanded unconditional disbandment of Transdniestrian guardsmen, withdrawal of all Cossack units and restoration of all Moldovan police offices in the Left-Bank as pre-conditions for talks on the further political status of the region. Dniester authorities would not negotiate and declared a next-in-turn railway blockade of the Right-Bank (NM, 3 April 1992).

Violent clashes in the Dubossary district escalated to rocketry fire-exchange, armed raids and assaults against military depots, fighting and terrorist acts along the whole frontier-line between the opposing parties in Transdniestrian. Many roads connecting Moldovan-populated villages with the cities of Bendery and Dubossary were reported to have been mined by

Transdniestrians with the aim to prevent supplies and cooperation between ethnic Moldovan rural population and the Moldovan police forces besieged in the cities. Several new agreements on cease-fire failed. The figures diffused by April, 17, stated that human losses since the beginning of violence in December 1991 had amounted to 42 killed and 130 wounded on the Moldovan side and 60 killed, 100 wounded and 60 lost on the Transdniestrian side (*Izvestiya*, 17 Apr. 1992). The number of registered refugees had grown to 20,000 Moldovans in the rump Moldova and 11,000 of Russophones in the Ukraine (*Kuranty*, 22 May, 4 Jun. 1992).

Ethnic hostilities reached a bloody stalemate in the Bendery battle in late May. For two months the city had been divided into two sectors, each controlled by the opposing armed groups. Reportedly, a next-in-turn armed assault by Transdniestrian guardsmen on the Bendery city police office on June 19 provoked the Moldovan government to send the army formations to restore control. Moldovan troops (reportedly, some 2,500 soldiers and officers) attacked the northern sector of Bendery controlled by the Transdniestrians. Trying to check rapid arrival of more guardsmen, Moldovan aviation air-bombed the bridge connecting Bendery city with the highway arriving from Tiraspol. Heavy artillery, reportedly, was widely employed by both sides, but it was the tanks, applied by Russophones and the support from the 14th army that, effectively, determined the outcome of the Bendery battle in favor of the Transdniestrians who regained the larger part of the city. The three-day combat resulted in hundreds of killed and wounded. Almost all buildings in Bendery were destroyed or severely damaged (*Kuranty*, 22 May, 23 May, 1992; *Izvestiya*, 22 Jun. 1992).

Though the command of opposing parties reached an agreement on cease-fire in Bendery on June, 22-23, the developments had gone beyond control and a potent wave of interethnic violence flared all along the frontier-line between Moldovan and Transdniestrian forces in the Left-Bank. The estimated figures of human losses, reported on June 24, amounted to 500 killed and 3,500 wounded from both sides in few days after the Bendery bloodshed. The number of Russophone refugees to Odessa region of the Ukraine totaled 30,000, thrice as much as during the previous months of warfare (*Kuranty*, 27 Jun., 8 Jul. 1992; *Izvestiya*, 26 Jun. 1992). The scope of members of military formations participating in the hostilities by some estimates comprised approximately 15,000 persons from each side, with approximately 400 of tanks and armored carriers and 300 artillery guns and mortars being employed. By the end of the month, the total number of refugees since the beginning of the conflict is officially reported to surpass 100,000 (*Kuranty*, 28 Jul. 1992).

Given the Russian military support for Transdniestrian, little possibility existed for Moldova to achieve its ends through the use of force. Continuation of hostilities enjoyed almost no support from a highly skeptical Moldovan population. The fledgling Moldovan state had proved almost absolutely inefficient in treating the separatist crisis in 1991-92 which, in fact, was managed mostly through third-parties' efforts. On June 25, during the Istanbul conference of the 11 Black sea countries, a special round of talks was held between presidents of Russia, Romania, the Ukraine, and Moldova. It was agreed to enforce cease fire and to separate opposing groups. Moldova's parliament was called upon to reconsider the status of the Left-Bank (*Izvestiya*, 26 Jun. 1992).

Since Moldovan authorities rejected direct negotiations with the separatists, peace-making talks were held between Moldova and Russia. The negotiations resulted the agreement 'On the principles of peace settlement of armed conflict in Transdniestrian districts of the Moldova republic' signed on 21 July by Presidents Yeltsyn and Snegur in Moscow. The Left-Bank delegation was headed by President Smirnov was present at the ceremony, although with no official status (*Izvestiya*, 22 Jul. 1992).

The accord envisaged creation of a separating line between the opposing armed formations to be supervised by military observers from Russia, Moldova, and Transdniestrian and gradual withdrawal of all troops from Transdniestria. The retirement of the 14th army to Russia linked to finding an agreeable resolution on the political status of Transdniestria within Moldova. Moldova assumed the obligation to grant to the population of the Left-Bank the right to express self-determination in Moldova should lose her independence. The accord was a success in suppressing violence and enforcing negative peace, yet it did not mean resolution of the crisis of stateness which was still awaiting for an appropriate institutional innovation.

Political Realignment as Crisis Management

As a consequence of popular attitudes concerning the war, political conditions in Moldova took a sharp turn. In the course of the following two weeks, resignations of Moldova's premier V.Muravschi, Minister of Internal Affairs I.Kostash and Minister of National Security Plugaru ousted the leaders of the 'party of war' from government positions. Another sign of the shifted balance of political forces was naming Petru Luchinsky, ex-

MCP First Secretary as Ambassador to Russia. Luchinski was rightfully believed to be able to use his access to the Moscow political elite to promote accommodation. A second prominent reform communist, Andrei Sangheli replaced prime minister Muravschi. Sangheli's new government promised a more efficient economic reform program, took a manifestly more flexible approach to the nationalities' question and, in fact, included within its ranks significantly improved minority representation (Crowther, 1997, p. 322).

In December 1992, President Snegur reintroduced the issue of 'Moldovanness' into the wide political debate by delivering a speech to the republican parliament in which he laid out a foreign policy course based on the pursuit of national independence. Snegur warned against the extremes of either unification with Romania or reintegration into a reinforced form of the CIS (Socor, 1992b; King, 1994). His public opposition to 'Pan-Romanianism' further soured relations between himself and the Popular Front, and at the same time sharpened divisions between moderates and more extreme nationalists within the Front itself. Few weeks later, Alexandru Moshanu, the chairman of the parliament, offered his resignation. Luchinsky took up the leadership of the parliament, replacing Moshanu and completing the realignment among the Moldovan leadership. 'The three top positions in the political hierarchy of the republic, the presidency, the prime ministership, and the parliamentary chair, were all held by reform communists, each a former member of the MCP politburo' (Crowther, 1997, p. 325).

Moderate intellectuals who had added tremendously to the Popular Front's prestige during its rise to power founded a competing organization, the 'Congress of Intellectuals'. Through the Congress, they sought to repair the damage done to their cause by the radicals, and to promote a less extreme nationalist agenda. As a consequence of these cardinal political changes, the parliamentary bloc of Agrarian deputies (*Viata Setului*) emerged as the single most influential force in Moldova's legislature. The shift in favor of the Agrarians and their Socialist Party allies in the legislature brought it into much closer compatibility with the government. At the same time, the obstructionist stances adopted by the Popular Front representatives had rendered it impossible to develop and implement a constructive legislative agenda. In October 1993, the Agrarian coalition finally managed to call early parliamentary elections for February of 1994.

The long-standing crisis of stateness and a de-facto partition of Moldova substantially complicated negotiations leading to the promulgation of the electoral law. An obvious danger was that if existing boundaries of territorial constituencies were used and elections were not successfully held in Transdniestrian, then the Tiraspol leadership could claim that the new legislature did not include its representatives, and hence was not legitimate. Trying to avoid this impasse the Moldovan leadership employed a single national electoral district. 'While not ensuring participation in the separatist region, this mechanism allowed elections to go forward, selecting a body of deputies whose constituency was the entire republic, regardless of their individual places of residence' (Crowther, 1997, p. 325).

During the elections, polling places were open in South Moldova by agreement with the Gagauz leadership, and voting went on there without disruption. Transdniestrian authorities refused to allow voting to take place on the territory that they controlled, but several thousand crossed the Dniester and voted in Right Bank polling places. The election results marked a sharp reversal from the politics of the previous period. The pro-Romanian forces were overwhelmingly rejected in favor of parties supporting Moldovan independence and closer alignment with the CIS. While 13 parties and party alliances plus 20 independent candidates were represented in the 27 February race, only four parties and electoral blocs garnered the 4% minimum vote necessary to win parliamentary seats. The Democratic Agrarian Party (PDAM) - made up largely of former communist elites - won with 43.2% of the votes, earning 56 parliamentary seats, while the Socialist Party and Unity Movement Bloc (BPSMUE) earned 22% (28 seats). The Peasants' and Intellectuals' Bloc (BTI) and the Christian Democratic Popular Front Alliance (AFPCD), winning only 9.2% (11 seats) and 7.5% (9 seats) (Mark, 1995, p. 57; Socor, 1994c).

Ethnopolitics in Moldova after Democratic Transition

Having carried out post-independence democratic legislative elections and enacted a new constitution, Moldova completed its democratic transition. Several important steps were made in 1994 on the way towards resolving the problem of stateness. They included referendum on Moldova's independence, new moderation in language issues, and a significant progress on the establishment of the Gagauz autonomy agreement.

Once in control of the main organs of government, moderate forces succeeded in reshaping the political discourse in the republic. They focused on issues that cut across nationality lines and on pursuing an ethnically inclusive strategy that could ensure the long-term stability of the

Moldovan state. Along with forceful assertion of national independence from Romania, this helped break both the foreign and domestic policy deadlocks, winning back the acceptance of minority communities and opening the way for serious negotiations with Moscow. Making a clear departure from both the pan-Romanianist and the 'Moldova-centered' (based on the pursuit of specifically Moldovan national goals) strategies that had charted the road to independence, the new consensus was intentionally meant to be more broadly based, cutting across ethnic lines. Altogether, these efforts succeeded in downgrading nationhood from the crisis level to a problem area that could be managed within the institutional framework of the emerging Moldovan state.

In early 1994 with a legislative majority and a high degree of policy consensus among the Agrarian government, President Snegur initiated the referendum on Moldova's independence (implying rejection of unification with Romania). Despite calls from the Popular Front for referendum boycotts, the March 6 referendum turnout was 75.1% of registered voters, 95% of whom rejected reunification with Romania in favor of an independent Republic of Moldova (Mark, 1995, p. 57).

The leadership of the self-styled Transdniestrian republic (PMR) was pleased with the overall election results and the referendum outcome, and expected greater cooperation from a new government. Soon after the referendum, a first round of talks between Chisinau and Tiraspol was organized by the CSCE and a Russian government-appointed mediator. On 28 April, President Snegur and the PMR leader Smirnov signed a joint declaration seeking a solution to the Transdniestrian issue, including granting the region a special status in accordance with the CSCE recommendations. Negotiations had not produced tangible results, in part because the PMR leadership still hoped to turn Moldova into a Transdniestrian-Moldovan confederation, while the Chisinau leaders found it far from easy to abandon the idea of a unitary state for a federative structure (Ionescu, 1995b; Duplain, 1995).

New moderation was displayed on language issues. On 17 June Moldovan government resolution revised the main points of the 1989 language laws which helped defuse political tension and calm the minorities.

The new constitution, adopted on 29 July, set the groundwork for Moldova to become a democratic republic, established a semi-presidential system with provision for separation of powers, and guaranteed basic human rights. It called for permanent neutrality and banned the basing of foreign troops on its territory. The constitution also reconfirmed the 'Moldovan' orientation of the new political majority. References to Romanian language and Romanian people that had appeared in the draft were removed in favor of Moldovan language and the Moldovan people).

The end of 1994 finally saw a breakthrough in managing the Gagauz part of the crisis of stateness. The weakening of pan-Romanian nationalists since mid-1992 had facilitated dialogue between Chisinau and Comrat. Already in 1993 significant progress was made with the help of third-party mediation. In its response to the tension in the Gagauz region, Ukraine had demonstrated its interest in upholding Moldova's territorial integrity. Turkey had also played a moderating and stabilizing role with regard to the Gagauz problem through its mission to Moldova. Turkish officials have sought to wean the Gagauz leaders away from their Russian political and cultural orientation and, at the same time, to encourage them to seek a compromise with Chisinau based on regional autonomy under Moldovan sovereignty. Development aid for the Gagauz region, offered by Turkey, was to be disbursed via Chisinau, and had been held up pending the Gagauz leaders' agreement with Chisinau (Socor, 1994a, p. 22).

Unlike the Transdniestrians, the Gagauz participated in both the parliamentary elections and the March referendum. The PDAM electoral victory was welcomed by Gagauz leaders as a clear step towards resolving the conflict. Under new Moldovan constitution, 'certain localities in South Moldova', essentially the region of the unrecognized Gagauz republic, were promised 'special status'. After tough, protracted negotiations, Gagauz representatives and the central government crafted an agreement on a special status for Gagauz-populated areas. A draft law was approved in first reading on 28 July 1994. On 28 December 1994, the law was approved in final reading.[6]

The law granted extensive rights to the Gagauz minority, creating 'an autonomous territorial unit'(Gagauz Yeri) as 'a form of self-determination for the Gagauz and 'a component part of the Republic of Moldova'. The preamble defines the Gagauzi as a 'people'(*popor*) and stipulates that South Moldova districts densely populated by the Gagauz be designated 'territorial-autonomous structures' with their own national symbols and legislative assembly. In these districts, Gagauz and Russian are recognized along with Moldovan as official languages. Since Bulgarians, Moldovans, Ukrainians, and Russians live alongside Gagauz in these areas, individual settlements were to hold referenda on whether the entire local population would be included in the autonomous territory. An important provision in the law explicitly guarantees the Gagauz a right to self-determination if Moldova should change its political status (unites with another state).

On 5 March, local residents participated in a referendum to decide whether their villages would join the new autonomous unit, and in May and June, voters returned to the polls to elect a governor and popular assembly for the region. By adopting this basic law on the Gagauz issue, Moldova became the first East European state to grant wide-ranging local autonomy to a restive ethnic minority and many observers have hailed Gagauz Yeri as a potential model for managing ethnic disputes in the former Soviet Union and beyond (Socor, 1994c). Some critics have pointed out that a number of serious obstacles, in fact, manifested as legislation on local autonomy moved from inception to implementation, particularly, the technical difficulties in determining the boundaries of the administrative unit by means of referenda in individual villages, and problems of administering such a new entity (King, 1995, p. 23). This should not deny the evident fact that the law on the Gagauz autonomy is much more than a mere bilateral deal. It actually has institutionalized a new pattern of relationship between the Gagauz and the Moldovan state, and therefore, has downgraded stateness from the level of crisis to the level of a problem area amenable to management within the framework of renewed institutions. It also helped derail the connection between the Gagauz radicals and Transdniestrian separatists (Socor, 1994a).

In the case of Transdniestrian, the management of the crisis of stateness has so far been short of any constructive institutional innovation and the conflict there remains basically untransformed. Its management represents a complex intersection between domestic and foreign policies. Starting in end 1992, round after round of negotiations were then held but with little progress. Moldova demanded complete withdrawal of the 14th Army, sovereignty over Transdniestrian, and no linkage between the two issues. Russia expected withdrawal to be linked to the fate of Transdniestrian, hedged on the question of transferring 14th Army assets to Transdniestrians, and pressed for an agreement on long term basing rights for the 14th Army on Moldovan territory. Finally the Transdniestrian authorities held out for federation with Moldova, which would, in essence, recognize their independent status. The deadlock was broken in the 10th round of negotiations only as a consequence of political realignment in Moldova. To many observers, Russia's policies towards resolution in Transdniestrian apparently continue to exert ambivalent effect upon the prospects of talks with the Left-Bank which end result, remains elusive (Duplain, 1995; Hanne, 1997).

Patterns of Ethnopolitical Crisis Management and Ethnic Peace: The Case of Moldova

Democratization in Moldova has been an extremely difficult process, severely aggravated by ethnopolitical tensions and minority separatism during democratic transition and efforts to proceed to democratic consolidation. The intensity of stress was redoubled by a profound identity crisis of 'Moldovanness' among the state-bearing Moldovans themselves.

At the stage of democratic transition which coincided with Moldova's transition to independence, mismanaged crisis of stateness erupted into disruptive ethnic strife. Ethnic violence escalated dramatically and assumed the pattern of ethnic warfare, complicated even more by conflict intervention of the ethnic kin on both sides. Management of crisis situations at the interactional level since their first occurrence in late 1990 represented a complex mix of both destructive and constructive patterns. By mid-1992 constructive patterns seem to have prevailed. Third-party mediation and political realignment among Moldovan elites succeeded in enforcing negative ethnic peace between the two banks of Moldova.

At the same time, it should be noted that, since then, negative ethnic peace in Transdniestria has stabilized and, given the current trends in Moldova's domestic and foreign developments, further eruptions of violent contentions can reasonably be deemed unlikely. It is important to point out at an important difference between Moldova and some other post-Soviet cases where negative ethnic peace has remained extremely unstable and alternated with reemerging violence (e.g., Georgia-South Ossetia, Georgia-Abkhazia, or Azerbaijan-Nagorny Karabakh) and where ethnic disruption contributed to the failure of completing democratic transitions or, at least, seriously undermined their chances in the foreseeable future. Unlike those cases, by mid-1990s Moldova has succeeded in completing its democratic transition.

The quality of ethnic peace that exists in different parts of Moldova has been contingent upon the patterns by which ethnopolitical crises and problem areas have been managed at the system level. These patterns have displayed a significant evolution. Initial attempts to ignore the necessity of coming out with institutional novations and re-adjustments had led to a nearly perilous cumulation of ethnopolitical crises of stateness and nationhood, as well as a serious aggravation of the problem of state effectiveness in the first year of Moldova's independence. The crises of stateness and nationhood resulted prolonged and difficult to manage. Realignment among ethnic Moldovan elites, radical change of nation-building ideologies and of the general public discourse which became manifest in 1994, effectively, have succeeded in downgrading nationhood to the level of problem-area amenable to management within the institutional framework of Moldovan state.

To date, generally harmonious ethnic relations predominate in the whole of the Right-Bank where ethnopolitics has been enlarging its positive dimension. Institutional innovation which introduced elements of federalism into Moldova's political system has succeeded in resolving the crisis of stateness in the Gagauz case where ethnic peace, though still rather unstable, has acquired an initial measure of positive quality.

Transdniestria remains an area of unresolved crisis of stateness. Actually, the de-facto partition of Moldova into the Right-Bank and the Left-Bank has entrenched since the end of the ethnic war in mid-1992. Though since 1994 some progress has been made in seeking rapprochement between Chisinau and Tiraspol and negotiations have been continuous, the final agreement on the status of Transdniestria remains elusive. An institutional innovation to pave the way out of the last crisis area of Moldova's stateness is still elusive. Ethnic peace in Transdniestrian can be assessed as a stabilized, but still negative and unstable. However, most observers agree that today's Moldova has made considerable progress in managing its ethnopolitical problem areas and crises.

Notes

1   On early stages of the Gagauz movement, see Cavanaugh (1992), Socor (1994b).
2   This section is adapted from Aklaev (1996a).
3   See Ionescu and Ruthland's characterization (1995, p. 3): 'The current situation in the 'Dniester Moldovan Republic' is a heady mixture of economic depression, rampant poverty, mafia-style criminality, and insecure weapons stocks, topped off with a residual communist mentality'.
4   On December 1, the separatist presidential elections and referenda on independence, reportedly, had the turnout of 78% in Transdniestrian and 80% in Gagauzia. In Transdniestrian, 90% of the voters expressed for independence, while 65,4% supported communist leader I. Smirnov to presidency. In Gagauz districts, reportedly, 76% voted for independence, while some 60% voted for the presidency of S. Topal, a radical Gagauz Halky leader. See *Nezavisimaya Moldova* (NM), 2 Nov., 9 Nov., 3 Dec. 1991.
5   A perceptive analysis of spiraling to ethnic war see in Kaufman (1996).
6   Gagauz Yeri stands for the 'Gagauz land'. The law was promulgated by Moldova's President Snegur on 13 January 1995. See more in Socor (1994a), King (1995).

10 Russian Federation

Structural and Demographic Background

The Russian Federation (RF) makes a unique case among post-Soviet successor states. The Soviet Union comprised 15 ethnically defined republics, of which the Russian Soviet Federative Socialist Republic (the RSFSR) was the largest. Though, besides Russia, four other union republics (Georgia, Azerbaijan, Uzbekhistan, and Tadjikistan), contained ethnically-based territorial subdivisions, of all these former Union republics, Russia's internal makeup was by far the most complex. In many respects, the RSFSR was structured like the Soviet Union. In addition to its purely territorial subdivisions (the regions, including *oblasts* and *krais)*, Russia comprised 16 autonomous republics (ASSRs), 5 autonomous oblasts (AOs), and 10 autonomous okrugs (AOKs). Complicating the situation even more was the fact that the lower-level ethnoterritorial autonomies (AOs and AOKs) were themselves territorial subdivisions of larger, non-ethnic regions. Another similarity was that many boundaries between ethnic territories were drawn purposely to reduce cohesiveness of ethnic groups. For instance, the Buryats were divided among Buryatia, Chita Krai, and Irkutsk oblast.

Since then, in response to the declarations of sovereignty, the formal status of all the autonomous republics has changed. After the amendments made to the Russia's Constitution on 15 December 1990 the 16 autonomous republics became simply 'republics within the Russian Federation'. On 3 July 1991 the RSFSR's Supreme Soviet adopted decrees under which four of the five autonomous oblasts (Adyghei, Gorno-Altai, Karachai-Cherkess, and Khakass) also became republics which total number increased to 20. It rose to 21 on 4 June 1992 when the Russian parliament sanctioned the splitting into two of the Chechen-Ingush republic.

As of today, the RF officially consists of twenty-one republics, six krais, forty-nine oblasts, and two federal cities. These differences in names of the 'subjects of the federation' reflect both ethnic and non-ethnic criteria.

Republics, initially delineated to recognize strong ethnic groups, typically have their own legislatures and most have their own presidents. The federal constitution grants republics the right to formulate their own constitutions (basic laws). Present-day republics within Russia are either former autonomous republics or former autonomous oblasts who have elevated their status. *Oblasts* and *Krais* are non-ethnically but territorially defined subunits. They do not have titular ethnic minorities and are predominantly composed of Russian ethnics. *Oblasts (Provinces)* are locally governed by legislative and executive bodies and, as of the 1993 Constitution, are entitled to formulate their charts (*ustavs*), a sort of local constitution. *Krais (Territories)* originally, were an arbitrary hybrid between republics and oblasts, delineated by containing one or more ethnically defined subunits that could be an autonomous oblast, autonomous okrug, or both. *Autonomous Oblasts and Okrugs* were designed as administrative units in the Soviet period to give small ethnic groups a political identity. They are found in sparsely populated regions, such as Siberia and the Russian Far East as constituents of krais and oblasts (see Tables 10.1 –10.3).

Together, the twenty-one republics of the RF account for 28.6% of the territory of the federation but for only 15.2% of its population. Of them, seven are in the North Caucasus (Adygeya, Chechnya, Dagestan, Ingushetia, Kabardino-Balkaria, Karachaevo-Cherkessia and North Ossetia); six are situated in the middle reaches of the Volga river and the Urals (Bashkortostan, Chuvasia, Mari-El, Mordovia, Tatarstan, Udmurtia), and five located in Siberia (Buriatia, Gornyi Altai, Khakassia, Sakha (Yakutia), and Tuva). The remaining three are Kalmykia, on the low reahces of the Volga; Karelia on the border with Finland, and Komi, in northern Russia.

Ethnic groups in all republics have been affected to different degrees by Russification and modernization, but many have preserved a strong sense of separate national identity. The peoples after whom the republics are named are all ethnically and culturally distinct from the Russians. They belong mainly to the North Caucasian, Turkic, Finno-Ugric, and Mongolian ethnic groups. Most of the North Caucasians as well as the Tatars and Bashkirs are traditionally Muslim, while Kalmyks and the peoples of Siberia are either Buddhist or shamanist.

The republics differ greatly from one another in many respects. The largest - Sakha (Yakutia) - covers more than 3.1. million sq. km, while the smallest -Adygheya - has an area of only 7600 sq. km. The most populous republics - Bashkortostan and Tatarstan - have roughly 4 million inhabitants each, while Gorny Altai has a population of fewer than 200,000. The most richly endowed is Sakha (Yakutia) which accounts for most of Russia's gold and diamond output, and Tatarstan and Bashkortostan, which are both major oil producers. Most of the republics depend heavily on subsidies from Moscow (Harris, 1993).

Table 10.1   Constituent units of the RSFSR

Terrtitorial-administrative units:
49 oblasts and 6 krais

Autonomous Soviet Socialist Republics- ASSRs

Bashkirian ASSR	Komi ASSR
Buryatian ASSR	Marian ASSR
Checheno-Inghush ASSR	Mordovian ASSR
Chuvashian ASSR	North Ossetian ASSR
Daghestan ASSR	Tatar ASSR
Kabardin-Balkar ASSR	Tuva ASSR
Karelian ASSR	Udmurt ASSR
Kalmykian ASSR	Yakutian ASSR

Autonomous Oblasts (Regions) - AOs

Adygeyan AO	Jewish AO
Gorno-Altai AO	Karachai-Cherkess AO
	Khakass AO

Autonomous Okrugs (Areas) - AOKs

Aga Buryat	Koryak
Chukchi	Nenets
Evenk	Taimyr
Khanty-Mansi	Ust-Orda Buryat
Komi Permyak	Yamal Nenets

Source: Constitution of the RSFSR adopted in 1978.

Table 10.2 Constituent units of the RF

Republics within Russia

Adygheya	Karelia
Altai	Khakassia
Bashkortostan	Komi
Buryatia	Marii El
Chechnya	Mordovia
Chuvash	North Ossetia-Alania
Daghestan	Sakha (Yakutia)
Inghush	Tatarstan
Kabardin-Balkar	Tuva
Kalmyk	Udmurt
Karachai-Cherkessia	

Autonomous Oblasts (Regions) - AOs
Jewish AO

Autonomous Okrugs (Areas) - AOKs

Aga Buryat	Koryak
Chukchi	Nenets
Evenk	Taimyr (Dolgan Nents)
Khanty-Mansi	Ust-Orda Buryat
Komi Permyak	Yamal Nenets

Krais (Territories)	*Oblasts (Regions)*
same as in the RSFSR	same as in the RSFSR

Source: Constitution of the RF adopted in 1993.

Several features of the RSFSR's structure persist as legacies that are particularly relevant for post-Soviet Russian ethnopolitics. First, the contradiction between the ethnofederal form and the unitary state substance. The RSFSR was never a true federation under the communist regime. For instance, in the 1978 Constitution of the RSFSR the article on the division of powers between the RSFSR and its constituent parts was vague to the extent of being meaningless; the article finished listing the central leadership's prerogatives by referring all embracingly to 'other

Table 10.3 Ethnic composition of republics within the RF

Republic	Total population, 1000s	%, Titular population	%, Russian population	%, Other minorities
Adygea	432	22	68	10
Bashkortostan	3943	22	39	39
Buryatia	1038	23	70	7
Chechnya	1270	58	23	19
Chuvash	1338	68	27	5
Daghestan	1802	80*	9	11
Gorno-Altay	191	31	60	9
Kabardino-Balkar	754	48	32	20
Kalmykia	323	45	38	17
Karachai-Cherkessia	414	31	42	27
Komi	1251	23	58	19
Mari-El	750	43	48	9
Mordovia	963	33	61	6
North-Ossetia	632	53	30	17
Tatarstan	3642	49	43	8
Tuva	309	64	32	4
Udmurtia	1606	31	59	10
Sakha (Yakutia)	1094	33	50	17

* This represents an amalgam of Dagestani peoples.

Source: USSR 1989 Census data.

issues of republican significance'. Post-Soviet Russia faces an inescapable challenge to make a transition to a real federalism.

Second, a basic institutional feature of federation in Russia was the principle of ethnic autonomy. Unlike Union republics within the USSR, autonomous republics within Russia were not officially defined as sovereign and had no right to secede. The titular nationalities in Russia'sautonomous units had fewer cultural amenities than did those of the Union republics, and their leaderships had fewer rights of decision-making than their counterparts in those republics (Tolz, 1993, p. 2). This, in fact, did provide some safeguards against the potential fragmentation of Russia. Yet, it also contributed to the almost naturally-set reference level of aspirations for ethnonational self-assertion of Russia's republics when the parade of sovereignties engulfed both the Union republics within the USSR and their constituent ethnic autonomies (Sheehy, 1993b).

Third, the structural asymmetry of the Russian Federation. Most of the constituent members of the RF, accounting for about 70% of its territory and more than 80% of the population, are territorial formations (oblasts and krais), which have traditionally enjoyed even fewer political and economic rights that Russia's ethnic republics. This asymmetricity of the RF's structure started to create problems since the *perestroika* period, when the leaders of the oblasts and krais acquired the right to express publicly their dissatisfaction over what they regarded as economic and political discrimination. The real problem is not so much that Russia consists of different kinds of administrative formations, but that these formations have to date been very unequal in status.

Ethnopolitical Problem Areas and Crises Under Democratization

Stages of Democratization in Russia

Overall, the dynamics of democratization in Russia falls into three distinct periods: 1) authoritarian decay in the late 1980s; 2) a prolonged period of democratic transition starting with the first free parliamentary elections in spring 1990 and first nation-wide presidential elections in summer 1991. The initial phase of post-Soviet experience (1992-93) was marked by intense power contentions between the President and the Supreme Soviet which culminated in serious civil strife and the downfall of the first Russian republic. The second republic in Russia came into existence after parliamentary elections and constitutional referendum held in December 1993; 3) attempts to consolidate democracy (from 1994 onwards).

Ethnopolitics in the Late 1980s-Early 1990s

The period of authoritarian decay in the Soviet Union in the late 1980s witnessed first wave of decentralization in the RSFSR accentuated by an increasing ethnopolitical mobilization in Russia's autonomies. During this period the institutions, identities and realms of justification associated with ethnic politics and center-periphery relations underwent massive transformation, as a previously stable set of institutional relations was disrupted by the end of the Communist party's monopoly of power in the face of *perestroika,* on the one hand, and a deep economic crisis of the still prevailing system of 'really existing socialism', on the other.

The first free elections to the RSFSR's parliament in spring 1990 changed the composition of Russia's republican authorities by bringing reform-oriented elites to power. Election of Boris Yeltsin to the position of the RSFSR Supreme Soviet's Chair and the adoption of the RSFSR's Declaration of Sovereignty marked the onset of a serious conflict between the new authorities of the RSFSR, the largest of the Soviet Union republics, and the central Soviet government. For the republics within Russia, the most pertinent aspect of this crisis became intense power struggles between Yeltsin and Gorbachev which personified the on-going contest for priority between republic- and union-levels of authority.

The Union center had already sought to channel the separatist ambitions of the ASSRs to its own purposes. With a decree of 26 April 1990, Gorbachev granted autonomous republics the right to participate in negotiations over the new Union Treaty as equal partners with the Union republics. Such a move threatened the territorial integrity of the Union republics - RSFSR in particular - and Russia's leaders faced the possibility that, under a future Union Treaty, the former ASSRs contained within the borders of Russia might evade the control of Russian authorities and answer only to the Union government. In his turn, Yeltsin tried to enlist the autonomous republics in his struggle against Gorbachev by offering to sign a Federation treaty that would serve as the basis for new Russia's constitution. During his visit to Tatarstan, Bashkortostan and the Komi autonomous republics in fall of 1990, Yeltsin encouraged local elites 'to take as much sovereignty as you can swallow', while simultaneously admonishing the autonomies to stick with the Russian government in opposition to Gorbachev and the odd Union center (Sheehy, 1993c, p. 36).

During the 1990-91 the autonomous republics within Russia had issued their declarations of sovereignty within Russia. The so-called 'parade of sovereignties' began with the North Ossetian ASSR on 20 July 1990 and culminated with that of the Kabardino-Balkaria ASSR on 30 January 1991. In this brief period, 14 of the 16 ASSRs declared their sovereignty and the remaining two republics issued somewhat milder statements upgrading their political status. All of them dropped the designation 'autonomous' and renamed themselves as either a soviet socialist republic, a socialist republic, or simply a republic. Somewhat later, 4 out of 5 autonomous oblasts (AOs) also declared their sovereignty, and were recognized as republics within the Russian Federation by the Russian Supreme Soviet on 3 July 1991 (Slider, 1994, p. 241). These declarations lagged behind those of the union republics by a year but made similar claims for the priority of local laws and control over natural resources and local economy. Unlike it was the case with the Union republics, the sovereignty declarations adopted in ASSRs within Russia did not became forerunners of declarations of independence and all 'sovereignizing' autonomies but Tatarstan and the Chechen-Ingushetia retained the phrasing 'within the Russian Federation'. As long as the Soviet Union existed, most of the former autonomies tended to limit their 'sovereignizing' ambitions to the modest aspiration to be treated as equal with Union republics partners in negotiations over new Union Treaty.

Russia at Independence (1991-92)

After the Soviet collapse Russia was left with a complex of ethnically charged political issues at least as intractable as those purportedly 'resolved' by the Communist party during its tenure as the leading and guiding force in the Soviet society.[1] All three ethnopolitical problem areas became salient and, in some respects politicized ethnicity in Russia has assumed a potentially more disruptive character than the ethnic factor had been to Gorbachev's radical reforms.

Stateness The problem of stateness had come to the fore in the first year of post-Soviet Russia. In the wake of the Soviet collapse, the public discourse became overwhelmingly apprehensive that disintegration processes would not stop at the level of former Union republics, but could damage the integrity of Russian territorial state, inducing further fractures along the boundaries of at least some of its ethnically defined republics. Though intensely perceived as problem area, stateness, however, did not become crisis at the system level. Despite initially widely diffused fears and present ethnically couched separatism, the country's structural and demographic context did prevent ethnoterritorial partition from coalescing into any significant threat to Russia's territorial integrity. Unlike the case of the former USSR, a number of important centripetal factors were acting that actually reduced the danger of the country's decomposition along ethnic lines (Kempton, 1996, p. 587; Teague, 1994c; Lynch and Lukic, 1996).

First, Russia had the advantage of being more ethnically homogeneous and ethnicity as such was unlikely to drive the search for economic and political autonomy in Russia to the same degree that it did in the republics of the Soviet Union. Whereas Russians constituted just 50% of the Soviet Union's population, and were declining relative to the non-Russian nations, ethnic Russians make up more than 80% of the total population of the Russian Federation. That figure was likely to increase further with the return of Russians from neighboring ex-Soviet republics. The ratio of ethnic Russians vs. ethnic non-Russians was generally positive even throughout the ethno-federal subdivisions. An important common demographic feature of republics within Russia has been the heavy presence of ethnic Russian population in almost all of them. As of the last census, taken in 1989, Russians accounted for 45.1% of the population of the 21 republics taken together, with the Russian share of the population ranging from 79.5% in Khakassia to 9.2% in Daghestan. As a rule, Russians are concentrated in the towns and work in industry, while the indigenous population remains to a large extent rural. In only six of the republics (mainly in the North Caucasus, also in Tuva and Chuvash republics) did the titular nationality or nationalities account for more than half the population. In Tatarstan, ethnic Tatars have only a slight margin over ethnic Russians (48.5 % to 43.3%). In the republics of Karelia, Komi, Khakassia, Udmurtia, Mordovia, Buriatia, and Sakha (Yakutia), ethnic Russians make almost two thirds of the total population, while in Bashkortostan and Marii-El, Russians are a plurality of the population.

Second, the asymmetricity of federation structure was working in the centripetal direction. While the immediate constituent parts of the Soviet Union were largely ethnically determined components, Russia includes both ethnically-defined and non-ethnically defined subdivisions and the latter outnumber the ethnic republics almost three times as much in both the number of units and population.

Third, geographic distribution of ethnically-defined republics within Russia was also different from the Soviet Union pattern where the main non-Russian nations were located along the periphery of the country bordering on foreign states or the sea. In the RF, by contrast, most ethnically defined republics are surrounded by Russian regions and do not have direct exit to the country's borders.

Fourth, particularly high degree of economic interdependence between sub-federal units had a centripetal effect. While the Soviet state was highly autarkic and self-sufficient in most resources, its lower-level components were not. The distribution of Russia's natural resources and seven decades of communist planning conspired to tightly integrate the components of the RF into the single economy (Kempton, 1996, p. 588). Those components of Russia that have large industrial bases or possess extensive agricultural lands are not well endowed with mineral resources. Conversely, those components that have vast deposits of raw materials (mostly in Siberia and the Urals) are generally dependent on the rest of Russia for both agricultural and industrial goods (Clark and Graham, 1995). Overall, the result of this economic interdependence is that the center maintains considerable economic leverage over Russia's components. For example, while Tatarstan, Russia's leading producer of crude oil, drills its own oil, it must send that oil to other parts of Russia for refining and re-export back. Politically, it is as if Tatarstan has no oil because without good relations with the central Russian state, it would lack the capacity to make use of it.

Fifth, political history of ethnically defined areas within Russia. Most of the non-Russian lands within the RF have been part of it for centuries. The memory of lost statehood, so important to the national revivals in the USSR (for example, among the Balts, Moldovans, and the West Ukrainians), is practically absent among the non-Russians of the RF which, with the arguable exception of Tatarstan and Tuva, have never known independent statehood (Barsamov, 1994; Monghush, 1993).

Finally, the factor of cultural proximity. There is a less marked differentiation in socio-cultural terms in Russia than there was in the Soviet Union. To a considerable extent, many of the non-Russian peoples belong to a Russian cultural and linguistic zone. For example, half of all Karelians say Russian is their native language. The same is true of about one-third of the Udmurts, Mordovians, and Komis, and of about one-fourth of all Chuvash, among other nationalities. Those figures increase by about

15% when considering only urban dwellers of the titular nation. A far greater tendency toward cultural assimilation is evident. In 1989, 42,000 titles of books were published in Russia in the Russian language. Tatarstan published the highest number of titles, 194, in a native language (Prazauskas, 1993, p. 15).

Though neither of the above factors ensured Russia's territorial integrity absolutely, yet, their cumulative effect helps account for the end-result, i.e., that despite these visible signs of breakdown, the RF has not succumbed to the Soviet pattern of disintegration.[2]

State effectiveness For post-Soviet Russia it was the effectiveness of the state and tasks of state-building that had become a real crisis of prime concern almost immediately at independence. Russia emerged from the breakup of the USSR as an essentially unitary state despite its self-description as a federation. Ethnopolitical dimension of the crisis of state effectiveness manifested as an acutely perceived need to find new institutional responses to develop alternative modes of center-local patterns of governance. Among all the successor states, Russia, perhaps, most emblematically encapsulates the essence of the dilemmas of state-formation, market transition and the maintenance of political order under conditions of intensely politicized ethnic consciousness. Effectiveness of the Russian state came to be increasingly overlapped with the challenges of competing ethnic nationalisms and local regionalisms within the RF itself.

Some observers in Russia have argued that in fact a return to the prerevolutionary administrative system of territorial formations (*gubernii*) enjoying local self-government and autonomous entities existing within a unitary state system was one of the options that Yeltsin leadership could have chosen. However, a number of politicians, including the leading members of the government, thought that the introduction of market-oriented reforms could be successful only if there were genuine cooperation from the republics and regions - a situation that could not be achieved unless all of the country's constituent members received sufficient rights to manage their own affairs (Tolz, 1993, p. 3).

A new, politically workable mode of governance was clearly necessary, and the general feeling was that a way out of the profound crisis of state effectiveness was to be sought in institutionalizing relations based on a real federalism which for Russia's political culture was a completely unexplored *terra incognita*.

Nationhood Nationhood became a serious problem area of ethnopolitical development, too, though degrees of its salience were different among the dominant ethnic Russian majority on the one hand, and non-Russian ethnics, on the other. As regards ethnic minorities, nationhood was unlikely to reach the level of crisis. Russia has always pursued broadly inclusive citizenship strategies aimed at integration and even Russification of all ethnic groups resident in its territory. Those tendencies toward cultural and linguistic assimilation give meaning to the distinction between the ethnic Russian nation (*Russkii*) and the broader cultural Russian people (*Rossiiski*), which has been incorporated into the title and constitution of the RF itself (*Rossiiskaya* Federatsiya). An important consequence of such policies has been the lack of serious minority grievances over citizenship policies.

As regards the Russian majority, nationhood has come to be linked with the post-Soviet crisis of 'Russianness' as national identity. Unlike all other parts of the former Soviet Union, where post-Communism was virtually synonymous with national liberation, Russia after the Soviet collapse felt less like a nation-state liberated from a multinational empire than like a deposed metropolitan power facing life without its colonies. While building their post-Soviet state Russians have had to contend with the arduous challenges of democratizing the regime, replacing a command with a market economy, and creating a sense of national identity broad enough to encompass the Russian majority and the many minority groups that reside within the borders of what is still the largest national territory in the world (Shevtsova, 1995, p. 57). At the same time, the rapid de-ideologization of the Russian popular psyche following the breakup of the USSR with necessity led Russians increasingly to view themselves as a discrete ethnic group rather than as 'Soviet people' (Dunlop, 1997).

The Federation Treaty (1992): Pros and Cons.

No issue in the uncertain days of Russian democracy was more prominent than that of federalism, especially as it touched on the status of Russia's ethnic republics. At the very start of post-Soviet history the search for institutional innovations to manage ethnopolitical problem areas and crises involved attempts to channel uncontrolled decentralization into a more ordered pattern by exploring the options offered by a federalist solution.

The late 1991- early 92 was the period of intensive center-periphery bargaining. By March 1992, these endeavors succeeded in the stipulation of a series of agreements - collectively referred to as the Federation Treaty (*Federativny Dogovor*) - which outlined the division of authority between the federal government and the so-called 'subjects of the federation'. These agreements founded a treaty-based federation in Russia. On March 13, 1992, representatives of 18 of the 20 republics within Russia initiated a treaty of federation with Moscow; a separate agreement was signed by representatives of the Federation's oblasts and krais the same week, followed by a third treaty with the autonomous okrugs. Then, on March 31, 1992, the three treaties, constituting the grand Federation Treaty, were formally signed into law (Abdulatipov, Boltenkova, and Iarov, 1993a).

Working out the new federative arrangement was a lengthy process that began in late 1990 (Boltenkova, 1992). In discussions over the treaty's final form, one of the prime sticking points was the unequal legal status of regions and republics. In December 1991, the territorially defined regions (oblasts and krais) of Russia manifestly objected to being permanently relegated to second-class status. During the talks preceding the conclusion of the Federation Treaty, four different solutions were debated (Abdulatipov, 1993, p. 4). One suggestion was to combine all Russian-majority regions into one ethnic Russian (*Russkaya*) republic, with a juridical status equal to that of the other republics within the RF. Depending on one's point of view, this would either elevate Russians by finally giving them their own ethnic territory or denigrate them by making their political status equal to that of the small nationalities. Anyway, the complexity of settlement patterns made this solution highly problematic.[3]

A second idea, one seemingly more popular among the incumbent elites and their coterie, was *gubernuizatsiya* which aimed at eliminating the ethno-territorial principle altogether and transforming all Russia's sub-federal units into what used to be *gubernii* (regions) of pre-revolutionary Russia.[4] This solution, however, was not realistic in the charged atmosphere of post-Soviet ethnopolitics.

A third solution was to equalize the status of regions and republics by increasing the rights and privileges of the regions, but this idea initially was seen both as an attack on republican sovereignty and as a step toward the 'disintegration of Russia into feuding principalities'.

Finally, another influential group of intellectuals and politicians suggested that the best idea might be to change almost nothing and that the RF should retain a Soviet-style structure with various levels of autonomy (Iljinskij, Krylov and Mikhaleva, 1993, p. 28). In that case, the very fact of signing the Treaty would be important as a pact-making on territorial integrity of Russia resolving the perceived crisis of stateness.

In its initial form, the Federation Treaty, as signed in March 1992, came closest to the last of these four proposals. The treaty consisted of three separate documents, each establishing the relationship between a given category of 'subject' and the federal government. The three types of subjects established by the treaty comprised: (1) sovereign republics within the Russian Federation; (2) krais, oblasts, and the federal cities of Moscow and St. Petersburg; (3) autonomous oblast and autonomous okrugs.

The Federation Treaty can be regarded an institutional innovation which permitted to resolve the perceived crisis of stateness and to defuse the fears that Russia might repeat the disintegration pattern of the former Soviet Union. In fact, the Federation Treaty became first serious sign of evident ethnopolitical legitimation of the central authorities and the country's territorial integrity on behalf of the overwhelming majority of 'subjects of the federation'. With the exclusion of Chechnya and Tatarstan, all other 19 republics signed the Federation Treaty. The Treaty was a step forward in federation-building. Most important, there have been created a new federation type, a treaty-based federation which now came to include not only republics, but also non-ethnically defined regions (oblasts and krais) as signatories, i.e. 'subjects of the federation', a status the latter had never enjoyed during the Soviet period. The treaty outlined the powers to be exercised by the federal government as well as the functions under the joint jurisdiction of federal and sub-federal governments.

The federal government was assigned responsibility for a number of governmental functions, most significantly foreign policy, defense and security policy, and citizenship and border issues (including the power to approve internal boundary changes). Joint center-provincial competencies included health, education, welfare, and protection of the minority rights. The functions left to the sole jurisdiction of the regions and republics were residual. Actually, such residual-power principle was regarded by most republics as largely meaningless owing to the comprehensiveness of the other jurisdictional clauses and was one of the reasons why republics demanded they be identified as 'sovereign states', with the presumption that this label would protect their autonomy. Finally, all of the republics demanded that they retain the authority to renegotiate bilaterally the particulars of their relationship with Moscow.

Though the Federation Treaty successfully resolved the perceived crisis of stateness, it turned out to be an insufficient innovation to resolve the actual crisis of state effectiveness. Exploring the option of federalism in Russia led to only relative stabilization and consolidation of Russia's statehood. Actually, the Federation Treaty legitimized the structure which permitted for one sovereign unit (republic) to be constituent sub-unit of another sovereign unit (Russian Federation as a whole). The treaty described the republics as 'sovereign', yet it said nothing about a right to secession, which was present in the USSR's constitution for the Union republics. Thus, while legitimizing further the notion of 'sovereignty', the treaty left unclear what specific rights this entailed (Bartsits, 1995).

The criticisms also focused on other features of the incomplete character of the federation reform. Although the real status and volume of competence of the regions and federal cities had been significantly extended (they have officially become 'subjects of the federation'), still, the treaty preserved and in some respects even reinforced the legal distinction between regions (krais and oblasts, predominantly ethnically Russian) and the non-Russian ethnically-defined republics. Republics enjoyed greater residual powers than regions; both regions and republics were given the right to conduct foreign economic relations, but only republics had a say in tax collection, and approval of federal declarations of states of emergency. Most problematically, 'sovereign' republics (but not regions) were granted formal ownership of the natural resources on their territory, although what was meant by the republics' ownership of land and natural resources was left unclear (Teague, 1994c, p. 36; Slocum, 1995, p. 17). The distribution of profits from exports between the center and the provinces, relative tax burdens, and the extent of subsidization of local budgets from the federal treasury were left to future negotiation or enacting legislation.

The Crisis of the Federal State (1993): Institutions and Interactions[5]

Shortly after the Federation Treaty had been stipulated, state effectiveness reemerged as acute crisis. Moreover, it manifested not only at the system level, but also at the level of strategic interactions. Ethnic and federation politics constituted the key dimension of the crisis. The interactional crisis occurred in the conditions of a 'dual authority' situation within the federal Center engaged into an acute conflict between its presidential and legislative branches, combined with contentions between the federal center and the republics. On top of that, political tensions between the federal center and non-ethnically defined regions (oblasts and krais) also reached its peak during the same period.

Effectiveness of the post-Soviet state had become the focal point of crisis interaction with unusually high likelihood of ensuing violence. Violence, in fact, did break out with dramatic events in Moscow in October 1993 which entailed the end of the first post-Soviet republic in Russia.

During 1992-mid 1993, attempts to consolidate Russia's statehood involved multiple negotiations over the contours of center-periphery relations, as peripheral units (regions and republics) of the Russian Federation mobilized new sets of political identities and claims to rights against the center. Regional leaders resented the higher status given the republics by the Federation treaty. While the privileged status of republics in the Russian federal bargaining game status was linked to their designation as ethnic homelands, it is important to note that, in the context of unfolding market reforms, regionalism and regional economic interests were increasingly moving to the fore. Russia has been a very special case in this trend, primarily because contemporary regional processes are being mainly driven by the ongoing transformation of the economic system, sometimes defined as 'administrative market'. The Soviet heritage in this sense is not just the artificial administrative/territorial division, but the very character of regional processes - in the course of which the regional elites were enabled to convert their former virtual property (administrative rights) into real property (control over natural resources, industrial bases, lands, etc).

Thus, federation subjects soon found themselves in the middle of the ongoing struggle between the Presidency and the Russian parliament (Supreme Soviet). Following the dissolution of the Soviet Union, Yeltsin no longer needed the autonomous republics as allies against Gorbachev, but he still needed regional support as long as he continued to face a stalemate with the obstructionist parliament. During this period, President tended to side with the republics to the extent that he defended their privileges vis-à-vis the regions and blocked regional attempts at self-promotion to the status of republic. This made many regions the natural allies of the Speaker of the Supreme Soviet, Ruslan Khasbulatov, in his escalating power struggle with President Yeltsin. The results of a nation-wide referendum in April of 1993 appeared to give Yeltsin the upper hand over parliament and Khazbulatov.[6]

Following Yetsin's overall success in the April referendum, attempts to devise a new constitutional foundation alternated between courting the intransigent republics and moves to take away their privileges. The site of the power struggles switched for a few months to the arena of constitution-drafting, where both Yeltsin and Khasbulatov sought to win over the regions and republics to their competing constitutional drafts. Yeltsin appeared to be inclined to make deals with the republics. The first presidential draft included the text of the Federation Treaty, with its in-built asymmetry between the rights of the republics, described 'sovereign states within the RF, accorded each the right to negotiate its relationship with Moscow bilaterally and required that the representation of the republics be increased to whatever extent necessary to ensure their control of the Federation Council. The only concession not granted to the republics was the right to secede (Ordeshok, 1995, p. 53).

This produced acute dissatisfaction among regional leaders and countermoves were made by local elites in oblasts and krais. In addition to consistently pressing the demand for a single standard of rights for all subjects of the federation, many regions that lacked republic status solved this problem unilaterally by staging referenda on the issue and then declaring themselves 'sovereign' republics (Payin, 1994b, p. 58-70). In this way regions tried to take advantage of the higher status guaranteed to the republics, apparently to be enshrined in the new constitution.

With their bargaining power salient, the republics became increasingly assertive. The leaders of the republics have focused on preserving the republics as a privileged class of subnational actors. While this distinction has been justified by reference to claims of cultural autonomy, its force has derived from the united front presented by all 20 republics, both the resource rich and the resource poor. Ethnic claims came to serve as a coordinating mechanism across different republics, distinguishing them from the Russian regions. When at the commissions of the Constitutional Convention, the regions (krais and oblasts) started to act as a mobilized force against the republics, most of the original 20 sovereign republics consistently maintained that they had no intention of agreeing to a new constitutional order whose provisions failed to incorporate their special standing. Though the Constitutional Convention settled on a compromise draft on 12 July, as of mid-August, no subject of the Federation had yet agreed to it (*Moscow News*, 20 Aug. 1993; Kononenko 1993).

Some of the influential officials in the center tried to manipulate this dissent between the subjects of the federation with the aim to increase the actual power of the federal center over the periphery. But since the federal authority was disrupted by internal struggles between its legislative and the executive branches, the regions and republics acquired large bargaining power in playing their support for the branch of the central authority that was promising them more. By August 1993 the conflict between the President and the Parliament reached its stalemate and, in order to get the upper hand over the parliament through marshaling the support of the subjects of the federation, the President attempted one more novation.

At his meeting on 12 August with regional and republican leaders in Petrozavodsk, Yeltsin proposed the creation of a new 'Council of Federation', conceived as a governmental body to be staffed, ex-officio, by leaders of the regional and republic administrations and legislatures (Chugaev, 1993; Solnick, 1996, p. 15, *Moscow News*, 15 Oct. 1993, p.6). In this way it was deemed to serve as the upper house of the new Russian parliament and was thought to be able to adopt (or at least to substantially legitimate) the Presidential draft Constitution, should the parliament refuse to accept it. While regional leaders distrusted Yeltsin, republican leaders particularly objected to the proposal's equal treatment of all federation subjects, which would have left them badly outnumbered by the predominantly Russian oblasts.

One month later with his decree No. 1400, the President dissolved the Supreme Soviet, setting in motion the string of events that touched off the bloodshed of 3-4 October in Moscow.[7] Once the parliament was defeated, the federal center wasted no time in asserting its authority over the subnational units (both the regions and republics) and in the process, recasting the rules of the federation game, as well as eventually reinventing the identities of Russian federalism (Slocum, 1995).

Once the president achieved the military victory over the Supreme Soviet, one of his first moves was to dismiss those regional heads of administration who had remained loyal to the parliament. Subsequently, the presidential authority turned its attention to the provincial legislatures. The regional and republican soviets were 'invited' to dissolve themselves, while the dissolution of elected councils at the city and district level was absolutely demanded. Finally, new legislative elections were ordered to be held in all of the regions (but not in the republics) by March 1994. The principle of direct presidential appointment of regional governors was reinforced; Yeltsin replaced some governors, and decreed that these appointed regional executives were to retain veto power and budgetary authority over the reconstituted regional soviets for a two-year period.

Along with calling for new elections in the regions, the President moved to disengage himself from his earlier accommodations to republican-level claims to sovereignty. In announcing that an elective Federation Council would form the upper house of the new parliament (*Federalnoye Sobraniye*), while at the same time dissolving the regional parliaments (Soviets), Yeltsin effectively abrogated the existing Council of Federation. Regional interests received a further blow when the Constitutional Convention was reshuffled to place both federal and regional working groups in a single chamber under the control of presidential representatives (RFE/RL Daily Report, 13 Oct. 1993).

The consolidation of a strong presidential regime, effectively, has shifted the balance of political authority in favor of the center. As the final form of the constitution took shape, it became increasingly clear that the President's team intended to substantially revise the Federation Treaty. Republic-level sovereignty claims that declared the priority of local legislation over federal law were nullified, and the unilateral self-promotion of a subject of the federation to a higher status was forbidden. Meanwhile, Leonid Smirnyagin, a member of the presidential council, wrote that 'by the middle of 1993 the words "sovereignty" and "Federation Treaty"... had become synonyms for a striving towards the disintegration of the state'(*Nezavisimaya Gazeta*, 30 Oct. 1993).

New constitutional principles declared by the presidential team, explicitly rejected confederalism or asymmetric federalism and called for a symmetric federalism which, though admitted different types of the sub-federal units, yet declared the legal equality of all subjects of the federation which was to be based on 'five bans': 1) a ban on secession, i.e., on exit from the federation; 2) a ban on unilateral changes in the status of subjects of the federation, in as much as this would affect the interests of other subjects and of the federation as a whole; 3) a ban on converting internal administrative borders into state or economic borders to ensure freedom of movement of people, goods, and information across the entire territory of the state; 4) the supremacy of federal legislation; 5) a single basis of government (subjects are forbidden from introducing non-democratic forms of government - theocracy, dictatorship, etc. (*Izvestiya*, 2 Nov. 1993)

On 8 November, Yeltsin presented a draft constitution that incorporated the principles of the symmetric, constitution-based federalism. The draft contained no mentioning of the republic-level sovereignty whatsoever. While not encompassing the text of the Federation Treaty, Art. 11.3 and Art. 1 in Section II make it clear that the Federation Treaty is still in force to the extent that it does not contradict the Constitution. The largest of these contradictions would appear to be exactly the issue of republican sovereignty. Whereas the Federation Treaty referred to the republics as 'sovereign republics within the Russian Federation', the Constitution said 'the sovereignty of the Russian Federation extends to the entirety of its territory', implying that sovereignty claims the sub-federal units are invalid. Significantly, the Constitution explicitly stated that all units of the Federation 'are equal members of the Russian Federation' (Art. 5, par. 1) which meant a considerable elevation of the status of regions (krais, oblasts) and extension of their rights.

On 12 December 1993, the new Constitution was passed at a referendum with 58.4% of the federation-wide vote.[8] The problem of ethno-political legitimation of new federative arrangements becomes obvious when one considers the breakdown of the referendum results. Official turnout was 54.8% of the registered voters, slightly more than the 50 % needed for a quorum. Opposition to the constitution was stronger in the ethnic republics than in the regions. In the regions, the majority of the electorate voted for the constitution, while only 23.6% supported it in the republics. Among all those voting in the republics, only 47.9 % voted for the constitution, compared with 60 % in the regions. Polling did not take place in Chechnya, where it was officially prohibited by local elites. In Tatarstan overall turnout was under 15%. Turnout was also below 50 % in three other republics - Udmurtia, Khakassia, and Komi - while for 21 republics as a whole, turnout was 49.2%. In the 16 republics where turnout exceeded 50%, a majority rejected the constitution in 7 (Adygeia, Bashkortostan, Dagestan, Karachai-Cherkessia, Mordova, Tuva, and Chuvashia).[9] Therefore, ratification appears to have been based solely on the federation-wide vote.

Ethnopolitics after 1994

Today's Russian democracy remains largely unconsolidated and faces demanding challenges in different spheres of post-Soviet transformations. Ethnic politics and issues of federalism are only some of such spheres, though by no means irrelevant ones for the overall success of the democratic project in Russia. The change of ethnopolitical scene that took place after the adoption of new constitution, can be characterized as consolidation of Russian statehood and partial stabilization of the center-periphery relations. Ethnopolitical problem areas have persisted.

Stateness Stateness remains a problem-area, although it is unlikely to reach critical salience for the RF at large. The hard-core political separatism has become a politically isolated phenomenon in nearly every other republic (Slocum, 1995, p. 25). The observers agree that the conditions for ethnically based civil wars in Russia do not exist, as there are no sharp socio-political cleavages with distinct national polarizations that could be formed into two opposing camps. The most serious nationalist challenges have come from the northern Caucasus, whose scale, however - 1% of total Russian territory - is unlikely to translate into a mortal threat to the Russian state.[10]

While regionalism and demands for a devolution of power from Moscow were and still remain strong forces, ethnic arguments are more frequently a justification rather than an actual case of contention (Kempton, 1996, p. 588). Sovereignty claims are increasingly put forth by pragmatic local leaders seeking to enhance their locality's economic standing within an evolving system of fiscal federalism (Gonchar and Goreglyad, 1995; Kototeyeva, 1996).

The latent preservation of the republics' special status remains a bone of contention for some regions, and the elimination of ethnically-defined units (the so-called *gubernizatsiya*) remains on the agenda for ardent advocates of strong Russian statehood, but the Yeltsin government has held firm in consistently rejecting any further 'self-promotions'. A sovereignty claim, in fact, has proved not to be a particularly fungible political commodity in new conditions. As the experience of the December 1995 parliamentary elections campaign showed, the sovereignty for the republics as a claim has been absent from electoral promises of any of all-Russian political parties. The focus of disputes over center-periphery relations within the RF has moved from political to economic issues. The political identities of the regions and republics seem to have coalesced around an understanding that the political disintegration of the RF would be an unlikely, unfeasible, and probably undesirable outcome. Actually, the principal divisions that have emerged within the Russian Federation over the last four years have been geographic and economic, not ethnic.

Today Russia's republics and regions are debating the costs and benefits of autonomy, testing their limits *within* the Federation, and trying to determine how much freedom they are willing to sacrifice in order to increase their benefits from the federation game. Despite the flaws in the current federation system, Moscow appears to be in a position to preserve the country's territorial integrity. What has been changing, and will continue to change, is the balance of power between Moscow and the rest of the RF.

As suggested by several analysts, perhaps, the most useful way of looking at the situation is as a group of nested, interconnected bargaining games (Slocum, 1995, p. 30). Whereas the political and economic demands of Russia's regions and republics have always been intimately linked, since 1993 a qualitatively new stage in center-periphery relations has emerged, marked by a change in the nature of the bargaining process from what has been termed as 'status game' to 'resource game' (Kempton, 1996).

Assessing the current state of the problem of *state effectiveness* in the context of federation politics, one needs to take into account a complex co-existence of two contradictory features in the period following the adoption of the new constitution in December 1993. On the one hand, inter-governmental relations remain very troubled in Russia. The extent of the autonomy of the regions and republics has yet to be clarified in practice. Joint competence, as stated in the Constitution, is often more nominal than real, because in many cases it is not accompanied by legislation specifying how it is to be implemented (Lysenko, 1998). Many of the constitutions of the republics contradict the provisions in the federal constitution of the RF, and complicated center-periphery relations have made efforts to work out an effective system of fiscal and budgetary federalism extremely difficult (e.g., Asochakov and Umnova, 1993; Wallich, 1994; Pastukhov, 1994; Aklaev, 1996b). Many observers have noted that Russian federalism quite often is used as a tool or even a bargaining chip in the political struggles of various forces (e.g., Kempton, 1996; Solnick, 1996). As far as the budget and other spheres are concerned, federalism is often a hollow declaration. In a country that for centuries has been a unitary state, federal relations and a 'federal mentality' do not spring out full-fledged overnight. No doubt, many attempts to substitute decentralization for federalism often occur.

On the other hand, the new constitutional order, while not resolving all tensions of the center-periphery relations, has provided a new institutional framework for managing these relations, a framework flexible enough to allow for center-periphery bargaining on some important issues, but rigid issues of sovereignty, succession, and the political status of the subjects. It has been correctly argued elsewhere that regimes in transition are wise to build flexibility into their constitutions. With respect to the RF, an important understanding of this point has been emphasized by Edward Walker (1995, p. 11-2) who argues that the very flexibility and indeterminacy of the constitutional ordering of center-periphery relations may be a necessary response to the uncertainty and institutional flux characterizing the Russian polity.

> What is unusual about the federation provisions in the Russian constitution, then, is that flexibility is built into the document in ways other than the amendment process. Within the limits of the general framework established by the 'five bans', a great deal is left open to negotiations between the federal government and the 'subjects of the federation'... Despite the difficulties this openness to negotiation will doubtless create in the future, it was preferable to 'legal dogmatism'.

The Constitution left open the possibility of concluding additional treaties between federal and republican or regional governments. In fact, this flexibility of constitutional arrangements did permit to explore new avenues for management of the center-periphery relations by institutionalizing the bilateral treaties stipulated between the authorities of the RF on one side, and the authorities of a specific 'subject of the federation', on the other.

The first bilateral treaty, *On Demarcation of Competencies Between the Government of the Russian Federation and the Government of the Republic of Tatarstan*, was signed on February 15, 1994. It can not be considered in isolation from the tense relations that existed between the federal authorities and those of the republic throughout 1990-93. Until early 1994 Tatarstan's political leadership held back from participation in Russian federal structures. President Shaimiyev called for a boycott of the December 1993 elections for the new Federal Assembly and the simultaneous referendum on Yeltsin's proposed constitution.

The treaty resulted from two years of negotiations which revealed the need to reach a compromise. Through this treaty and 11 agreements, the federal center has delegated a much larger number of powers and benefits to Tatarstan than to other subjects of the Russian Federation. Furthermore, Tatarstan has received a number of the federal government's exclusive authorities. The treaty, on the whole, satisfied Kazan's long-standing demand to be granted a special treatment and, in effect, healed the rift that had been created by Tatarstan's refusal to sign the Federation Treaty in 1992. At the same time, the Treaty with Tatarstan did not remove serious contradictions between federal and republic constitutions. The treaty contained neither a provision stating that Tatarstan is a constituent republic of the Russian Federation, nor recognition of the federal constitution's and federal laws' superiority over republic laws. The treaty had elements of both an international and an intra-state treaty, and hence it deviated from the principle of equality of all subjects of the Federation, suggesting a return to the practices of asymmetrical federalism.

The significance of the Russia-Tatarstan treaty has been subject to varying interpretations (See its critique e.g. Lysenko, 1995, p. 119; Iskhakov, 1995, p. 23). Within Tatarstan, the Tatar nationalist opposition to Shaimiyev split over the issue of support for the treaty, thus further consolidating the power base and authority of the president. For most political observers at the center, the treaty signified that Tatarstan had at last agreed to join the Federation and renounced its prior claims to sovereignty. Many Tatar nationalists in effect accepted this interpretation, seeing the treaty as a betrayal by Shaimiyev of Tatarstan's sovereignty and their own hopes for the republic's ultimate political independence. Shaimiyev himself insisted that the agreement was a treaty 'between two sovereign states', and that henceforth the Constitution of Tatarstan and the treaty with Russia would serve side by side as the basic law of Tatarstan. Using these strategies, Shaimiyev appears to have skillfully manipulated the local debate over the treaty, marginalizing hard-core separatists within Tatarstan and shifting the focus to negotiations over concrete economic interests, rather than more abstract conflicts over Tatarstan's political status. On the whole, the move satisfied Kazan's long-standing demand for a special treatment but what remains of Tatarstan's 'sovereignty' is in the eye of the beholder.

Following the signing of the power-sharing treaty, Tatarstan held special elections to fill its seats in the Federal Assembly. When Tatarstan, the penultimate holdout among Russia's republics, thus agreed to play by the rules of the game, an important phase in the consolidation of the Russian statehood had come to an end. In 1995 the events in Chechnya provided a vivid demonstration of what the price for refusing to join the federation may eventually be. Today it is evident that the treaty eased the growing tensions and brought Tatarstan back within the political and legal space of the RF. As observed by Slocum (1995, p. 27): '[Just] as the ambiguity surrounding the relationship between the Federation Treaty and the December 1993 Constitution seems to have served as a stabilizing factor in the overall pattern of center-periphery relations, similar ambiguity surrounding the implications of the Russia-Tatarstan treaty added a degree of stability in the relations between these two entities'.

The treaty with Tatarstan reopened the door for other subjects of the federation to demand special treatment. Despite repeated avowals that no more bilateral treaties would be signed, by the end of 1995 Moscow had signed similar documents with six other republics: Kabardino-Balkaria, Bashkortostan, North Ossetia, Sakha-Yakutia, Buriatia, and Udmurtia. A positive effect was that the separatist and nationalist trends in ethnic republics lost much of their momentum following the conclusion of the treaties. All republics came to recognize and abide by the federal legislation.[11] Republican legislation has made progress in demarcating joint competencies, as well as accumulating positive experience in the development of treaty-based relations in various spheres.

Analysts consider Moscow's strategy in pushing ad hoc regional treaties as probably serving a dual purpose. In addition to placating restive regions, the center may have also weakened the coordinating mechanism that permitted the republics to act collectively since 1990. If Tatarstan or Sakha (Yakutia), for instance, derives special benefits from its bilateral treaty rather than from its status as a republic, then perhaps it will be less likely to defend the interests of other republics (Solnick, 1996, p. 23).

Through 1995 only ethnic republics were offered treaties with the center, thus increasing the perceived inequality between republics and regions. These practices, logically, were bound to change once the majority of regions (oblasts and krais) finally held gubernatorial elections (starting in mid 1996). As central authorities started to lose the power to replace regional leaders, a control by means of granting treaties increasingly turned out a reasonable option to be considered by the federal center. In January 1996, almost two years after the signing of the first treaty, the federal authorities declared ready 'to balance the treaty-making process' and agreed to sign treaties and agreements with a number of oblasts and krais. Bilateral treaties with regions began with Sverdlovsk, Kaliningrad, Orenburg, Krasnodar Krai, and Khabarovsk Krai. The treaty with Sverdlovsk in January 1996 granted the oblast important concessions in the area of personnel appointments and fiscal administration. Since then, for republics and oblasts alike the bilateral treaties represented real shifts of jurisdictional authority from the center to the signatory region or republic. The pace of concluding bilateral treaties accelerated through the June of 1996 presidential election campaign.

By mid-1996, over 15 treaties and 150 agreements on demarcation of powers in specific spheres had been signed. New signatories included Chuvashia and Komi republics, Kaliningrad, Orenburg, Perm, Rostov,

Sverdlovsk, Irkutsk and Leningrad oblasts, Krasnodar and Khabarovsk regions, St. Petersburg as a city of federal jurisdiction, and constituent okrugs of regions (Ust'-Ordynsk Buriat okrug and Komi-Permyatsk okrug). By end 1997, the number of bilateral treaties has risen to forty.

From the viewpoint of management system-level ethnopolitical problem area, institutionalization of bilateral treaties has meant a choice made in favor of a new re-adjustment of federation-building strategies, now including a mixture of both constitutional and treaty approaches.[12] Attempt to institutionalize federation management through the practice of bilateral treaties are even more impressive when on the background of the dramatic developments in Chechnya. On the one hand, these treaties provide a constructive alternative to the use of brute force and suggest that post-Soviet elites at the federal government in Russia have learned something about constructive management of center-periphery disputes. On the other hand, this practice of bilateral treaties, instead of constitutional amendments, means that, obviously, the federalization process and institutional innovations required for a successful management of state effectiveness as well as the search for a center-periphery balance is far from complete.

In this respect, today's RF represents a case for the model of imperfect federalism that requires a prolonged period of power delimitation before its federal-like arrangements take a fully-fledged shape. Deal-making over jurisdictional prerogatives is likely to further undermine the ambiguous federal provisions of the 1993 constitution and to make achieving consensus on constitutional revisions even more unlikely. Moreover, an expressed concern has been that the ongoing bilateral negotiations may ultimately supersede any constitutional norms for power-sharing in Russia, provided that the center abides by the terms of its deals. If it does, however, the Russian constitution may soon give way to a patchwork of ad hoc agreements - published and unpublished - that are constantly in the process of renegotiation (e.g. Lysenko, 1998).

Consequentially, effectiveness of the post-Soviet federal state in Russia is likely to remain a serious problem area in the foreseeable future. Today the treaties put subjects of the federation in unequal positions and thus run counter to the principle of equality as stipulated in the Russian constitution. In the prevailing circumstances, the most important task is formulating the 'standard rules of the game' that would be accepted by all subjects of the Federation and the federal center. As long as there are no such rules, or they are not recognized, or the game is run by the rules set between Moscow and individual subjects, the positions of constitutionalism, a basic component of *Rechtstaat*, are likely to remain unconsolidated. In short, although Moscow has begun to establish a more coherent federal structure - through the 1992 Federation treaty and the 1993 Constitution - the federation continues to be held together by a series of bilateral treaties and agreements between Moscow and the constituent republics, regions, and krais.

Nationhood Nationhood so far, has been a problem area without any serious potential for translating into interactional crisis in relations between the Russian majority and non-Russian ethnic minorities. At the same time, promotion of multiple identities and search for an adequate balance between civic and ethnic definitions of nationhood is likely to represent a salient task along the way of democratic consolidation. Particular importance needs be attributed to forging a liberal civic conception of Russian nationhood which could counterbalance attempts to promote neo-imperial etatist definitions (*derzhava*), advocated by reactionary forces of Russian 'national-patriots' on the one hand, and Soviet era communist nostalgics on the other.[13] Some positive trends at promoting non-ethnic, civic definitions of nationhood have manifested at the level of some of republics within Russia, as evidenced in the concepts of *Tatarstantsy* in Tatarstan and *Yakutiane* in Sakha (Yakutia). The high degree of cultural assimilation in those republics, as well as the fact that political struggles have been framed as center-periphery rivalries rather than interethnic ones have contributed to a strong sense of the respective civic identities (Hanauer, 1996, p. 82-3; Aklaev, 1996b, pp. 144-7).

Patterns of Ethnopolitical Crisis Management and Ethnic Peace: The Case of Russian Federation

Overall, Russia succeeded to preserve ethnic peace on the vast majority of its territory during its extremely complicated democratic transition. The only two serious cases of sustained ethnic violence reported since the collapse of the former Soviet Union occurred in parts of North Caucasus whose total scale does not exceed 1% of the RF's territory. One of them, Ossete-Inghush armed hostilities in 1992, is a case of long-standing animosities with roots in the history of forced population transfer in the 1940s (territorial attribution of the Prigorodny district) and thus is not directly related to the democratization processes. The federal center succeeded to enforce negative peace by suppressing the hostilities and separating opposing armed formations. At the same time, there has been little change in transforming the conflict since then.

The case of Chechnya has obviously been a grave one and besides its historical roots, is directly related to ethnopolitics of stateness under transition. Yet is has also been an isolated case of outright ethnoterritorial separatism in the RF. The problem area of stateness in the rest of Russia is unlikely to exacerbate because of that. The patterns applied in managing the Chechnya crisis during 1991-96 were mostly destructive and culminated in prolonged violent confrontation escalating to warfare between the federal forces and the rebel republic. In mid-1996 outright violence was suspended and since then a series of negotiations have been underway. Though negative peace has been a fact for the last years or so, the talks thus far have failed to produce any substantial compromise agreement.

The interactional crisis which did involve the whole of Russia during the first years of the country's post-Soviet transition was related to the effectiveness of post-Soviet Russian federative state and acute power struggles within the federal center. In 1992-93, the effectiveness of new Russian state manifestly became the focal point of interactions in both ethnopolitics and larger politics of democratization. Patterns, by which the crisis of 1992-93 was actually managed, have exerted a profound and ambivalent impact on the whole structure of Russia's institutions, principles of federalism and ethnopolitical dynamics at large. Crisis management strategies ranged from bargaining to coercive imposition and have succeeded in defusing the lingering impasse between the two branches of the central authority as well as in winning the time to search for more constructive approaches to managing federation disputes.

The quality of ethnic peace in today's Russia has been a function of the specific configuration of ethnopolitical problem areas and crises at the system level, kinds of institutional choices and applied patterns of crisis management. With the exception of Chechnya and Tatarstan, stateness has never reached the level of crisis. Differential patterns applied in managing the two crises (coercive violent repression in the case of Chechnya, and power-sharing negotiations and pact-making in the case of Tatarstan) account for differential outcomes.

For Russia it is the problem area of state effectiveness of its federal state that is most likely to determine the prospects of the consolidation of democratizing ethnic peace. Management of ethnopolitical challenges to the effectiveness of the federal state proceeded along the ways of exploring the federalist solution and included a series of try-and-see endeavors with different institutional arrangements of federalist type in the attempts to tailor the ones more adaptable to the Russian scene. Those have ranged from an asymmetric federation based on multilateral treaty agreements (as reflected in the 1992 Federation Treaty), through constitution-based de jure symmetric federation (as reflected in the December 1993 federal constitution) to a mixed type of a de-facto asymmetricity of federal arrangements based on constitutional flexibility negotiated bilateral treaties between the federal center and selected 'subjects of federation'. All these institutional innovations and adjustments have been partial in their nature, incomplete in the degree of achieved institutionalization and often even ambivalent in realization. At the same time, probably, exactly these features can account for the apparent short-term success in resolving the crisis of state effectiveness and in keeping ethnopolitical relations short of high level of tension (with the obvious exception of Chechnya).

In fact, given the situational, dynamic and somewhat volatile nature of post-Soviet politics, Russian authorities in the center face a delicate dilemma of balancing general legal principles with highly specific negotiated compromises. In this sense, a well-managed federalism promises to become the best antidote against virulent forms of nationalism (Balzer and Vinokurova, 1996, p. 116). It also means that the tasks of federation-building and institutionalizing relations of real federalism loom large on the agenda of democratic consolidation in Russia.

Overall, in the overwhelming majority of Russia's territory, excluding the area of North Caucasus (where stable negative peace has been enforced in Ossetia-Inghushetia case and unstable negative peace is fledgling in Chechnya), today's ethnic peace can be assessed as displaying some initial measure of a positive quality. It has been based on the overall prevalence of non-violent patterns of conflict management which have only become possible after a completed democratic transition. The increase of positive quality of ethnic peace will strongly depend upon continuation of power-sharing negotiations and federation rearrangements. Yet, to a great extent, it is still a largely uninstitutionalized and therefore, inherently unstable relationship of peace. Perhaps more than for other post-Soviet cases, it is evident that in Russia consolidation of ethnic peace is directly contingent upon continuing progress in building institutions of democratic federalism.

Notes

1. See e.g. the assessments of scenarios of Russia's political development after the Soviet collapse in Pugachev (1992, pp. 27-35).
2. Lynch and Lukic (1996) argue that if a challenge to the integrity of the Russian state were to emerge, it would have to come from the Russians themselves. Ethno-federal secessions or realignments would most likely follow or reflect civil conflict among Russians rather than cause the conflict.
3. For juridical arguments against the idea of formation of Russian Republic see Ebzeyev and Karapetyan (1995).
4. See, e.g., interview with O. Rumyantsev, president of the Russia's Supreme Soviet Constitutional Group in *Moscow News* (1991, no. 10, p. 5) interview with G. Popov in *Izvestiya* (3 Oct. 1991), also Cheshko (1993, p. 29-45).
5. This section is adapted from Slocum (1995).
6. The referendum had four questions. The exact wording and nationwide vote totals for each question were: question 1, 'Do you have confidence in the President of the Russian Federation, B. Yeltsin?' (58.7% yes, 39.2% no); question 2, 'Do you approve of the social and economic policy carried out by the President of the Russian Federation since 1992?' (53% yes, 44.6% no); question 3, 'Do you consider it necessary to hold an early election for the President of the Russian Federation?' (49.5% yes, 30.2% no); question 4, 'Do you consider it necessary to hold early elections for the Congress of People's Deputies of the Russian Federation?' (67.2% yes, 19.3% no). The overall turnout was around 64% (Clem and Craumer, 1993, p. 482).
7. For a detailed analysis of regional (in *krais* and *oblasts*) aspect of the September-October 1993 crisis see Kasimov and Senatova (1993, pp. 183-7).
8. See the official results of the referendum in *Bulletin of the Central Election Committee of the Russian Federation*, Vol. 1, No. 12; the regional and republican distribution of the election results see Guboglo (1994, p. 34).
9. For instance, the results of the referendum show that the draft constitution received 'no' in Adygeia - 61.1%, in Bashkortostan . 57. 99%, in Daghestan - 79, 14%, in Karachaevo-Cherkessia - 72%, in Mordovia - 62.86%, in Chuvashia - 58.4%, see Bartsis (1995, p. 56).
10. Lynch and Lukic (1996, p.17) observe in this respect: 'The fact that the Russian government tolerated Chechnya's declaration of independence for three years before addressing the issue suggests the low significance of the area for the integrity of the state. The danger of Chechnya is not one of Russia's impending ethnic disintegration but rather that, by dramatizing the collapse of Russia's effective civil and military institutions, it could accelerate and transform a fragmentation of authority within Russia that is already advanced'.
11. In exchange for certain benefits, Tatarstan and Bashkortostan have abandoned their single-channel tax system (by which they could unilaterally halt the flow of taxes collected on their territory to the federal budget) in favor of a multi-channel system of taxation.
12. On two principles towards Russian federation-building see e.g., Mukhametshin (1994), Khakimov (1996), critique in Hanauer (1996), Umnova (1998).
13. This issue has received its special treatment in Simonsen (1996).

Conclusion

The case studies surveyed in Part III suggest that the emergence of ethnopolitical problem areas and crises has been an invariable concomitant of both democratic transition and early phases of democratic consolidation in the examined multiethnic post-communist systems. The state and quality of the peace relationship between ethnic groups have tended to depend not only and not so much upon past legacies. Even more important have been institutional and strategic choices made at the onset and at critical junctions of democratization process. By way of conclusion, this chapter aims to summarize major observations concerning specific features of democratizing ethnic peace and the role that ethnopolitical crisis management has to play in the dynamics and prospects of its development.

Features of Democratizing Ethnic Peace

Analyzing specific features of democratizing ethnic peace as a category in its own right gives a better understanding of the nature of the relationship and the complexity of tasks that democratization in multiethnic setting is faced with. Three important features stand out in this connection.

First, as regards its quality, it is a *positive* peace. The very movement away from coercive rule is a catharsis. It takes away the burden of double oppression toward the ethnic subordinates, broadens the perceived limits of freedom and promotes interethnic cooperative efforts in the pursuit of justice and civility. A completed democratic transition brings about the promise of a higher quality life and evolutionary political growth, as well as generates the will to proact for this positive change among all groups irrespective of their ethnic identities.

Second, as regards its potential for endurance, this relationship of peace is fragile, very *unstable* and has low threshold of breakdown. Unfolding democratization means a process by which all relevant political actors agree upon, and start to pursue, new rules of the political game which make the non-violent mode of conflict resolution possible. Post-transitional peace among ethnic groups is extremely volatile precisely because the new rules of non-violent contestation, moderation and compromise have not yet become, in Juan Linz's words, the 'only game in town' even in intragroup relations (within ethnic dominants or ethnic subordinates), while the uncertainties of the evolving democratic change sharply increase collective ethnic apprehensions and provide incentives for radicalization of outbidding elites.

Third, as regards its processual attributes, democratizing ethnic peace is an extremely *elusive* and *crisis-prone* relationship. These features come as product of a complex, ambivalent and dynamic interplay between ethnic politics and politics of democratization. Democratization, in fact, often exacerbates existing ethnic problems and dangers of situational politics. The change associated with transitions involves extremely profound, comprehensive and rapidly evolving socio-political transformations that engulf all spheres of life in post-authoritarian societies. Imperfect operation of conflict management institutions and practices in transitional systems engenders intensely perceived communal apprehensions. The resulting stress, if left unmanaged, can easily coalesce into an ultimate threat to both ethnic peace and the prospects of the democratic project.

Transition to new institutions that make constructive conflict management possible is by no means an easy enterprise. A lot depends upon specific interactions between the state and/or ethnic groups and - what is even more important - upon the critical choices made by salient elites. Ultimately, the persistence and the quality of the ethnic peace relationship are contingent upon the ability of the forces promoting democracy to instill new norms and institutionalize new patterns of interaction in a specific multiethnic milieu besieged by entrenched legacies of the past.

Ethnopolitical Crisis Management and Democratizing Ethnic Peace

The crisis-prone attribute of ethnic peace more often than not has tended to come to the fore in ethnopolitical dynamics of all of the above-reviewed cases of post-Soviet democratization. At both the system and the interactional levels, problems of democratizing ethnic peace have, in fact, been coterminous with the tasks of ethnopolitical crisis management.

Our cases give evidence that suggests several important lines of linkage between patterns of crisis management and the resultant state and quality of the peace relationship between ethnic groups. First, the very fact of preservation of ethnic peace (or, conversely, its breakdown) has been the result of the crisis management patterns applied at the interactional level and the respective policy choices. Second, the quality of the preserved ethnic peace (negative or more positive) has been the result of the crisis management patterns applied at the system level and the respective choices made in the realm of political institutions. Third, at both levels of crisis management, the prospects for the endurance of the peace relationship (the degree of its potential sustainability) have tended to be strongly related to the application of constructive patterns of ethnopolitical crisis management.

As observed in our cases, the degree of salience of a specific ethnopolitical problem area (stateness, state effectiveness, nationhood) to the crisis level has varied with the configuration of ethnic groups in individual cases, structuring of interactions between the state and political ethnic actors, and the types of cleavages that antedated democratization. For the Soviet Union-Lithuania, Moldova-Transdniestria, and Moldova-Gagauz cases it was the problem of stateness that had reached the level of crisis, for Estonia it was nationhood, for the Russian Federation it was the effectiveness of the federal state.

Success in downgrading a certain ethnopolitical crisis to the level of a problem area strongly depends upon the progress reached in building new institutions and promoting new practices of conflict management. There are no general solutions to ethnopolitical crises. Each case differs from others in terms of its possible amenability to particular strategies of accommodation. Yet, the cross-case comparison points in the direction that strategies built on democratic *and* liberal foundations have a far better chance of producing sustainable interethnic security and fostering stable peace.

Successful democratization in multiethnic systems is called upon to transform ethnic politics into a positive and sustainable relationship of peace. The essence of this transformation is the replacement of previous patterns of conflict management with new institutions that have the capacity to process ethnic conflict peacefully and constructively. Efforts to preserve and foster peace cannot be separated from those meant to manage and resolve conflict. The central challenge on the agenda of post-authoritarian ethnopolitical development is to realize a transition to such patterns of conflict management that are compatible with liberal democracy. In this sense, multiethnic democracy is reached in stages along with the successful resolution of ethnopolitical crises and institutionalization of management of respective problem areas. Democratizing ethnic peace can be considered as democratic peace-in-becoming.

The change in the patterns of conflict management comes in stages and includes: 1) institutional choice at the stage of democratic transition that can be achieved as the product of interethnic pact-making, and 2) institution-building and institutional re-adjustment at the stage of democratic consolidation and the habituation to conflict management practices that provide for the well-being of ethnic minorities and respect for their rights.

Crisis management, though different from both conflict management and conflict resolution, may serve as an initial, solid step towards achieving either goal. If the institutional innovation is appropriate, the ethnopolitical crisis is downgraded to the level of a problem area and becomes amenable to management within the newly created or re-adjusted institutional framework. Progress in institution-building effectively promotes the system's capacity to deal with ethnopolitical problem areas by peaceful means.

Towards Consolidated Ethnic Peace

Reflections over the future of democratizing ethnic peace pose the issues of peace consolidation to the fore of the unfolding research and policy agenda. What new factors come to influence the conditions and character of ethnic peace after multiethnic polities have survived the founding experience? What new challenges arise on the agenda of ethnic peace as the democratization process moves from a riveting phase of transition to one of a laborious and seemingly unexciting routine of consolidation? What are the ethnically relevant configurations that exist in post-transitional conflicts over power, the state, nationhood and citizenship and how, out of these contestations, can democratic ethnopolitical practices become 'the only game in town'? Under what conditions can fledgling democracies acquire the skills to channel ethnic mobilization in directions that expand avenues of democratic participation without undermining democratic stability?

Having survived the founding experience, ethnic peace in new democracies is by no means surely on the road to consolidation. The paths for the evolution of the relationship in post-transitional setting are multiple. It is not only the danger of its *breakdown*, often to be followed by reimposition of the coercive rule, or the promise of its *progression* to stable liberal peace. At least two other alternatives are also possible and have become manifest in a number of cases: 1) a hybrid relationship that combines elements of stability in the short- to middle-run with the illiberal treatment of minorities, often thorough the hegemonic control that reproduces the incivility of structured ethnic dominance (a partially stable but mostly illiberal ethnic peace); 2) a persistent but unconsolidated relationship that fails to develop institutionalized power-sharing and safeguards for minorities rights (a partially liberal but mostly unstable and unsustainable ethnic peace). In any single case, unless relevant circumstances culminate in the extreme, the end result is not inescapable, and issues of craft loom large.

It is politically and conceptually important to understand the specific tasks of crafting consolidated ethnic peace. The relationship needs to have in place three interacting and mutually reinforcing components in order for such consolidation to exist: institutions, culture, and constituency of ethnic peace which reflect the respective (institutional, attitudinal, and behavioral) dimensions of the consolidation process.

The building of democratic institutions capable of constructively processing ethnic conflict is the most crucial, albeit complicated and frustratingly slow component of the challenges on the agenda of democratizing ethnic peace. Ultimately, institutionalization which is implied by successful democratic consolidation is the irreducible requisite for achieving both positive and sustainable ethnic peace as well. Only when there is a fundamental acknowledgment of the basic need of all ethnopolitical groups for security, identity, and participation, and only when that acknowledgment is implemented in a corresponding institutional form, will lasting ethnic peace be achieved.

Democratic institutions of ethnic peace have to be not only created but crafted, nurtured, and developed. The legitimation and consolidation of democratic power-sharing institutions (in either consociational or integrative options) are not necessarily permanent achievements but may require continuous adjustment, reform, and renewal to maintain. The danger is to expect too much of what might be called political engineering since, in reality, the success of democratic institutions has been organic, not mechanical. They work only if they can live and grow in the common acceptance and rooted affection of the community and its culture from which they take their form.

As a matter of fact, at the earlier phases of democratic consolidation the diffusion of norms of non-violent conflict management is more important for promoting ethnic peace than any particular institutional structure or formal constitutional provisions. At the same time, the invariable feature of democratizing systems is that institutions precede the development of norms in the polity, which makes the basis for restraint on violent outbursts less secure.

Only at the later stages of democratic consolidation when the normative structure of ethnic peace is internalized, can the institutional conditions of the relationship become truly sustainable. In the immediate aftermath of transitions the oft-present danger is to expect too much of what might be called political engineering. In reality, the success of democratic institutions has always been organic, not mechanical. They work only if they can live and grow in the common acceptance and rooted affection of the community and its culture from which they take their form. Shifts in the political culture that will result supportive of peace between ethnic groups in a multiethnic polity require the growth of liberal values and norms of civility that reinforce multiple identities, engrounding of transethnic loyalties and tolerance, reaching complementarity of the civic and the ethnic realms of nationhood.

Successful and viable power-sharing is not the cause of the liberal spirit of tolerance, moderation and compromise, but their result. Democratically crafted power sharing (in either consociational or integrative options) is actually the mechanism adopted to give expression to the prior readiness of ethnic political actors to eschew exclusive politics in the interests of mutually beneficial outcomes. Only in this way can multiethnic political community develop institutionalized intergroup trust which, in turn, makes the emergence of an interethnic social contract possible.

Realistically thinking, it is to be acknowledged that the creation of an inclusively pluralistic 'culture of ethnic peace' can only occur at the end of a long process of changes in attitudes, collective identities, and institutions. An interim step along this path and its irreducible requisite is the establishment of the ethnic peace constituency.

At the system level the tasks of such a constituency have to do with the diffusion and engrounding of civilized norms. In new democracies (re)emergent civil society (democratic citizenry) can be conceptualized as such constituency promoting ethnic peace. The principles of civil society - such as the equality of human beings cannot deny the immense variability of human experience and identities. Civil society represents a crucial arena for the development of important attributes of multiethnic democracy, such as tolerance, moderation, a willingness to compromise and a respect for opposing viewpoints. These values and norms become stable only when they emerge through cooperative experience of democratic consolidation.

At the level of interactions ethnic peace constituencies are also crucial for promoting interethnic consensus and cooperation. Negotiated inter-elite agreements on power-sharing institutions represent attempts to institutionalize non-violent ethnic conflict management. At the same time, they require a wider social consensus to prove viable. It has been pointed out that elites might be able to negotiate a conflict management system that makes violence unnecessary only if they are able to induce their followers to support them (Nordlinger 1972). This brings about the issue of actors and constituencies. The combined impact of internal actors and external third parties should be organized such that - as Lederach (1996) has put it - peace constituencies emerge on the ground. This suggests that, in terms of political interactions, the ethnic peace constituency implies networks of individuals who, firstly, have a personal interest in the lasting ethnic peace, and, secondly, have the influence and means to make this interest a reality.

Recent thinking on the matter has conceptualized the term 'peace constituencies' as a back-reference to 'war constituencies', i.e. those social and economic structures that take shape within the affected society in the course of a lengthy military altercation and which - often independently of the original causes of the war - foster the continuation of violence. Such constituencies, include, most importantly, the 'immediate winners' in the militarized conditions as well as all those who profit from the more or less impoverished 'war economy' and/or can exploit the shattered structures and corrupt conditions. Ropers (1997, pp. 30-1) observes that creating 'peace constituencies', accordingly, means lending support, within societies, to interests, networks, institutions, and attitudes of an opposite kind to those cited as well as promoting the 'culture of peace'.

As we move into the next century, it becomes increasingly clear that peace, both internationally and nationally, is no longer acceptable on any terms; it has come to be intimately linked with the notions of justice and freedom. Conflict resolution is not measured simply by the absence of bloodshed; it is assessed by the moral quality of the outcome. In this connection, the areas of concern of the two approaches to dealing with conflict (conflict management on the one hand, and democratization on the other), actually, merge. As noted by Pauline Baker (1997, p. 566),

Conflict managers tend to concentrate on short-term solutions that address the precipitous events that sparked the conflict; above all, they seek a swift and expedient end to violence. Democratizers tend to concentrate on longer-term solutions that address the root causes of the conflict; they search for enduring democratic stability. The former see peace as a precondition for democracy; the latter see democracy as a precondition for peace.

In no other realm of today's world has this linkage become so manifestly evident and manifest as in the realm of democratizing ethnic politics. Not only is democracy conducive to peace among states, but it also holds the keys to improving the quality and sustainability of the relationship among ethnic groups within states. Free peoples make good neighbors both internationally and domestically. Amidst the drift and doubt of post-transition, democracy needs to be seen not as part of the problem of ethnic conflict, but as the basis for its solution.

Promoting multiethnic democracy as a set of viable institutions and a liberal culture of inclusive pluralism is the path leading toward the relationship of positive, stable and sustainable ethnic peace at the subnational level of multiethnic states. Liberal democracy inheres in sustainable positive ethnic peace, is implicit in it, as the concept of health is implicit in life. Consolidation of sustainable ethnic peace in post-transitional multiethnic systems effectively, hinges upon consolidation of their democracy.

Bibliography

Abdulatipov, R. (1995), 'Federalizatsiya Rossii i vzaimosvyaz regionalnoj i natsionalnoj politiki' (Federalization of Russia and interconnection between regional and national politics'), *Etnopoliticheskij Vestnik (Ethnopolitical Herald)*, no.1, pp. 5-23.

Abdulatipov, R.G., Boltenkova, L.F. and Yarov, Y. (1993), *Federalism v Istorii Rossii (Federalism in Russia's History)*, Moscow, Supreme Soviet Press.

Acton, J. (1956), *Essays on Freedom and Power*, Thames and Hudson, London.

Afanasyev, M. (1994), 'Izmenenye v Mekhanizme Funktsionirovaniya Pravyashikh Regionalnykh Elit' (Regional Incumbent Elites: Changes in the Mechanism of Functioning'), *Polis*, no. 6, pp. 59-67.

Aklaev, A. R. (1996a) 'Dynamics of the Moldova - Trans-Dniester Ethnic Conflict (late 1980s to early 1990s)', in K. Rupersinghe and V. Tishkov (eds), *Ethnicity and Power in the Contemporary World*, The United Nations University Press, New York, pp.83-115.

Aklaev, A. R. (1996b), 'Ethnopoliticheskoje Razvitije i Legitimnost Vlasti' ('Ethnopolitical Development and Legitimacy', ch. 2 in L. M. Drobizheva, A.R. Aklaev, V.V. Koroteyeva, and G.U. Soldatova, *Demokratizatsija i 'Litsa" Natsionalizma v Menyajushejsya Rossijskoj Federatsii nachala 1990 godov (Democratization and 'Faces" of Nationalism in Changing Russian Federation of the early 1990s)*, Mysl Publishers, Moscow, pp. 103-59.

Aklaev, A. R. (1996c), 'Novyje Konstitutsii Respublic : Osnova Stabilizatsii i Faktory Konflikta' ('New Constitutions of Republics: Bases of Stabilization and Factors of Conflict'), ch. 3 in L. M. Drobizheva, A.R. Aklaev, V.V. Koroteyeva, and G.U. Soldatova, *Demokratizatsija i 'Litsa" Natsionalizma v Menyajushejsya Rossijskoj Federatsii nachala 1990 godov (Democratization and 'Faces" of Nationalism in Changing Russian Federation of the early 1990s)*, Mysl Publishers, Moscow, pp. 160-203.

Allardt, E. (1979), *Implications of the Ethnic Revival in Modern Industrialised Society*, Commentationes Scientiarum Socialium 12, Societas Scientiarum Fennica, Helsinki.

Almond, G. and Verba, S (1980), *The Civic Culture Revisited*, Little, Brown, Boston.

Almond, G. and Verba, S. (1963), *The Civic Culture*, Little, Brown, Boston.

Anderson, B. (1983), *Imagined Communities: Reflections on the Origin and Spread of Nationalism*, Verso Books, London.
Archer, C. (1996), 'The Nordic Area as a "Zone of Peace"', *Journal of Peace Research*, vol. 33, pp. 451-67.
Armstrong, J. (1982), *Nations Before Nationalism*, University of North Carolina Press, Chapel Hill.
Aron, R. (1966), *Peace and War*, Doubleday, New York.
Asochakov, A. and Umnova, I. (1995), 'Ot Dogovora k Konstitusii: O Trudnostiakh Zarozhdenija Novogo Rossijskogo Federalisma'('From the Treaty to the Constitution: On the Difficulties of Birth of the New Russian Federalism'), *Rossijskaja Federatsjja*, 1995, no. 12, pp. 20-3.
Atgimimas (Vilnius), newspaper
Ayoob, M. (1997), 'State Making, State Breaking, State Failure', in Ch. A. Crocker, O.F. Hampson, with P. Ayall (eds), *Managing Global Chaos*, USIP Press, Washington, DC, pp. 37-51.
Azar, E.E. (1972), 'Conflict Escalation and Conflict Reduction in an International Crisis: Suez, 1956', *Journal of Conflict Resolution*, vol. 16, no. 2, pp. 183-201.
Azar, E.E. (1990a), *The Management of Protracted Social Conflict. Theory and Cases*, Dartmouth, Aldershot.
Azar, E.E. (1990b), 'Protracted international conflicts: Ten propositions', in J.W. Burton and F. Dukes (eds), *Conflict: Readings in Management and Resolution*, St. Martin's, New York, pp. 145-55.
Azar, E.E. and Burton, J. W. (1986), *International Conflict Resolution: Theory and Practice*, Lynne Rienner. Boulder, CO.
Babst, D. V. (1964), 'Effective Governments - a Force for Peace', *The Wisconsin Sociologist*, vol. 3, no. 1, pp. 9-14.
Babst, D. V. (1972), 'A Force for Peace', *Industrial Research*, vol. 14 pp. 55-58.
Badie, B. and Birnbaum, P. (1979), *The Sociology of the State*, University of Chicago Press, Chicago.
Baker, P. (1997), 'Conflict Resolution Versus Democratic Governance. Divergent Paths To Peace?', in Ch.A. Crocker, and F.O. Hampson with P. Aall (eds), *Managing Global Chaos*, USIP Press, Washington, DC, pp. 563-71.
Balzer, M. M. and Vinokurova, U.A. (1996), 'Nationalism, Interethnic Relations and Federalism: The Case of the Sakha Republic (Yakutia)', *Europe-Asia Studies*, vol. 48, no.1, pp. 101-20.
Bandara, A. (1986), *Social Foundations of Thought and Action: A Social Cognitive Theory*, Prentice Hall, Englewood Cliffs, NJ.
Banton, M. (1983), *Racial and Ethnic Competition*, Cambridge University Press, Cambridge.
Banton, M. (1995), 'Rational Choice Theories', *American Behavioral Scientist*, vol. 38, no. 3, pp. 478-97.
Barrington, L. (1995), 'The Domestic and International Consequences of Citizenship in the Soviet Successor States', *Europe-Asia Studies*, vol. 47, pp. 731-63.

Barsamov, V. (1994), 'Natsionalnaya Politika v Rossijskikh Respublikakh: Evolutsiya Poslednikh let i Perspektivy' ('Nationalities' Politics in Russia's Republics: Evolution in Recent Years and Prospects'), *Obshestvennyje Nauki i Sovremennost (Social Sciences and Modernity)*, no. 6: 103-11.

Barth, F. (1969), (ed), *Ethnic Groups and Boundaries*, Little, Brown, Boston.

Bartsits, I. (1995), 'Kontseptsija Suvereniteta v Konstitutsii Rossii' ('The Conception of Sovereignty in the Russia's Constitution'), *Rossijskaja Federatsija (Russian Federation)*, no. 2, pp. 56-9.

Bater, J.H. (1989), *The Soviet Scene: A Geographical Perspective*, Armonk, New York.

Bates, R. (1983), 'Modernization, Ethnic Competition, and the Rationality of Politics in Contemporary Africa', in D. Rothschild and V. Olorunsola (eds), *State vs. Ethnic Claims: African Policy Dilemmas*, Westview, Boulder, pp. 152-171.

Beissinger, M. R. (1995), 'The persisting ambiguity of empire', *Post-Soviet Affairs*, Vol. 11, no. 2, pp. 149-84.

Bell, C. (1971), *The Conventions of Crisis: A Study in Diplomatic Management*, Oxford University Press, London.

Bendor, J., Kramer, R.M., and Stout, S. (1991), 'When in Doubt... Cooperation in a Noisy Prisoner's Dilemma', *Journal of Conflict Resolution*, vol. 36, no. 2, pp. 309-41.

Benvenisti, M. (1984), *The West Bank Data Project: A Survey of Israeli's Policies*, American Enterprise Institute, Washington, DC.

Bermeo, N. (1990), 'Rethinking Regime Change', *Comparative Politics*, vol. 22, no. 4, pp. 359-77.

Binder, L. (1971), 'Crises of Political Development', in L. Binder et al., *Crises and Sequences in Political Development*, Princeton University Press, Princeton, pp. 3-72.

Binder, L., Coleman, J.S., La Palombara, J., Pye, L.W., Verba, S., and Weiner, M. (1971), *Crises and Sequences in Political Development*, Princeton University Press: Princeton.

Bingham Powell, G. (1982), *Contemporary Democracies: Participation, Stability and Violence*, Harvard University Press, Cambridge, MA.

Birch, A. H. (1994), *Concepts and Theories of Modern Democracy*, Routledge, London.

Birckenbach, H-M. (1997), *Preventive Diplomacy Through Fact-Finding: How International Organisations Review the Conflict over Citizenship in Estonia and Latvia*, Lit Verlag, Hamburg.

Boardman, S. K. and Horowitz, S.V. (1994), 'Constructive Conflict Management and Social Problems: An Introduction', *Journal of Social Issues*, vol. 50, no. 1, pp. 1-13.

Bogacheva, O. (1995), 'Stanovleniye Rossijskoj Modeli Budzhetnogo Federalizma' ('Establishment of the Russia's Model of Budgetary Federalizm'), *Voprosy Ekonomiki (Issues of Economics)*, no. 8, pp. 30-40.

Bok, S. (1989), *A Strategy for Peace*, Pantheon, New York.
Boltenkova, L.(1992), 'K Istorii i Soderzhaniju Federativnogo Dogovora', ('On the History and Contents of the Federation Treaty'), *Ethnopolis*, no. 2, pp. 33-5.
Bose, S. (1995), 'State Crises and Nationalities Conflict in Sri Lanka and Yugoslavia', *Comparative Political Studies*, vol. 28, no. 1, pp. 87-116.
Boulding, K. (1978), *Stable Peace*, University of Texas Press, Austin, TX.
Bova, R. (1991), 'Political Dynamics of the Post-Communist Transition: A Comparative Perspective', *World Politics*, vol. 44, no. 1, pp. 113-38.
Bowers, S.(1992), *Ethnic Politics in Eastern Europe*, Institute for the Study of Conflict and Terrorism, London.
Brass, P. R. (1991), *Ethnicity and Nationalism: Theory and Comparison*, Sage Publications, London.
Brass, P.R. (1974), *Language, Religion, and Politics in North India*, Cambridge University Press, New York.
Brass, P.R. (1985), (ed), *Ethnic Groups and the State*, Barnes and Noble Books, Totowa, NJ.
Braumoeller, B. F. (1997), 'Deadly Doves: Liberal Nationalism and the Democratic Peace in the Soviet Successor States', *International Studies Quarterly*, vol. 41, no. 3, pp. 375-402.
Brecher, M. (1977), 'Towards a Theory of International Crisis Behavior', *Political Studies Quarterly*, vol. 21, no. 1, pp. 39-74.
Brecher, M. (1978), (ed), *Studies in Crisis Behavior*, Transaction Books, New Brunswick, NJ.
Brecher, M. (1993), *Crises in World Politics: Theory and Reality*, Pergamon, Oxford.
Brecher, M. and James, P. (1986), 'Patterns of Crisis Management', *Journal of Conflict Resolution*, vol. 32, no. 3.
Brecher, M. and Wilkenfield, J. (1989), *Crises in the Twentieth Century*, Pergamon, New York.
Bremer, S. A. (1992), 'Dangerous Dyads: Conditions, Affecting the Likelihood of Interstate War, 1816-1965', *Journal of Conflict Resolution*, vol. 36, no.4, pp. 309-41.
Bremer, S. A. (1993), 'Democracy and militarized interstate conflict, 1816-1965'. *International Interactions*, vol. 18, no.3, pp. 231-50.
Bremmer, I. (1997), 'Post Soviet nationalities theory: Past, present, and future', in I. Bremmer and R. Taras (eds), (1997), *New States, New Politics: Building the Post-Soviet Nations*, Cambridge University Press, Cambridge, pp. 3-28.
Bremmer, I. and Taras, R. (1993), (eds), *Nations and Politics in the Soviet Successor States*, Cambridge University Press, Cambridge.
Breuilly, J. (1982), *Nationalism and the State*, Manchester University Press, Manchester.

Brown, M. (1993), 'Causes and Implications of Ethnic Conflict' in M.Brown (ed) *Ethnic Conflict and International Security*, Princeton University Press, Princeton, NJ, pp. 3-27.
Brubacker, R. (1992a), *Citizenship and Nationhood in France and Germany*. Harvard University Press, Cambridge, MA.
Brubacker, R. (1992b), 'Citizenship Struggles in Soviet Successor States', *International Migration Review*, vol. 26, no. 2, pp. 269-91.
Brubacker, R. (1994), 'Nationhood and the National Question in the Soviet Union and post-Soviet Eurasia: An Institutional Account', *Theory and Society*, vol. 23, no. 1, pp. 47-58.
Brubacker, R. (1995), 'Aftermaths of Empire and the Unmixing of Peoples: Historical and Comparative Perspectives', *Ethnic and Racial Studies*, vol. 18, no. 2, pp. 189-218.
Brunner, G. (1982), 'Legitimacy Doctrines and Legitimation Procedures in East European Systems', in T.H. Rigby and F. Feher (eds), *Political Legitimation in Communist States*, MacMillan, London.
Bueno de Mesquita, B. and Lalman, D. (1992), *War and Reason*, Yale University Press, New Haven.
Bunce, V. (1995a),. 'Should Transitologists Be Grounded?', *Slavic Review*, vol. 54, no. 1, pp. 111-27.
Bunce, V. (1995b), 'Paper Curtains and Paper Tigers', *Slavic Review*, vol. 54, no. 4, pp. 979-87.
Bungs, D. (1993), 'Elections and Restoring Democracy in Baltic States', *RFE/RL Report*, vol. 2, no. 38, pp. 12-6.
Burant, S. (1997), 'Overcoming the Past: Polish-Lithuanian Relations, 1990-1995', *Journal of Baltic Studies*, vol. 27, no. 4, pp. 309-29.
Canovan, M. (1996), *Nationhood and Political Theory*, Edward Elgar: Chetlenham.
Chan, S. (1984), 'Mirror, Mirror on the Wall..: Are Freer Countries More Pacific?', *Journal of Conflict Resolution*, vol. 28, no. 4, pp. 617-48.
Chan, S. (1993), 'Democracy and War: Some Thoughts on Future Research Agenda'. *International Interactions*, vol. 18.
Cheshko, S.(1993), 'Konstitutsinnaya Reforma i Natsionalnyye Problemy v Rossii' ('Constitutional Reform and Nationalities' Problems in Russia'), *Etnograficheskoye Obozreniye (Ethnographic Review)*, no. 6, pp. 29-45.
Chinn, J. and Truex, L.A. (1996), 'The Question of Citizenship in the Baltics', *Journal of Democracy*, vol. 7, no. 1, pp. 133-47.
Chirot, D. (1995), 'National Liberation and Nationalist nightmares: The Consequences of the End of Empires in Eastern Europe in the 20th century', in B. Crawford (ed), *Markets, States, and Democracy: The Political Economy of Post-Communist Transformation*, Westview, Boulder, pp. 43-71.
Cirtautas, A.M. (1995), 'The Post-Leninist State: A Conceptual and Empirical Examination', *Communist and Post-Communist Studies*, vol. 28, no.4, pp. 372-92.

Clark, S. and Graham, D. (1995), 'The Russian Federation's Fight for Survival', *Orbis*, vol. 39, no. 3, pp. 329-52.

Clark, T. (1995), 'The Lithuanian Political Party System', *East European Politcs and Societies*, vol. 9, no.1, pp. 41-62.

Clem, R. S. and. Craumer, P.R. (1993), 'The Geography of the April 25 [1993] Russian Referendum', *Post-Soviet Geography*, vol. 34, no. 8, pp. 481-96.

Clemens, W. C. (1994), 'Estonia Rebuilds: The Second Year of Independence, 1992-1993', *Nationalities Papers*, vol. 22, no.2, pp.393-403.

Clemens, W. C. (1997), 'Who or What Killed the Soviet Union? How Three Davids Undermined Goliath', *Nationalism and Ethnic Politics*, vol. 3, no. 1, pp. 136-58.

Clutterbuck, R. (1993), *International Crisis and Conflict*, St Martin's, New York.

Coakley, J. (1993), 'Introduction: The Territorial Management of Ethnic Conflict' in J. Coakley (ed), *The Territorial Management of Ethnic Conflict*, Frank Cass, London, pp. 1-23.

Collier, D. and Levitsky, S. (1997), 'Democracy with Adjectives: Conceptual Innovation in Comparative Research', *World Politics*, vol. 49, pp. 430-51.

Colomer, J.M. (1995), 'Institutions and Incentives', *Journal of Democracy*, vol. 6, no. 2.

Comisso, E. (1995), 'Legacies of the Past or New Institutions? The Struggle Over Redistribution in Hungary', *Comparative Political Studies*, vol. 28, no. 2, pp. 200-38.

Comisso, E. (1997), 'Is the Glass Half Full or Half Empty? Reflections on Five Years of Competitive Politics in Eastern Europe', *Communist and Post-Communist Studies*, vol. 30, no.1, pp. 1-22.

Conquest, R. (1990), *The Great Terror: A Reassessment*, Oxford University Press, Oxford.

Conversi, D. (1995), 'Reassessing Current Theories of Nationalism: Nationalism as Boundary Maintenance and Creation', *Nationalism and Ethnic Politics*, vol. 1, no. 1, pp. 73-85.

Coser, L. A. (1956), *The Functions of Social Conflict*, Free Press, New York.

Crawford, B. (1995), (ed), *Markets, States, and Democracy: The Political Economy of Post-Communist Transformation*, Westview, Boulder.

Crawford, B. and Lijphart, A. (1995), 'Explaining Political and Economic Change in Post-Communist Eastern Europe: Old Legacies, New institutions, Hegemonic norms, and International Pressures', *Comparative Political Studies*, vol. 28, no. 2, pp. 171-99.

Crowther, W. (1997), 'Moldova: Caught Between Nation and Empire', in I. Bremmer and R. Taras (eds), *New States, New Politics: Building the Post-Soviet Nations*. Cambridge University Press, Cambridge, pp. 316-49.

Dahl, R. A. (1971), *Polyarchy: Participation and Opposition*, Yale University Press, New Haven.

Dahl, R. A. (1989), *Democracy and Its Critics*, Yale University Press: New Haven.

Dahl, R. A. (1994), 'A Democratic Dilemma: System Effectiveness versus Citizen Participation', *Political Science Quarterly*, vol. 109, no. 1, pp. 23-35.

Dahrendorf, R. (1959), *Class and Class Conflict in Industrial Society*, Stanford University Press, Stanford, CA.

Dahrendorf, R. (1990), *Reflections on the Revolution in Europe*, Times Books, Random House, New York.

Dawisha, K. and Parrott, B. (1994), *Russia and the New States of Eurasia*. Cambridge University Press, Cambridge.

De Nevers, R. (1993), 'Democratization and Ethnic Conflict', in Brown, M. (ed), *Ethnic Conflict and International Security*, Princeton University Press, Princeton, pp. 61-78.

Deletant, D. (1992), 'The Rights of Ethnic Minorities in Eastern Europe: Some Considerations', in R. Beddard and D.M. Hill (eds), *Emerging Right in the New Europe*, University of Southampton, Southampton.

Demographic Data Collections of Estonia, Latvia, Lithuania (1998), Statistikaamet, Tallinn.

Deutsch, K. W. (1953), *Nationalism and Social Communication*, M.I.T. Press, Cambridge.

Deutsch, K. W. et al. (1957), *Political Community and the North Atlantic Area*, Princeton University Press: Princeton, NJ.

Deutsch, M. (1968), 'Conflicts: Constructive and Destructive', *Journal of Social Issues*, vol. 25, no.1, pp. 7-41.

Deutsch, M. (1973), *The Resolution of Conflict, Constructive and Destructive Processes*, Yale University Press, New Haven.

Deutsch, M. (1987), 'Theoretical Perspectives on Conflict and Conflict Resolution', in D.J. Sandole and I. Sandole-Staroste (eds), *Conflict Management and Power Sharing: Interpersonal to International*, New York University Press, New York.

Deurtch, M. (1994), 'Constructive Conflict Resolution: Principles, Training, and Research', *Journal of Social Issues*, vol. 50, no. 1, pp. 13-32.

Di Palma, G. (1990), *To Craft Democracies. An Essay on Democratic Transitions*, University of California Press, Berkeley, CA.

Di Palma, G. (1991), 'Why Democracy Can Work in Eastern Europe', *Journal of Democracy*, Vol. 2, no. 1, pp. 21-31.

Diamond, L. (1990), 'Three Paradoxes of Democracy', *Journal of Democracy*, vol. 1, no. 3, pp. 48-60.

Diamond, L. (1993a), 'Causes and Effects', in Diamond, L. (ed), *Political Culture and Democracy in Developing Countries*, Lynne Rienner Publishers: Boulder, pp. 411-436.

Diamond, L. (1993b), 'Democracy as Paradox', in E. Sprinzak and L. Diamond. (eds), *Israeli Democracy Under Stress*, Lynne Rienner Publishers, Boulder, pp. 21-43.

Diamond, L. (1994). 'Rethinking Civil Society: Towards Democratic Consolidation', *Journal of Democracy*, vol. 5, no. 3, pp. 4-13.

Diamond, L. (1995), *Promoting Democracy in the 1990s: Actors and Instruments, Issues and Imperatives*. A Report to the Carnegie Commission on Preventing Deadly Conflict, Carnegie Corporation: Washington, DC.

Diamond, L. (1996), 'Is the Third Wave Over?', *Journal of Democracy*, vol. 7, no. 3.

Diamond, L. and Plattner, M.F. (1994), 'Introduction', in L. Diamond and M.F. Plattner (eds), *Nationalism, Ethnic Conflict, and Democracy*, Johns Hopkins University Press, Baltimore, MD.

Diamond, L., Linz, J.J., and Lipset S.M. (1995a), 'Introduction: What Makes for Democracy?', in Diamond, L., Linz, J.J., and Lipset S.M. (eds), (1995), *Politics in Developing Countries: Comparing Experiences with Democracy*, Lynne Rienner: Boulder, CO, pp. 1-66.

Dima, N.(1991), *From Moldavia to Moldova*, Columbia University Press, New York.

Dixon, W. J. (1993), 'Democracy and the Management of International Conflict', *Journal of Conflict Resolution*, vol. 37, no.1, pp. 42-68.

Dixon, W. J. (1994), 'Democracy and the Peaceful Settlement of International Conflict', *American Political Science Review*, vol. 88, no.1, pp. 14-32.

DiZereuga, G. (1995), 'Democracies and Peace: The Self-organizing Foundation for the Democratic Peace', *The Review of Politics*, vol. 57, no. 2, pp. 279-309.

Dmitriev, C. (1996), 'Hostages of the (former) Soviet Empire', *Transition*, no. 12, pp. 18-21.

Domke, W. K. (1988), *War and the Changing Global System*, Yale University Press, New Haven.

Doyle, M. (1983), 'Kant, Liberal Legacies and Foreign Affairs, Parts 1 and 2, *Philosophy and Public Affairs*, Vol. 12, nos. 3 and 4, pp. 205-35, 323-53.

Doyle, M. (1986), 'Liberalism and World Politics', *American Political Science Review*, vol. 80, no. 4, pp. 1151-69.

Doyle, Michael. (1996), 'Reflections on the Liberal Peace and its Critics', in M. E. Brown, S. M. Lynn-Jones and S. E. Miller (eds), *Debating the Democratic Peace*, The MIT Press: Cambridge, MA, pp. 358-63.

Driessen, B. (1994), 'Slav non-citizens in the Baltics', *International Journal of Group Rights*, vol. 2, no. 1, pp. 113-37.

Dryzek, J.S. (1996), 'Political Inclusion and the Dynamics of Democratization', *American Political Science Review*, vol. 90, no. 1, pp. 475-487.

Dunlop, J. (1997), 'Russia in search of an identity', in I. Bremmer and R. Taras (eds), *New States, New Politics: Building the Post-Soviet Nations*, Cambridge University Press, Cambridge, pp. 29-96.

Duplain, J. (1995), 'Chisinau's and Tiraspol's Faltering Quest for Accord', *Transition*, 20 October 1995, pp. 10-3.

Eberwein, W.-D. (1981), 'The Quantitative Study of International Conflict: Quantity and Quality?', *Journal of Peace Research*, vol. 18, no.1, pp. 19-38.

Ebzeyev, B. and Karapetyan, L. (1995), 'Rossijskij Federalizm: Ravnopraviye i Assimmetriya Konstitutsionnogo Statusa' ('Russian Federalism: Equality and

Asimmetricity of the Constitutional Status of Federation Subjects'), *Gosudarstvo i Pravo (State and Law)*, no. 3, pp. 3-12.

Edelman, M. (1964), *The Symbolic Uses of Politics*, University of Illinois Press, Urbana, IL.

Eisenstadt, S.N. (1992), 'The Breakdown of Communist Regimes', *Daedalus*, vol. 121, no.2, pp. 21-43.

Ekho Litvy (Vilnius), newspaper.

Ekiert, G. (1991), 'Democratization Processes in East Central Europe: A Theoretical Reconsideration', *British Journal of Political Science*, vol. 21, no.2, pp. 285-313.

Ellingsen, T. and Gleiditsch, N.P. (1997), 'Democracy and Armed Conflict in the Third World', in D. Smith and Volden, K. (eds), *Causes of Conflict in the Third World*, International Peace Research Institute, Oslo.

Elster, J. and Slagstad, R. (eds), (1988), *Constitutionalism and Democracy*, Cambridge University Press, Cambridge, pp. 1-18.

Ember M., Ember C., and Russett, B. (1992), 'Peace Between Participatory Polities: A Cross-Cultural Test of the 'Democracies Rarely Fight Each Other's Hypothesis', *World Politics*, vol. 44, no.4, pp. 573-99.

Emizet, K. and V. Hesli, 'The Disposition to Secede: An Analysis of the Soviet Case', *Comparative Political Studies*, vol.24, no.4 (January 1995): 493-536.

Erikson, E. (1958), *Young Man Luther*, Norton, New York.

Erikson, E. (1963), *Childhood and Society*, Norton, New York.

Erikson, E. (1968), *Identity, Youth and Crisis*, Norton, New York.

Esman, M. J.(ed.) (1977), *Ethnic Conflict in the Western World*, Cornell University Press, Ithaca, NY.

Esman, M.J. (1990), 'Political and Psychological Factors in Ethnic Conflict', in J.V. Montville (ed) *Conflict and Peacemaking in Multiethnic Societies*, Lexington Books: Lexington, pp. 53-64.

Esman, M.J. (1994), *Ethnic Politics*, Cornell University Press, Ithaca, NY.

Esman, M.J. (1995), 'Ethnic Actors in International Politics', *Nationalism and Ethnic Politics*, Vol. 1, no. 1, pp. 111-125.

Estonia (Tallinn), newspaper.

Evans, P. (1992), 'The State as Problem and Solution: Predation, Embedded Autonomy, and Structural Change', in S. Haggard and R. Kaufman (eds), *The Politics of Economic Adjustment*, Princeton University Press, Princeton, pp.139-81.

Evans, P.B., Rueschemeyer, D., and Skocpol, T. (1985), *Bringing the State Back In*, Cambridge University Press, Cambridge.

Fane, D. (1993), 'Moldova: Breaking Loose From Moscow', in I. Bremmer and R. Taras (eds), *Nations and Politics in the Soviet Successor States*, Cambridge University Press, Cambridge.

Fleron, F. J. and Hoffman, E.P. (1993), (eds.), *Post-Communist Studies and Political Science*, Westview, Boulder.

Franke, M. F.N. (1995), 'Immanuel Kant and the (Im)Possibility of International Relations Theory', *Alternatives*, vol. 20, no.3, pp. 279-323.
Freedom House (1995), *Freedom in the World: The Annual Survey of Political Rights and Civil Liberties, 1994-95*, Freedom House, New York.
Fukuyama, F. (1995), 'Confucianism and democracy', *Journal of Democracy*, Vol. 6, no. 2, pp.20-33.
Furnivall, J.S. (1947), *Colonial Policy and Practice*, Cambridge University Press, London.
Furnivall, J.S. (1986), *Netherlands India: A Study of Plural Economy*, B.M. Israel: Amsterdam.
Galtung, J. (1969), 'Violence, Peace and Peace Research', *Journal of Peace Research*, Vol. 6, no. 3, pp. 167-191.
Galtung, J. (1981), 'The Specific Contribution of Peace Research to the Study of Violence: Typologies', in J.M. Domenach et al. (eds), *Violence and Its Causes*, Unesco, Paris.
Gaubatz, K. T. (1996), 'Kant, Democracy, and History', *Journal of Democracy*, Vol. 7, no. 4, pp. 136-149.
Geddes, B. (1995), 'A Comparative Perspective on the Leninist Legacy in Eastern Europe', *Comparative Political Studies*, vol. 28, no. 2, pp. 239-74.
Geertz C. (1963), 'The Integrative Revolution: Primordial Sentiments and Civil Politics in the New States', in C. Geertz (ed.), *Old Societies and New States*, The Free Press, Glencoe, IL.
Geller, D. (1985), *Domestic Factors in Foreign Policy: A Cross-National Statistical Analysis*, Shenkman Books, Cambridge, MA.
Gellner, E. (1983), *Nations and Nationalism*, Cornell University Press, Ithaca, NY.
Gellner, E. (1991), 'Civil Society in Historical Context', *International Social Science Journal*, vol. 43, no. 3, pp. 463-482.
Genov, N. (1991), 'The Transition to Democracy in Eastern Europe: Trends and Paradoxes of Social Rationalization', *International Social Science Journal*, vol. 128.
George, A. L. (1991), (ed.), *Avoiding War: Problems of Crisis Management*, Westview, Boulder.
Geremek, B. (1992), 'Civil Society Then and Now', *Journal of Democracy*, vol. 3, no. 2, pp. 3-12.
Gerner, K. and Hedlund, S. (1993), *The Baltic States and the End of the Soviet Empire*, Routledge, London.
Girnius, S. (1991), 'The Lithuanian Citizenship Law', *RFE/RL Research Report*, 19 Sept. 1991, pp. 21-3.
Girnius, S. (1993), 'Establishing Currencies in the Baltic states', *RFE/RL Report*, vol. 2, no. 22, pp. 35-9.
Glazer, N. and Moynihan, D.P. (1975), (eds), *Ethnicity: Theory and Experience*, Harvard University Press, Cambridge, MA.
Gleditsch, N. P. (1992), 'Democracy and Peace', *Journal of Peace Research*, vol. 29, no. 4: 369-376.

Gleditsch, N. P. and Hegre, H. (1997), 'Peace and Democracy: Three Levels of Analysis', *Journal of Conflict Resolution*, vol. 41, no. 2, pp. 283-310.

Gleditsch, N.P. (1995), 'Democracy and the Future of European Peace', *European Journal of International Relations*, vol. 1, no. 4, pp. 539-72.

Gonchar, N. and Goreglyad, V. 'Budzhetny Federalizm: Realii i Perspektivy' (Budgetary Federalism: Realities and Prospects), *Ethnopolis*, no.2, pp. 52-65.

Gray, V. (1996), 'Identity and democracy in the Baltics', *Democratization*, vol. 3, no. 2, pp. 69-91.

Greenfeld, L. (1993), *Nationalism: Five Roads to Modernity*, Harvard University Press, Cambridge.

Grew, R. (1978) (ed), *Crises of Political Development in Europe and the U.S*, Princeton University Press, Princeton, NJ.

Groom, A.J.R. (1990), 'Paradigms in Conflict', in J. Burton and F. Dukes (eds), *Conflict: Readings in Management and Resolution*, St. Martin's, New York.

Groom, A.J.R. (1991), 'No compromise: Power Sharing in a Theoretical Perspective', *International Social Science Journal*, vol. 127, pp. 77-86.

Grosby, S. (1994), 'Verdict of History: The Inexpungeable Tie of Primordialiyt', *Ethnic and Racial Studies*, vol. 17, no. 1, pp. 164-96.

Guboglo, M. (1994), (ed.), *Yazyk i Natsionalism v Postsovetskikh Respublikakh (Langauge and Nationalism in Post-Soviet Republics)*, Institute of Ethnology Press, Moscow.

Gurr, T.R. (1970), *Why Men Rebel*, Princeton University Press, Princeton.

Gurr, T.R. (1988), 'War, Revolution and the Growth of the Coercive State', *Comparative Political Studies*, vol. 21, no. 1, pp. 45-65.

Gurr, T.R. (1993), *Minorities At Risk: A Global View of Ethnopolitical Conflicts*, USIP Press, Washington, DC.

Haas, A. (1996), 'Non-Violence in Ethnic Relations in Estonia', *Journal of Baltic Studies*, vol. 27, no. 1, pp. 47-76.

Haas, M. (1986), 'Research on International Crisis: Obsolescence of an Approach?', *International Interactions*, vol. 13, no. 1, pp. 23-58.

Hammarstrom, M. (1995), 'Theory-building in the Study of Crises', *Journal of Peace Research*, vol. 32, no 2 pp. 233-8.

Hanauer, L. S. 'Tatarstan and the Prospects for Federalism in Russia: A Commentary', *Security Dialogue*, vol. 27, no.1, pp. 82-7.

Hanne, G. (1997), 'Playing Two Different Tunes, as Usual, in Moldova: Still at an Impasse with the Dniester "Republic"', *Transitions*, vol. 4, no. 7, pp. 68-72.

Hanson, P. (1993), 'Estonia's Narva problem, Narva's Estonia Problem', *RFE/RL Report*, vol. 2, no. 18, pp. 17-23.

Hanson, P. (1994), 'The center versus the Periphery in Russian Economic Relations', RFE/RL Research Report, vol. 3, no. 2, pp. 23-8.

Harris, C. (1993),'A Geographic Analysis of Non-Russian Minorities in Russia and its Ethnic Homelands', *Post-Soviet Geography*, no. 1, pp. 543-597.

Hayden, R. (1992), 'Constitutional Nationalism in the Formerly Yugoslav Republics', *Slavic Review*, vol. 51, pp. 655-66.

Heisler, M. O. (1991), 'Ethnicity and Ethnic Relations in the Modern West', in J.V. Montville (ed), *Conflict and Peacemaking in Multiethnic Societies*, D.C. Heath and Company, Lexington, MA, pp. 5-20.

Held, D. (1995), 'Cosmopolitan Democracy and the Global Order: Reflections on the 200th Anniversary of Kant's "Perpetual Peace"', *Alternatives*, vol. 20, no. 4, pp. 415-31.

Heper, M. (1992), 'The Strong State as a Problem for the Consolidation of Democracy: Turkey and Germany Compared', *Comparative Political Studies*, vol. 25, no. 2, pp. 169-94.

Hermann, C. (1969), *Crises in Foreign Policy: A Situational Analysis*. Bobbs-Merrill, Indianapolis.

Hermann, M.G. and Kegley, C.W. (1995), 'Rethinking Democracy and International Peace: Perspectives from Political Psychology', *International Studies Quarterly*, Vol. 39, no. 4, pp. 511-33.

Hiden, J. and Salmon, P. (1994), *The Baltic Nations and Europe. Estonia, Latvia and Lithuania in the Twentieth Century*, London: Longman, 2nd ed.

Highley, J. and Gunther, R. (eds), (1992), *Elites and Democratic Consolidation in Latin America and Southern Europe*, Columbia University Press, New York.

Hirshman, A. O. (1994), 'Social Conflicts as Pillars of Democratic Market Society', *Political Theory*. vol. 22, no. 2, pp. 203-19.

Hislope, R. (1998), 'Ethnic Conflict and the "Generosity Moment"', *Journal of Democracy*, vol. 9, no. 1, pp.140-53.

Hobsbawn E.J. (1982), *Nations and Nationalism Since 1780*, Cambridge University Press, Cambridge.

Hofstede, G. (1989), 'Cultural Predictions of National Negotiation Styles', in F. Mautner-Markhof (ed), *Processes of International Negotiations*, Westview: Boulder, pp. 193-201.

Holsti, O. R. (1972), *Crisis, Escalation and War*, McGill University, Montreal.

Holsti, O. R. (1980), 'Historians, Social Scientists and Crisis Management: An Alternative View', *Journal of Conflict Resolution*, vol. 24, no. 4, pp. 665-82.

Holsti, O. R. (1989), 'Theories of Crisis Decision Making', in Lauren, P.G. (ed), *History Theory, and Policy,* Free Press, New York.

Hopple, G. W. and Rossa, P.J. (1981), 'International Crisis Analysis: Recent Developments and Future Directions', in T. Hoppman, D.A. Zinnes, and J.D. Singer (eds), *Cumulation in International Relations Research,* Monograph Series in World Affairs, Denver, CO, pp. 65-97.

Horowitz, D. (1985), *Ethnic Groups in Conflict*, University of California Press, Berkeley, CA.

Horowitz, D. (1990a), 'Making Moderation Pay', in J.V. Montville (ed), *Conflict and Peacemaking in Multiethnic Societies*, D.C. Heath and Company, Lexington, MA, pp. 451-74.

Horowitz, D. (1990b), 'Ethnic Conflict Management for Policymakers', in J.V. Montville (ed), *Conflict and Peacemaking in Multiethnic Societies*, D.C. Heath and Company, Lexington, MA, pp. 115-126.

Horowitz, D. (1991), *A Democratic South Africa? Constitutional Engineering in a Divided Society*, University of California Press, Berkeley.
Horowitz, D. (1992), 'How to begin thinking theoretically about Soviet ethnic problems', in A. Motyl (ed), *Thinking Theoretically About Soviet Nationalities. History and Comparison in the Study of the USSR*, Columbia University Press, New York.
Horowitz, D. (1993), 'Democracy in Divided Societies.' *Journal of Democracy*, vol. 4, no.4, pp. 1-38.
Huntington, S. P. (1968), *Political Order in Changing Societies*, Yale University Press, New Haven.
Huntington, S. P. (1981), 'Reform and Stability in a Modernizing, Multi-Ethnic Siociety', *Politikon*, vol. 8, no. 2, pp. 8-26.
Huntington, S. P. (1984), 'Will More Countries Become Democratic?', *Political Science Quarterly*, vol.99, no. 2.
Huntington, S. P. (1991), *The Third Wave: Democratization in the Late Twentieth Century*, University of Oklahoma Press: Norman, OK.
Huntington, S. P. (1996), 'Democracy for the Long Haul', *Journal of Democracy*, vol. 7, no. 2, pp. 3-13.
Huntington, S.P. (1993), 'The Clash of Civilizations?', *Foreign Affairs*, vol. 72, pp. 22-49.
Huntington, S.P. (1996), *The Clash of Civilizations and the Remaking of the World Order*, Simon and Schuster, New York.
Huntley, W. L. (1995), 'Kant's Third Image: Systemic Sources of the Liberal Peace', *International Studies Quarterly*, vol. 40, no. 1, pp. 45-76.
Iljinsky, I., Krylov, B. and Mikhaleva, N. (1993), 'Novoje Federativnoje Ustroistvo Rossii' ('New Federation Structure in Russia'), *Ethnopolis*, no.3, pp. 27-35.
Inglehart, R. (1990), *Culture Shift in Advanced Industrial Countries*, Princeton University Press, Princeton.
Ionescu, D. (1995), 'Russia's Long Arm and the Dniester Impasse', *Transition*, vol. 1, no. 19, pp. 14-15.
Ionescu, D. and Ruthland, P. (1995), 'Russia and the Near Abroad', *Transition*, vol. 1, no. 19, pp. 2-3.
Iskhakov, D. (1995), 'Model Tatarstana: Za i Protiv'('The Tatarstan Model: Pros and Cons'), *Panorama-Forum*, no. 1, pp. 56-72.
Izvestiya (Moscow), newspaper.
Jackson, W. D. (1994), 'Imperial temptations: Ethnics abroad', *Orbis*, Vol. 38, no. 1, pp. 1-18.
Janos, A. C. (1991), 'Social science, communism, and the dynamics of political change', *World Politics*, vol. 44, no. 1, pp. 81-112.
Joffe, J. (1990), 'Tocqueville Revisited: Are Good democracies Bad Players in the Game of Nations?', in B. Roberts (ed) *The New Democracies: Global Change and U.S. Policy*, The MIT Press: Cambridge, MA, pp. 124-34.

Jönnson, C. (1990), *Communication in International Bargaining*, St Martin's, New York.
Jowitt, K. (1991), 'The Leninist extinction', in D. Chirot (ed.), *The Crisis of Leninism and the Decline of the Left: The Revolutions of 1989*, University of Washington Press, Seattle, pp. 74-99.
Jowitt, K. (1992), *New World Disorder: The Leninist Extinction*, University of California Press, Berkeley.
Käärid, L. and Valter,E. (1997), *Integrating Non-Estonians into Estonian Society: Setting the Course*, UNDP Office Press, Tallinn.
Kacowicz, A.M. (1995), 'Explaining Zones of Peace: Democracies as Satisfied Powers?', *Journal of Peace Research*, vol. 32, no. 3, pp. 263-76.
Kant, I[1795], *Zum ewigen Frieden,* Transl. in H. Reiss (ed) 1970, *Kant's Political Writings*. Cambridge University Press, Cambridge.
Kaplan, C. (1993), 'Estonia: A Plural Society on the Road to Independence', in I. Bremmer and R. Taras (eds), *Nation and Politics in the Soviet Successor States*, Cambridge University Press, Cambridge, pp. 206-21.
Karl, T. (1990), 'Dilemmas of Democratization in Latin America', *Comparative Politics*, vol. 23, no. 1, pp. 1-21.
Karl, T. and Schmitter, P.C. (1991), 'Modes of Transition in Latin America, Southern and Eastern Europe', *International Social Science Journal*, vol. 128, pp. 269-4.
Karl, T. and Schmitter, P.C. (1992), 'The types of democracy emerging in Southern Europe and South and Central America', in P. Volten (ed), *Bound to Change: Consolidating Democracy in Central Europe*, Institute for East-West Security Studies, New York, pp. 42-68.
Karl, T. and Schmitter, P.C. (1995), 'From an Iron Curtain to a Paper Tiger: Grounding Transitologists or Students of Postcommunism?', *Slavic Review*, Vol. 54, no. 4, pp. 965-78.
Kasimov, A. and O. Senatova (1993), 'Moskovskoje Porazhenije Rossijskogo Federalizma' ('The Moscow Defeat of Russian Federalism'), *Vek XX i Mir (XX-th Century and the World)*, no.7-12, pp. 183-91.
Kask, P. (1994), 'National Radicalization in Estonia: Legislation on Citizenship and Related Issues', *Nationalities Papers*, vol. 22, no. 2, pp. 379-90.
Katz, M. N. (1993), 'The Legacy of Empire in International Relations', *Comparative Strategy*, vol. 12, no. 4, pp. 365-84.
Katz, M.N. (1997), 'Collapsed Empires', in Ch.A. Crocker, and F.O. Hampson with P. Aall (eds), *Managing Global Chaos*, USIP Press, Washington, DC, pp. 185-96.
Kaufman, S. J. (1996), 'Spiraling to Ethnic War: Elites, Masses, and Moscow in Moldova's civil war', *International Security*, vol. 21, no. 2, pp. 108-38.
Keane, J. (ed), (1988), *Civil Society and the State: New European Perspectives*, Verso, London.
Keens-Soper, M. (1989), 'The Liberal State and Nationalism in Post-war Europe', *History of European Ideas*, vol.10, no. 1, pp. 698-703.

Kempton, D. R. (1996), 'The Republic of Sakha (Yakutia): The Evolution of Center-Periphery Relations in the Russian Federation', *Europe-Asia Studies*, vol. 48, no. 4, pp. 587-613.

Kertzer, K.I. (1988), *Ritual, Politics, and Power*, Yale University Press, New Haven.

Khakimov, Raphael S. 'Prospects of Federalism in Russia: A View from Tatarstan', *Security Dialogue*, vol. 27, no.1, pp. 69-81.

Kiionka, R. (1991), 'Who Should Become a Citizen of Estonia?', *RFE?RL Report on the USSR*, 27 Sept., pp. 23-6.

Kiionka, R. (1992), 'Drafting New Constitutions: Estonia', *RFE/RL Research Report*, vol. 1, no. 27, pp. 57-61.

King, C. (1994a), 'Post-Sovietology: Area Studies or Social Science?', *International Affairs*, vol. 70, no. 2, pp. 291-7.

King, C. (1994b), 'Moldovan Identity and the Politics of Pan-Romanianism', *Slavic Review*, vol. 53, no. 2, pp. 345-68.

King, C. (1995), 'Gagauz Yeri and the Dilemmas of Self-Determination', *Transition*, vol. 1, no. 19, pp. 21-5.

Kirch, A. (1994), 'From a Change of Evaluation to a Change of Paradigms: Estonia 1940-1993', in A. Kirch (ed), *Changing Identities in Estonia. Sociological Facts and Commentaries*, Estonian Science Foundation, Tallinn, pp. 6-10.

Kirch, A. (1997), (ed), *The Integration of Non-Estonians into Estonian Society: History, Problems, and Trends*, Estonian Academy Publishers, Tallinn.

Kirch, A. and Kirch,M. (1996), 'Russians in Contemporary Estonia: From Adaptation to Integration', *Proceedings of the Estonian Academy of Sciences: Humanities and Social Sciences*, vol. 45, no. 2, p. 202-24.

Kivirahk, J. (1992), 'The Twilight of Socialism in Man's Consciousness', EMOR-Reports, vol. 3, no. 3, EMOR, Tallinn.

Klatt, M. (1994), 'Russians in the 'Near Abroad'', *RFE/RL Report*, vol. 3, no.32, pp. 33-44.

Knock, T. J. (1992), *To End All Wars: Woodrow Wilson and the Quest for a New World Order*, Oxford University Press, New York.

Kobeckaite, H. (1992), *National Minorities in Lithuania*, Center for National Research, Vilnius.

Kolstoe, P. (1993), 'The New Russian Diaspora: Minority Protection in the Soviet Successor States', *Journal of Peace Research*, vol. 13, no. 2, pp. 197-217.

Kolstoe, P. (1995), *Russians in the Former Soviet Republics*, Indiana University Press, Bloomington.

Kolstoe, P. (1996), 'Nation-Building in the Former USSR'. *Journal of Democracy*. vol. 7, no. 1, pp. 118-47.

Komjaunimo Tiesa (Vilnius), newspaper.

Kononenko, V. (1993) 'Sovet Federatsii, verojatno, Budet ne Uchrezhden, a Samouchrezhden' ('The Federation Council Will Probably Be Not Constituted, but Self-Constituted'), *Izvestiya*, 23 Aug.

Koroteyeva, V.V. (1996), 'Respubliki RF mezhdu Etnoregionalizmom i Ekonomicheskim Natsionalizmom'('Republics within the RF: Between Ethnoregionalism and Economic Nationalism'), ch. 5 in L. M. Drobizheva, A.R. Aklaev, V.V. Koroteyeva, and G.U. Soldatova, *Demokratizatsija i "Litsa" Natsionalizma v Menyajushejsya Rossijskoj Federatsii nachala 1990 godov (Democratization and "Faces" of Nationalism in Changing Russian Federation of the early 1990s)*, Mysl Publishers, Moscow, pp. 204-249.

Kozlov, V. (1992), *Natsionalnosti SSSR (Nationalities of the USSR)*, Nauka, Moscow.

Krasnov, V. (1995) 'Ot Vyborov 1993 k Vyboram 1995' ('From 1993 elections to 1995 elections'), *Svobodnaya Mysl (Free Thought)*, no. 10, pp. 12-26.

Kriesberg, L. (1982), *Social Conflicts,* Syracusae University Press, Syracusae, NY.

Kriesberg, L. (1991), 'Introduction: Timing Conditions, Strategies and Errors', in L. Kriesberg and S.J. Thorson (eds), *Timing the De-Escalation of International Conflicts*, Syracusae University Press, Syracusae, NY, pp. 1-27.

Krikus, R. (1993), 'Lithuania: Nationalism in the modern era', in I. Bremmer and R. Taras (eds), *Nations and Politics in the Soviet Successor States*, Cambridge University Press, Cambridge, 157-81.

Kupchan, C. (1995), 'Introduction: Nationalism Resurgent', in in C. A. Kupchan (ed), *Nationalism and Nationalities in the New Europe*, Cornell University Press, Ithaca, NY, pp. 1-14.

Kuranty (Moscow), newspaper.

Kymlicka, W. (1995), *Multicultural Citizenship: A Liberal Theory of Minority Rights,* Oxford University Press, Oxford.

Laar, M. (1996), 'Estonia's Success Story', *Journal of Democracy*, vol. 7, no. 1, pp. 96-101.

Lake, D. A. (1992), 'Powerful Pacifists: Democratic States and War', *American Political Science Review*, vol. 86, no. 1, pp. 24-37.

Lake, D. A. and Rothschild, D. (1996), 'Containing Fear: The Origins and Management of Ethnic Conflict', *International Security*, vol.21, no.2, pp.41-75.

Lane, R. (1994), 'Structural Functionalism Reconsidered: A Proposed Research Model', *Comparative Politics*, vol. 24, no. 4, pp. 461-77.

Lange, F. (1994), 'The Baltic States and the CSCE', *Journal of Baltic Studies*, vol. 25, no. 3, pp. 233-47.

Laue, J. H. (1991), 'Contributions to the Emerging Field of Conflict Resolution', in W. S. Thompson et al. (eds), *Approaches to Peace*, USIP Press, Washington.

Lauristin, M. and Vihalem, P. (1997), *Return to the Western World. Cultural and Political Perspectives on the Estonian Post-Communist Transformation*, Tartu University Press, Tartu.

Lederach, J.P. (1996) 'Conflict transformation in protracted internal conflicts: The case for a comprehensive framework', in K. Rupersinghe (ed), *Conflict Transformation*, St Martin's, New York, pp. 201-22.

Leng, R.J. (1993), 'Reciprocating Influence Startegies in International Crisis Bargaining', *Journal of Conflict Resolution*, vol. 37, no. 1, pp. 3-41.
Levine, R.A. and Campbell, D. (1972), *Ethnocentrism. Theories of Conflict, Ethnic Attitudes, and Group Behavior*, Wiley, New York.
Levy, J. S. (1988), 'Domestic Politics and War' *Journal of Interdisciplinary History*, vol. 18, no. 3, pp. 345-69.
Lieven, A. (1993), *The Baltic Revolution*, Yale University Press, New Haven.
Lijphart, A. (1968), *The Politics of Accommodation: Pluralism and Democracy in the Netherlands*, University of California Press, Berkeley.
Lijphart, A. (1969), 'Consociational Democracy', *World Politics*, vol. 21, no. 4, pp.: 207-25.
Lijphart, A. (1977), *Democracy in Plural Societies: A Comparative Exploration*, Yale University Press: New Haven, CT.
Lijphart, A. (1990), 'Majority Rule versus Consociationalism in Deeply Divided Societies', *Politikon*, vol. 4, pp. 68-84.
Lijphart, A. (1991), 'Majority Rule in Theory and Practice: The Tenacity of a Flawed Paradigm', *International Social Science Journal*, vol. 43, no. 3, pp. 463-82.
Linz, J. and Stepan A. (1992), 'Political Identities and Electoral Sequences: SPayin, the Soviet Union and Yugoslavia', *Daedalus*, 121-39.
Linz, J. J. (1975), 'Totalitarian and authoritarian regimes', in F.I. Greenstein and N. W. Polby (eds), *Handbook of Political Science*, Addison-Westley, Reading, MA.
Linz, J. J. and Stepan, A. (1996), *Problems of Democratic Transition and Consolidation: Southern Europe, South America and Post-Communist Europe*, The Johns Hopkins University Press: Baltimore, MD.
Lipset, S. M. (1959), *Political Man: The Social Bases of Politics*, Johns Hopkins University Press, Baltimore, MD, 1-st ed.
Lipset, S. M. (1981), *Political Man: The Social Bases of Politics*, Johns Hopkins University Press, Baltimore, MD, 2-nd ed.
Liuhto, K. (1996), 'Entrepreneurial Transition in Post-Soviet Republics: The Estonian path', *Europe-Asia Studies*, vol. 48, no. 1, pp. 121-140.
Lustick, I. (1979), 'Stability in Deeply Divided Societies: Consociationalism vs Control', *World Politics*, vol. 31, no. 1, pp. 325-44.
Lustick, I. (1980), *Arabs in the Jewish State: Israel's Control of a National Minority*, University of Texas Press, Austin, TX.
Lustick, I. (1997), 'Lijphart, Lakatos, and Consociationalism', *World Politics*, vol. 50, no. 1, pp. 88-118.
Lustik, I. (1993), *Unsettled States, Disputed Lands, Britain and Ireland, France and Algeria, Israel and the West Bank-Gaza*. Cornell University Press, Ithaca, NY.
Luterbacher, U. (1984), 'Last Words Abour War?', *Journal of Conflict Resolution*, vol. 28, no.1, pp. 165-82.

Lynch, A. and Lukic, R. (1996), 'The Russian Federation will remain united', *Transition*, 12 January, pp. 14-17.
Lynn-Jones, S. (1996), 'Preface', in M. E. Brown, S. M. Lynn-Jones and S. E. Miller (eds), *Debating the Democratic Peace*, The MIT Press, Cambridge, MA, pp. i-xxxiii.
Lysenko, V. (1995), *Ot Tatarstana do Chechni. Stanovlenije Novogo Rossijskogo Federalizma (From Tatarstan to Chechnya. Beginnings of new Russian Federalism)*, Moscow, 1995.
Lysenko, V.N. (1998), 'Distribution of Power: The Experience of the Russian Federation', in G. Lapidus and S. Tsalik (eds), *Preventing Deadly Conflicts: Strategies and Institutions*, Proceedings of a Conference in Moscow, Carnegie Corporation of New York, Washington, DC, pp. 97-115.
Mainwaring, S. (1992), 'Transition to Democracy and Democratic Consolidation: Theoretical and Comparative Issues', in S. Mainwaring, G. O'Donnell, and J. S. Valenzuela (eds), *Issues in Democratic Consolidation: The New South American Democracies in Comparative Perspective*, University of Notre Dame Press, Notre Dame, IN.
Mansfield, E. D. and Snyder, J. (1995), 'Democratization and the Danger of War', *International Security*, vol. 20, no.1, pp. 5-38.
Mansfield, E. D. and Snyder, J. (1996), 'The Effects of Democratization on War', *International Security*, vol. 21, no. 1, pp. 196-207.
Maoz, Z. and N. Abdolali. (1989), 'Regime Types and International Conflict: 1815-1976', *Journal of Conflict Resolution*, vol. 33, no.1, pp. 3-35.
Maoz, Z. and Russett, B. (1992), 'Alliances, Wealth, Contiguity and Political Stability: Is the Lack of Conflict Between Democracies a Statistical Artifact?', *International Interactions*, vol. 17, pp. 245-67.
Maoz, Z. and Russett, B. (1993), 'Normative and Structural Causes of Democratic Peace, 1946-86', *American Political Science Review*, vol. 87, no. 3, pp. 624-38.
Mark, R. A. (1995), 'Moldova: Progress Amid Crisis', *Transition*, no.3, pp. 57-60.
Mayo, H. B. (1960), *An Introduction to Democratic Theory*, Oxford University Press, New York.
McClelland, Ch. (1968), 'Access to Berlin: The Quantity and Variety of Events, 1948-63', in J.D. Singer (ed), *Quantitative International Politics: Insights and Evidence*, Free Press, New York pp. 159-86.
McClelland, Ch. (1972), 'The Beginning, Duration and Abatement of International Crises: Comparison of Two Conflict Arenas', in C.F. Hermann (ed), *International Crises: Insights From Behavioral Research*, Free Press: New York, pp. 83-105.
McDonough, P., Barnes, S.H. and Pina, A.N, 'The Nature of Political Support and Legitimacy in Spain', *Comparative Political Studies*, vol. 27, no. 3, pp. 349-80.

McGarry, J. and O'Leary, B. (1993), 'Introduction: the Macro-Political Regulation of Ethnic Conflict', in J. McGarry, and B. O'Leary (eds), *The Politics of Ethnic Conflict Regulation*, Routledge, London, pp. 1-40.

McRae, K. (1990), 'Theories of Power Sharing and Conflict Management', in J. Montville (ed), *Conflict and Peacekeeping in Multiethnic Socieites*, Lexington Books, Lexington, MA, pp. 93-106.

Medvedev, R. (1989), *Let History Judge, The Origins and Consequences of Stalinism*, Columbia University Press, New York.

Metcalf, L.K. (1996), 'Outbidding to Radical Nationalists: Minority Policy in Estonia, 1988-1993', *Nations and Nationalism*, vol. 2, no.2, pp. 213-34.

Midlarsky, M.I. (1992), *The Internationalization of Communal Strife*, Unwin and Hyman, London.

Mikhailov, V. (1995), 'Nats'izm' v zerkale Natsiyaza' ('Naz'izm' in the Mirror of the Nazispeak), *Polis*, no. 4, pp. 77-86.

Mikhaleva, N. (1995), 'Konstitutsionnyje Reformy v Respublikakh-Subjektakh Rossijskoj Federatsii' ('Constitutional Reforms in the Republics - Subjects of the Russian Federation'), *Gosudarstvo i Pravo (State and Law)*, no. 4, pp. 3-11.

Miljan, T. (1989), 'The Proposal to Establish Economic Autonomy in Estonia', *Journal of Baltic Studies* , vol. 20, no. 1, pp. 154-60.

Mill, J. S. (1958), *Considerations on Representative Government*, Liberal Arts Press, New York.

Miller, N. R. (1983), 'Pluralism and Social Choice', *American Political Science Review*, vol. 77, no. 3, pp. 734-47.

Misiunas, R. J. and Taagepera, R. (1983), *The Baltic States: Years of Dependence, 1940-1980*, University of California Press, Berkeley.

Modelski, G. (1964), 'International Settlement of Internal War', in J. Rosenau (ed), *International Aspects of Civil Strife*, Princeton University Press, Princeton.

Molodezh Estonii (Tallinn), newspaper.

Mongush, M. (1993), 'The Annexation of Tannu-Tuva and the Formation of the Tuvinskaya ASSR', *Nationalities Papers*, vol. 21, no. 2, pp. 47-52.

Moreno, L. (1995), 'Multiple Ethnoterritorial Concurrence in Spain', *Nationalism and Ethnic Politics*, vol. 1, no. 1, pp. 11-32.

Morgan, T. C. and Schwebach, V. (1992), 'Take Two Democracies and Call Me in the Morning: A Prescription for Peace?', *International Interactions*, vol. 17, no. 4, pp. 305-20.

Morgan, T.C. and Campbell, S.H. (1991), 'Domestic Structure, Decisional Constraints, and War: So Why Kant Democracies Fight?', in *Journal of Conflict Resolution*, vol. 35, no. 2, pp. 187-211.

Moscow News (Moscow), newspaper.

Moynihan, D. P. (1993*)*, *Pandaemonium: Ethnicity and International Politics*, Oxford University Press, New York.

Muiznieks, N.R. (1995), 'The influence of the Baltic popular movements on the process of Soviet Disintegration', *Europe-Asia Studies*, vol. 47, no. 1, pp. 3-27.

Mukhametshin, F. (1994), 'Rossijskij Federalizm: Problemy Formirovaniya Otnoshenoj Nvogo Tpa' ('Russian Federalism: The Problems of Formation of a New Type of Relations'), *Gosudarstvo i Pravo (State and Law)*, no.3, pp. 49-59.

Muller, E.N. and Weede, (1990), 'Cross-national Variation in Political Violence: A Rational Action Approach', *Journal of Conflict Resolution*, vol. 34, no. 4, pp. 624-51.

Mullerson, R. (1994), *International Law, Rights and Politics: Developments in Eastern Europe and the CIS*, Routledge, London.

Munck, G. (1994), 'Democratic Transitions in Comparative Perspective', *Comparative Politics*, vol. 27, no. 2, pp. 355-74.

Munck, G. (1997), 'Bringing Post-Communist Societies into Democratization Studies', *Slavic Review*, vol. 56, no. 3, pp. 542-50.

Muravchik, J. (1997), 'Promoting peace through democracy', in Ch. A. Crocker, O.F. Hampson, with P. Ayall (eds), *Managing Global Chaos*, USIP Press, Washington, DC, pp. 573-85.

Newman, S and Piroth, S. (1996), 'The Use of Ballots, Boms and Bullets by Ethnoregional Movements in Advanced Industrial Democracies', *Nationalism and Ethnic Politics*, vol. 2, no. 3, pp.381-414.

Newman, S. (1991), 'Does Modernization Breed Ethnic Political Conflict?', *World Politics*, vol. 43, no. 3, pp. 451-78.

Newman, S. (1996), *Ethnoregional Conflict in Democracies. Mostly Ballots, Rarely Bullets*, Greenwood Press, Westport, CT.

Newman, S. (1997), 'Ideological Trends among Ethnoregional Parties in Post-Industrial Democracies', *Nationalism and Ethnic Politics*, vol. 3, no. 1, pp.28-60.

Nezavisimaya Gazeta (Moscow), newspaper.

Nezavisimaya Moldova (Chisinau), newspaper.

Nodia, G. (1992), 'Nationalism and Democracy', *Journal of Democracy*, vol. 3, no. 4.

Nodia, G. (1996), 'How Different are Post-Communist Transitions?', *Journal of Democracy*, vol. 7, no.4, pp. 15-29.

Nordlinger, E.A. (1972), *Conflict Regulation in Divided Societies*, Harvard Studies in International Affairs, Cambridge, MA.

Norgaard, O. (1996), *The Baltic States after Independence*, Edward Elgar, Cheltenham.

Novak, J. (1997), 'The Precarious Triumph of Civil Society', *Transition*, no.1, pp. 11-13.

Nutt, M. (1990), 'Politicheskaya Shkala Sovremennosti' ('Political Spectrum of Contemporaneity'), *Raduga*, no. 6, pp. 33-42.

O'Connell, J. (1971), 'Authority and Community in Nigeria', in R. Melson and H. Wolpe (eds), *Nigeria: Modernization and the Politics of Communalism*, Michigan State University Press, East Lansing.
O'Donnell, G. (1994), 'Delegative Democracy', *Journal of Democracy*, vol. 5, no.1, pp. 60-9.
O'Donnell, G. and Schmitter, Ph. (1986), *Transitions from Authoritarian Rule: Tentative Conclusions about Uncertain Democracy*, Johns Hopkins University Press, Baltimore, MD.
O'Leary, B. and McGarry, J. (1993), *The politics of Antagonism: Understanding Northern Ireland*, Athlone, London..
O'Neal, J.R., O'Neal, F.H., Zeev, M. and Russett, B. (1996), 'The Liberal Peace: Interdependence, Democracy, and International Conflict, 1950-1985', *Journal of Peace Research*, vol.33, no. 1, pp. 11-28.
Obershall, A. (1973), *Social Conflict and Social Movements*, Prentice-Hall, Englewood Cliffs, NJ.
Offe, C. (1991), 'Capitalism by Democratic Design? Democratic theory facing the triple transition in East Central Europe', *Social Research*, vol. 58, pp. 865-92.
Ordeshook, P.C. (1995), 'Reexamining Russia: Institutions and Incentives', *Journal of Democracy*, vol. 6, no. 2, pp.46-60.
Ott, A.F., Kirch, A. And Kirch, M. (1996), 'Ethnic anxiety: A case study of resident aliens in Estonia, 1990-92', *Journal of Baltic Studies*, vol. 27, no. 1, pp. 21-45.
Owen, J.M. (1994), 'How Liberalism Produces Democratic Peace', *International Security*, vol. 19, no. 2, pp. 87-125.
Park, A. (1993), 'Ideological Dimension of the Post-Communist Domestic Conflicts', *Communist and Post-Communist Studies*, vol. 26, no. 3, pp. 265-76.
Pastukhov, V. (1994), 'Novyj Federalism dlya Rossii: Institutsionalizatsiya Svobody' ('New Federalism for Russia: Institutionalization of Freedom'), *Polis*, no. 3, pp. 95-105.
Patrash, M. (1990), 'Migration: The state of the problem and the path to its resolution under conditions of self-financing', *Literatura si Arta*, no. 6, February, pp. 6-7.
Patterson, O. (1977), *Ethnic Chauvinism: The Reactionary Impulse*, Stein and Day, New York.
Payin, E. (1994), 'The disintegration of the empire and the fate of the 'imperial minority', in V. Schlapentokh, M. Sendich and E. Payin (eds), *The New Russian Diaspora: Russian Minorities in the Former Soviet Republics*, M.E. Sharpe, Armonk, pp. 21-36.
Payin, E. (1995), 'Separatizm i Federalism v Sovremennoj Rossiyi' ('Separatism and Federalism in Contemporary Russia'), in T.I. Zaslavskaya and L.A. Arutyunyan (eds) *Kuda Idet Rossiya? Alternativy Obshestvennogo Razvitiya (Whiter Russia? Alternatives of Social Development)*, Interpraks, Moscow, pp.159-71.

Peled, Y. (1992), 'Ethnic Democracy and the Legal Construction of Citizenship: Arab Citizens of the Jewish State', *American Political Science Review*, vol. 86, no. 2, pp. 432-43.

Poortinga, Y.H. and Hendriks, E.C. (1989), 'Culture as a Factor in International Negotiations: A Proposed Research Project from a Psychological Perspective', in F. Mautner-Markhof (ed), *Processes of International Negotiations*, Westview, Boulder, CO, pp. 203-12.

Porter, B. D. and Saivetz, C.R. (1994), 'The Once and Future Empire: Russia and the Near Abroad', *The Washington Quarterly*, vol. 17, no. 3, pp. 75-90.

Posen, B. R. (1993), 'The Security Dilemma and Ethnic Conflict', in M.Brown (ed.). *Ethnic Conflict and International Security*, Princeton University, Princeton, pp. 103-125.

Pravda (Moscow), newspaper.

Prazauskas, A. (1993), 'Raspadetsya li Rossijskaya Federatsiya?' ('Will Russian Federation Disintegrate?'), *Aktualnaya Politika*, nos 2-6: 11-17.

Premdas, R. R. 'The Internationalization of Ethnic Conflict: Some Theoretical Consideations', in De Silva, K. M. and R. J. May (eds), *Internationalization of Ethnic Conflict*, Pinter Publishers, London, pp. 10-25.

Pruitt, D. and Rubin, J. (1986), *Social Conflict: Escalation, Stalemate, and Settlement*, Random House, New York.

Przeworski, A. (1988), 'Democracy as a Contingent Outcome of Conflicts', in J. Elster, and R. Slagstad (eds), *Constitutionalism and Democracy*, Cambridge University Press, Cambridge, pp. 59-80.

Przeworski, A. (1991), *Democracy and the Market*, Cambridge University Press, Cambridge.

Przeworski, A., Alvarez, M. Cheibub, J.A., and Limongi, F. (1996), 'What Makes Democracies Endure?', *Journal of Democracy*, vol. 7, no 1, pp. 39-55.

Pugachev, B. (1992), 'Puti Stanovlenija Rossijskoj Gosudarstvennosti'('Ways of Establishing the Russian Statehood'), *Ethnopolis*, no. 2, pp. 27-35.

Putnam, R. D. (1993), *Making Democracy Work: Civic Traditions in Modern Italy*, Princeton University Press, Princeton, NJ.

Pye, L. W. (1971), 'The Legitimacy Crisis', in Binder et al. (1971), pp.101-135.

Pye, L.W. (1990), 'Political Science and the Crisis of Authoritarianism', *American Political Science Review*, vol. 84, no.1, pp. 3-17.

Ra'anan, U. (1990), 'The Nation-State Fallacy', in J.V. Montville (ed), *Conflict and Peacemaking in Multiethnic Societies*, Heath and Co, Lexington, MA, pp. 5-20.

Rabie, M. (1994), *Conflict Resolution and Ethnicity*, Praeger, Westport, CT.

Rabushka, A. and Shepsle, K. (1972*)*, *Politics in Plural Societies: A Theory of Democratic Instability*, Charles E. Merrill, Columbus, OH.

Rae, D. (1969), 'Decision Rules and Individual Values in Constitutional Choice', *American Political Science Review*, vol. 63, no. 1, pp. 40-56.

Raun, T. (1987), *Estonia and the Estonians*, Stanford, Hoover Institution Press.

Raun, T. (1994), 'Post-Soviet Estonia, 1991-1993', *Journal of Baltic Studies*, vol. 25, no.4, pp. 73-80.
Raun, T. (1995), 'The Estonian SSR Language Law (1989): Background and implementation', *Nationalities Papers*, vol. 23, pp. 515-34.
Raun, T. (1997a), 'Estonia: Independence Redefined', in I. Bremmer and R. Taras (eds.), *New States, New Politics: Building the Post-Soviet Nations*, Cambridge University Press, Cambridge, pp. 402-433.
Raun, T. (1997b), 'Democratization and Political Development in Estonia, 1987-96', in K. Dawisha and B. Parrott (eds.), *The Consolidation of Democracy in East-Central Europe*, Cambridge University Press, Cambridge, pp. 334-74.
Ray, J. L. (1993), 'Wars Between Democracies: Rare or Nonexistent?', *International Interactions*, vol. 18, no. 3, pp. 251-76.
Ray, J. L. (1995a), 'Global Trends, State-Specific Factors and Regime Transitions, 1825-1993', *Journal of Peace Research*, vol. 32, no. 1, pp. 49-63.
Ray, J. L. (1995b), *Democracy and International Conflict. An Evaluation of the Democratic Peace Proposition*, University of South Carolina Press: Columbia.
Ray, J.L. (1997), 'The Democratic Path to Peace', *Journal of Democracy*, vol. 8, no. 2, pp. 49-64.
Raymond, G. A. (1994), 'Democracies, Disputes, and Third-Party Intermediaries', *Journal of Conflict Resolution*, vol. 38, no. 1, pp. 24-42.
Raz, J. (1986), *The Morality of Freedom*, Oxford University Press, Oxford.
Remmer, K. L. (1995), 'New Theoretical Perspectives on Democratization', *Comparative Politics*, vol. 28, no. 1, pp. 103-22.
Remmer, K. L. (1997), 'Theoretical Decay and Theoretical Development: The Resurgence of Institutional Analysis', *World Politics*, vol. 50, no. 1, pp. 34-61.
Resler, T. J. (1997), 'Dilemmas of democratization: Safeguariding minorities in Russia, Ukraine, Lithuania', *Europe-Asia Studies*, vol. 49, no.1, pp. 89-106.
Richardson, J. L. (1994), *Crisis Diplomacy: The Great Powers Since the Mid-Nineteenth Century*, Cambridge University Press, Cambridge.
Richardson, L.F. (1960), *Statistics of Deadly Quarrels*, Boxwood and Quadrangle, Chicago.
Risse-Kappen, T. (1995), 'Democratic Peace - Warlike Democracies? A Social Constructivist Interpretation of the Liberal Argument', *European Journal of International Relations*, vol. 1, no. 4, pp. 491-518.
Ropers, N. (1997), *Roles and Functions of Third Parties in the Constructive Management of Ethnopolitical Conflicts*, Berghof Occasional Paper No. 14, Berghof Resesrach Center for Constructive Conflict Management, Berlin.
Rose, R. and Maley, J. (1994), 'Conflict or Compromise in the Baltic states?', *RFE/RL Report*, vol. 3, no.28, pp. 26- 35.
Rossijskaya Gazeta (newspaper), Moscow.
Rothschild, D. (1986), 'Hegemonial Exchange: An alternative Model for Managing Conflict in Middle Africa', in D.L. Thompson, and D. Roven (eds), *Ethnicity, Politics and Development*, Lynne Rienner, Boulder, CO.

Rothschild, J. (1982) *Ethnopolitics: A Conceptual Framework*, Columbia University Press, New York.
Rousseau, D. L., Gelpi, Ch., Reiter, D., and Huth, P.K. (1996), 'Assessing the Dyadic Nature of the Democratic Peace, 1918-88', *American Political Science Review*, vol. 90, no. 3.
Rubin, J. Z. (1994), 'Models of Conflict Management', *Journal of Social Issues*, Vol. 50, no.1, pp. 33-46.
Rubin, J.Z., Pruitt, D.G. and Kim, S. H. (1994), *Social Conflict: Escalation, Stalemate, and Settlement*, McGraw-Hill, New York.
Rule, J.B. (1988), *Theories of Civil Violence*, University of California Press, Berkeley.
Rummel, R.J. (1979), *Understanding Conflict and War: Vol. 4, War, Power, and Peace*. Sage Publications, Los Angeles.
Rummel, R. J. (1983), 'Libertarianism and international violence', *Journal of Conflict resolution*, vol. 27, no. 1, March, pp. 27-71.
Rupersinghe, K. (1995), 'Conflict Transformation', in K. Rupersinghe, (ed) *Conflict Transformation*, St. Martin's, New York, pp. 65-91.
Russett, B. (1990), *Controlling the Sword: The Democratic Governance of National Security*, Harvard University Press, Cambridge, MA.
Russett, B. (1993), *Grasping the Democratic Peace: Principles for a Post-Cold War World*, Princeton University Press, Princeton, NJ.
Russett, B. and Antholis, W. (1992), 'Do Democracies Fight Each Other? Evidence from the Peloponnesian War', *Journal of Peace Research*, vol. 29, no. 4, pp. 415-34.
Rustow, D. A. (1970), 'Transitions to Democracy: Toward a Dynamic Model', *Comparative Politics*, vol. 2, no. 3, pp. 337-64.
Ruthland, P. (1994), 'Has Democracy Failed in Russia?', *The National Interest*, vol. 38, pp. 8-10.
Ruthland, P. (1996), 'The Enigma of Ethnicity', *Transition*, no. 1, p. 4.
Ryan, M. and Prentice, R. (1987), *Social Trends in the Soviet Union From 1950*, St. Martin's, New York.
Ryan, S. (1995), *Ethnic Conflict and International Relations*, Dartmouth, Aldershot, 2nd ed.
Saar, A. (1991), 'What did the Plebiscite and Referendum in Estonia reveal about the Statehood of Estonia and the Soviet Union', *The Monthly Survey of Estonian and Soviet Politics*. Panor, Tallinn, pp. 12-16.
Safran, W. (1991), 'Ethnicity and Pluralism: Comparative and Theoretical Perspectives', *Canadian Review of Studies in Nationalism*, vol. 18, no2.1-2, pp. 1-12.
Samorodny, O. (1989),'Politichesky Spektr Estonii' ('Political Spetrum of Estonia', *Raduga*, no. 12, pp. 45-56.
Sampson, S. (1986), 'The Informal Sector in Eastern Europe', *Telos*, vol. 66, pp. 44-66.

Sartori, G. (1987), *The Theory of Democracy Revisited*, Chatham House Publishers, Chatham.
Sartori, G. (1995), 'How Far Can Free Government Travel?', *Journal of Democracy*, vol. 6, no.3, pp. 101-11.
Sartori, G. (1997), 'Understanding Pluralism, vol. 8 no. 4, pp. 58-69.
Saunders, H. H. (1992), 'Political Settlement and the Gulf Crisis', *Mediterranean Quarterly*, vol. 2, no. 2, pp. 1-11.
Schechterman, B. and Slann, M. (eds) (1993), *The Ethnic Dimension in International Relations*, Praeger, New York.
Schedler, A. (1998), 'What Is Democratic Consolidation ?', *Journal of Democracy*, vol. 9, no. 2, pp. 91-107.
Scherer, K.R., R.P. Abeles and C.S. Fisher. (1975), *Human Aggression and Conflict. Interdisciplinary Perspectives*, Prentice-Hall, Englewood Cliffs, NJ.
Schmitter, P. C. and Karl, T. L. (1994), 'The Conceptual Travel of Transitologists and Consolidologists: How Far to the East Should They Attempt to Go?,' *Slavic Review*, vol. 53, no.1, pp. 173-85.
Schmitter, P.C. and Karl, T. L. (1991), 'What Democracy Is ... and Is Not,' *Journal of Democracy*, vol. 2, no.3, pp. 75-88.
Schmitter, P. (1994), 'Dangers and Dilemmas of Democracy', *Journal of Democracy*, vol. 5, no. 1, pp. 57-74.
Schöpflin, G. (1994), 'Postcommunism: The Problems of Democratic Construction', *Daedalus*, vol. 123, no.3, pp. 127-141.
Schöpflin, G. (1995a),. 'Nationalism and Ethnicity in Europe, East and West', in C. A. Kupchan (ed), *Nationalism and Nationalities in the New Europe*, Cornell University Press, Ithaca, NY, pp. 37-65.
Schöpflin, G. (1995b), 'Nationhood, Communism and State Legitimation', *Nations and Nationalism*, vol. 1, , pp. 81-92.
Schumpeter, J. A. (1947), *Capitalism, Socialism, and Democracy*, Harper, New York.
Senese, P. D. (1997), 'Between Dispute and War: The Effect of Joint Democracy on Interstate Conflict Escalation', *The Journal of Politics*, vol. 59, no. 1, pp. 1-27.
Senn, A.E. (1990), *Lithuania Awakening*, Berkeley, University of California Press.
Senn, A.E. (1991), *Crisis in Lithuania: January 1991*, Chicago, Akiraciai.
Senn, A.E. (1992), 'The Political Culture of Independent Lithuania: A Review Essay', *Journal of Baltic Studies*, vol. 23, no. 3, pp. 307-316.
Senn, A.E. (1994), 'Lithuania's First Two Years of Independence', *Journal of Baltic Studies*, vol. 25, no. 1, pp. 81-88.
Senn, A.E. (1997), 'Lithuania: Rights and Responsibilities of Independence', in I. Bremmer and R. Taras (eds.), *New States, New Politics: Building the Post-Soviet Nations*, Cambridge University Press, Cambridge, pp. 353-75.
Senn, A.E. and Motulaite, V. (1993), 'The Lithuanian concept of statehood', *Nationalities Papers*, vol. 21, no.2, pp. 25-34.
Sfatul Tserij (Chisinau), newspaper.

Sharlet, R. (1994), 'The Prospects for Federalism in Russian Constitutional Politics', *Publius*, vol. 24, no. 1, pp. 115-27.
Sheehy, A. (1993a), 'The Estonian Law on Aliens', *RFE/RL Research Report*, vol. 2, no. 28, pp. 7-11.
Sheehy, A. (1993b), 'Russia's Republics: A Threat to its Territorial Integrity?' vol. 2, no. 20, pp. 34-40.
Sheffer, G. (1994), 'Ethnonational Diasporas and Security', *Survival*, vol. 36, no. 1, pp. 60-79.
Shevtsova, L. (1995), 'The Two Sides of the New Russia', *Journal of Democracy*, vol. 6, no. 3, pp. 56-72.
Shibutani, T. and Kwan, K. M. (1965), *Ethnic Stratification: A Comparative Approach*, Macmillan, London.
Shils, E. A. (1957), 'Primordial, Personal, Sacred and Civil Ties', *British Journal of Sociology*, vol. 8, no. 1, pp. 130-45.
Shils, E. A. (1991), 'The Virtue of Civil Society', *Government and Opposition*, vol. 26, no. 1, pp. 3-20.
Shin, D. C. (1994), 'On the Third Wave of Democratization: A Synthesis and Evaluation of Recent Theory and Research', *World Politics*, vol. 47, no. 1, pp. 135-70.
Simonsen, S.G. (1996), 'Raising the "the Russian Question": Ethnicity and Statehood - Russkie and Rossiya', *Nationalism and Ethnic Politics*, vol. 2, no. 1, pp. 91-110.
Sisk, T. D. (1995), *Democratization in South Africa: The Elusive Social Contract*, Princeton University Press, Princeton.
Sisk, T.D. (1996), *Power Sharing and International Mediation in Ethnic Conflicts*, USIP Press, Washington, DC.
Sklar, R. L. (1987), 'Developmental Democracy', *Comparative Studies in Society and History*, vol. 29, no. 4, pp. 686-714.
Sklar, R.L. (1996), 'Towards a Theory of Developmental Democracy', in A. Leftwich (ed), *Democracy and Development: Theory and Practice*, Polity Press, Cambridge.
Slider, D. (1994), 'Federalism, Discord, and Accommodation: Intergovernmental Relations in Post-Soviet Russia', in Th. Friedgut and J. Hahn (eds), *Local Power and Post-Soviet Politics*, M.E. Sharpe, Armonk, NY.
Slocum, J. W. (1995), *Disintegration and Consolidation: National Separatism and the Evolution of Center-Periphery Relations in the Russian Federation*, Occasional Paper No. 19 of the Peace Studies Program, Cornell University Press, Ithaca, NY.
Small, M. and Singer, J. D. (1976), 'The War-Proneness of Democratic Regimes', *Jerusalem Journal of International Relations*, vol. 1, no. 1, pp. 50-69.
Smith, A. D. (1986), *The Ethnic Origins of Nations*, Blackwell, Oxford.
Smith, A. D. (1991), *National Identity*, Penguin Books, Harmondsworth.
Smith, M.G. (1965), *The Plural Soociety in the British West Indies*, University of California Press, Berkeley.

Smith, M.G. (1969), 'Some Developments in the Analytic Study of Pluralism', in L. Kuper and M.G. Smith (eds), *Pluralism in Africa*, University of California Press, Berkeley.

Smith, M.G. (1986), 'Pluralism, Violence and the Modern State', in A. Kazancigil (ed), *The State in Global Perspective*, Gower/UNESCO, Paris.

Smith, M.G. (1988), 'Pluralism, Race and Ethnicity in Selected African Countries', in J. Rex and D. Mason (eds), *Theories of Race and Ethnic Relations*, Cambridge University Press, Cambridge.

Smolar, A. (1996), 'Civil Society after Communism: From Opposition to Atomization', *Journal of Democracy*, vol. 7, no.1, pp. 24-38.

Smooha, S. (1990), 'Minority Status in an Ethnic Democracy: The Status of the Arab Minority in Israel', *Ethnic and Racial Studies*, vol. 13, no. 2, pp. 389-413.

Smooha, S. (1992), *Arabs and Jews in Mutual Intolerance*, Westview Press, San Francisco.

Smooha, S. and Hanf, Th. (1992), 'The Diverse Modes of Conflict Regulation in Deeply Divided Societies', *International Journal of Comparative Sociology*, vol. 33, nos 1-2.

Snyder, J. (1993), 'Nationalism and the Crisis of the Post-Soviet State', in: M.Brown (ed), *Ethnic Conflict and International Security*, Princeton University Press, Princeton, pp. 79-103.

Socor, V. (1989), 'The Moldavian Democratic Movement: Structure, Program, and Initial Impact', RFE/RL Report on the USSR, vol. 1, no. 8, pp. 31-4.

Socor, V. (1993), 'Moldova's 'Dniester' Ulcer', *RFE/RL Research Report*, vol. 2, no. 10, pp. 12-6.

Socor, V. (1994a), 'Gagauz Autonomy in Moldova: A Precedent for Eastern Europe', *RFE/RL Report*, vol. 3, no. 33, pp. 20-8.

Socor, V. (1994b), 'Five Countries Look at Ethnic Problems in Southern Moldova', *RFE/RL Report*, vol. 3, no. 32, pp. 19-23.

Socor, V. (1994c), 'Moldova's Political Lanscape: Profiles of the Parties', *RFE/RE Research Report*, vol. 3, no.10, pp. 6-14.

Soglasiye (Vilnius), newspaper.

Solnick, S. (1996), ' The Political Economy of Russian Federalism: A Framework for Analysis', *Problems of Post-Communism*, vol. 43, no.6, pp. 13-26.

Sorensen, G. (1992), 'Kant and Processes of Democratization: Consequences for Neorealist Thought', *Journal of Peace Research*, vol. 29, no. 4, pp. 397-410.

Sorensen, G. (1993), *Democracy and Democratization. Processes and Prospects in a Changing World*, Westview Press, Boulder, CO.

Sovetskaya Estonia (Tallinn), newspaper

Sovetskaya Litva (Vilnius), newspaper.

Sovetskaya Moldova (Chisinau), newspaper.

Starr, H. (1991), 'Democratic Dominoes. Diffusion Approaches to the Spread of Democracy in the International System', *Journal of Conflict Resolution*, vol. 35, no. 2, pp. 356-381.

Starr, H. (1992), 'Democracy and War: Choice, Learning and Security Communities', *Journal of Peace Research*, vol. 29, no. 2, pp. 207-213.

Starr, H. (1997), 'Democracy and Integration: Why Democracies Don't Fight Each Other', *Journal of Peace Research*, vol. 32, no. 2, pp. 153-162.

Steen, A. (1996), 'Consolidation and Competence: Research on the Politics of Recruiting Political Elites in the Baltic States', *Journal of Baltic Studies*, vol. 27, no.2, pp. 143-56.

Steen, A. (1997), 'The New Elites in the Baltic States: Recirculation and Change', *Scandinavian Political Studies*, vol. 20, no. 1, pp. 91-112.

Streit, C. (1938). *Union Now: A Proposal for a Federal Union of the Leading Democracies,* Harpers, New York.

Sztompka, P. (1991), 'The Intangibles and Imponderables of the Transition to Democracy', *Studies in Comparative Communism*, vol. 24, no. 3, pp. 295-311.

Taagepera, R. (1989), 'Estonia's Road to Independence', *Problems of Communism* vol. 38, no.6, pp. 11-9.

Taagepera, R. (1992), 'Ethnic Relations in Estonia, 1991', *Journal of Baltic Studies*, vol. 23, no. 2, pp. 121-32.

Taagepera, R. (1994), 'Estonia's Constitutional Assembly, 1991-1992', *Journal of Baltic Studies*, vol. 25, no. 3, pp. 211-31.

Taylor, C. (1998), 'The Dynamics of Democratic Exclusion', *Journal of Democracy*, vol. 9, no. 4, pp. 143-56.

Teague, E. (1993), 'North-South Divide: Yeltsin and Russia's Provincial Leaders'. *RFE/RL Research Report*, vol. 2, no. 47, pp. 7-23.

Teague, E. (1994a), 'Russia's local elections begin', *RFE/RL Research Report* vol. 3, no. 7, pp. 1-4.

Teague, E. (1994b), 'Russia and Tatarstan Sign Power-Sharing Treaty', *RFE/RL Research Report*, vol. 3, no. 14, pp. 19-27.

Teague, E. (1994c), 'Center-periphery relations in the Russian Federation', in R. Szporluk (ed.), *National Identity and Ethnicity in Russia and the New States of Eurasia*, M.E. Sharpe, Armonk, NY, pp. 21-57.

Tedin, K.L. (1994), 'Popular Support for Competitive Elections in the Soviet Union', *Comparartive Political Studies*, vol. 27, no. 2, pp. 241-71.

Terry, S.M. (1993), 'Thinking About Post-Communist Transitions: How Different Are They?', *Slavic Review*, vol. 52, no 2, pp. 333-37.

The Baltic States: A Reference Book (1991), Encyclopedia Publishers, Tallinn.

Thompson, W.R. and Tucker, R. (1997), 'A Tale of Two Democratic Peace Critiques', *Journal of Conflict Resolution,* vol. 41, no. 3, pp. 428-54.

Tilly, Ch. (1978), *From Mobilization to Revolution*, Addison-Wesley, Reading.

Tilly, Ch., Tilly, L. and Tilly, R. (1975), *The Rebellious Century*, Harvard University Press, Cambridge.

Tishkov, V.A. (1997), *Ethnicity, Nationalism and Conflict in and after the Soviet Union*, Sage, London.

Tolz, V. (1993), 'Thorny Road Toward Federalism in Russia', *RFE/RL Research Report*, vol. 2, no.48, pp. 1-8.

Tong, Y. (1995), 'Mass Alienation under State Socialism and After', *Communist and Post-Communist Studies*, vol. 28, no. 2, pp. 215-37.
Touval, S. and Zartman, I.W. (eds) (1985), *International Mediation in Theory and Practice*, Westview Press, Boulder.
Umnova, I.A. (1998), *Konstitutsionnyje Osnovy Sovremennogo Rossijskogo Federalizma (Constitutional Foundations of Contemporary Russian Federalism)*, Delo Publishers, Moscow.
Vaitiekus, S. (1994), 'Multicultural Environment and System of Education in Lithuania', *Baltic News*, vol. 8, no. 77, pp. 33-35.
Valenzuela, J.S. (1992), 'Democratic Consoliadtion in Post-Transitional Settings: Notion, Process and Facilitating Conditions', in S. Mainwaring, G. O'Donnell, and J.S. Valenzuela (eds), *Issues in Democratic Consolidation: The New South American Democracies in Comparative Perspective*, University of Notre Dame Press, Notre Dame, IN.
Van den Berghe, P. (1981), *The Ethnic Phenomenon*, Elsevier, Oxford.
Vance, C. (1983), *Hard Choices*, Simon and Schuster, New York.
Vasquez, J. (1993), *The War Puzzle*, Cambridge University Press, Cambridge.
Vebra, R. (1994), 'Political Rebirth in Lithuania, 1990-91: Events and Problems', *Journal of Baltic Studies*, vol. 25, no. 2, pp. 183-88.
Verba S. (1971), 'Sequences and Development', in Binder et al. (1971), pp. 283-316.
Verba, S. (1965), 'Comparative Political Culture', in L. W. Pye and S. Verba (eds), *Political Culture and Political Development*, Princeton University Press: Princeton, NJ, pp. 512-560.
Verdery, K. (1993) 'Whither "Nation" and "Nationalism"?', *Daedalus*, vol. 122, no. 3, pp. 37-46.
Vetik, R. (1993), 'Ethnic Conflict and Accommodation in Post-Communist Estonia', *Journal of Peace Research*, vol. 30, no.3, pp. 271-80.
Vetik, R. (1994), 'Russians in Estonia: New Development Trends', *Changing Identities in Estonia: Sociological Facts and Commentaries*, Estonian Science Foundation, Tallinn, pp. 72-9.
Vetik, R. (1995), 'Identity Development and Political Adjustment in Estonia: Research Note', *World Affairs*, vol. 157, no.3.
Walker, E.W. (1995), 'Federalism Russian Style. The Federation Provisions in Russia's New Constitution', *Problems of Post-Communism*, vol.42, pp. 3-12.
Wallich, C., (ed) (1994), *Russia and the Challenge of Fiscal Federalism*, The World Bank, Waschington, DC.
Weart, S.R. (1994), 'Peace Among Democratic and Oligarchic Republics', *Journal of Peace Research*, vol. 31, no. 3, pp. 299-316.
Weber, M. (1968), *Economy and Society*, G. Roth and C. Wittich (eds), Bedminster, New York.
Weede, E. (1984), 'Democracy and War Involvement', *Journal of Conflict Resolution*, vol. 28, no.4, pp. 649-64.

Weede, E. (1992), 'Some Simple Calculations on Democracy and War Involvement', *Journal of Peace Research*, vol. 29, no. 4, pp. 377-83.
Weffort, F. C. (1993), 'What is a *New* Democracy?', *International Journal of Social Sciences*, vol. 136, pp. 245-55.
Weigant, M. H. (1995), 'The Russian minority in Estonia', International Journal on Group Rights, vol. 3, no. 1, pp. 109-143.
Weigle, M. A. and Butterfield, J. (1992) 'Civil Society in Reforming Communist Regimes: The Logic of Emergence', *Comparative Politics*, vol. 25, no. 1, pp. 1-25.
Weiner, M. (1978), *Sons of the Soil: Migration and Ethnic Conflict in India*, Princeton University Press, Princeton, NJ.
Welsh, H.A. (1994), 'Political Transition Processes in Central and Eastern Europe', *Comparative Politics*, vol. 26, no. 3, pp. 379-93.
Whitehead, L. (1989), 'The Consolidation of Fragile Democracies', in R.A. Pastor, (ed), *Democracy in the Americas*, Holmes and Meier, New York.
Winn, N. (1996), *European Crisis Management in the 1980s*, Dartmouth, Aldershot.
Wright, Q. (1965), *A Study of War*, University of Chicago Press, Chicago, IL.
Young, C. (1976), *The Politics of Cultural Pluralism*, University of Wisconsin Press, Madison.
Young, O. (1968), *The Politics of Force*, Princeton University Press, Princeton.
Zakaria, F. (1997), 'The Rise of Illiberal Democracy', *Foreign Affairs*, vol. 76, no. 6, pp. 22-43.
Zartman, W. (1985), *Ripe for Resolution: Conflict and Intervention in Africa*, Oxford University Press, New York.
Zartman, W. (1991), 'Conflict and Resolution: Contest, Cost and Change', *The Annals of the AAPSS*, vol. 518, pp. 11-23.
Zartman, W.I. (1990), 'Negotiations and Prenegotiations in Ethnic Conflict', in Montville (ed) *Conflict and Peacemaking in Multiethnic Societies*, Lexington Books: Lexington, pp. 511-34.
Zaslavsky, V. (1992), 'Nationalism and Democratic Transition in Post-Communist Societies', *Daedalus*, vol. 121, no. 2, pp. 97-122.
Zaslavsky, V. (1993), 'Success and Collapse: Traditional Soviet Nationality Policy', in I. Bremmer and R. Taras (eds), *Nations and Politics in the Soviet Successor States*, Cambridge University Press, Cambridge, pp. 29-42.
Zhang, B. (1994), 'Corporatism, Totalitarianism, and Transitions to Democracy', *Comparartive Political Studies*, vol. 27, no. 1, pp. 108-36.
Zimmerman, E. (1983), *Political Violence, Crises, and Revolution*, Schenkman, Cambridge.
Zubek, V. (1993), 'New Poland's Old Dilemma: The Polish minority in Lithuania', *Ethnic and Racial Studies*, vol. 16, no.4, pp. 657-82.
Zvidrins, P. (1994), 'Changes of Ethnic Composition in the Baltic States', *Nationalities Papers*, vol. 22, no. 2, pp. 365-77.

Index

Conflict
    conflict stages 35-8
    conflict escalation/deescalations 36-7
Constructive conflict management 20-1
Crisis
    concept of 39-40, 43
    of political development 40-1
    in international relations 42-3
Crisis management 47
Cross-cutting cleavages 31-3
Civility-building 95
Civil society
    and ethnic conflict 59-60
    under post-communism 104-7
Civic/ethnic value balance 67-8, 91, 95-6
Democracy
    conceptualizations of 49-52
    as conflict management 20-1, 65-6
    and nationalism 52-4, 56
    and nation-state 52-3
    problems in plural societies 56-64
    and liberalism 51-2
    and positive peace 21-2, 65-66, 79-81
    in developmental terms 86
Democracy-building 135-6
Democratic Consolidation 83-4, 86
Democratic Craft 80-1
Democratic Ethnic Peace
    concept of 23-5
    cultural conditions of 66-70
    institutional conditions of 70-6
Democratic Peace
    phenomenon of 9-10
    proposition of 10
    emergence of a theory 11-3
    levels of analysis 18
    intellectual roots 10
    normative explanations 14-5
    cultural explanations 13-4
    progressive research agenda 16-7
    and democratization 2, 3, 17-8
    ethnic dimension 2-4, 17-8
Democratic transition 82
Democratization
    conceptualizations of 78-82
    as conflict management 85
    as crisis management 85-7
    third wave of 78-9
    stages of 82-5
    preconditions vs. craft 80-1
    processes and modes of 81, 95-6
    and ethnic conflict 87
Democratizing Ethnic Peace
    concept of 23-5, 254
    features of 97-8, 254-5, 258
    and ethnopolitical crisis management 97-9, 255-7
    contextual factors of 88-9
    stage-specific factors of 89-97
Estonia
    historical background 143
    demographic background 143-6
    stages of democratization 146
    ethnopolitical mobilization under *perestroika* 146-52
    Popular Front of Estonia 147
    Intermovent 149
    OSTK 149
    Estonian Citizens' Committees 151-2
    declaration on sovereignty 147-8
    elections of 1990 152-3

elections of 1992 160
elections of 1995 171
restoration of independence 152-3, 155, 158
ethnopolitical crisis interaction 162-67
ethnopolitical problem areas (crises)
   stateness 155
   state effectiveness 155
   nationhood 156-62, 167-71
legislation on citizenship 158-60
issues of inclusion/exclusion 157-60
Law on Aliens 162-3
third-party mediation 164-7
policies of integration 167-70, 172-3
quality of ethnic peace 173-5
'Ethnic democracy' 75-6
Ethnicity
   approaches to 26-9
      primordialism 27
      instrumentalism 27-8
   and society 31-3, 58-9
   and the state 33-4
Ethnic inclusion/exclusion 60, 69
Ethnic outbidding 58, 62-3
Ethnic peace
   and type of rule 18-25, 66
   culture of 260-1
   institutions of 259-60
   issues of consolidation of 257-61
   sustainability of ethnic peace 23-4, 260-1
Ethnic peace constituency 259-60
Ethnopolitical conflict
   nature of 26, 28-31, 58
   factors of 31-4
   dynamics of 34-6
   psychology and politics 28-31
   structure of 31, 34
   and social change 36-9
Ethnopolitical crises
   types of 43
   levels of 43
   interactional 42-5
   systemic 43-6
      of stateness 114-6
      of state effectiveness 116-9
      of nationhood 119-22
   sequences of 122-3

Ethnopolitical crisis mangement
   levels of 48
   patterns of 48-59, 146-9
   menu of choice 136-9
   and ethnic peace 48-9
   Hegemonic control 75-6
   Institutional innovation as crisis management 42, 45, 86-7, 93-6, 98-9, 137-9
Intergroup perceptions 70, 91-2
Intergroup tolerance 69-70
Lithuania
   historical background 178-80
   demographic background 179
   stages of democratization 180
   ethnopolitical mobilization under *perestroika* 180-4
   Sajudis 181
   Yedinstvo 183
   Declaration on Sovereignty 182
   restoration of independence 185-6, 190-1
   elections of 1989 182
   elections of 1990 185
   elections of 1992 190
   ethnopolitical crisis interaction 162-7
   ethnopolitical problem areas (crises)
      stateness 185-6, 190-1
      state effectiveness 191
      nationhood 191
   legislation on citizenship 192-3
   politicies of multicututralism 191, 193-5
   policies of integration 193-5
   quality of ethnic peace 195-6
Minorities' rights vs. individual rights 59-60, 67, 94-5
Moldova
   historical background 197-9
   demographic background 198-9
   Right-Bank Moldova 197
   Left Bank Moldova 197
   stages of democratization 200
   ethnopolitical mobilization under *perestroika* 200-3
   Moldova Popular Front 200
   Gagauz Halky 200, 205
   Gagauz Yeri 220-1

Yedinstvo 201
Declaration on sovereignty 204
elections of 1990 203
elections of 1994 219
ethnopolitical crisis interaction 205-6, 211-3
ethnopolitical problem areas (crises)
  stateness 208-10, 220, 223
  state effectiveness 210-1
  nationhood 210-1
Moldovanness/Romanianness debate 210-11, 217-8
cumulation of crises 208-11
restoration of independence 208
ethnic civil war 212-8
third parties' mediation 211-5, 217
political realignment of 1994 217-8
legislation on citizenship 210
quality of ethnic peace 222-3
Multiple identities 32-3, 67, 88
Nation-building 94-5, 134-5
Nationalism and nationhood
  civic conceptions of 55-6, 67-8
  ethnic conceptions of 56-7
New democarcies 79, 84
Peace
  concept of 18-9
  positive vs. negative peace 18-22
  stable vs. unstable peace 22-4
  causes of stable peace 23
Pluralism 60, 69-70
Post-Communist transitions
  specific features 103-9
  legacies of the past 103-7
  tasks on the agenda 107
  role of nationalism 108
  international context 109
  compasrativists vs anticomparativists' debate 109-13
  legacies vs imperatives debate 113-4

Post-Soviet ethnopolitics
  features of 128-9
  past legacies 130-1
  lagacies of metaconflict 131
  lagacies of empire 131
  Russian diaspora 131-3
  post-Soviet state-building 133-4
  post-Soviet nation-building 134-5
  post-Soviet democracy-building 136
Power-Sharing
  consociational patterns 72-3
  integrative patterns 73-4
  institutions of 71-2
Russian Federation
  demographic background 227-8
  republics within Russia 224-7, 229
  stages of democratization 229-30
  Russia at independence 231-2
  centripetal factors 232-4
  Federation Treaty 235-8
  ethnopolitical crisis interaction 239-42
  ethnopolitical problem areas (crises)
    stateness 231-2
    state effectiveness 234, 239-41
    nationhood 235, 250
  Constituional convention 240-1
  1993 Constituion 242-3
  post-1993 federation politics 243-50
  bilateral treaties 246-9
  asymmetricity of federalism 237, 239
  quality of ethnic peace 250-2
Security community 16-7, 24-5
State-building 93-4, 133-4
Supraethnic integration 23-4
USSR
  Soviet 'federalism' 125-7
  titular nationalities 126
  institutionalization of ethnicity 125-6
  patterns of ethnopolitics 126-9